Bolivia

a travel survival kit

Deanna Swaney

Bolivia - a travel survival kit
1st edition

Published by
Lonely Planet Publications
Head Office: PO Box 88, South Yarra, Victoria 3141, Australia
US Office: PO Box 2001A, Berkeley, CA 94702, USA

Printed by
Colorcraft, Hong Kong

Photographs by
Ward Hulbert (WH)
Todd Miner (TM)
Vincent Neussl (VN)
Deanna Swaney (DS)
Tony Wheeler (TW)
Cover: Alpacas in the Cordillera Real (TM)

Published
December 1988

National Library of Australia Cataloguing in Publication Data

Swaney, Deanna.
Bolivia, a travel survival kit.

1st ed.
Includes index.
ISBN 0 86442 033 1.

1. Bolivia - Description and travel - 1981 - -
Guide-books. I. Title.

918.4'0452

Deanna Swaney

Deanna Swaney made the obligatory European tour after graduating from university and she has been addicted to travel ever since. Although she has wandered around six continents, she is particularly fascinated by the diversity and beauty of Latin America.

Deanna makes her home base in Anchorage, Alaska, where she finances her trips by writing funny coded messages to a Basic IV 8000 mini-computer. She derives her inspiration from the writings of Lao-Tzu and Ayn Rand, and the Alaskan wilderness.

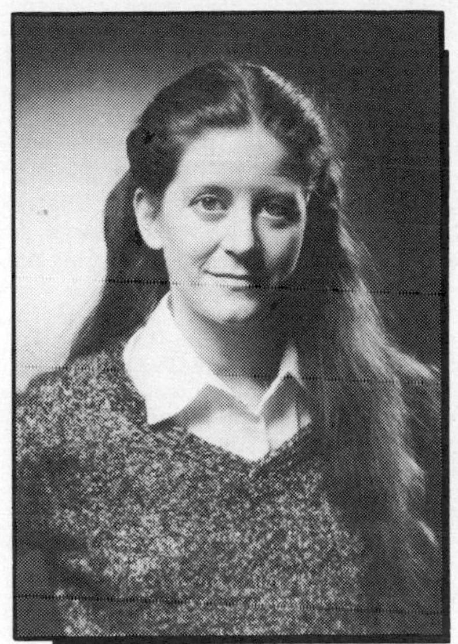

Lonely Planet Credits

Editors	Lindy Cameron Katie Cody Tom Smallman
Maps & cover design	Valerie Tellini
Design & Illustrations	Margaret Jung
Typesetting	Ann Jeffree

Thanks also to Anne Logan for additional typesetting.

Acknowledgements

When all my exposed film – the product of five month's research in Bolivia – was stolen in Brazil, I was understandably devastated. However, thanks to three very good friends and a comforting letter from Tony Wheeler, the project wasn't abandoned. My sincerest appreciation goes to Ward Hulbert and Todd Miner, both of Anchorage, Alaska, and to Vincent Neussl of Köln, West Germany, for happily providing some beautiful slides.

I'm also grateful to Becky Zaborac of Sanctuary Travel in Anchorage, who spent some of her valuable time looking up airfares for me on their *sabre* system.

Tom Sadowski of Tom Sadowski Films in Anchorage broke away from his funky postcards long enough to take a very difficult subject and work wonders with it. Many thanks to Tom for the considerable time and talent he expended in producing the photo of me to go with my bio.

Down in Bolivia, Donald and Mavis Randall of Tarija and Albert, Eileen and Paul Randall of Tupiza provided me with transportation, loads of info, and the best Kiwi meals to be found anywhere on the continent – all of which were greatly appreciated.

Thanks also to: Dr. Pat McLoughlin of La Jolla, California, who helped me with the Health Section; Dr. Dale Stevens of Orem, Utah, who dug up some maps and information on Bolivian Geography; Olga Castrillo of the Bolivian Embassy in Washington DC, who provided some valuable information on Bolivian immigration laws; Mark Delaney of Anchorage, Kenneth and Doris Swaney of Ruskin, Florida, and J Earl Swaney of Braderton, Florida for babysitting some rather cumbersome belongings while I was off traipsing around.

Special love and thanks to: my father, Earl Swaney, of Santa Clara, California, who bailed me out of a few potentially disastrous situations; Thomas Stack of Herxheim, West Germany, whose company in Bolivia was very much enjoyed; and to J Earl Swaney of Braderton, Florida, and David Dault of Anchorage, both of whom provided quiet and stress-free environments in which to grind out this project.

I'd also like to thank the following travellers and Bolivians who shared invaluable insights and experiences as well as their homes or company during the researching of this book:

Bart Ruiter (N), Claus Otto (D), Hans (D), Vincent Neussl (D), Claire Best (UK), Terry Terrill (C), David McGuire (UK), Caspar Baltazar Condori (B), Eckard Kühne (S), Padré José (B), Ciro Montero Vaca (B), Elsa Bernal (B), Grover & Santusa Choque de Callpa (B), Luis Araya (B), Jorge Luksic (B), Alexandra Blake (UK), Victoria Hipps (UK), Eduardo Garnica Fajardo (B), Julio Ortuño (B), Carlos Galíen (B), Carol Mattix (B), Maggie Pereira (USA),Jan Enguall (Sw), 'Don Conejo' (B), Gloria de Robles (B), Willie & Ray Hill (B), Zelso & Robertino Montenegro (B), Jorge & Duby Pol (B), Rosendo & Rosita Ateaga (B), René Machado Rocha (B), Manfred Auer (D), Rickey Rogers (USA), Vincente Melcón Flores (B), Betty Espinosa (B), Richard Olguín (B), Antonio Torrico (B), Bernard Obelliane (F), Bill Collard (UK), Mark Lawton (USA), Andy Lees (UK), Jim Bourke (USA), Barbel Tiemann (D), Klaus-Stephen Hwinrich (D), Antonio Uven Campaña (A), Leslie McTyre Gutierrez (B), Guillermo Aquila Paz (B), Jean-Luc Moreau (F), Ramón Catari (B), Paulino Estéban (B), Fabio Castañedo Torres (C)

A - Argentina, B - Bolivia, C - Colobia, D - West Germany, F - France, N - Netherlands, S - Switzerland, Sw - Sweden, UK - UK

A Warning & a Request

Things change – prices go up, schedules change, good places go bad and bad places go bankrupt – nothing stays the same. So if you find things better or worse, recently opened or long since closed, please write and tell us and help make the next edition better! All information is greatly appreciated and the best letters will receive a free copy of the next edition, or any other Lonely Planet book of your choice.

Extracts from the best letters are also included in the *Lonely Planet Update*. The *Update* helps us make useful information available to you as soon as possible – it's like reading an up-to-date notice board or postcards from a friend. Each edition contains hundreds of useful tips, and advice from the best possible source of information – other travellers. The *Lonely Planet Update* is published quarterly in paperback and is available from bookshops and by subscription. Turn to the back pages of this book for more details.

Dedication This book is lovingly dedicated to my father, Earl Swaney, and his best friend, Ehu Manu Nui, who are at home together in high places.

Contents

Introduction

Lying astride the widest point of the Andean Cordillera and spilling down through a maze of tortured hills and valleys into the Amazon and Paraná Basins, Bolivia is the poorest, highest, most isolated and least developed of all the Latin American republics.

Mention the name 'Bolivia' to anyone not personally acquainted with the country and it immediately conjures up images of scar-faced mafiosos smuggling the magic powder from jungle laboratories, pushers battling for space on filthy street corners, and revolution-torn landscapes littered with the corpses of the innocent masses.

Bolivia has suffered lately from a lot of bad press generated by its reputation for frequent shuffling and scuffling at the top and by the increasing worldwide consumption of its most popular export.

But, while cocaine does supply about 60% of the nation's trade revenue, relatively very few of Bolivia's 6½ million inhabitants benefit from it and most are involved in more down-to-earth economic activities, such as mining, herding and agriculture.

As for the political situation, the Bolivian presidency is as stable a position as that of bun-warmer at McDonald's. Apart from the odd state-of-emergency declaration (when travel is restricted or controlled) or the imposition of curfews, the visible effect of revolution upon José Blow is negligible.

For the traveller, Bolivia is a magnificent blend of mind-blowing landscapes, colonial treasures, colourful indigenous cultures and remnants of mysterious ancient civilisations.

It is also the home of a semi-existent transportation system (with non-existent schedules), cold (or electrifying!) showers, and possibly the most corrupt and disorganised bunch of officials and politicos on the face of the earth.

Every traveller in Bolivia – guided tourist, backpacker, mountain climber or whatever – will need to be equipped with not only a sense of adventure but also a keen wit, a long fuse and a willingness to accept and appreciate the unexpected. A smile and a few encouraging words will often serve to calm the savage bureaucratic beast, while a few $$ will work miracles!

But, while the corruption and inefficiency of the powers that be will probably carry you to the proverbial breaking point, you'll find that the average Bolivian is an honest and friendly individual who will enjoy making your acquaintance and learning something about your neck-of-the-woods.

Despite the political strife, Bolivia is a

relatively safe country for the foreign visitor. The sneaky thievery, guerrilla sabotage, armed robbery and violent assault so legendary in some neighbouring countries are practically non-existent here and the most annoying element you're likely to encounter in the civilian society is the amorous or obnoxious inebriate.

With 65% of the population belonging to the Quechua, Aymará and a score of other indigenous groups, Bolivia is the most 'Indian' nation in South America. It is also the one least affected by outside customs and values, and only recently has big-time tourism taken advantage of its appeal.

Notwithstanding the troubles of a turbulent, landlocked republic, this is a land of surprises awaiting discovery. In every corner of this little-known country, the willing adventurer will find a wealth of diverse cultures, natural beauty and the kind of unforgettable experiences that motivate travellers.

Some of the best of everything awaits you in Bolivia, so wherever you travel – from the windswept deserts of the Altiplano to the jungle-choked northern waterways, or from the busy, colourful cities to the remote Andean valleys and forgotten villages – slow down, observe and savour.

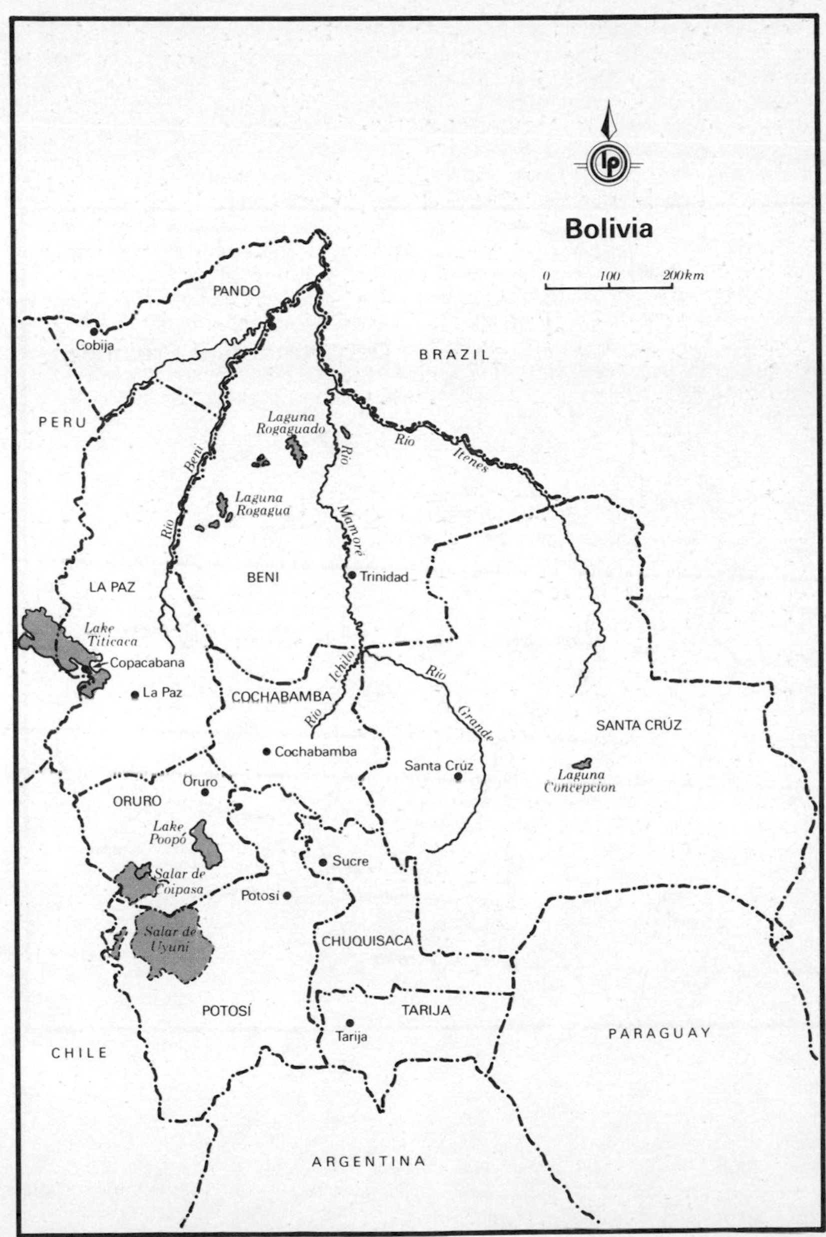
Bolivia
0
100
200km
PANDO
Cobija
BRAZIL
PERU
Laguna
Rogaguado
Río
Itenes
Río
Beni
Laguna
Rogagua
Río
Mamoré
BENI
Trinidad
LA PAZ
Lake
Titicaca
Copacabana
La Paz
COCHABAMBA
Río
Ichilo
Río
Grande
SANTA CRÚZ
Cochabamba
Santa Crúz
Laguna
Concepcion
Oruro
ORURO
Lake
Poopó
Sucre
Salar de
Coipasa
Potosí
Salar de
Uyuni
CHUQUISACA
POTOSÍ
TARIJA
Tarija
PARAGUAY
CHILE
ARGENTINA

Departments & Provinces
PANDO
Cobija
Riberalta
BENI
Trinidad
LA PAZ
Lake Titicaca
La Paz
COCHABAMBA
Cochabamba
SANTA CRÚZ
Santa Crúz
Oruro
ORURO
Sucre
Potosí
CHUQUISACA
POTOSÍ
Tarija
TARIJA

1 Tahuamanu (Suarez)
2 Abunã
3 Manuripi
4 Madre de Dios
5 Vaca Diez
6 Ballivián
7 Yacuma
8 Mamoré
9 Iténez
10 Cercado
11 Marbán
12 Moxos
13 Ayopaya
14 Chapare
15 Tapacarí
16 Quillacollo
17 Arque
18 Capinota
19 Cercado
20 Jordan (Cliza)
21 Arani
22 Punata
23 Arce
24 Mizque
25 Carrasco
26 Campero
27 Ichilo
28 Gutierrez
29 Santiesteban
30 Warnes
31 Nuflo de Chávez
32 Velasco
33 Sandoval
34 Chiquitos
35 Ibañez
36 Florida
37 Vallegrande
38 Charcas
39 Oropeza
40 Siles
41 Yamparáez
42 Zudañez
43 Boeto
44 Tomina
45 Azurduy
46 Nor Cinti
47 Sud Cinti
48 Azero
49 Calvo
50 Gran Chaco
51 O'Conor
52 Arce
53 Cercado
54 Mendez
55 Avilez
56 Sud Chichas
57 Sud Lipez
58 Daniel Campos
59 Nor Lípez
60 Nor Chicas
61 Quijarro
62 Linares
63 Cornelio Saavedra
64 Frías
65 Chayanta
66 Charcas
67 General Bilbao
68 Alonzo de Ibañez
69 Bustillos
70 Abaroa
71 Cabrera
72 Sabaya
73 Carangas
74 Poopó
75 Dalence
76 Cercado
77 Sajama
78 Pacajes
79 Aroma
80 Inquisivi
81 Loaiza
82 Ingavi
83 Los Andes
84 Manco Kapaj
85 Omasuyos
86 Murillo
87 Nor Yungas
88 Sud Yungas
89 Larecaja
90 Muíecas
91 Camacho
92 Saavedra
93 Caupolican
94 Iturralde

Facts about the Country

HISTORY

Bolivia has a history that reads somewhat like a soap opera, for it seems almost unlikely that one country could be beset by such a diverse and seemingly never-ending series of problems.

Bolivians today, more than 50% of whom are of pure Indian blood, are a rugged and determined people with a strong spirit born of surviving hundreds of years of oppression and exploitation.

Even the characteristic bowler hats and voluminous skirts worn by the women were imposed on them in the 18th century by the Spanish king and the customary centre-parting of the hair was the result of a decree by the Viceroy Toledo.

Although it seems that Bolivians simply accepted almost any kind of iniquity meted out, this has not been the case.

Resistance to Spanish rule in South America began first in Bolivia, with mestizo revolts in 1661 and 1780, and Indian insurrections between 1776 and 1780. Earlier than that, many of the dispersed communities of Aymará-speaking Indians – whose kingdoms were once centred on the Altiplano – fought historic battles against the cultural dominance and oppression of the expanding Inca empire. And one of the most influential cultures of pre-colonial times originated and flourished in Bolivia.

The Central Andes

The largest expanse of level, cultivable land in the Andes is the great altiplano which extends from present-day Bolivia into southern Peru. This region has been inhabited for thousands of years and its people experienced great changes as the political, artistic and religious influences of the earliest organised states crossed back and forth over the mountains and the great plain, extending their power north as far as Ecuador and south to Chile.

The earliest history of Bolivia therefore, is pretty much interchangeable with that of Peru. It is in fact the history of the Central Andes as there were no such political borders then, only the boundaries of regional kingdoms and chiefdoms.

Perhaps the greatest, pre-Columbian, influence which swept across the altiplano shaping, in particular, the history of Bolivia was exerted by the imperial designs of two major empires – the Tiahuanaco culture of Bolivia and the Inca of Peru.

Most archaeologists define the ancient history of the Central Andes in terms of 'horizons', determined by the era when a particular art form was practised over a wide area. This is mostly because the influence of individual Andean cultures on each other, from earliest times, can best be seen in the interrelationship of art forms and styles of architecture throughout the area.

The things that influenced the development of different regions and cultures were brought about by peaceful exchange, often between nomadic tribes, or by the expansionist activities of powerful and well organised societies. They resulted, ultimately, in making the Central Andes the centre of most of South America's highest cultural achievements.

Early Horizons

The Andes' earliest people were nomadic hunters but around the middle of the 3rd century BC, as permanent settlements were becoming more common, fishing and farming began to take on more importance.

The Initial Period, up to about 1400 BC, saw the establishment of villages and ceremonial centres and there was also a certain amount of trade between coastal fishing communities and the farming villages of the highlands.

The so-called Early Horizon, from about 1400 BC to 400 BC, marked the spread of the Chavín style of art and was an era of great architectural activity. The culmination of the Chavín style, and its best preserved example, is the ruins of the temple complex at Chavín de Huantar, on the eastern slopes of the Andes in Peru.

It is also thought that during the Early Horizon period a wave of Aymará-speaking Indians, possibly from the mountains of central Peru, swept across into the Bolivian Andes and occupied the Altiplano, probably driving out many of the region's original settlers.

The Chavín influences, which were felt far and wide, and even for quite some time after the decline of the society that had promoted it, contributed to the developing regional styles of the following Early Intermediate period, from 400 BC to 500 AD.

The centuries of the Middle Horizon, from about 500 AD to 900 AD, were marked by the imperial expansion of the Tiahuanaco-Hauri culture.

Tiahuanaco

The township of Tiahuanaco, on the shores of Lake Titicaca in Bolivia, grew and prospered throughout the Middle Horizon period as it developed into the religious and political centre for all the Altiplano villages.

Tiahuanaco and its outpost, or political counterpart, of Hauri in the Ayacucho Valley (now Peru) developed into a well-organised, prosperous and ambitious society. Though the relationship between the two towns, separated as they were by such a great distance, is not really clear, the architecture and the iconography in the changing artforms of the Middle Horizon demonstrate very close cultural ties.

While it may have been that they were dual capitals, many of the theories regarding the connection between the two towns seem to favour the idea that Tiahuanaco was the real power behind this empire. It's architecture and sculpture were apparently more refined than that of Hauri so it's possible that Tiahuanaco was the ceremonial and political centre and Hauri was its strategic military outpost in the north.

Whatever the relationship the Tiahuanaco-Hauri expansion, as it is known, extended throughout the Central Andes and as far north as Ecuador, spreading, sharing and imposing its art and architecture on the conquered regions. It's also believed that Tiahuanaco introduced and encouraged the extensive planting of maize for ceremonial purposes.

The town had been inhabited since about 1500 BC and was still occupied as late as 1200 AD but its real power only lasted till about the 9th century. (Hauri was abandoned sometime before 800 AD.) Although the Tiahuanaco people produced technically impressive work, the most notable being the township of Tiahuanaco itself, many of their stone carvings and hieroglyphs remain undeciphered.

The civilisation was gradually supplanted by another period of regional strongholds and art styles, which thrived till the coming of the Incas. One theory speculates that the Tiahuanaco people were displaced by a lowering of the level of Lake Titicaca, which left their lakeside settlement far from the shore. Some believe that these people wandered southward to develop into the unique Chipaya tribe of the western Oruro Department.

Today, collections of Tiahuanaco relics may be found in museums throughout the country and the ruins of Tiahuanaco, on the plain between La Paz and the south shore of Lake Titicaca, can be visited.

The Inca Conquest

The Late Horizon, from 1476 AD to 1534 AD, defines the pinnacle of Inca civilisation in the Andes. For all its greatness however, the Inca Empire, or political state, lasted less than a century before falling to the might of the invading Spanish.

The last of South America's indigenous conquerors, the Incas pushed their Tahuantisuyu empire from its seat of power in Cuzco (Peru) eastwards into Bolivia, south to the northern reaches of Argentina and Chile and all the way up to Ecuador.

The Inca people began their march into history as a minor Cuzco chiefdom, a family that became an empire-building clan who managed, in the space of little more than 50 years, to establish a highly unified state.

Although the Inca had inhabited the Cuzco region since the 12th century it wasn't until about 1440 that they began seriously extending their political boundaries beyond the immediate neighbourhood.

While their origins are the stuff of myths and legends their achievements certainly were not. Renowned for their great stone cities and their craftsmanship in gold and silver, the Incas also set up a hierarchy of governmental and agricultural overseers, a viable social welfare scheme and a complex road network and communication system that defied the difficult terrain of their far-flung empire.

The Inca Manco, the founder of the Inca line, and his sister Mama Huaca were believed to be the children of the Sun god. Their progeny were the first of the Inca noble family which, to keep the line and the growing number of related Inca clans pure, adopted a very structured system of marriage.

Because of this, each Inca ruler, or Sapa Inca, was naturally a direct descendant of the Sun God and, while having an unlimited number of wives (whose children were legitimate Inca nobles), was always married to his sister in order to perpetuate the divine lineage from the Sun.

While the mythical history of the Inca is the most romantic there are of course more down to earth theories regarding their origins, including that of the 17th century Spanish chronicler Fernando Montesinos. He believed the Incas were descended from a line of wise men from the ancient Bolivian city of Tiahuanaco.

Manco Capac

Whatever their origins, the Inca belief in the intrinsic power and good qualities of the Sun god, of which they were naturally endowed, enabled them to achieve extraordinary levels of social organisation. Their manner of government could be described as an imperialist socialist dictatorship. The Sapa Inca was the reigning monarch, head of the noble family and the extended Inca clan, and unquestionably in charge of the state.

The state technically owned all property within its vast and expanding realm and taxes usually took the form of labour. At the same time the Inca family also organised a system of mutual aid, so that if necessary relief supplies from prosperous areas could be sent to others suffering from local misfortune.

This system of benevolent rule was largely due to the influence of the eighth true Inca, Viracocha, who believed that the mandate from the Sun god was not just to conquer, plunder and enslave but to organise the defeated tribes so they too could benefit from the benevolence of the Sun god.

When the Incas came a-conquering into Kolla-Suyo (present-day Bolivia) they assimilated numerous tribes, as they had done elsewhere, by imposing taxation, religion and their own Quechua language, as the *lingua franca*, upon the inhabitants of the region.

The stubborn Aymará of the Bolivian Altiplano, who fought the Inca onslaught in vain, were permitted, as were most of the conquered tribes throughout the Andes, to retain some facets of their culture including their own language for daily speech.

Although, by the late 1520s, internal rivalries had begun to take their toll on the Inca empire, it was the arrival of outsiders, first thought to be emissaries from the Sun god, who ultimately dealt the final blow. The Spanish landed in *their* New World in 1531 and within a year had pushed inland towards Cuzco, in search of land, wealth and adventure.

The Spanish Conquest

When Francisco Pizarro, Diego de Almagro and their bands of merry conquistadors arrived in Cuzco in 1532, the Inca emperor Atahualpa reigned as the supreme leader of a vast empire.

Atahualpa, although a son of the previous Sapa Inca, was not the true descendant of the Sun god. In a brief civil war, over the division of lands, Atahualpa had imprisoned his half-brother, the true Inca king, and taken the throne as his own.

When the Spanish appeared, the Incas believed they had been sent by the great Viracocha Inca as revenge for the seizure of the throne. In fear Atahualpa ordered the murder of the real king which, not only effectively ended the true bloodline of the Inca dynasty, but brought a certain amount of shame on the family, shattering the strength of the Inca hierarchy.

The Spanish obviously couldn't care less about the death of the true Inca, except in as much as they could use the Inca's guilt to their advantage. Between Atahualpa's shame at having killed the divine descendant of the Sun, and the Inca nobility's initial trust in the Spanish 'gods', the conquistadors in a sense had it easy.

Within two years the government had been conquered, the Inca empire was no more and the invaders divided the land and booty between the two leaders of the Spanish forces.

Alto Perú, as the Spanish then called Bolivia, fell for a brief period into the possession of Diego de Almagro, although he didn't live long enough to make the most of his prize as he was assassinated in 1538. (He was joined three years later by Pizzaro who suffered the same fate at the hands of his own followers.)

In the meantime, the Spanish set about exploring and settling their newly-conquered land. In 1538, the township of La Plata was founded, as the Spanish capital of the Charcas region. This town, later renamed Chuquisaca and finally Sucre, became the administrative, religious and educational centre of the eastern Spanish territories.

By the time the wandering Indian, Diego Huallpa, revealed his earth-shattering discovery at Potosí in 1544, the Spanish

Atahualpa

conquerors had already firmly implanted their language, religion and customs upon the remnants of Atahualpa's empire.

Spanish Potosí, or the 'Villa Imperial de Carlos V', was founded in 1545 when the riches of *Cerro Rico*, the 'Silver Mountain,' were already on their way to the Spanish treasuries.

The Potosí mine quickly became the most prolific the world has ever known and the silver extracted from it underwrote the Spanish economy, particularly the extravagance of its monarchy, for about two centuries and spawned a legendary maritime crime wave on the Caribbean Sea.

Atrocious conditions in the gold and silver mines of Potosí guaranteed a short life span not only for the local Indian population, who were herded into work gangs, but the millions of African slaves impressed into labour there as well. Those not actually worked to death or killed through accidents, succumbed to pulmonary silicosis within just a few years.

The Spanish soldiers, administrators, settlers, adventurers and miners who poured into the region also helped establish a powerful land-owning aristocracy. The indigenous peoples became tenant farmers, subservient to their Spanish lords, and were required to supply their conquerors with food and labour in exchange for subsistence-sized plots of land.

The city of La Paz was founded in 1548, by Captain Alonzo de Mendoza, as a centre for the local gold mines and as an administrative and strategic staging post for the huge shipments of silver en route from Potosí to the Peruvian ports on the Pacific.

Santa Crúz de la Sierra was founded in 1561 by Spaniards who had migrated from Paraguay.

Increased agricultural productivity and the growing prosperity of the Spanish landowners also promoted the growth of farming townships. The city of Cochabamba was founded in 1574 and soon became the granary of Bolivia, while the foundation of Tarija in the same year also served as a defence post against incursions by the independent Indians of the region.

It was the discovery of silver, once again, that elevated the village of Oruro to the status of a town in 1606. In the 18th century it was producing nearly 50% of Bolivia's silver, and still later, its prosperity (and that of Potosí) was revived by the re-working of the mines for tin.

In 1781, a futile attempt was made to expel the Spaniards and re-establish the Inca Empire. Some 30 years later, in May of 1809, the first independence movement in Spanish America was under way in Chuquisaca (Sucre) and a local government was established there. Other major Bolivian cities quickly followed the example and the powder keg exploded.

During the first quarter of the 19th century, the South American soldier and liberator General Simón Bolívar, succeeded in liberating Venezuela and Colombia from the Spanish. In 1822 he dispatched Mariscal (major-general) Antonio José de Sucre to Ecuador to defeat the Royalists at the battle of Pichincha.

In 1824, following years of local guerrilla action against the Spanish, Peru finally won its independence, also thanks to the intervention of Bolívar and Sucre during the battles of Junín (6 August) and Ayacucho (9 December).

Sucre then called on the people of upper Peru to declare their own independence and exactly one year later, Alto Peru became the new Republic of Bolivia, named after the man who even today is honoured (and practically deified) throughout the Latin American republics. Bolívar and Sucre, incidentally, became the first and second presidents of the new republic.

After a brief attempt on the part of the third president, Andres Santa Cruz, to form a confederation with Peru things began to go awry. One military junta after another usurped power from its predecessor and started a pattern of political strife that would haunt the nation for the next 162 years.

Few of the 188 governments to date have remained in power long enough to have had much intentional effect. Some were more than a little eccentric too. One colourful leader, General Mariano Melgarejo who ruled by the bottle from 1865 to 1871, drunkenly set off with his army on an overland march to the aid of France at the outset of the Franco-Prussian War. History has it that he was sobered up by a sudden downpour and abandoned the project (to the relief of the Prussians, I'm sure).

Shrinking Territory

Bolivia's misfortunes during this period, however, were not limited to internal strife. At the time of independence her boundaries encompassed well over two million square km. By the time Bolivia's neighbours had finished paring away at her territory, only half the original land area remained.

The first and most significant loss occurred as a result of the War of the Pacific. Between 1879 and 1884, Chile took 350 km of coastline from allies Peru and Bolivia. This meant the loss of the valuable Littoral Department, including the port of Antofagasta and the copper and nitrate rich sands of the Atacama Desert.

Although Chile did attempt to recompense the loss by building a railroad from La Paz to the coast and allowing Bolivia free port privileges in Antofagasta, Bolivians have never gotten over the devastating *enclaustromiento* which left them without an outlet to the sea. Even now, the government uses the issue as a rallying cry whenever it wants to unite the people behind a common cause.

During the years that followed, Peru, Brazil and Argentina each had their turn hacking away at Bolivia's borders.

The next major loss was in 1903 when, during a rubber boom, Brazil annexed the remote Acre Territory immediately upon its secession from the Bolivian Republic – which it had done with Brazil's encouragement.

Both countries had been ransacking the forests of the Acre, which stretched from Bolivia's present Amazonian borders to about half-way up Peru's eastern border, but the area was so rich in rubber trees that Brazil engineered a dispute over sovereignty and sent in its army.

Brazil also attempted to compensate Bolivia's loss with a new railway. This one was to open up the remote northern reaches of the country but the unfinished project never even reached Bolivian soil. The line ended at Guajará Mirim, on the Brazilian bank of the Mamoré River, and is now used only infrequently as a tourist novelty.

In 1932, a border dispute with Paraguay (the boundaries between the two countries had never been formally defined) for control of the Chaco erupted into full-scale warfare.

This time the conflict was partly caused by rival western oil companies which had their eye on concessions should their prospecting activities reveal huge deposits of oil in the Chaco. In a bid to secure favourable franchises a quarrel was engineered with Standard Oil supporting Bolivia and Shell siding with Paraguay.

On the other hand Paraguay, badly beaten after taking on Argentina, Uruguay and Brazil in the War of the Triple Alliancè, needed an outlet to avenge its loss. Victory in this respect would also guarantee a prosperous economic future – if the oil companies were right.

So Bolivia fell victim to Paraguayan pride and within three years had lost another 225,000 square km, 40,000 young men and a dubious outlet to the sea via the Paraguay River. No oil was found in the Chaco, however, so even Paraguay lost out.

Modern Problems

While defeat at the hands of Paraguay promoted an upsurge in national feeling in Bolivia, it also had revolutionary repercussions. After the Chaco War, the friction between the peasant miners and their absentee big-business bosses in the tin industry, centred in Oruro, began to escalate.

The miners' complaints against outrageous working conditions, pitifully low compensation and the export of profits raised the trade union and political consciousness of Bolivian workers.

Radicals gathered together under the banner of the Movimiento Nacional Revolucionario (MNR), led by Victor Paz Estenssoro. The general unrest brought the MNR to power in the general elections of 1951 but a military coup, which prevented them from actually taking power, provoked an armed revolt by the miners.

After the heavy fighting of the April Revolution in 1952, the military was defeated and Estenssoro and the MNR took the helm for the first time.

He quickly nationalised the mines, evicted the tin barons, and set up the Corporación Minera de Bolivia (COMIBOL), the state corporation to be in charge of mining interests.

The reformists, who were also concerned with agrarian and educational reform and universal suffrage, pressed ahead with a programme of wide ranging reforms. This included the redistribution of the large estates amongst the peasants who had been working the land and the restructuring of the education system to provide schooling for everyone.

The long-isolated areas of the country, particularly those in the east, were also brought closer into the national picture through the construction of roads, such as the one between Santa Cruz and Cochabamba.

All these social and economic reforms, aimed at ensuring the participation of all sections of the population, had the effect of making the miners and peasants feel that they were part of the nation, and the relatively popular government of the MNR lasted an incredible 12 years under various presidents. Estenssoro himself served three non-consecutive terms of varying lengths.

However, even with US support, the MNR was unable to substantially raise the standard of living or increase food production. Estenssoro was forced to become more and more autocratic as the dissension in his own ranks began to increase.

In 1964 the whole mob, weakened by the internal quarrels, was overthrown by a military junta headed by General René Barrientos Ortuño.

From the start of this fresh round of military rule there was strong opposition throughout the country, led mostly by students and miners. One of General Barrientos' first actions had been to attack the miners, as they were the principal strength behind the deposed MNR.

In 1967, still during the regime of Barrientos, the Marxist folk hero Ché Guevara, who had been training guerrillas in southern Bolivia, was executed by a

US-backed military delegation and the Bolivian Armed Forces. It was thought the Argentinian-born soldier politician was heading a peasant revolt in the south-east.

In the same year there was a massacre, by government military forces, of miners who had gathered at Catavi to form an anti-government front.

Following the death of President Barrientos in a helicopter crash in 1969, governments again began to come and go like the subway, as the familiar pattern of coups replaced one military officer with another.

General Hugo Banzer Suáres, head of a right-wing coalition, took over in 1971 and served a turbulent term until 1978 when he mandated a return to democratic process and scheduled general elections. Although he lost the elections, the results were ignored on the grounds that serious tampering had occurred.

Soon after, however, Banzer was forced to step down when his opponent General Juan Pereda Asbún assumed power. Juan Pereda, in turn, had the top job snatched from him in the same year by General David Perdilla, who at least had the support of the democratic opposition.

It wasn't until 1982 though, that the military regime finally ended when the civilian left-wing leader of the Communist-supported MIR, Dr Hernán Siles Zuazo, took over.

His term was beleaguered with labour disputes, ruthless government spending and monetary devaluation. The result of all this was a staggering inflation rate that at one point reached 35,000% annually!

When Siles Zuazo gave up after three years and called general elections, Victor Paz Estenssoro returned to politics to become president for the fourth time. He immediately set about stabilising the shattered economy by ousting labour unions and deploying armed forces to keep the peace.

Today, Estenssoro remains in power and is committed to programmes which he hopes will return his nationalised government mines to private cooperatives and develop the largely uninhabited lowland regions of the north and east.

Inflation has subsided, but spiralling unemployment, especially in the poor mining areas of the Altiplano, seriously threatens the stability of the current government. It remains to be seen whether or not the military will take advantage of the growing stress and again seize power from elected officials.

GEOGRAPHY

Bolivia currently encompasses 1,098,000 square km. It is 3½ times the size of the British Isles, slightly smaller than Alaska and just less than half the size of Western Australia.

It is bordered on the west by Chile and Peru, on the north and east by Brazil, and on the south by Argentina and Paraguay. The country is shaped roughly like an equilateral triangle. From east to west it measures 1300 km at its widest point and it's 1500 km from north to south.

Much of Bolivia's appeal for the visitor lies in its awesome geography. Physically, the land is divided into five basic and diverse regions: the high Altiplano, the highland valleys, the Yungas, the Grán Chaco, and the jungled lowlands of the Amazon and Paraná Basins.

Altiplano

The Altiplano is the most heavily populated region of the country but it is by no means crowded. The word *altiplano* means 'high plain' and this great plateau, which runs from the Peruvian border north of Lake Titicaca southward to the Argentine border, also spills over into neighbouring Peru, Chile and Argentina.

Despite its name, however, the Altiplano is anything but flat. The city of La Paz, for instance, sits in a deep canyon beneath its rim.

Basin altitudes range from 3500 to 4000 metres but the snow-capped peaks of the Cordillera Real, the Cordillera de Chichas and the many isolated volcanic summits of the Cordillera Occidental reach much higher. Mt Sajama near the Chilean border, for instance, is disputably Bolivia's highest peak and rises 6520 metres above sea level; while the average elevation of the Cordillera Real, near La Paz, is 5500 metres.

The Altiplano itself is a rather haunting place – a cold, windy, treeless land where horizons and distant mountains seem to melt into the sky, or into each other; and where phantom lakes appear and disappear, or suddenly just change size. Above it all, building clouds or trailing wisps of windblown snow, the great white-capped giants loom like sentinels over the chameleon-like landscape. The entire impression is one of grave solitude and observers are left wondering what they're actually seeing.

Bolivia's 'great lakes' are also found on the Altiplano. Lake Titicaca, the most important and beautiful of them, is the second largest in South America, after Venezuela's Lake Maracaibo. It is also the highest navigable lake in the world. Lakes Uru Uru and Poopó, south of Oruro, are little more than giant puddles, just a few metres deep.

South of the lakes, where the land becomes drier and less populated, are the remnants of two other lakes, the Salar de Uyuni and the Salar de Coipasa. These two salt deserts and the surrounding salty plains form an eerie expanse of as near to nothing as one can imagine. Certainly the vistas there won't soon be forgotten.

Highland Valleys

The highland valleys just east of the Altiplano boast the most hospitable living conditions in the country. The climate enjoyed by the people of Cochabamba, Sucre, Tupiza and Tarija is the envy of Bolivians elsewhere. In this region only Potosí suffers from unfavourable temperatures (mostly because of its poor location).

This is the Cordillera Central, an area of scrambled hills and valleys, fertile basins and intense agriculture. With a kind of backward Mediterranean climate – rain falls in summer instead of winter – the people there can grow olives, nuts, wheat, maize and grapes. Wine is produced in Tarija.

Yungas

To the north of Cochabamba and La Paz, where the Andes fall away into the

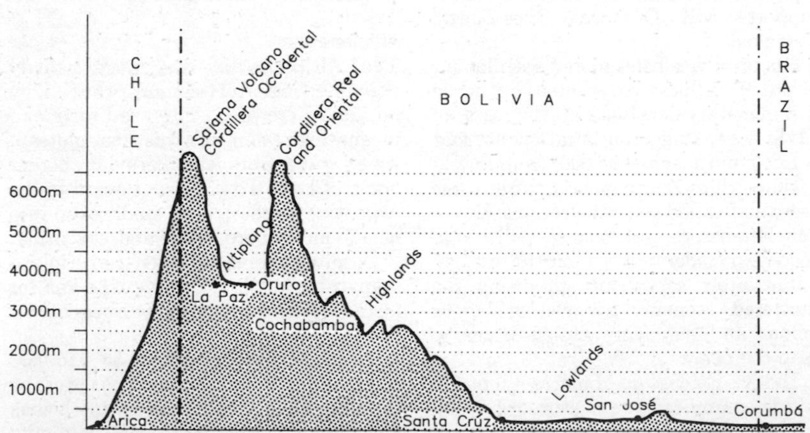

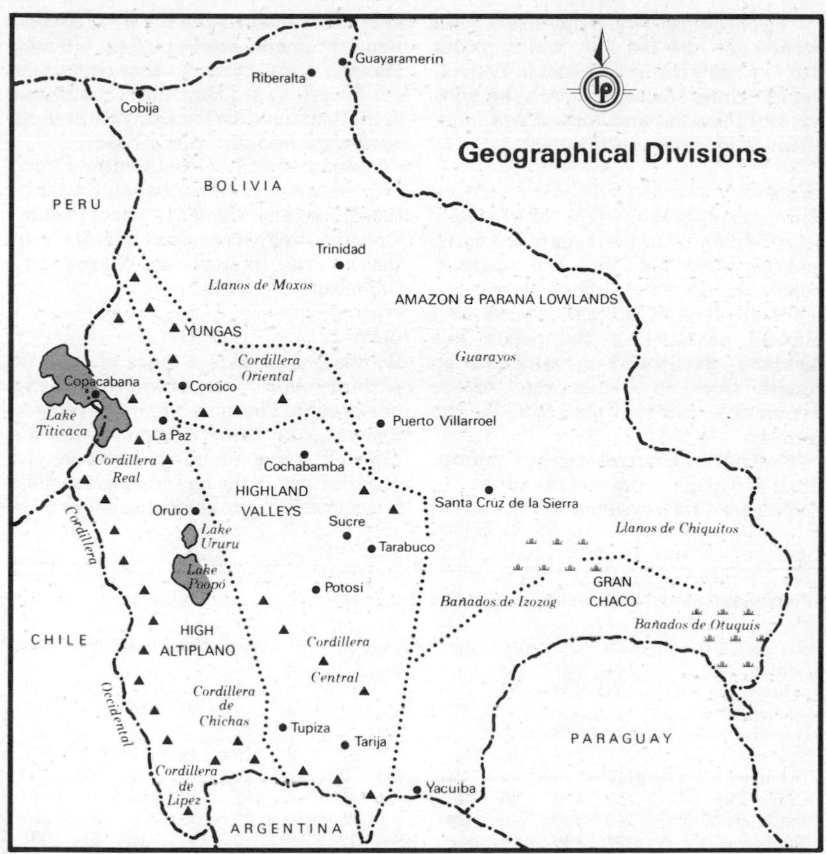

Amazon Basin, is the Yungas – the transition zone between dry highlands and humid lowlands. The name simply means 'valleys'.

Above the steaming, jungled depths rise the near-vertical slopes of the Cordillera Oriental which halt Altiplano-bound clouds, causing them to deposit bounteous rainfall on the Yungas. Vegetation is therefore abundant and tropical fruits, coffee, sugar, coca, cacao, vegetables and tobacco grow practically by themselves.

Chaco

In the south-east corner of Bolivia, along the Paraguayan and Argentine borders, lies the flat, nearly impenetrable scrubland of the Grán Chaco. The level terrain is covered by a tangled thicket of small thorny trees and cactus.

As the region is almost completely uninhabited, native flora and fauna thrive there undisturbed. The Chaco provides a refuge for some rare animal species, such as the jaguar and peccary, which have been displaced in other parts of the country.

The only settlement of any size is Villa Montes, on the rail line, which prides itself on being the hottest spot in Bolivia. Temperatures frequently reach the mid-40s and thick red dust (or if it's raining, sticky mud) covers everything.

Lowlands

Encompassing about 60% of Bolivia's total land area, the lowlands of the north and east are hot, flat and sparsely populated. Recently, efforts have been made to develop the agricultural and mineral potential of the region but highland dwellers seem reluctant to resettle there, so a large sector of the population comes from outside the country.

The land is comprised largely of swamp-land, low jungle scrub and rainforest.

Two great river systems drain this vast area. The Acre, Madre de Diós, Abunã, Beni, Mamoré, Ichilo, Ibaré, Grande, Paragua and a score of other rivers flow northward toward Brazil into tributaries of the Amazon. The Paraguay River flows southward into the Paraná Basin.

In South-west Beni and Central Santa Crúz Departments exist the only breaks in the flat green monotony, where natural monoliths and ranges of low hills rise from the Llanos (plains) de Moxos and Chiquitos.

CLIMATE

Bolivia has as wide a range of climatic patterns as it has of elevation and topography. The most important thing to remember on the Altiplano is that it's probably going to be colder than you expect. Even in the humid jungle regions frosts and sub-zero temperatures are not

Precipitation in millimetres (approximate averages)

	Jan	*Feb*	*Mar*	*Apr*	*May*	*Jun*	*Jul*	*Aug*	*Sep*	*Oct*	*Nov*	*Dec*
La Paz	138	87	80	32	2	2	2	3	25	50	51	88
Oruro	158	138	80	9	3	0	3	5	15	25	25	42
Cochabamba	121	137	133	23	7	2	0	0	0	10	130	137
Potosí	180	119	100	9	5	2	2	2	5	12	12	81
Sucre	151	137	118	37	2	3	9	19	44	48	98	117
Tarija	115	75	64	34	2	2	11	14	18	40	108	129
Santa Crúz	84	159	40	48	50	81	43	118	120	324	125	119
Trinidad	260	140	140	23	9	29	16	49	50	130	165	169
Cobija	257	290	346	130	129	42	0	0	146	412	400	307

Temperatures in degrees C (average high and low)

	Jan	*Feb*	*Mar*	*Apr*	*May*	*Jun*	*Jul*	*Aug*	*Sep*	*Oct*	*Nov*	*Dec*
La Paz	18	18	18	19	17	17	17	17	18	19	19	19
	6	6	6	5	3	2	1	2	3	5	6	6
Cochabamba *	20	20	19	19	18	17	18	19	19	21	21	20
Sucre	24	23	24	24	23	22	21	23	23	24	23	22
	11	11	10	10	6	5	5	6	7	8	9	10
Santa Crúz	31	31	30	28	25	23	24	28	29	30	31	31
	21	21	20	19	16	15	15	16	19	20	20	21
Villazón *	14	14	14	13	6	2	2	6	9	10	14	14
Trinidad *	27	27	27	27	27	27	26	26	27	28	28	28

* Only Average temperatures available.

unheard of when a *surazo*, or pampa wind from the south, is blowing.

As for the rest of the country, although you're as near to the equator as you would be in Tahiti or Hawaii, the higher elevations and unprotected expanses all contribute to variable weather.

The two poles of climatic misery in Bolivia are Puerto Suárez for its stifling, humid heat, and Uyuni for its near-Arctic cold and icy winds. But even then there are no absolutes in the Bolivian climate; I have sunbathed in Uyuni and nearly frozen stiff in Puerto Suárez.

The rainy period lasts from November to March in most of the country. This is summer in Bolivia.

In La Paz, mists swirl through the streets and the city is literally wrapped in the clouds; rain falls daily and cold air currents sweep down the canyon from the Altiplano.

Above, on the high plain, the lakes swell to devour the landscape and livestock stand in knee-deep puddles.

In the flooding of 1985-86, Lake Titicaca rose several metres and flooded roads, homes and villages. In Bolivia and in neighbouring Peru an estimated 200,000 people lost their homes and crops in this disaster. In the jungle areas to the north, where violent electrical storms and tropical downpours can usually be expected during the summer, many deaths during the same period were attributed to the disease and the raging rivers that were the result of the deluge.

Throughout the country, night-time temperatures drop dramatically and, on the high Altiplano, the sun just has to pass behind a cloud for a significant temperature difference to be noticed.

Of the major cities, only Potosí consistently receives snow in the winter (May to August), but in Oruro and La Paz it is not uncommon. Sub-zero temperatures are frequent, especially at night, and precipitation is still common but of shorter duration than during the rainy season.

In Cochabamba, Sucre and Tarija, this is the time of clear, beautiful skies and optimum temperatures. There is hardly a more ideal climate on earth, in my opinion. In the winter, the lowlands experience hot, sunny days and an occasional 10-minute shower to cool things off and settle the dust. In the Yungas, plan on some rain nearly every day of the year.

When considering seasons, remember that Bolivia is in the southern hemisphere. On the Altiplano, dress as you would in Scotland or southern New Zealand in the respective season. In the highland valleys, the climate is similar to that of Madrid, Los Angeles or Perth, but a little cooler and with the seasons reversed. That is, summer in those cities corresponds to winter in Cochabamba or Sucre and vice versa. The lowlands experience a climate similar to that of Miami or Darwin.

WILDLIFE

Due to its relatively sparse population, lack of extensive development and diverse geography, Bolivia is the best place on the continent for viewing South American wildlife. Of course, you'll need to venture beyond the cities for the opportunity but that doesn't mean you'll have to slog through snow, swamp and jungle to catch a glimpse of Bolivia's wild kingdom. You'll be able to see an enormous variety of animal life from the windows or decks of the country's buses, trains and boats.

On the Altiplano, for instance, you're bound to see plenty of llamas and alpacas. Although they're hardly qualified as wild, having been domesticated for centuries in these highlands, they are unusual and interesting to see. Despite their cute and cuddly appearance, however, they have a nasty reputation for biting and spitting, so beware if you plan to observe at close range.

These ill-tempered cameloid domesticates, cousins of the equally ill-tempered dromedaries and bactrians of Africa and Asia, also have other cousins in the New

World. Guanacos and the delicate little vicuñas are often seen along the railway line between Uyuni and the Chilean border.

Vicuñas are unfortunately in trouble these days. Their incredibly soft and fuzzy little hides fetch a king's ransom on the illicit market and Bolivia has been a bit lax about trying to keep them in their skins. The best place to see them is actually just across the border in Chile's Lauca National Park, where they survive in their thousands and are zealously protected.

The Altiplano is also the favourite habitat for an incredible number of flamingos. Just look for any shallow lake and it will probably be full of them.

Not so abundant, but still relatively common, are the rhea, or South American ostrich, and the *viscacha*. The latter are cute long-tailed rabbits which spend most of their time huddled under rocks. They're very docile but unless you approach quietly they probably won't stick around. Until I actually saw one, I thought the viscacha was just a Bolivian version of the fabled Yankee jackalope.

If you're very lucky, you might see a cóndor or two in your travels around the highland regions of the country. Highly revered by the Incas, these rare New World vultures are the world's largest flying birds. They have a wingspan of over three metres and have been known to effortlessly drag a carcass weighing 20 kg.

In the more humid regions, there is an incredible variety of such things as lizards, noisy green parrots, monkeys, snakes, butterflies, fish and bugs by the zillions!

If you're travelling by river in the Amazon Basin you're almost sure to spot capybaras (large amphibious rodents), turtles, alligators and pink dolphins. It's not unusual to see giant anacondas in the waters of the Beni and if you're travelling overland you'll come across armadillos, *jochi* (or agouti – agile long-legged rodents), rheas and sloths.

Many of these more common animals wind up in the stewpot. Locals roast turtles in the shell and eat their eggs. Jochi and armadillo are considered staples in some areas and a great many of the latter are also turned into *charangos*, a Bolivian ukulele-type instrument.

There are numerous other species lurking about which are unfortunately rather more difficult to observe, either because they hide well or exist only in small numbers.

The puma, native throughout the Americas, was considered sacred by many of the tribes conquered by the Incas and in fact the Inca capital of Cuzco was laid out in the shape of this feline deity. Even today, many Bolivians believe that a lunar eclipse occurs whenever a hungry puma begins nibbling at the moon, which is also a deity. On such occasions, they make all kinds of racket, hoping to frighten it away. At any rate, the puma is a reclusive creature and there's not much chance you'll run across one without a great deal of effort.

The jaguar, tapir and *javelí* (peccary), which occupy the nearly inaccessible expanses of the Grán Chaco, are also very elusive. Slightly more common is the giant anteater which sometimes may be spotted along the railway line east of Santa Crúz.

GOVERNMENT

In theory only, this is how it works: Bolivia is a republic, much like the USA, with legislative, executive and judicial branches of government. The first two convene in La Paz, the de facto capital, and the Supreme Court sits in Sucre, the legal capital.

The president is elected to a four-year term by popular vote and cannot hold more than one consecutive term. Once elected, the president appoints a cabinet of 15 members and also selects departmental and local government officers.

The Legislature consists of a Senate and a Chamber of Deputies which convenes in legislative session for 90 days per year. Each department (there are nine of them) sends three elected senators for terms of six years, with one-third elected every two years. The Chamber of Deputies has 102 members who are elected to four-year terms.

In actual fact things very rarely work out this way. In a land that's had more leaders than years of independence and has been ruled by military juntas for much of its existence, such democratic processes may seem a bit foreign.

ECONOMY

With world tin markets declining and internal strife between miners' unions, cooperatives and the state, the days of the supremacy of tin as Bolivia's mainstay export are over for the time being. However, raw natural resources still make up most of the nation's legal annual export revenue of US$400 million.

In the far south-west there are rich deposits of sulphur, antimony, bismuth and lead/zinc. Further north and west are the famed silver and gold mines of Potosí, still working after over four centuries, and around Oruro there are the troubled tin mines.

Due to lack of skill and capital, governmental corruption and ludicrous disorganisation, most of Bolivia's mineral exports leave the nation in raw form. Not only does this increase transport costs, but it also hinders Bolivia's ability to compete effectively on world markets. Cooperatives bear the burden of this loss through low wages and appalling working conditions for the miners.

The nation is currently looking toward the *Oriente*, the humid lowlands, where significant deposits of natural gas, iron manganese and petroleum have been discovered.

Agriculturally, Bolivia is a subsistence country. That is, most of the food products grown or raised there remain within its borders with only a few notable exceptions. A small amount of Yungas coffee is exported and a moderate quantity of sugar, grown in Tarija and Santa Crúz Departments, is also exported, mostly to Argentina. And then, of course, there's cocaine . . .

In 1986 alone, Bolivia's star export brought US$600 million into the country – that's US$200 million more than all legal exports combined. It also brought down the wrath of the US government, which seems to think that a well-placed bomb is the solution to any problem.

Despite the 1984 kidnapping of President Hernan Siles Zuazo by a US-backed guerrilla group, as well as threats to cut off foreign aid to the country and a rather bungled attempt at disintegrating a few cocaine-processing laboratories in the Beni region, the situation hasn't changed much over the past few years.

While the police busy themselves hassling tourists and coca-growing Indians to satisfy the US government, the big guys just keep right on quietly paying off the right people.

The fact is that Bolivia, as it is, cannot survive without drug money and as long as there's a demand for the evil powder, Bolivia will continue to produce. Today, at least 20,000 hectares of coca are under cultivation, primarily in the Yungas and Chapare regions. In 1986, this was turned into 100,000 kg of cocaine.

Of late, Bolivia has been trying to boost its weak economy by promoting tourism, but budgets are small and the kind of facilities which would attract big money are lacking outside of La Paz. It also seems that any gains made by the Bolivian Tourism Institute are quickly negated by corrupt officials who see tourists as a lucrative form of personal revenue and, consequently, squeamish visitors are easily put off.

POPULATION

Bolivia has a population of about 6.5 million, 70% of whom live on the bleak Altiplano near the western boundary of the country. Most of these people are concentrated in the northern end of this region in the environs of La Paz, Lake Titicaca and Oruro.

Between 50% and 60% of the total population is of pure Indian stock and most speak either Quechua or Aymará as a first language.

About 35% are *mestizo*, people of Spanish American and American Indian parentage or descent. They are locally known as *cholo*, but the term is misleading because it has also come to connote anyone, even pure-blooded Indian, who has moved to the city and still wears ethnic dress.

About 1% of the population is of African heritage, mostly descended from the slaves conscripted to work the mines of Potosí.

The remainder of the population is of European descent, with a wide variety of origins. Some are obviously descendants of the early conquerors, but one also finds colonies of *Platt-Deutch* speaking Mennonites from Canada, missionaries of several dozen foreign churches, escaped Nazi war criminals and disillusioned ex-pats from all over the world.

A small Asian minority has also taken root in the east, centred around the colony of Okinawa in Santa Crúz Department. At this time, there is relatively little mixing between the various groups.

Bolivia is generally considered to be the poorest country in South America and the second poorest in the western hemisphere (after Haiti), with a gross national product that reflects annual earnings of only US$318 per inhabitant. Fortunately, this is not as severe as it sounds because a good many rural Bolivians operate outside the currency system and enjoy relatively comfortable subsistence lifestyles.

Education, though technically compulsory, is either poor or non-existent in much of the country and the literacy rate is the lowest in South America. A friend of mine who took to visiting schools in Bolivia reported that a good deal of educational time is spent memorising and chanting military drill, which reflects the state of affairs in this nation where the armed forces wield so much power.

The state of health care, particularly in rural areas, is also quite poor. It's estimated that 15% of infants born in Bolivia can be expected to die before the age of one. Similarly, the average life-expectancy in the country is only 51 years compared with 70 to 75 years in most developed nations.

CHOLA DRESS

Anyone who's had any contact with Bolivia should be familiar with the stereotypical Aymará women's dress. Both colourful and utilitarian, this interesting ensemble has come to represent Bolivia to the rest of the world.

The most noticeable characteristic of the traditional Aymará dress is the ubiquitous dark green, black or brown bowler hat that would seem more at home on a London street than in the heart of the former Spanish colonies. Despite their oppressive origins you'd be hard pressed to find a *chola* or a *campesina* without one.

The women normally braid their hair into two long plaits which are joined by a tuft of black wool known as a *pocacha*.

The short *pollera* skirts they wear are constructed of several horizontal bands tucked under each other. This garment tends to make most of the women appear overweight, especially when they wear several layers of these skirts.

On top, the outfit consists of a factory-made blouse, a woollen *chompa* (pullover/jumper), a short vest-like jacket, a cotton apron, or a combination of all of these. Usually, the women will add a woollen shawl known as a *phullu*.

Slung across the back and tied around the neck is the *ahuayo*, a rectangle of manufactured or hand-woven cloth decorated with brilliantly-coloured horizontal bands. It is used as a carryall and is filled with everything from coca or groceries to babies.

The Quechua of the highlands east of the Altiplano wear equally colourful but not so universally recognised attire. The hat, called a *montera*, is a flat-topped affair made of white wool. It's taller and broader than the bowlers worn by the Aymará. The men's montera looks something like an old-time football or warriors' helmet but it's made of finely woven wool.

RELIGION & SUPERSTITION

With 95% of the population following it to varying degrees, Roman Catholicism is accepted almost universally throughout Bolivia. In the Indian community and in rural areas, however, the beliefs and rituals of the Incas and Aymarás blend with the Christianity of their conquerors into an interesting conglomeration of doctrines, rites and superstitions.

The most obvious aspect of native religion is the belief in various gods. A diverse array of beneficent and malevolent characters seem to have their fingers into everything and expect constant appeasement by their subjects.

If a person has a problem with a particular god then the *yatiri*, or witch doctor, will often be able to help. If you'd like to know what sort of harm may befall you, a visit to the *thaliri*, or fortune-teller, is in order. This will give the yatiri an idea of what he's supposed to prevent from happening and which god he can bribe to prevent it.

There is however, a particularly insidious night phantom called *Kharisiri* who preys on sleeping humans. Once a person is on his bad side not even the best yatiri can help.

Ekeko, which means 'dwarf' in Aymará, is the good little household god of abundance. He is responsible for finding spouses for the single, homes for the homeless and success for business people. He's a whimsical little creature and a good friend to have. The *Alasitas* festival in La Paz is dedicated to Ekeko and there's even a monument in his honour in that same city.

The evil *Happiñuñoz* are dreaded, however. The personification of beautiful women, these characters seduce men, cause them to lose their powers of reason and then steal their souls. The inevitable result is death for the poor victim.

The rainbow is called *Cuharmi* and will bring bad luck if you point at it or allow your children to look at it.

The most important of all the deities is *Pachamama*, the earth mother. She shares herself with human beings, helps bring forth abundant crops and distributes riches to those who venerate her. She seems to have quite an appetite for such things as coca, alcohol and the blood of animals, particularly llamas. The people must remember to apologise to her should they need to disturb the earth for any reason, such as ploughing, construction, mining or whatever.

In the mines of Oruro and Potosí, a number of superstitions and beliefs have developed and persisted over the years because miners believe that they need luck in order to be productive in the mines. Luck, they assume, is brought on by avoidance of certain 'unlucky' practices.

Women, for instance, may not enter certain mines. Miners may not whistle or eat toasted *aba* beans while in the mine; and if llama meat is eaten inside the mine, the miners may not use salt to season it. Breaking any of these taboos, the miners believe, would surely bring bad luck and low mineral production.

FIESTAS & HOLIDAYS

Bolivian holidays and fiestas are invariably of religious or political origin. They usually commemorate a Christian or Indian saint or god, or a political event such as a battle. They typically include lots of folk music, dancing, food, alcohol, ritual and general unrestrained behaviour. Water balloons and fireworks are also popular on these occasions.

For the traveller, they can be lots of fun and anyone who wants a better understanding of Bolivian cultures should try to attend at least one.

The following is only a partial list of the most significant or interesting annual events throughout the country. As every Bolivian town stages a fiesta as frequently as any excuse arises, with a little effort you'll probably be able to catch two or three during even a short visit.

As with everything in Bolivia, the dates given here are subject to change, so be sure to check before going too far out of your way to attend one. Many of the fiestas listed are celebrated nationwide and the city identified is just the most famous celebration of it.

January

Alasitas Fair, or Festival of Abundance (24th). This dates from Inca times and is dedicated to Ekeko, the little household god of abundance. (La Paz)

February

Virgin of Candelaria (2nd) A weeklong festival and cattle market. (Aiquile) And, yet another excuse for a big blowout in Copacabana!

Carnival * Celebrations nationwide, but the most spectacular event is staged in Oruro.

March

Phujllay * (Pookh'yai), which means 'play' in Quechua. This festival commemorates the Battle of Lumbati and is one of the three major festivals in Bolivia. (Tarabuco)

Semana Santa * Holy Week activities nationwide, taking place in either March or April. The most impressive event is the Good Friday fiesta in Copacabana, where hundreds of pilgrims make the 158 km walk from La Paz.

April

Fiesta de la Papa (4th & 5th) Folkloric festival dedicated to the potato (I've heard this one is great!). (Betanzos)

May

Fiesta de la Crúz (3rd) Commemorating the cross on which Christ was crucified – 15 days of music, parades, and alcohol consumption. (Tarija)

Commemorative Festival (25th) Celebrates the Independence movement of 1809, the first in Latin America. (Sucre)

Fiesta de la Santísima Trinidad * Occurs in either May or June with indigenous dancing and musical instruments featured. (Trinidad)

Día de la Madre * Mother's Day honours women and children who defended their cities and homes during battle. Celebrated nationwide.

June

Festividad de Nuestro Señor Jesús del Grán Poder * One of Bolivia's three major

festivals, dedicated to the 'great power of Jesus Christ'. (La Paz)
Llama sacrifice to Pachamama * Takes place on the last three Saturdays of June. (Potosí)

July
Fiesta (31st) Local festival in a unique jungle Indian community. (San Ignacio de Moxos)

August
Llama sacrifice to Pachamama * Takes place the first Saturday of the month. (Potosí)
Independence Day Fiesta (3rd-10th) Excessive raging! (Copacabana and nationwide)
Virgen de Urcupiña (15th) Folkloric singing and dancing. This is the biggest festival in the Cochabamba Department. (Quillacollo)
Virgen de Chaguaya (15th) Dedicated to Christian faith. This is the only Bolivian fiesta I know of that prohibits the drinking of alcohol. (Chaguaya)
Fiesta de San Roque (16th) Participants wear brightly-coloured clothing, feathers and belts. San Roque is the patron saint of dogs, so they take part too. Unique music is performed. (Tarija)

September
Department of Santa Crúz civic holiday (24th) Buildings, statues and monuments are dedicated and hot air flies. (Santa Crúz)

October
Virgen del Rosario * Masses, bullfights, folk music and market activities. (Tarabuco)

November
All-Saints' Day (1st, 2nd) Cemetery visits and decoration of graves nationwide.

December
Christmas (25th)

* Dates differ each year.

LANGUAGE

The official language of Bolivia is Spanish, but only 60 to 70% of the people actually speak it, and then often as a second language. The remainder speak Quechua, the language of the Incas, or Aymará, the pre-Incaic language of the Altiplano. A host of other minor indigenous tongues are used in limited areas throughout the country.

Most travellers in South America either arrive with at least a basic knowledge of Spanish or very quickly acquire a workable vocabulary of say 300 to 500 words. English in Bolivia is about as useful as Mandarin in the USA, but fortunately it's not difficult to learn the basics of Spanish. With a short night course or self-teaching programme, you won't be carrying on philosophical or political discussions right away, but you will be communicating and gaining a basis on which to build.

For those who haven't had the opportunity to study Spanish before travelling, the following is a brief run-down of basic grammar and pronunciation and commonly-used words and phrases.

Pronunciation

Vowel pronunciation in Bolivian Spanish is easy and consistent. In the following vowel list the nearest equivalent English vowel is highlighted:

a is similar to 'f**a**ther'
e is similar to 'w**ay**'
i is similar to 'b**ea**n'
o is similar to '**o**ld'
u is similar to 'p**oo**l'
y is the same as *i*

Spanish consonants are more or less the same as their English counterparts but there are a few variations:

c is only soft before *i* or *e* (ie like an 's')
d is a cross between English 'd' and 'th'
g is only soft before *i* or *e* (ie like German 'ch', something like an English 'h' only with more friction)
h is never (under any circumstances) pronounced
j is pronounced like English 'h', only with more friction
ll is pronounced more or less like the 'll y' in 'will you' but *ll* often sounds more like a simple English 'y'
ñ is the equivalent of English 'ny' as in 'canyon'

gu and *qu* are used to get the hard consonant sound (ie like English 'g' and 'k' in 'get' and 'kit') in front of *e* or *i*. In this case, the *u* is silent unless it is altered with an umlaut. In front of *a* or *o* the *u* is pronounced like an English 'w'.
rr is a rolled or trilled 'r'.
r is a slap of the tongue against the palate and sounds like a very quickly spoken 'd' or 't' as in 'ladder' or 'matter'. At the beginning of a word, some Bolivians pronounce it 'zh'
v is a cross between English 'v' and 'b'
x is pronounced as in 'taxi'
z is pronounced as 's'

Emphasis in Spanish is always placed on the second last syllable unless an accent mark is employed to alter it. Accents also serve to break up vowel sounds in a diphthong.

Grammar
Articles, adjectives and demonstrative pronouns must agree with the noun in both gender and number. Nouns ending in *a* are generally feminine and the corresponding articles are *la* (singular) and *las* (plural). Those ending in *o* are usually masculine and require the articles *el* (singular) and *los* (plural).

There are, however, hundreds of exceptions to these guidelines which can only be memorised or deduced by the referent of the word. Plurals are formed by adding *s* to words ending in a vowel and *es* to those ending in a consonant.

In addition to using all the familiar English tenses, Spanish also uses the imperfect tense and two subjunctive tenses (past and present). Tenses are formed either by adding a myriad of endings to the root verb or preceding the participle form by some variation of the verb *haber* (to have/to exist).

There are verb endings for first, second and third person singular and plural. Second person singular and plural are divided into formal and familiar modes. If that's not enough, there are three types of verbs – those ending in 'ar', 'er' and 'ir' – which are all conjugated differently. There are also a whole slough of stem-changing rules and irregularities which must be memorised.

Common courtesies
good morning
buén día
good afternoon (or good evening)
buenas tardes
yes
sí
no
no
hello
holá
See you later.
hasta luego
good-bye
Usually just *ciao*. The familiar *adios* is rarely used in Bolivia.
How are you?
que tal?, *como estás?* (familiar) or *como está?* (formal)
please
por favor
thank you
gracias
It's a pleasure.
con mucho gusto

Some useful phrases
Do you speak Spanish?
habla usted castellano?
Where do you come from?
de donde es ustéd?
What is your country?
cual es su país?
Where are you staying?
donde estás alojado?
What is your profession?
cuál es su profesión?
What time do you have?
que hora tiene?
Don't you have smaller change?
no tiene sencillo?
Do you understand? (polite)
me explico?

Do you understand? (casual)
me entiendes?
Where can I change money/travellers' cheques?
donde se cambia monedas/cheques de viajeros?
Where is the .... ?
donde está el/la .... ?
How much is this?
There are fortunately several variations on this well-worn phrase: *a como?*, *por cuanto sale esto?*, *cuanto cuesta esto?*, *cuanto vale esto?*
too expensive
demasiado caro
cheaper
más barato
I'll take it.
lo llevo
What's the weather like?
que tiempo hace?
Buy from me!
comprame!
to the right
a la derecha
to the left
a la izquiereda
Continue straight ahead.
siga derecho
I don't understand.
no entiendo
more or less
más o menos
when?
cuando?
how?
como?
How's that again?
como?
where?
donde?
What time does the next plane/bus/train leave for .... ?
a que hora sale el próximo avión/bús/trén para .... ?
where from?
de donde?
around there
para allá
around here
para acá
It's hot/cold.
hace calor/frío

Some useful words

airport
aeropuerto
bank
banco
block
cuadra
boyfriend/girlfriend
enamorado/a
bus station
terminal terrestre
church
templo, *catedrál*, *iglesia*
city
ciudád
downhill
para abajo
exchange house
casa de cambio
here
aquí
husband/wife
marido/esposa
Indian/peasant
campesino (or *cholo* if they live in the city)
mother/father
madre/padre
people
la gente
police
policía
post office
correo
rain
lluvia
snow
nieve
there
allí
town square
plaza
train station
estación de ferrocarriles

uphill
para arriba
wind
viento

Time & dates
What time is it?
que hora es? or *que horas son?*
It is one o'clock.
es la una
It is two o'clock.
son las dos
midnight
medianoche
noon
mediodia
in the afternoon
de la tarde
in the morning
de la mañana
at night
de la noche
half past two
dos y media
quarter past two
dos y cuarto
two twenty-five
dos con veinticinco minutos
twenty to two
veinte para las dos

Sunday
domingo
Monday
lunes
Tuesday
martes
Wednesday
miércoles
Thursday
jueves
Friday
viernes
Saturday
sábado

Spring
la primavera
Summer
el verano
Autumn
el otoño
Winter
el invierno

today
hoy
tomorrow
mañana
yesterday
ayer

Quechua & Aymará
For your interest, the following is a list of Quechua and Aymará words and phrases relating to things that may be useful in areas where these languages are spoken.

The grammar and pronunciation of these languages are quite difficult for native English speakers. If you're serious about learning them, or will be spending a lot of time in remote areas, you should look around in La Paz for a good course.

Dictionaries and phrasebooks are available through Los Amigos del Libro and larger bookstores in La Paz, but a fairly sound knowledge of Spanish will be needed to use them.

Lonely Planet's 'Quechua phrasebook', available in 1989, is primarily for travellers to Peru but will be of use to travellers who visit the Bolivian highlands. This phrasebook provides useful phrases and vocabulary in the Cuzco dialect.

Pronunciation of the following words and phrases will be similar to the way they would be pronounced in Spanish. An underlined letter signifies an explosive delivery of that letter. An apostrophe is a glottal stop (the 'sound' in the middle of 'oh-oh!').

Some Useful Phrases

English	Aymará	Quechua
Where is ....?	*kaukasa .... ?*	*maypi .... ?*
to the left	*chchekaru*	*lokeman*

to the right	*cupiru*	*pañaman*
How do you say .... ?	*cun sañasa uca'ha .... ?*	*imainata nincha chaita .... ?*
It is called	*ucan sutipa'h ....*	*chaipa'g sutin'ha ....*
Please repeat.	*uastata sita*	*ua'manta niway*
It's a pleasure.	*take chuima'hampi*	*tucuy sokoywan*
What does that mean?	*cuna sañasa muniucha'ha?*	*imata'nita munanchai'ja?*
I don't know.	*janiwa yatkti*	*mana yachanichu*
I am hungry.	*mankatawa hiu'ta*	*yarkaimanta wañusianiña*
How much?	*k'gauka?*	*maik'ata'g?*

Some Useful Words

be	*ucanquir*	*kaskai*
cheap	*pisitaqui*	*pisillapa'g*
condor	*malku*	*cóndor*
distant	*haya*	*caru*
downhill	*aynacha*	*uray*
father	*auqui*	*tata*
food	*manka*	*mikíuy*
friend	*kgochu*	*kgochu*
give	*churaña*	*koi*
go (travel)	*saraña*	*purina*
grandfather	*achachila*	*awicho-machu*
grandmother	*hacha-mama*	*paya*
hello!	*laphi!*	*raphi!*
house	*uta*	*huasi*
I	*haya*	*ñoka*
learn	*yatiña*	*yachaska*
llama	*yama-karhua*	*karhua*
lodging	*korpa*	*pascana*
man	*chacha*	*k'gari*
miner	*koyiri*	*koya'g*
moon	*pha'gsi*	*kiya*
mother	*taica*	*mama*
near	*maka*	*kailla*
no	*janiwa*	*mana*
river	*jawira*	*mayu*
ruins	*champir*	*champir*
snowy peak	*kollu*	*riti-orko*
sun	*yinti*	*inti*
teacher	*yatichiri*	*yachachi'g*
thirst	*phara*	*chchaqui*
to work	*irnakaña*	*lank'ana*
trail	*tapu*	*chakiñan*
very near	*hakítaqui*	*kaillitalla*
water	*uma*	*yacu*
when?	*cunapacha?*	*haiká'g?*
woman	*warmi*	*warmi*
yes	*jisa*	*ari*
you	*huma*	*khan*

Numbers

Number	Spanish	Aymará	Quechua
1	*uno*	*maya*	*u'*
2	*dos*	*paya*	*iskai*
3	*tres*	*quimsa*	*quinsa*
4	*cuatro*	*pusi*	*tahua*
5	*cinco*	*pesca*	*phiska*
6	*seis*	*zo'hta*	*so'gta*
7	*siete*	*pakalko*	*khanchis*
8	*ocho*	*quimsakalko*	*pusa'g*
9	*nueve*	*yatunca*	*iskon*
10	*diéz*	*tunca*	*chunca*
11	*once*	*tuncamayani*	*chunca u'niyo'g*
12	*doce*	*tuncapayani*	*chunca iskai'niyo'g*
13	*trece*	*tuncaquimsani*	*chunca quinsa'niyo'g*
14	*catorce*	*tuncapusini*	*chunca tahua'yo'g*
15	*quince*	*tuncapescani*	*chunca phiska'nio'g*
16	*dieciseis*	*tunca zo'htani*	*chunca so'gta'nio'g*
17	*diecisiete*	*tuncapakalkoni*	*chunca khanchisniyo'g*
18	*dieciocho*	*tunca quimsalalkoni*	*chunca pusa'gniyo'g*
19	*diecinueve*	*tunca yatuncani*	*chunca iskoniyo'g*
20	*veinte*	*pa tunka*	*iskai chunca*
21	*veintiuno*	*pa tunk mayani*	*iskai chunca u'niyo'g*
30	*treinta*	*quimsa tunca*	*quinsa chunca*
40	*cuarenta*	*pusi tunca*	*tahua chunca*
50	*cincuenta*	*pesca tunca*	*phiska chunca*
60	*sesenta*	*zo'hta tunca*	*so'gta chunca*
70	*setenta*	*pakalka tunca*	*khanchi chunca*
80	*ochenta*	*quimsakalko tunca*	*pusa'g chunca*
90	*noventa*	*yatunk tunca*	*iskon chunca*
100	*cién*	*pataca*	*pacha'g*
101	*ciento uno*	*pataca mayani*	*pach'u'niyo'g*
200	*dos cientos*	*papataca*	*iskaipacha'*
201	*dos cientos uno*	*papataca mayani*	*iskaipacha'u'niyo'g*
300	*tres cientos*	*quimsapataca*	*quinsapacha'*
400	*quatrocientos*	*pusipataca*	*tahuapacha'*
500	*quinientos*	*pescapataca*	*phiskapacha'*
600	*seis cientos*	*zo'htapataca*	*so'gtapacha'*
700	*setecientos*	*pakalkapataca*	*khanchispacha'*
800	*ochocientos*	*quimsakalkopataca*	*pusa'pacha'*
900	*novecientos*	*yatuncapataca*	*iskonpacha'*
1000	*mil*	*waranka*	*huaranca*
100,000	*cien mil*	*pataca waranka*	*pacha'g-huaranca*
1,000,000	*un millon*	*mapacha'*	*hunu*

Facts for the Visitor

VISAS & DOCUMENTS

Countries whose citizens do not require tourism or transit visas for entrance into Bolivia are West Germany, Austria, Belgium, Spain, the Netherlands, Ireland, Great Britain, Italy, Norway, Portugal, Sweden, Switzerland, Israel, Canada, Peru, Uruguay, the Dominican Republic, Ecuador and the USA.

Everyone else must obtain a visa from a Bolivian Consulate either in their home country or in a neighbouring South American country. In addition to a visa, citizens of most Asian, African and Communist countries officially require 'personal permission' by cable from Bolivian immigration before a visa will be issued.

The fact is that Bolivian officials' knowledge of geography is very sketchy. I met countless folks from countries requiring visas who were allowed in without one. To be on the safe side, though, it's best to play by the rules or they could catch up to you when you try to leave.

Officially, your passport must be valid for one year beyond your date of entry into the country though I was once given a 90-day entry stamp just one month before my passport expired. Again, however, it's probably best not to take chances.

Minors under 18 not travelling with both parents may be required to produce a notarised letter from the parent(s) not accompanying them to Bolivia, which grants permission to travel and guarantees financial responsibility. An official-looking statement that the missing parent is deceased will replace this requirement.

Everyone travelling to Bolivia for business purposes is required to obtain a visa. You will need a passport, letter of intent and a financial guarantee from your employer. A business visa costs US$50 and is valid for a visit of 90 days.

Most border crossing officials will give only 30-day entrance stamps. Villazón and Copacabana are the only ports of entry that actually have 90-day stamps. All lengths of stay may be extended in major cities by the federal police. The fee at the time of writing was US$25 but travellers have reported that it is negotiable, most often in favour of the officials.

A certificate of yellow fever vaccination is required of anyone entering from an infected area. This is usually interpreted as Sub-Saharan Africa, some parts of Central America, the Caribbean and the Guianas. Officially, a yellow fever certificate is also required for travel in Santa Crúz Department, but I've never been asked for one.

If you plan to enter Brazil from Bolivia, you'll need one or be required to get one at the border. At Corumbá, the vaccination clinic is open only from 9 to 10 am, Monday to Saturday. At Guajará-mirim, there is a clinic at the port, open daily. At Brasilia and Cáceres, however, there are no such facilities and you'll have to get the certificate before arriving at the border.

Personal documents (passports, visas, *cédulas*) must be carried at all times. Police checks are frequently encountered and the penalty for being caught without documents is US$50 and several lost hours while paperwork is shuffled at the police station. This is strictly enforced in lowland regions where drug trafficking is rife.

Diplomatic, official, student and missionary visas are issued free of charge. Permanent residence and work visas are also available through consulates abroad, but be prepared to wait or pay exorbitant sums to get such complex paperwork 'in order'.

Visas for Adjoining Countries
Visas may be obtained at the following consulates in Bolivia:

Chile
La Paz: Avenida 6 de Agosto 2932 (tel 322201); open 8:30 am to noon weekdays.
Argentina
La Paz: Banco de la Nación Argentina (tel 353089); open 9 am to 2 pm weekdays.
Santa Crúz: Banco de la Nación Argentina Junín 22
Cochabamba: Avenida Pando 1329 (tel 48268); open 9 am to 1 pm weekdays.
Tarija: Corner of Ballivián and Bolívar
Paraguay
La Paz: Avenida Arce 2105 (tel 322018); open 8.30 am to 12.30 pm.
Santa Crúz: Sucre 677
Peru
La Paz: Avenida Mariscal Santa Crúz 1285 (tel 352031)
Cochabamba: Avenida Pando 1143 (tel 43276); open 9 am to noon and 2 to 5 pm weekdays.
Santa Crúz: Calle La Paz 726
Brazil
La Paz: Fernando Guachalla 494 (tel 35718); open 10 am to noon and 2 to 4 pm weekdays.
Santa Crúz: Suárez de Figueroa 127 (tel 44400)
Cochabamba: Calle Potosí 14455 (tel 45702)
Cobija: Corner of Beni and Molina
Guayaramerín: Calle Beni

Visa and passport photos are available in 10 minutes from Rapid Fotocolor in the basement of Edificio La Primera which is on 16 de Julio, half a block from the La Paz tourist office. You pay only US$5 for six black-and-white photos.

MONEY

Bolivia's unit of currency is the Boliviano and is represented by B$. At the time of writing, US$1 = B$2.

The Boliviano has only been in existence for a short time. 'Every Bolivian is a millionaire', one *Paceño* told me before its advent on 1 January, 1987. The new unit of currency is the product of eliminating six zeros from the massively inflated peso denomination. Since the end of 1985, US$1 had been equivalent to B$2,000,000.

Thus, amazingly, Bolivian currency has remained stable for almost two years now! Even so, all prices in this book, unless otherwise noted, will be quoted in US dollars.

Bolivianos come in .01, .05, .1, .5, 1, 5 and 10 denomination notes. These are actually old peso notes which are sometimes, but not always overstamped with the new denominations. This all gets incredibly confusing at first because B$1 may be referred to as 1,000,000 pesos, 1000 pesos, one peso, one boliviano, 50 dollar cents, or 1000 bolivianos. You'll catch on after awhile.

All that odd-looking money you'll find littering the streets is not left over from some Bolivian version of Monopoly. Old peso notes of small denominations – 100s, 1000s and 5000s – are discarded as worthless paper. Old peso coins are used only as telephone tokens.

Bolivian currency of any kind is worthless outside Bolivia. If it can be exchanged at all, the rate given will be so poor that the cash is worth more in souvenir value – after all, where else will you ever see so many zeros?

Changing Money The black market in currency was abolished in late 1985 and since the official rate currently represents the currency's actual value, a parallel market remains unnecessary. This is, of course, subject to change.

As a rule, the best currency to carry is US dollars. Pounds sterling, Swiss francs and Japanese yen may be more stable, but the greenback is the only foreign currency accepted throughout Bolivia. Currencies of neighbouring countries may be exchanged at border areas.

If you're carrying travellers' cheques, which is a good idea, American Express

seem to be the most widely accepted. Other brands, however, won't cause you significant problems.

Bolivian banks do not, as a rule, exchange money although I found several who would do so in a pinch for a very poor rate. In the largest cities, you can find *casas de cambio* (exchange houses) that will change bills. Some will also change travellers' cheques.

The best rates can be found at travel agencies, jewellery and appliance stores, pharmacies and any place that carries on a lot of trade with the USA. Their foreign transactions must be made in US dollars and merchants are happy to get them. Many of these places will exchange travellers' cheques too. Finer hotels and restaurants may accept travellers' cheques as payment for services, but will generally not exchange them outright.

If you'll be travelling outside of La Paz, Cochabamba or Santa Crúz, I strongly recommend that you carry enough cash to get you back to one of those cities. Markets for travellers' cheques vary and if merchants don't desperately need dollars, you'll probably only be able to exchange cash in the smaller cities. Since merchants must wait 20 business days to receive cash for your travellers' cheques, you have to expect to exchange them for 5% to 10% less than cash.

Casas de Cambio and merchants usually open at around 9 am and close at 6 pm. They close for midday break at noon and re-open sometime between 2 and 3 pm. Street changers will provide round-the-clock exchange services, but they give the same rates as everyone else.

Never hand over your cash before receiving and counting the money they give you. If you're not familiar with Bolivian notes, be sure to count zeros, as 50000 looks an awful lot like 500000 and 1000000 is easily confused with 10000000.

In La Paz and Cochabamba several merchants and casas de cambio will exchange travellers' cheques for cash dollars and take a 1% to 3% commission.

This is a good way to get hold of some dollars if you're headed to Brazil where, due to the parallel market, travellers' cheques currently receive 30% to 35% less than cash.

Credit Cards Major cards, such as Visa, Master Charge and American Express, may be used in larger cities at first-rate hotels, restaurants and tour agencies. Buying cash with credit cards is a major hassle and should be avoided unless you have several days to spare.

Bargaining In Bolivia, as in most of Latin America, few prices are fixed. Almost everything is negotiable, not only for *artesanía* (local handicrafts), but also for food, transport and even lodging.

Bolivians expect to haggle over prices but some of the high, so-called 'gringo pricing' is caused by foreigners who seem to be willing to pay any price named. Many foreigners seem to be plagued by guilty feelings that they have so much more money than the locals that it won't hurt them to pay a little more than market price.

Bolivians don't usually understand this kind of thinking and they take it as ignorance rather than altruism. So don't worry about short-changing the merchants – they have a price below which they will not sell. It's your job to find that price.

In Bolivia, the original asking price is usually more realistic than it would be in neighbouring Peru, for instance. Expect to pay 80 to 90% of what is initially quoted.

Bills & Change Bills with tiny pieces missing, repaired with opaque tape, sewed with thread or even reconstructed from several other bills, are quite common.

In La Paz and Oruro, vendors and consumers engage in a battle of wits over these notes. Vendors employ sneaky methods of giving them as change, particularly to ignorant foreigners and inattentive Bolivians. So check your change and return any mangled bills, or you'll end up using them as toilet paper if you can't think up an equally sneaky method of tricking another vendor into accepting them.

Another problem is change; nobody has it. When you exchange money, you will invariably be given B$5 and B$10 notes, but just *try* to use one of them to buy a B$1 bottle of soda.

If you hand one of these notes to a vendor he will become flustered and will wander aimlessly around to other vendors, hopelessly begging change, which no one will have. In the end he will return defeated and report that there is no change. You've derailed the whole system. If you've already consumed the product you're trying to purchase, prepare to settle in for a wait while the vendor combs the city searching for change.

It may be a hassle to lug around a pile of near-worthless bills, but if you're planning a trip to the market or to any other place where prices are very low, it will save a lot of time to have some small bills on hand.

COSTS

Overall, prices for food, services, hotels and transportation are slightly higher than in other Andean Republics but lower than in Brazil, Argentina and Uruguay. Although, thanks to drug money, Santa Crúz de la Sierra may be the most expensive South American city outside of Patagonia.

Throughout Bolivia, there is a whopping import duty on consumer goods produced outside the country. Automobiles, electronics and camera equipment, film and books from outside will cost at least twice what they would in Australia or North America. For example, a paperback novel will cost US$10 to US$12, a box of corn flakes up to US$5 and electronic equipment prices will be astronomical.

A practice you may run across, especially

in the cities, is 'gringo pricing'. An attitude somewhere between acceptance and paranoia is advised when dealing with situations of suspected overcharging. If you want to avoid an unpleasant scene, it's a good idea to agree on food, accommodation and transportation prices before the goods or services are consumed.

TIPPING

Except in four and five star hotels and exclusive restaurants or clubs, it is not done at all. Restaurants will add a service charge of 10% to your bill anyway, so further tipping is unnecessary. Bus and taxi drivers, as a rule, are not tipped either.

TOURIST INFORMATION

Bolivia is not yet a traditional tourist destination. With no Machu Picchu or Rio de Janeiro to promote and recommend it, the Bolivian tourist industry is still very much in its formative stages.

This doesn't mean, however, that there's not a lot to see and do. It only means that the government hasn't spent a lot of money developing and touting the country's numerous attractions, which many travellers prefer anyway.

The cities of La Paz, Oruro, Cochabamba, Sucre, Tarija, Potosí, Santa Crúz and Trinidad all have offices of the *Instituto Boliviano de Turismo* (IBT).

These range in quality from very helpful to practically worthless, but all will provide you with a street plan of their respective city and can answer simple questions about local transport and attractions. The offices in Sucre and Oruro are particularly friendly and knowledgeable and a visit would be well worth the time.

Locations of tourist offices will be marked on city maps where applicable. They tend to be moved around frequently however, particularly in Tarija and Trinidad, so you may have to track them down anyway. If you find that one has moved, please let us know.

Instituto Boliviano de Turismo

Opening hours are officially 9 am to noon and 2 to 6 pm, but you'll be lucky to find most of them attended for more than a couple of hours each day. As with most Bolivian government operations, the functioning is left largely to the whims of the employees.

GENERAL INFORMATION

Post

Postales, or post cards, to the rest of the Americas and Europe cost 20c, and to anywhere else in the world they're 30c. *Cartas*, or airmail letters, cost 30c to the Americas and Europe and 40c to Australia and the rest of the world.

To a destination within Bolivia, a letter costs 20c or it can be sent for 30c via *Expreso*, express mail. For 50c extra, any piece of mail to anywhere in the world may be certified. Special precautions are taken to ensure that these aren't lost or pilfered and even locals reckon it's worth the price.

Never mail anything from small town post offices. In some towns, such as Montero, sacks of mail lie around for months just waiting for vehicles to take them to larger postal centres.

Parcels, *encomiendas* or *paquetes*, are a little more tricky to send. First of all, the unwrapped parcel must be taken to the *aduana*, or customs office, for inspection. There will sometimes be a customs agent working in the post office itself, but in some cities, such as Oruro, it is across town.

You will have to wrap and seal the parcel in the presence of the customs official, so be sure to take along a box, paper, tape, string and the address. Once the parcel is ready to mail, the customs official stamps it and it's ready for the post office.

A one kg package costs US$15 to send to any foreign destination in the Americas or Europe, making Bolivia's by far the most expensive postal system in Latin America. Certification of the package is recommended and costs 50c more.

Once the fees are paid, you have to take the package to a *revisor* who determines whether or not you've paid enough, which you usually haven't. As soon as the postal clerk and the revisor agree that it contains enough postage, the package will be accepted.

The chances of arrival of any posted parcel increase inversely in proportion to its value and to the number of 'inspections' to which it is subjected. In other words, don't post anything you can't risk losing.

Receiving Mail General Delivery services in Bolivia are called *Poste Restante*; not the French pronunciation, but POS-tay ray-STAN-tay. *Lista de Correos*, the term used in most of Latin America, would also be understood.

A letter sent this way should include the name of the addressee, 'Poste Restante, Correo Central' and the name of the city, department and country. Including the department is helpful because city and town names are repeated. There is a San Ignacio in both Beni and Santa Crúz departments, and a Santa Ana in Beni and La Paz.

While most international mail will be only to the well-known larger cities, innocent misspelling or careless handwriting may render 'Cochabamba' and 'Copacabana' or 'Tarija' and 'Tupiza' indistinguishable, so the department name will help clarify them.

Poste Restante letters will be delivered to the main post office in the city and will be held for 90 days before being returned to the sender. In order to receive mail, a passport must be presented.

Names in Bolivia, as in all Latin countries, are constructed of any number of given and acquired names followed by the father's family name and the mother's maiden name. The *apellido*, or surname, is therefore not the 'last' name used. This can lead to all kinds of confusion in receiving mail filed or listed alphabetically.

For instance, a letter to the president of Bolivia, Victor Paz Estenssoro, would be filed under 'P' for 'Paz'. Likewise, a letter addressed to Mary Ann Smith would most likely end up with the As. Given the way things tend to work in Bolivia, though, Mary would be wise to check under the Ms and the Ss, also. Even capitalising and underlining the surname will not always alleviate the confusion.

In addition to Poste Restante, mail may also be received at an American Express agency or representative office. They keep a list of letters received and you will be required to show your passport and some proof that you are a customer of theirs – a few travellers' cheques or an American Express card will suffice. The American Express representative in La Paz is Magriturismo Limitada (tel 341201) at Avenida 16 de Julio 149, Piso 5 Edificio Avenida, La Paz, Bolivia. Limited English is spoken in the office.

Some, but not all consulates and embassies will receive and hold mail for citizens of their home country, so check beforehand. I know that the Netherlands, Norway, West Germany, Canada, the USA, France and Austria currently provide this service. Australia and New Zealand are represented in Bolivia by the British consulate which will not receive mail.

Telephones

All major and minor cities throughout the country have both ENTEL, or *Empresa Nacional de Telecomunicaciones*, and post offices, *Correos de Bolivia*.

Local Telephone Calls Don't waste your time searching for public telephone boxes; I've only seen two or three in the entire country.

Local calls can be made from ENTEL offices and cost 5c. Since coins are not in regular circulation, old peso coins are sold as *fichas*, or tokens, and are used in public pay telephones.

Alternatively, small street kiosks are often equipped with telephones which may be used for brief local calls. These will cost from 5c to 15c. Hotels and restaurants also allow the public to use their telephones and charge about the same price as the kiosks.

International Calls From private telephones, normal or reverse charge international calls may be made by phoning the International Operator and providing the country code, area or city code and the phone number desired. If you'd like to reverse the charges, explain that the call is *por cobrar*. ENTEL offices will not accept reverse charge calls.

A three-minute telephone call to North America currently costs US$6 station-to-station and US$8 person-to-person. To Europe and the rest of the world, expect to pay at least 30% more.

To make a call from the ENTEL office, you must first fill out a form detailing the city, country, person and number you wish to call. You must leave your passport at the desk while the call is being made. ENTEL will then make the call for you, call your name when it is ready for you to talk and return your passport after you've paid the bill.

All international calls made from Bolivia must be routed through La Paz. At the La Paz ENTEL office, a half-hour wait can be expected. Outside of La Paz, delays of two or three hours are possible.

Long distance calls to locations within Bolivia are inexpensive and can be made from ENTEL offices in less than 10 minutes.

Electricity

Bolivia uses a standard current of 220 volts at 50 cycles except in a few selected locations in La Paz and Potosí. Be sure to ask before you plug in.

In many small towns like Copacabana and Camiri, demand for power exceeds the power stations' ability to supply it. Outages are frequent and in some places are even scheduled during hours of high usage. In some large cities, the water and power are routinely turned off between midnight and 5 am, so if you're a night owl, be sure to have a torch on hand.

Time

Bolivian time is four hours behind Greenwich Mean Time. When it's noon in La Paz, it is 4 pm in London, 11 am in New York, 8 am in San Francisco, 4 am the following day in Auckland and 2 am the following day in Sydney and Melbourne.

Those impressive-looking world clocks in the La Paz ENTEL office should be ignored. It cannot simultaneously be 12.15 in La Paz and 7.40 in New York!

Plumbing

Most of the plumbing in Bolivia is jerry-built or poorly installed and inferior to what developed nations consider acceptable. Therefore, some explanation and instruction for use may be helpful.

First of all, bathtubs are rare outside of expensive tourist hotels, as are hot and cold running water.

It is possible however, to have hot, or tepid, showers thanks to a frightening and deadly-looking device that attaches to the shower head and electrically heats the water as it passes through. Bare wires dangle from the ceiling or run into the shower head.

The dangling variety indicates that you're not going to get a hot shower because the device is broken, as many are. Don't bother getting undressed until you've verified that it's working.

On the wall, you will find a lever that looks suspiciously like an old-time electrocutioner's switch. You have to flip the switch after the water is running (yes, really), so it's best to leave your shoes on and not get wet until this is done.

When the heater is activated, it will begin to emit an electrical humming sound and the lights in the room will dim or go out altogether. This is because the heater requires a great deal of electricity to operate effectively.

The temperature of the water can then be adjusted by increasing or decreasing its flow. A larger volume of water cannot be adequately heated in the time it takes to pass through the shower head, so often, a shower of a bearable temperature is nothing but a pressureless drip.

When it's time to turn the water off, don't touch the controls until you've dried off and have your shoes on. This may be tricky, especially if the shower stall is small. Before turning the water off, flip the switch on the wall and then close the valve.

The WC is usually called *el baño* but it's also often misnamed *servicio sanitario* or *servicio higiénico*. Usually neither sanitary nor hygienic, it can be quite a shock for the newly-arrived visitor. Even foreigners lodging in tourist-class hotels will invariably encounter a typical Bolivian toilet sometime during their visit so it's useful to be prepared for the worst.

In markets and transportation terminals, use of the facilities will usually cost 5c to 10c. At the train station in Quijarro they charge a whopping 25c! In return, you will receive two sheets of one-ply toilet paper which, if you are normal, will not be enough. Toilet paper is almost never provided in public facilities, not even in top class restaurants (or the Bolivian embassy in Washington, DC, for that matter!), so Bolivians carry a roll with them wherever they go.

Since water pressure is very weak, the toilets often cannot even choke down shit, let alone such things as tampons or toilet paper. Therefore, a wastebasket is normally provided in public facilities. If there is no receptacle or if it is already full, just throw the used toilet paper on the floor and someone may get around to cleaning it up. If you think this is disgusting or unhealthy, just wait till you've experienced a clogged and overflowing toilet.

In rural areas, toilets tend to be more basic: a hole in the ground or a corner of a pig sty. So much for eating porkchops in Bolivia . . .

Weights & Measurements

Although the metric system is prevalent, imperial measurements are sometimes used in Bolivia. I have consistently use metric measurements throughout this book, but any fellow Yanks who want to know how high those mountains really are can refer to the conversion chart at the back of this book.

MEDIA

Newspapers

Cochabamba, La Paz, Potosí, Oruro and Santa Crúz all have daily newspapers. The most comprehensive are *El Diario, Hoy, Última Hora* in La Paz, *La Patria* in Oruro, *El Mundo* in Santa Crúz and *Los Tiempos* in Cochabamba. Associated Press, Deutsche Presse Agentur, Reuters and United Press International all have representatives in La Paz.

Radio & Television

The country has 162 radio stations broadcasting in Spanish, Quechua and Aymará.

The government operates television stations in La Paz, Cochabamba, Trinidad, Oruro, Potosí, Tarija and Santa Crúz. The same cities and Sucre are also served by the University Television Network. Smaller cities have private television stations and in some cities in the south such as Tarija, some foreign stations are received.

HEALTH

Although your chances of contracting a serious illness in Bolivia are slim, you'll be exposed to environmental factors, foods and sanitation standards that are probably quite different from what you're used to. All of these factors can significantly affect the travel experience.

This run-down of the health risks includes some preventative measures, symptom descriptions and suggestions about what to do if there is a problem. This isn't meant to replace professional diagnosis or prescription however, and visitors to the third world should discuss with their physician the most up-to-date methods used to prevent and treat the threats to health which may be encountered.

In addition, all travellers should be aware of any drug allergies they may have and avoid using them or their derivatives while travelling in Bolivia. Since common names of prescription medicines in Bolivia are likely to be different from the ones you're used to, ask a pharmacist before taking anything you're not sure about.

It's not necessary to take with you every remedy for every illness you might conceivably contract during your trip. Just about everything available at home can also be found in Bolivian pharmacies and pharmaceutical drugs are available without a prescription. They are a bit lax about storage however, so be sure to check the expiry dates before buying. It would also be a good idea to take along a sufficient supply of any prescriptions that you must take habitually, including contraceptive pills and vitamin tablets.

Pharmacies in Bolivia are known as *farmacias* and medicines are called *medicamentos*. The word for doctor is *medico* and medicine tablets are known as *pastillas*.

Vaccinations

A yellow fever vaccination and related documentation is strongly recommended for every traveller in Bolivia and is legally required for travel in Santa Crúz Department. In addition, Brazilian authorities will not grant entrance from Bolivia without it. The vaccination certificate remains effective for 10 years.

A cholera vaccine is advised only if you plan to travel in remote areas. It consists of two jabs given at one-week intervals two months before departure and is valid for six months. Similarly, the typhoid vaccine is only necessary if you'll be spending time in rural areas. It is given in two shots one month apart.

Plague and rabies vaccines are available but not usually advised unless serious outbreaks are reported in areas where you plan to be travelling.

If you haven't had a complete series of oral polio vaccines or a tetanus-DPT vaccine as a matter of course, they should both be considered essential before a visit to developing countries. In addition, a tetanus-DPT booster should be taken every five to 10 years.

You should also consider a gamma globulin shot as a precaution against hepatitis. It is only effective for 90 to 120 days or so and does not guarantee that you won't contract hepatitis anyway, but it is still recommended, particularly if you have come in contact with someone who has the disease.

Travel Insurance

Even if you normally carry health or hospitalisation insurance or live in a country where health care is provided by the government it's still a good idea to buy some inexpensive travellers' insurance that covers both health and loss of baggage.

Make sure the policy includes health care and medication in the countries you plan to visit and includes a flight home for you and anyone you're travelling with, should your condition warrant it.

Medical Kit

It is always a good idea to travel with a basic first aid kit. Some of the items which should be included are: Band-Aids, a sterilised gauze bandage, elastoplast, cotton wool, a thermometer, tweezers, scissors, antibiotic cream and ointment, an antiseptic agent (Dettol or Betadine), burn cream (Caladryl is good for sun burn, minor burns and itchy bites), insect repellent and multi vitamins.

Don't forget water sterilisation tablets or iodine; anti-malarial tablets; any medication you're already taking; some sort of diarrhoea medication; paracetamol (Panadol), for pain and fever; a course of antibiotics (check with your doctor); and contraceptives, if necessary.

Food & Water

Local water supplies in Bolivia do not measure up to European or North American standards and since dysentery, and other more serious diseases such as typhoid and hepatitis, may be found lurking there, the age-old advice 'don't drink the water' holds good. Dishes and food products washed in the water as well as ice in drinks may also cause problems.

You should only drink water that has been boiled, filtered or treated with tincture of iodine or purification tablets. Tap water sterilised by one of these methods should be OK and the bottled water, available commercially in Bolivia, is free of contaminants and is safe to drink.

Water purification tablets and instructions for use are available commercially in outdoor equipment stores throughout Europe, North America and Australia. The most effective type is an iodine-based product like Potable Agua which kills amoebas as well as bacteria. It's major drawback is that it leaves the water tasting unpleasant. This can be remedied by adding the juice of two small lemons to each litre treated. Chemical contamination of water can only be removed with a charcoal filtering system.

When it comes to food, what you eat or don't eat should be a personal decision. Some travellers insist upon avoiding all dairy products, meat, fish, salads and even hot drinks which contain milk or unboiled water. They subsist on bottled drinks, bread and personally-peeled fruits and vegetables. Some still get the trots.

I love milk, salads, cheese and fish and, while travelling, only avoid them if they look or smell odd. I spent a year in South America and never had dysentery. Although I met other travellers who sampled everything, ate indiscriminately at markets and even drank untreated water without ill effects, I don't recommend going that far. Use your own best judgement.

Health Risks & Precautions

Common Ailments Few travellers escape the inevitable misery of *Montezuma's Revenge* and there is very little you can do to prevent the onslaught. Also called *turista*, and known by a dozen other descriptive nicknames, there is no escaping the fact that it is just plain old travellers' diarrhoea and it can happen to you anywhere.

This problem is not caused by lack of sanitation or 'bad' food but primarily by a change in diet and a lack of resistance to local strains of bacteria. The first thing to remember is that every case of diarrhoea is not dysentery, so don't panic and start stuffing yourself with pills.

The best regimen is to rest, for two or three days if possible; drink plenty of 'safe' liquids, such as unsweetened tea or bottled water (not milk, coffee, strong tea, soft drinks or cocoa); and stick to a fat-free diet – dry toast is best. After a couple or days a healthy person should develop an immunity and will be able to resume activity.

Taking antibiotics in this case can do more harm than good. If the bacteria in your body are able to build up immunity to them, the antibiotics may not work when you really need them.

It's interesting that, in addition to the initial 'shakedown' I normally go through each time I arrive in South America, I experience it again upon arriving home. I therefore suspect that South Americans may have similar discomforts when they visit us (the Yankee Quickstep or the Wallaby Hops?) thanks to unfamiliar diet and bacteria.

Dysentery This is, unfortunately, also quite common among travellers. There are two types of dysentery, characterised by diarrhoea containing blood and lots of mucus.

Bacillary dysentery, the most common variety, is an intestinal infection caused by ingestion of contaminated food or water. It hits suddenly and lays you out with intestinal cramps, diarrhoea, nausea and fever.

As it's caused by bacteria it responds well to antibiotics and is usually treated symptomatically with a kaolin and pectin or a bismuth compound. On the other hand, since the symptoms themselves are actually the best treatment – diarrhoea and fever are both trying to rid the body of the infection – it may be best to just hole up for a few days and let it run its course. If activity or travel is absolutely necessary during the infection, you can take either Imodium or Lomotil to 'plug the drain', so to speak, until reaching a more convenient location to R & R (rest and run).

Amoebic dysentery, or amoebiasis, is a much more serious variety. It is caused by protozoans, or amoebic parasites, called *Endamoeba histolytica* which are also transmitted through contaminated food or water. Once they've invaded, they live in the lower intestinal tract and cause heavy and often bloody diarrhoea, fever, tenderness in the liver area and intense abdominal pain. It builds up more slowly than bacillary dysentery and can't be starved out.

If left untreated, ulceration and inflammation of the colon and rectum can become very serious. If you suspect amoebic dysentery, you should see a doctor. If that's not possible, try the antiparasitic *Flagyl* (metronidazole). You'll need three tablets three or four times daily for 10 days to rid yourself of the condition. Flagyl should not be taken by pregnant women.

The best method of preventing dysentery is, of course, to avoid eating or drinking contaminated items.

Hepatitis This incapacitating disease is caused by a virus which attacks the liver. Hepatitis is contracted through contact with contaminated food, water, toilets or individuals. The victim's eyes and skin will turn a sickly yellow and urine will be orange or brown. An infected person will also experience a tenderness in the right side of the abdomen and a loss of appetite.

If you contract infectious hepatitis (Hepatitis A) during a short trip to Bolivia, you probably should make arrangements to go home. If you can afford the time however, and have a reliable companion who can bring food and water, the best cure is to stay where you are, find a few good books and only leave bed to go the bathroom. After a month or so, you should feel like living again. Drink lots of fluids and keep to a diet high in proteins and vitamins. Avoid alcohol and cigarettes absolutely!

Type A can be caught by eating food, drinking water or using cutlery or crockery contaminated by an infected person.

Hepatitis B, or serum hepatitis, can only be caught by having sex with an infected person or by using the same syringe. If Type B is diagnosed, fatal liver failure is a real possibility and the victim should be sent home and/or hospitalised immediately.

The best preventative measure available is a gamma globulin shot before departure from home and booster shots every three or four months thereafter while you're away. (Beware of unsanitary needles!) A jab is also in order if you come in contact with any infected person; and if *you* come down with hepatitis, anyone who has had recent contact with you should take the shot, too.

Malaria If you will only be travelling in highland Bolivia, that is above 2800 metres or so, anti-malarial precautions are not necessary. If you plan to visit the jungle lowlands, Yungas or Chaco areas, however, some concern is warranted.

Malaria is an infectious disease characterised by recurring attacks of chills and fever. It is caused by the parasite *plasmodium* which is transmitted through the bite of an infected anopheles mosquito.

Malaria sporozites enter the bloodstream and travel to the liver where they mature, infect the red blood cells and begin to multiply. This process takes between one and five weeks. Only when the infected cells re-enter the bloodstream and burst do the dramatic symptoms begin.

For this reason, malaria can be extremely dangerous because the victim by this time has often left the malarial area, so the disease is not suspected and therefore is improperly treated.

All strains of malaria, *falciparum, vivax* and *ovale*, are characterised in their early stages by growing fatigue and a gradual loss of appetite. At the time of attack, headache, diarrhoea, nausea and periodic high fever, sweating and chills are present. In addition, the dangerous falciparum strain is accompanied by hallucinations and delirium.

In all cases, medical attention is essential. Diagnosis is confirmed by a blood test in which the plasmodium and its strain can be identified.

The most effective form of malaria prevention, of course, is to avoid being bitten. When travelling in tropical areas, it's best to sleep under a mosquito net or at least light a mosquito coil. A powerful insect repellent, one consisting 95% or more of *diethylmeta-toluamide*, is the most effective defence though. The best I've ever run across is called Jungle Juice

Area of Malaria Risk

100 and is available through REI Inc, PO Box C-88126, Seattle, WA 98188 USA.

Since it is impossible to guarantee that you won't be bitten, various drugs are available to inhibit the development of malaria.

Chloroquine (marketed under various trade names) is generally regarded as the safest but, with continued use, even it has been known to cause harmful side-effects and it shouldn't be taken over long periods of time. There are also some areas where the malaria parasite has developed an immunity to chloroquine-based drugs. The usual dosage is one tablet per week two weeks before, each week during and six weeks after visiting an area where malaria is present.

Traditionally, Fansidar was prescribed for travel to areas where plasmodium falciparum and chloroquine-resistant strains were found, but now it is illegal in many developed countries and is rarely used as a preventative drug. It is feared that overuse of Fansidar will generate development of Fansidar-resistant strains. It has also been known to cause, on rare occasions, some very disagreeable side-effects, including death.

These days it is used primarily as a treatment for chloroquine-resistant forms of malaria. Other treatments for all types include quinine-based drugs taken in combination with an antibiotic such as tetracycline.

Chagas' Disease There is a very small possibility of contracting this disease. It is caused by a parasite which lives in the faeces of the *vinchuca* beetle which, in turn, lives in the thatching of dirty huts in the lowland and Chaco regions of Bolivia, Argentina, Paraguay and Brazil.

The disease, transmitted through the bite of this beetle, more colourfully called the assassin bug, causes progressive constriction and hardening of blood vessels, which places increasing strain on the heart. At present there is no cure and Chagas' is always fatal over a period of years.

I've read mind-boggling estimates that up to 25% of Bolivia's population suffers from it. Whether this is true or not, researchers in developed countries seem to be largely unaware of this serious disease. In Argentina, however, a private campaign is underway to eradicate the beetle and effect a cure.

The best prevention is to use a mosquito net if you'll be sleeping in thatched buildings. If you are bitten, wash the affected area well and don't scratch the bite, or the faeces and consequently the parasite will be rubbed into the wound.

Haemorrhagic Fever Incidences of this illness have been reported in low-lying jungle areas, especially in Beni and Pando departments. It is transmitted by mosquitoes and can be prevented by using the same mosquito protection recommended against malaria.

The most salient symptom is an odd pinprick-type rash which is caused by capillary haemorrhaging. Accompanying symptoms include chills, fever, fatigue, congestion and other influenza-like symptoms. It can be very dangerous and professional attention, preferably in a hospital, should be immediately sought.

Worms The most common form you're likely to contract are hookworms. They are usually caught by walking barefoot on infected soil. They bore through the skin, attach themselves to the inner wall of the intestine and proceed to suck the blood. Abdominal pain and sometimes anaemia are the result.

Threadworms, or *strongyloidiasis*, are also found in low lying areas and operate very much like hookworms, but symptoms are more visible and can include diarrhoea and vomiting.

Worms may be treated with thiabendazole or mabendazole taken orally twice daily for three or four days. As usual, however, medical advice is best because the symptoms of worms so closely resemble those of other, more serious conditions.

Skin Lesions & Infections The warm, moist conditions of the tropical lowlands invite and promote the growth of 'wee beasties' that would be thwarted in more temperate climates. Because of this, even a small cut or scratch can become painfully infected and lead to more serious problems.

Since bacterial immunity to certain antibiotics can build-up, it's not wise to take these medicines indiscriminately or as a preventative measure.

The best treatment for cuts is to frequently cleanse the affected area with soap and water and apply mercurachrome or an antiseptic creme, such as garamycin. If, despite this, the wound becomes tender and inflamed then use of an antibiotic is warranted, especially if you also develop a mild fever. Try 150 mg tablets of erythromycin twice daily until the infection has subsided.

Animals & Insects It's highly unlikely that you'll ever see a deadly-venomous snake in Bolivia unless you're going to be tramping quietly through the deepest jungles. There, you may come across two insidious species – the *bushmaster*, called *verdugo* or 'executioner' in Spanish, and the *fer-de-lance*.

There's not much use prescribing any subsequent action in the case of a bite by either of these devils because, even if an antivenene were available, the victim wouldn't have time to reach it anyway. So if you're planning any Indiana Jones-type activities, watch your step. Anyone else can forget this was ever mentioned.

For bite victims of other types of poisonous snakes, spiders and scorpions, standard first-aid measures should be taken and medical attention sought. In the lowlands, be sure to check shoes, clothing and sleeping bags before use.

Body lice and scabies mites are also common in South America so a number of shampoos and creams are available to eliminate them. In addition to hair and skin, clothing and bedding should be washed thoroughly to prevent further infestation.

Throughout Bolivia, but especially in the humid lowlands, rodents and bats carry the rabies virus and pass it on to larger animals and humans. The usual advice applies. Avoid any animal that appears to be foaming at the mouth or acting strangely. Bats, especially vampire bats, are common in the Amazon Basin and are notorious carriers of rabies. Be sure to cover all parts of your body at night, especially your feet and scalp.

If you do get bitten, try to capture or kill the offending animal so that it may be tested. If that's impossible, then you must assume the animal is rabid. The rabies virus incubates in its victim in a minimum of three weeks, so while medical attention isn't urgent, it still shouldn't be delayed.

Ants, gnats, mosquitoes, bees and flies will be just as annoying in Bolivia as they are at home. If you're going walking in humid or densely-foliated areas, wear light cotton trousers and shoes, not shorts and sandals or thongs. Regardless of temperature, never wear shorts or thongs in the jungle and remember to carry an effective insect repellent.

Soroche (Altitude Sickness) Due to extreme altitude, the oxygen density in the highland and Altiplano regions is much lower than most foreigners are accustomed to.

The atmospheric density at Potosí, at 4070 metres, is less than ⅔ its value at sea level; and at Mt Chacaltaya near La Paz, the summit of which lies at 5600 metres, it is only about half. Water on the Altiplano boils at about 90°C and planes landing at La Paz's Kennedy Airport reach stall speed at nearly twice the velocity they would in Santa Crúz at only 437 metres.

The human body is also affected by an increase in altitude. On a rapid ascent to high altitude, say a flight from Lima at sea level to La Paz at 3686 metres, the body is not given time to adapt to the lower oxygen concentration. Newly-arrived visitors will invariably experience a condition known as *soroche* or altitude sickness.

As the body attempts to compensate for the decreasing availability of life-sustaining oxygen, respiration is deepened and accelerated. At first, this hyperventilation causes an overabundance of carbon dioxide in the blood. This acid/base imbalance causes a feeling of fatigue and lethargy until the kidney kicks into action to correct it.

Mental capacity is reduced and the victim experiences a persistent headache, loss of appetite, weakness and shortness of breath after even minor activity. These symptoms are sometimes accompanied by nausea and vomiting. Chewing coca leaves or drinking *mate de coca* (coca leaf tea) will relieve some of the discomfort, but the best remedy is a day or two of rest while the body begins its acclimatisation process. Drinking large quantities of water, about two or three litres daily, is essential.

After a week or so at high altitude, 80% of the acclimatisation process is complete. After about two more weeks, the bone marrow is stimulated to produce more red blood cells and the oxygen-carrying capacity of the blood is increased by 25%. Further acclimatisation goes on over longer periods of time, but nobody ever reaches more than about 95% of their sea level capacity.

If you are travelling quickly to high altitudes and won't have the opportunity to acclimatise, a drug called Diamox (Acetazolamide) will prevent altitude discomfort. It should be taken in 250mg doses four times daily, four days before and six days after ascent.

In order to prevent the formation of kidney stones, it is very important to drink lots of water (at least 1½ litres) after the first dosage each day. For ascents to even higher altitudes, Micoren tablets, which are available in pharmacies, may be taken two or three times daily. They stimulate the respiratory functions and relieve immediate symptoms. For headache, taking aspirin will only aggravate the acclimatisation process by lowering the blood's capacity to carry oxygen. A non-aspirin pain-reliever such as Tylenol (acetaminophen) should be used.

Most of Bolivia's population lives above 3000 metres. The most lofty city is Potosí and the highest population I'm aware of is a small group of scientists living at 5300 metres on the slopes of Mt Chacaltaya. This is at the outer limit of human endurance; above this altitude, the body will not adapt sufficiently to allow permanent habitation.

Acute Mountain Sickness (AMS) A more serious condition than soroche, AMS is experienced among climbers and hikers who spend time above the acclimatisation threshold. The only hope for victims is administration of oxygen and immediate descent to lower altitude.

Tell-tale signs include dizziness, disorientation and loss of judgement in addition to those symptoms present with soroche. Breathing becomes laboured due to pulmonary oedema, a concentration of fluids in the lungs. Brain cells may also retain water (cerebral oedema) which eventually leads to unconsciousness and death.

Above 5600 metres or so, tiny blood vessels in the retina and the brain begin to haemorrhage slightly and vision or brain function can temporarily be affected. Abnormal clotting of blood can also affect the brain and the heart.

Anyone planning to ascend to altitudes of over 5000 metres for any length of time (longer than a few hours of skiing at Chacaltaya that is) should first seek medical advice and be familiar with methods and rules used by expedition climbers to deal with AMS. Those with a history of cardiac, pulmonary or circulatory problems should consult a physician before travelling to Bolivia at all.

Hypothermia Hypothermia is a dangerous lowering of the body temperature. It is caused by exhaustion and exposure to cold, wet or windy weather, which can occur anywhere in Bolivia. Hypothermia is a threat whenever a person is exposed to the elements at temperatures below 10°.

The best treatment is of course to get the victim to shelter and give them warm drinks and a hot bath if possible, which it probably won't be in Bolivia. Wet clothing should be changed or removed – no clothing at all, is better than wet garments.

The patient should lie down, wrapped in a sleeping bag or blanket to preserve body heat. Another person may lie down with them in order to provide as much warmth as possible. If no improvement is noticed within a few minutes, seek help but don't leave the victim alone while doing so. The body heat of another person is immediately more important than medical attention.

Heat & Sunburn The Altiplano and much of the highland regions of Bolivia lie within the tropics at elevations greater than 3000 metres. The atmosphere there is too thin to screen out much of the dangerous ultraviolet radiation that is absorbed and deflected at lower altitudes.

So, it may be cold and windy or even overcast but the UV effect is still hazardous and the use of a strong sunscreen is essential because serious burns can occur after even brief exposure.

Don't neglect to apply it to any area of exposed skin, especially if you're near water or snow. On Lake Titicaca and in the high mountains, reflected rays can burn as badly as those directly from space.

As sunscreen is one of those items that is quite expensive in Bolivia, and it's also difficult to find one with a rating greater than six or so, I recommend you bring some from home. In addition, a hat will serve to shade your face and protect your scalp. Sunglasses will prevent eye irritation (especially if you wear contact lenses).

Some people also experience a rash caused by photosensitivity in high altitudes. It can be treated with light applications of cortisone cream to affected areas (never use cortisone near your eyes, however).

In the tropical lowlands, Yungas and Chaco regions, heat combined with humidity and exposure to the sun can be oppressive and leave you feeling lethargic, irritable and dazed. A cool swim or lazy afternoon in the shade will do wonders to improve your mood. You'll also need to drink lots of liquids and eat salty foods in order to replenish your supply of these products lost during sweating.

Motion Sickness If you're prone to motion sickness at all, then come prepared because the roads and railroads in Bolivia aren't exactly smooth. If Dramamine works for you, take some along.

The best relief I can recommend, however, is *transdermal scopalomine.* I've used it a few times and have been able to read and even eat during storms at sea, so it should stand the test of Bolivian bumping. It will dilate the pupils if it accidentally comes in contact with the eyes and has been known to cause drowsiness, so due caution should be exercised.

WOMEN TRAVELLING ALONE

Bolivia is still very much a man's country and for a single woman travelling alone, this can be a frustrating problem. The mere fact you seem to be unmarried and far from your home and family will cause you to appear suspiciously disreputable.

Because most young South American men have become acquainted with foreign women through such reliable media as North American television, the concept of *gringa fácil*, which roughly means 'loose chick' has developed. Since Bolivia has its cultural roots in southern Europe, it has been subjected to over four centuries of *machismo*. By many, therefore, you will be considered fair and willing game.

Most of the ignorant and ridiculous abuse, passes and comments a lone woman will have to endure are harmless. On only one occasion did I have a more serious problem, which, considering all possibilities, was still relatively minor. I was walking alone in a residential area and a gang of five teenagers began throwing rocks. I'm still not sure whether it was an exhibition of machismo or just more anti-US sentiment.

Many women travellers, when subjected to machismo in any form, simply ignore the perpetrator or eye him disgustedly. This is what 'well-bred' Bolivian girls would be expected to do under the same circumstances, but it does nothing to remedy the underlying problem. The pea-brains interpret this to mean that the subject is actually taking them seriously.

A woman who simply mutters *casada* and keeps on walking leaves the guys believing that she would take them up on the offer if she were not trapped by marriage. The hopeful lads then set about finding an unmarried one.

A method which has worked for me is telling them that I am an intelligent person and would have nothing in common with someone who makes such ignorant comments. I've left some shocked faces with this one – they were expecting disgust or success, not blatant arrogance.

Those who prefer to be a bit more civil about it can explain that in their culture, women are considered equal to men and that such behaviour is not appreciated. This approach is actually much better than mine because it serves to educate rather than insult.

Another option which is 100% effective is to find a male travelling companion. Thousands of foreigners, especially men, are travelling solo through Latin America these days and many lasting friendships are made between travellers who just happen to be going the same way for a while.

For those women who insist upon travelling alone for whatever reason, it's a good idea to avoid such male domains as bars, sports matches, mines, construction sites and the like.

DRUGS

Cocaine

Bolivia may be the land of cocaine, but anyone under the impression that a cheap and abundant supply is readily available to the general public will probably be disappointed. Refined cocaine is highly illegal in Bolivia and unless you've got a healthy supply of cash to pay off the arresting officer, it's best left alone.

The big guys get away with processing and exporting because they pay. Young backpacking foreigners and coca-producing Indians become statistics to wave before the US government as proof, if you will, that Bolivia is doing something about the drug problem.

Although young foreigners are searched less frequently than they were a year ago (perhaps the police have realised they don't carry all that much money), it's still not wise to carry drugs of any kind, even in small quantities. The consequences are simply too costly.

If you choose to ignore this advice and the worst happens - you're caught with drugs and arrested - the safest bet is to immediately pay off the arresting officer(s) before more officials learn about your plight and want to be cut in on the deal. This recommendation may seem a bit unethical to you, but once you've seen the inside of a Bolivian jail, you'll know what unethical is.

It's best not to call your payoff a bribe per se. Ask something like: *como podemos arreglar este asunto?* - 'how can we put this matter right?' They'll understand what you mean.

If the officer refuses and hauls you to jail, then you're on your own. Foreign embassies aren't usually interested in such hard luck stories. They may provide you with a lawyer and see that you're treated as fairly as any Bolivian would be under the same circumstances, but beyond that, they're powerless.

Coca Leaves

While cocaine, marijuana, hashish and heroin, etc, are all illegal, the coca leaf, which is the source of cocaine and related drugs, is chewed daily and even venerated by native peoples.

Mama Coca is the daughter of *Pachamama*, the earth mother, and coca was a gift to the people to be used in driving evil forces out of their homes and fields.

Both the Quechua and Aymará make sacrifices of coca leaves when planting or mining in order to ensure a good harvest or a lucky strike. The *yatiri*, or witch doctors, use them in their healing and exorcising rituals and in remote rural areas the leaves are often used in place of money. If you're going walking in the mountains or countryside, carry some along as a gift to helpful locals. The gesture will be enormously appreciated.

Coca is an appetite suppressent and a central nervous system stimulant. The conquering Spaniards found that those who chewed the leaf became more dedicated workers so they promoted its use among the peasants. Today, nearly all campesinos and cholos, men and women alike, take advantage of its benefits.

The Indians use it while working to lessen the effects of altitude and eliminate the necessity of a lunch break. They also chew it recreationally or socially in much the way we would smoke cigarettes or drink coffee. In fact, among Bolivian miners, the 'coca break' has come to be an institution. Those of European origin, however, still regard chewing coca as a disgusting 'Indian' habit and avoid its use.

The leaf itself grows on bushes which are cultivated in the Yungas and Upper Chapare regions at altitudes between 1000 and 2000 metres. They are sold by the kg in just about every market in Bolivia along with *legía*, an alkaloid usually made of potato and *quinoa* ash, which is used to draw the drug from the leaves when chewed. There are two kinds of legía: *achura*, which is sweet, and *cuta*, which is salty.

The Indians normally chew about 30 to 35 leaves at a time. If you want to try it, the process involves placing a few leaves, five to 10, between your gums and cheek until they soften. Repeat the process placing a little legia between some of the leaves. Don't start chewing, however, until you've stuffed in the desired amount. Once you've chewed it into a pulpy mess, you're supposed to swallow the bitter-tasting juice. This will numb your mouth and throat. (Novocaine and related anaesthetics are coca derivatives.)

The effects of coca-chewing are not startling by any description. It will leave you feeling a little detached, reflective or even melancholy. It's a pleasantly peaceful feeling and it's easy to understand why the people enjoy it so much.

Mushrooms & Cacti

Psilocyben or 'magic mushrooms' are

available, as they are in most of the world, in places where livestock leave things lying around. They're not illegal – South Americans don't seem to even be aware of them – but be sure that what you're eating is the real thing.

Choma, or San Pedro cactus, grows throughout the deserts of south-western Bolivia. It may be found most conveniently in the *Valle de la Luna* (Valley of the Moon), near La Paz. The natives report that, after being cooked for several hours, the juice of its flesh will 'send you flying'. Which is not surprising as the active ingredient is mescaline. Currently, its use is also quite legal (or rather, it's not criminal) in Bolivia. If you're interested, ask a local to point it out for you.

Drug Plants

These are not a rumour. Some unscrupulous and poorly-paid officials are always looking for methods of extorting money from anyone who may be caught off guard. If you are travelling alone and look rich enough to cough up a few thousand dollars or so to avoid spending a year in prison awaiting trial, you may be victimised.

During a routine search, when you're not paying attention, an officer may triumphantly 'find' a container of suspicious-looking white powder in your luggage. You'll probably never know whether it is actually cocaine or not because such things as laboratory tests are not considered important. The officer says it's cocaine and so it is.

He will, at this point, offer to make a deal: you pay him US$5000 and he will agree to overlook the matter. For what it's worth, I haven't actually heard of anyone going to prison because they couldn't pay. The officials will probably be happy to take whatever you've got.

Principled individuals who have gone to prison rather than admit to a crime they did not commit, often agree to pay the fine after a few days of incarceration. Unfortunately this only fuels the flame of corruption and since foreign embassies seem to want nothing to do with drug-related charges, innocent victims are more or less on their own.

This practice is fortunately not too common. While you'll probably never have this problem, some precautions are warranted.

Whenever you're subjected to customs or police searches, especially at Santa Crúz airport where this practice has been reported, watch carefully while the officers are pawing through your luggage. If possible, keep a friend on hand who could serve as a witness, and make conversation with the official conducting the search.

If you're carrying a piece of luggage on public transportation, lock all latches and zippers to prevent tampering when you're not looking.

If things still manage to go awry, don't touch the contraband they've 'found' in your luggage, don't sign anything that might be an admission of guilt and ask for the name of the offending officer. Most importantly, don't panic. This is easier said than done, of course, but you'll need to be thinking clearly.

Remember, both you and the police officer know that you're innocent and you may be able to turn this to your advantage. If this happens to someone you know, report and publicise the barbarity to consulates, government officials and other travellers who may be venturing into the jurisdiction of such corruption.

Above all else, don't let this remote possibility prevent you from travelling to Bolivia. Chances of this happening are very slim indeed and an alert individual can practically be guaranteed that no such thing will occur.

BEGGARS

For some, one of the most disconcerting aspects of travel in Bolivia is the constant presence of beggars. With no social welfare system to sustain them, the elderly, blind, crippled and jobless take to the streets and try to arouse sympathy in any way they can.

Some travellers choose to give to only the most pathetic cases or to those enterprising individuals who provide some value for the money, such as by singing or playing a musical instrument. Others simply feel that any contribution they might make only serves to fuel the machine that creates beggars so they ignore the whiny and obsequious cries for *plata*.

As everyone has a different idea of an appropriate response to this behaviour I hesitate to make recommendations. I do know that if I'd given even a pittance to every beggar I encountered in Bolivia, I'd have to go begging myself. As a rule, I generally try to help those who are making an effort to change their situation, to do something other than sit and wait for a handout. For the ones who go begging for bones and scraps in the market I would buy a hot meal or a bowl of soup. It may cost only a quarter, but even that is well outside the budget of poorer Bolivians, and such small gestures are greatly appreciated.

The physically impaired are always underemployed and are frequently left to such tasks as selling lottery tickets and telephone tokens, but they are at least able to earn something. Therefore I'd be inclined to offer something to others, such as the very elderly or mentally indigent, who would appear to have no other possible means of support.

Regarding the numerous children who beg, it's probably best not to give them money since it can lead to their exploitation and give them the impression that something can be had for nothing. If a child appears to be truly hungry, however, there's nothing wrong with giving away something to eat provided it's more nutritious than a piece of candy.

FILM & PHOTOGRAPHY

Both cameras and film are available in Bolivia but at exorbitant prices and not always where and when you need them. Certain types of film, such as Kodachrome or Polaroid, are difficult to find. Those who plan to take photographs should carry all necessary equipment and supplies from home.

A lot of photographic paraphernalia can become quite a liability, so consider carefully which lenses, filters, tripods and attachments are indispensable and which ones will probably never be used. And again, don't take anything you can't risk losing. Your equipment is as safe in Bolivia as it would be in Los Angeles or Sydney (safer in some cases), but in any part of the world, if theft of valuable equipment is convenient, someone may seize the opportunity.

The average Bolivian can't afford Nikons, Minoltas and all the trimmings, so if you carry one, expect to be labelled as a 'rich tourist'. This isn't necessarily negative, but it does carry a slightly different connotation from 'penny-pinching *mochilero*' (backpacker). If you carry a camera, more people will try to sell you things and those who are superstitious about cameras will react differently to you, also.

While some Bolivians will enjoy having their picture taken, others will be put off by your attempts to get that perfect 'people shot'. They may be superstitious about your camera or suspicious of your motives.

Once, in a remote village, a local girl burst into angry tears when one of my companions snapped a photo of her. She explained that the mountain people were tired of being exploited by photographers who would sell pictures of them and not share any of the profit.

On another occasion, I was successful in sneakily taking some photos of the *mercado de hechiceria*, or witches' market, in La Paz, hoping to include some interesting shots in this book. Taking photos there is taboo, more or less, because of superstitions dealing with such things. One of the vendors saw me and angrily told me that I'd regret the indiscretion. A month later, all my exposed film of Bolivia, about 30 rolls, was stolen and tossed into the Amazon in Brazil. Of course this was just a coincidence, but . . .

The main point is that you must try to respect the wishes of those locals, however photogenic or colourful, who may be camera-shy for one reason or another. Be sure to ask permission to photograph if a candid shot can't be made and don't insist or snap a picture anyway if permission is denied. There will be plenty of willing subjects who can provide other equally interesting 'people shots'.

Limited camera repairs can be made in La Paz. *Casa Kavlin* at Calle Potosí 1130 is reputable and will repair and service Kodak products. Japanese cameras must be taken to *Fuji* which is two blocks away on the same street. There, the technician is available from 10.30 am to noon on weekdays.

The quality of film processing in Bolivia is rather poor so I'd recommend you either wait until you get home to process it or have someone else carry it home for you. It's not a good idea to subject your precious film to the postal system unless you don't really care whether it arrives or not.

ACCOMMODATION

The Bolivian Tourism Institute (IBT) has a hotel rating system that rates hotels with zero to five stars and divides other accommodation into categories which are, in descending order, *hostales, casas de huéspedes* (guest houses), *residenciales, alojamientos* and *posadas*.

Hotels

I am aware of only three five-star hotels in the country – two in La Paz and one in Santa Crúz. These would probably rate about three stars on a worldwide scale, but still, you can expect clean rooms, fine restaurants with bars and entertainment, room service, laundry service (albeit expensive), hot and cold running water, a telephone, refrigerator and all the usual amenities – for about half the price you'd pay at such an establishment in London or Sydney.

A one-star hotel, on the other hand, would probably have only cold water – possibly with a hot shower attachment (see the section on plumbing), a snack bar, shabby but clean linen and an overall rather 'seedy' appearance.

Two, three and four-star hotels would, of course, fall somewhere in between. No stars at all would indicate that the establishment is called a hotel but would actually belong in a lower category. Heat or air conditioning are unheard of below the three-star level.

Hostales, casas de heúspedes and residenciales all serve as finer budget hotels. A guest will have the option of a *baño privado* – private bath, or *baño común* – shared bath, which will have a hot water attachment on the shower head. These places will also have flush toilets, some kind of laundry sink or even a maid, who will wash your clothes for a very reasonable rate, and usually a restaurant or snack bar where you can buy coffee, breakfast or sandwiches. These hotels will cost between US$5 and US$10 per person with a private bath and about 30% less without.

Alojamientos are basic budget accommodation. Alojamiento means 'lodge', and that's about all it is – a place to crash. Few have hot water in any form, some are clean and some are disgustingly dirty and they rarely have private baths or restaurants, though sometimes a laundry sink is provided. Rates are usually charged per person rather than per room so there's no advantage to showing up with a large group. Double beds are sometimes hard to find. Prices range from 75c per person in Copacabana to US$6 in Santa Crúz.

Posadas are the dirt-cheapest basic roof and bed you're going to find. They vary in quality, but usually that means bad to worse. In all fairness, there are a few clean ones but in most you could scrape off the scum with a putty knife. Most don't have showers, a select few don't even have toilets and those that do often keep down costs by closing the door and forgetting that they exist. (Unfortunately, some alojamientos have been known to employ the same methods.)

Posadas range in price from US$1 to US$3 per person for a bed that may have been slept in for a month without a change of sheets – another cost-cutting measure. For those on the tightest of bare-bones budgets, however, this will be the way to go.

Another type of hotel which may be found away from the larger cities is the *Hotel Prefectural*. The idea behind these government-run hotels is to provide a bit of luxury in small towns of tourist interest. They are sterile-looking buildings, which remind me of well-groomed mental institutions, normally tucked away in the countryside just outside of populated areas. They do, however, offer a quality of accommodation previously not available in such small places as Coroico and Copacabana.

In this book, 'Places to Stay' will be broken down into: top end, middle and bottom end. A top end hotel will typically cost more than US$30 for a double and will include almost everything of three stars and above on the Bolivian rating scale. Middle range hotels will run from US$10 to US$30 for two people, whether the rate is charged per person or per room. Everything under US$5 per person will be considered bottom end.

In a few cities, such as Santa Crúz, where prices are much higher than in the rest of the country, this scale will have to be altered slightly or the cheapest alojamiento would fall into the middle range category.

Hotels that are above average, recommended or frequented by budget travellers will be identified as such.

In some larger cities, you will undoubtedly notice an odd two or three-tier pricing structure in effect. Bolivians, called *nacionales* on price lists, pay one price; other South Americans, who are supposed to be richer than the Bolivians, pay a slightly higher price; and foreigners, called *extranjeros*, who are of course very rich, pay the highest price of all.

In some places, the 'other South Americans' are lumped together with the *extranjeros* but, whatever the grouping, rooms and service are the same for everyone – only the prices vary. If you are put off by such discriminatory practices, take heart that I found one lovely *residenciál* in Cochabamba where foreigners actually pay less than Bolivians.

The vast majority of hotel owners are friendly, honest people and they demand the same of their staff. Competition is such that a hotel can't afford to get a bad reputation, so your belongings should be safe left in the room. For what it's worth, I've never had a single item stolen anywhere in Bolivia.

If you still have a healthy concern, however, it's best not to leave valuable things just lying around in hotel rooms. Money or jewellery may be checked at the hotel desk (always get a receipt!), but they would probably be safer stored in some obscure corner of a locked pack.

In many lower-priced hotels, doors will not lock from either side and there's sometimes a window beside the door that can be easily opened from the outside. If you do find yourself in such a place, be sure that you can trust the proprietor to keep an eye on things while you are away.

In a few cities, visitors are requested to register with the police upon their arrival. No one has ever been able to give me a viable reason for this, so I've just ignored it. In only one town, Camiri, will hotel owners refuse you a room without police sanction.

In some towns, proprietors are required to provide the police with lists of guests and their personal document numbers. Often, especially in Cochabamba, police make routine searches of hotels where foreigners tend to stay. These usually occur at excruciatingly early hours of the morning and get to be a damned nuisance.

Just about all hotels, if you stay for a day or two, will watch your luggage free of charge if you plan to be away for a few days. This service ranges from a very informal area behind the hotel counter to a locked room designated specifically for that purpose.

Those travelling alone should note that *simples*, or single rooms, are sometimes not available or cost only slightly less than a *doble*, or double room. In some cases, if they give you a double you will be expected to pay for both beds. (If you want to get even you can muss them both up.)

In the less expensive places *camas matrimoniales*, or double beds, are also scarce. Rooms with three or four beds are available almost everywhere, but they will cost the same per bed as smaller rooms unless you can talk the owner into a 'high-occupancy discount'.

Room availability should be no problem at all except during major fiestas when prices double and rooms are quickly occupied by visiting nationals. At these times, however, private homeowners will let out rooms in order to bring in some extra cash.

Keep in mind that water and electric utilities throughout the country are sporadic to begin with, but that most inexpensive hotels only turn on the power and water to the rooms for several hours in the morning and evening. Some establishments expect you to let them know when you will be wanting a shower so they can accommodate you.

Some final advice – never accept a room without inspecting it first. The most cheery reception areas can shelter some pretty dank and dingy rooms. If you're not satisfied with the room you're first shown, ask to see another. Most proprietors welcome travellers and are eager to please.

Camping

This is fairly easy all over Bolivia, but that doesn't mean there are chains of caravan parks with clubhouses, showers and all the trimmings. Campers will have to sleep in a tent or beneath the stars, or clouds.

It is a little difficult to camp near large cities, but I've tried to include at least one suggestion near each large population centre for those who'd like to escape all the bustle and that infernal horn-honking for awhile. In most cases, there will be no reliable nearby water supply, so you'll have to carry water.

If you're hiking or trekking you'll find that camping is possible just about anywhere as long as it's not in someone's pasture or potato field. Another option is to ask around in villages – sometimes locals will put you up for a small fee, say 50c or so. If you're sleeping in huts in the more humid areas, read the warnings about Chagas' Disease in the Health section.

FOOD

Bolivian food is as diverse as its regions. The fare of the Altiplano tends to be starchy and loaded with carbohydrates while in the lowlands, fish, vegetables and fruits figure more prominently.

Meat of some kind will invariably predominate in every meal and will usually be accompanied by rice, potatoes (or another starchy tuber) and shredded lettuce. Sometimes the whole affair will be covered with *llajhua*, a hot sauce made from tomatoes and hot yellow peppers. In the Amazon Basin, and occasionally elsewhere, the tuber will be replaced by steamed or fried plantain or manioc.

Meals

Lunch is the main meal of the day and restaurants will offer an *almuerzo completo* or complete lunch. This is the daily special and will consist of a soup, bread, *segundo* (main course), coffee or tea and, most of the time, will include a simple dessert.

The almuerzo completo will change each day and is normally dirt cheap. If you don't like what they're serving, you can order something from the regular menu which will cost about twice as much as the special.

La cena is the evening meal and operates much the way as lunch, but is less elaborate. It is usually eaten after 7 pm.

Breakfast is called *desayuno* and often consists of nothing more than coffee and a roll or some kind of pastry.

Fast Foods

The original Bolivian mid-morning snack food is the *salteña*, a football-shaped (US football, that is) meat and vegetable pie. It is stuffed with chicken or beef, olives, eggs, potato, onion, peas, carrots and whatever else may have been on hand. It is normally heavily spiced and is absolutely delicious.

Empanadas are ubiquitous throughout South America. They are filled, in varying quantities, with meat (normally beef) and called *empanadas de carne*, chicken – *empanadas de pollo*, or cheese – *empanadas de queso*, and are either baked in bread or deep-fried in fat. Sometimes other ingredients, such as those going into salteñas, are added to the meat varieties.

Humintas (sometimes spelled *humitas*) are cornmeal tamales filled with spiced beef, vegetables and potatoes. They are wrapped in a maize husk and fried, grilled or baked. A similar concoction, called a *relleno*, is similar to the American corn fritter.

Meats

The most common dishes are derived from beef, chicken or fish. The poorer campesinos eat a lot of mutton (*cordero*), goat (*cabrito*) or llama. Pork (*carne de chancho*) is considered a delicacy and is only eaten on special occasions.

Typical beef dishes include barbecued or grilled beef (*asado* or *parillada*); back (*lomo*), shoulder (*brazuelo*), steak (*churrasco*), tripe (*panza*) and dried beef (*charqui*). Other concoctions include *thimpu*, a kind of spicy meat and vegetable stew, and *falso conejo* (false rabbit?), a very greasy and rubbery substance that appears to be animal-based.

A dish called *pique macho*, which is thinly sliced beef served with onions, is popular in Sucre and Potosí. *Anticuchos*, or beef-heart shish-kebabs, are a specialty in La Paz.

Chicken is either fried, broiled or grilled and is commonly served as *pollo a la canasta* – chicken in the basket, with mustard, chips and *ají*, a picante or hot sauce.

The most popular types of fish (*pescado*) are *trucha*, or trout from Lake Titicaca, and a host of other fresh-water varieties such as the *dorado, sábalo* and *surabí* found in the Oriente. I'm convinced that surabí, a kind of catfish, is the most delicious fish on the face of the earth – try it!

In addition, armadillo, jochi (or agouti; a delicacy), alligator and a multitude of other critters are also eaten in certain areas.

Dairy

Sheep's milk cheese is made all over the Altiplano and is delicious provided it isn't made with too much salt. Vendors will normally let you have a sample before buying. It is more inexpensive and, I believe, better than cow's milk cheese which is considered more prestigious among the campesinos.

Chaco cheese from the eastern Tarija and western Santa Crúz departments is coveted all over Bolivia as the finest produced in the country. The Mennonite colonies of Santa Crúz make some very nice European-style cheeses.

Fresh milk is available through PIL, the national dairy, in the largest cities. In some places, however, it's rather difficult to find. Any store displaying a picture of a happy cow licking its lips will have milk for sale. Some markets also sell raw (unpasteurised and unhomogenised) milk.

Fruits, Vegetables & Cereals

Tuberous plants make up a great percentage of the vegetable diet of most Bolivians. Potatoes come in dozens of varieties, most of which are small and colourful. Freeze-dried potatoes, called *chuños* or *tunto*, are sometimes eaten as snacks or with meals. Most foreigners don't like them because they have the appearance and consistency of styrofoam.

Ocas are tough, purple, potato-like tubers. They taste pretty good when they're fried or roasted, but boiled ocas will take some getting used to. Another tuber sold in markets everywhere is the *añu*, a purple, yellow and white stalagmite-shaped thing that tastes like a parsnip and is usually boiled.

In the Oriente, the potato and its relatives are replaced by the root of the ubiquitous *manioc* (another name for cassava), which is very good if it's cooked long enough.

Two other common foods include *choclo*, a large kernel maize which is eaten everywhere on the Altiplano, and *abas*, the beans of the *palqui* plant which grow wild and are eaten roasted or added to stews. It is also used to make a coffee-like beverage.

Quinoa and *tarhui*, grains unique to the area, are high in protein and used to make flour and thicken stews. Quinoa is similar in most respects to soya, but it grows on a stalk and looks a bit like caviar when it's in the field.

In addition to familiar fruits like oranges and bananas, quite a few other varieties are grown and eaten, some of which I'd never heard of before visiting Bolivia.

Chirimoya, a type of custard apple, is a green, scaly-looking fruit which can be found in markets in most parts of the country. The flesh inside looks and tastes like custard pudding.

The fruit of the prickly pear cactus (*tuna*) is eaten in the highlands as it is all over the Andes. In the lowlands, there are scores of exotic tropical fruits available. *Ambaiba*, which is shaped like a hand, and *quaypurú* are quite good. There are also variations on the orange and the banana. Mandarins (*mandarinas*), plantains (*plátanos*) and finger bananas (*quineos*) are available everywhere.

Restaurants

Restaurants in Bolivia don't tend to serve that vast array of health foods, ethnic cuisines, fast foods and smorgasbords that you may be accustomed to at home. Most Bolivians have never heard of quiche, salad bars, teppan-yaki and the like, though there is a bit of variety available in the larger urban centres.

The sort of restaurants that serve typical European or North American foods are usually near the large tourist hotels, embassies and wealthy neighbourhoods. There are some pseudo fast-food joints in La Paz and Cochabamba, including a couple that try very hard to look like some popular US-based chains.

Chifas, or Chinese restaurants, exist in all the major cities and even some more off-the-wall cuisines (for Bolivia), such as Indian, Mexican and Japanese, are represented on a small scale.

Local restaurants range from *confiterias*, where you can get a snack or a cup of coffee, to classy sidewalk cafés where you can sit beside a palm-lined boulevard and eat steak. There are back-street cubbyholes, greasy-spoon truckstops and hundreds of Mom & Pop operations of varying quality in every major population centre.

In the smaller of these establishments there are no menus; the day's offerings are normally written on a chalkboard posted at the entrance. If they do have a menu, it's usually just a list of what the owner wishes was available rather than a true representation of what can be had. In a lot of cases, it's better to ignore the menu and just ask what they do have.

If you're on a strict budget or if you'd just like to sample a bit of local culture, the main market of every city and town has food stalls where filling and usually tasty bargain-basement meals are served.

DRINKS

Apart from the usual black tea, coffee and chocolate, other hot drinks such as *mate de coca* (coca leaf tea), *mate de manzanilla* (camomile tea) and *api* are served during or after meals. Api is a very syrupy drink made from sweet maize, lemon, cinnamon and staggering amounts of white sugar.

Many of the usual soft and bubbly imports like Coke, Sprite, Pepsi and Fanta are available. For some unimaginable reason, locals have also been known to enjoy a high-calorie sugar rush called Inca Cola, which tastes like liquefied bubble gum. Just one sip is all it takes to convince most people that they don't want another.

Grapes are grown in the vicinity of Tarija and some acceptable wines are produced. A very popular and inexpensive type of low-grade wine (it's actually drunk more as a spirit) called *singani* is made from poor quality grapes and grape skins.

There are several very good Bolivian beers available. *Pilsener* and *Paceña* are brewed in La Paz and *Sureña* comes from Sucre.

Without question, the favourite alcoholic drink consumed by the Bolivian masses is an industrial-strength maize liquor known as *chicha*. It's production is centred around Cochabamba and all those white plastic flags you see flying on long poles around there signify that chicha is for sale. There are a lot or rumours flying around Bolivia concerning its ingredients, but I recommend you ignore them if you plan to drink it. It's quite good and is guaranteed to affect you, even when taken in small doses.

When drinking alcoholic beverages, keep in mind that altitude intensifies the effects. In La Paz, you can get good and laid out after just three beers and will quite likely be unconscious after the fourth.

Another warning: when Bolivians gather to drink alcohol, whether it's beer, wine, chicha or whatever, it's serious; they intend to get plastered. So before

accepting an invitation to drink with locals, consider that you will be expected to do the same. In fact, Bolivians seem to get very offended if any person in their party is able to walk out of a bar under their own steam.

BOOKS & BOOKSHOPS

English, German and some French language books are available from Los Amigos del Libro which has outlets in La Paz, Cochabamba, Potosí and Santa Crúz. They tend to be quite pricey, but they have a good selection of popular paperbacks, guidebooks, dictionaries and histories as well as glossy coffee-table books dealing with the anthropology, archaeology and scenery of Bolivia.

The bookshop at Kennedy International Airport in La Paz also sells guides and souvenir books, but at staggering and immovable prices.

Other bookshops often have a shelf or a box of used English-language paperbacks stashed away somewhere, so even if you don't find them displayed, it's worth asking.

Newsweek and *Time* are available in La Paz and sometimes in Santa Crúz and Cochabamba.

If you read Spanish, classic literature and popular novels may also be found at Los Amigos del Libro and similar shops. The majority of *livrerias* (bookshops) and street sellers, however, sell only pulpy local publications, comics and school texts.

If you'd like to read further about Bolivia and related topics, the following list may offer some suggestions.

People & Society

At Play in the Fields of the Lord, Peter Matthiessen. A fictional work by the man who has become somewhat of a hero to world-roaming travellers. It's a story about missionaries in the Amazon jungles.

One Hundred Years of Solitude, Gabriél Garcia Marquez (Picador 1978). The Nobel Prize-winning author's classic tale of South American life.

We Eat the Mines and the Mines Eat Us, June Nash (Columbia University Press 1979). An anthropologist's study of life and death in the Bolivian tin mines. Recommended.

The Bridge of San Luis Ray, Thornton Wilder (Grosset & Dunlap 1927). This story takes place in Peru, but is an interesting fictional classic dealing with characters and ideals found in the Andes.

History

Selected Writings of Bolivar I & II, compiled by the Bank of Venezuela Colonial Press 1951. Voluminous edition of Bolivar's articles and letters. South American history buffs will love it. It includes such revealing anachronistic quotes as: 'Hapless Bolivia has had four different leaders in less than two weeks! Only the kingdom of Hell could offer so appalling a picture discrediting humanity!'

Ché Guevara, Daniel James (Stein & Day 1969). Very interesting, slightly right-wing biography of the folk hero with

emphasis upon his activities and ultimate demise in Bolivia.
The Incredible Incas & Their Timeless Land, Loren McIntyre (National Geographic Society Press 1975). Easily-digested account of Inca history and description of Inca lands in modern times by someone who has lived in Peru and Bolivia for many years. Typical informal 'Geographic' style and lots of colour photos and illustrations.
Tales of Potosí, Bartolomé Arzáns de Orsua y Vela (Brown University Press 1975). An anthology of stories about the city whose history reads more like fiction than fact. It's a very good insight into colonial life in Bolivia.

General
Land Above the Clouds, Tony Morrison (Andre Deutsch 1974). A study of the land and wildlife of the Andes.
The History of Coca 'The divine Plant of the Incas', W Golden Mortimer, MD (And/OR Press, 1974). All about the Andean wonder drug. Originally published in 1901.
The Old Patagonia Express, Paul Theroux (Pocket Books 1980). The tale of a train journey from Boston to Patagonia. Theroux takes a rather poor attitude toward budget travellers and doesn't seem to much enjoy his trip, but it's an interesting story.
The Incredible Voyage, Tristan Jones (Sheed Andrews & McMeel, Inc. 1977). Includes narrative about several months sailing and exploring on Lake Titicaca.
The Ra Expeditions, Thor Heyerdahl (Doubleday & Co. 1971). Has some interesting discussions of reed boats, not only those from Lake Titicaca, but also from other far-flung places.

Language
University of Chicago Spanish-English/English-Spanish Dictionary (Pocket Books 1972). Emphasises Latin American usage and pronunciation.

Lonely Planet's *Quechua phrasebook*, available in 1989, gives useful phrases and words in the Cuzco dialect (also spoken in the Bolivian highlands).

Travel Guides
South America on a Shoestring, Geoff Crowther (Lonely Planet). Regularly updated general guide for those travelling on a budget throughout South America, Central America and Mexico. Lots of maps and plenty of info in a well-organised format.
Along the Gringo Trail, Jack Epstien (And/Or Press 1977). An often humorous budget guide which covers the 'Gringo Trail', the well-worn route from the US/Mexico border to Tierra del Fuego.
A Traveller's Guide to El Dorado & the Inca Empire, Lynn Meisch (Penguin Books 3rd printing 1980). A thoroughly entertaining and informative book providing background information about Colombia, Peru, Ecuador and Bolivia. I highly recommend it!
Adventuring in the Andes, Charles Frazier (Sierra Club Books 1985). Off-the-beaten-path travel in Bolivia, Ecuador and Peru. Bolivia is only given 18 pages, but it contains some valuable info.
Backpacking & Trekking in Peru & Bolivia, Hilary and George Bradt (Bradt Enterprises 1980). Excellent rundown of hikes in both countries although, as usual, Bolivia gets second billing. All recommended hikes are limited to the Cordillera Real and the Yungas, but it does include some invaluable background information for those primarily interested in hiking and trekking.
South America Handbook, edited by John Brooks (Trade & Travel Publications, 63rd edition, 1986). Voluminous and pricey guide covering everything between the Río Grande and Antarctica (even the Caribbean). It's the best general guide around and though it lacks good maps, it contains a mind-boggling amount of information which is presented in a confusing but space-conscious format. It's interesting reading, too, if you're captivated

by telephone directories. A lot of info on Bolivia I found hopelessly outdated, but I still got enough out of it to justify the price and weight.

If you'll be travelling in other South American countries, Lonely Planet's Travel Survival Kits on *Chile & Easter Island*, by Alan Samagalski, and *Peru* and *Ecuador & the Galapagos Islands*, both by Rob Rachowiecki, are recommended. Currently in the works at Lonely Planet are guides covering Argentina, Brazil and Colombia by other authors.

MAPS

A number of maps are available in La Paz, Cochabamba and Santa Crúz through *Los Amigos del Libro*. Other bookshops and stationery stores sell national cartographic publications and, in many places, street vendors even sell poster-like thematic maps of the country.

All of these, though, are of such poor quality that they are of marginal use. The colour plates used to print them were so badly misaligned in most cases that blue rivers and red highways become green and orange lines on yellow backgrounds and city names are far enough from their locations to cause confusion.

A widely-available road map called *Red de Caminos* (Highway Network) is a highly optimistic representation of every highway commissioner's wildest dreams. Many roads drawn in on this map haven't even been planned yet, and those in the planning stages are shown as major routes.

The government mapping office is in a small, unassuming cubbyhole at Avenida 16 de Julio 1471 in La Paz. They produce reasonable topographic sheets of most of the country, which are available to the public for US$6 each. Unfortunately, they are frequently out of the more popular ones, such as treks, peaks and Lake Titicaca, etc.

They also publish an excellent map of the entire country which is available in several sizes. The smallest costs US$8 and shows significant populations, political divisions, transport routes and physical features. This is undoubtedly the best map available in Bolivia, but it's also often in short supply.

These government maps are sometimes available in bookshops. They're easily recognisable because they contain the name of the president in power when the map was commissioned below the title. Before buying, however, be sure to check the publication date as there are still a lot of 1937 and 1952 maps floating around.

City street plans are available from tourist offices in major cities. These vary in quality and accuracy. All of them were produced on very low budgets and most are outdated, but they can still be very useful. In smaller cities, street plans can be bought at the *alcaldía* (city hall) for about US$10. They are often quite optimistic and emphasise economic and civic accomplishments rather than tourist facilities.

Climbing maps of major Bolivian peaks are available from Club Andino Boliviano (tel 324682) at Calle México 1638, La Paz. Their mailing address is Casilla 1346, La Paz, Bolivia.

WHAT TO BRING

By the time most travellers get to Bolivia, they are already seasoned enough to know the sort of things they need to travel in such developing countries. For those who have chosen Bolivia as a first destination, however, or for those who, like myself, have managed to stumble through 50 countries beneath as many haphazardly-packed kgs, here are a few guidelines.

Bags The type of luggage you should carry will depend largely upon your style of travel. If you prefer prearranged tours, finer hotels and consistently use taxis around town, it's a safe bet to say that traditional but strong suitcases or shoulder bags will be just fine.

If you're planning to travel more casually,

an internal frame backpack or a pack that zips into a suitcase would be more suitable because you will probably be carrying it longer distances. The most important factors to consider are comfort, strength, weight and manageability. A flimsy, bulky or awkward piece of luggage will quickly become a nightmare of repairs or back pains and bodily contortions.

Essentials The most important advice is to travel light and only take along that which is indispensable. Unfortunately, everyone has a different idea about what that means. One person's automatic drip coffee-maker is another person's morning 'fix'. And what appears to be a puffy sleping bag is in reality a 'five-kg-30 rated Hollofil Andean Survival System'.

As for travelling light, I'm not much of an authority. On my last trip to South America, among hundreds of other travellers' packs I discovered that mine was as heavy as any two of their combined. I don't know how it got that way (one never does), but it was not a pleasant realisation. There were times when I even wished it would be stolen.

To help you try to avoid this the following is a checklist of items which are either difficult to obtain in Bolivia or will be used often enough to justify their weight throughout your trip.

First Aid Kit
Malaria tablets
Travel alarm clock
Small flashlight and extra batteries
Water bottle – aluminium is better than plastic because it does not flavour the water or allow light to pass through and stimulate the growth of bacteria.
Water purification tablets – iodine-based if possible
Swiss Army type pocket knife with bottle opener, corkscrew, scissors, can opener, etc.
Spare glasses and a copy of optical prescription
Towel
Clothesline – two or three metres of cord is useful for all sorts of things.
Sewing kit
Writing implements – few South American pens will function on airmail paper.
Spanish/English Dictionary
Contraceptives
Tampons – Napkins are available everywhere, but tampons are scarce and very expensive
Any prescription medications you normally take.

Clothing Without going completely overboard and carrying your entire wardrobe around in your pack, you do need to be reasonably prepared for the extremes of Bolivia's climate.

The minimum I would recommend carrying for the cold is a warm jacket suitable for freezing temperatures, a fuzzy pullover, a pair of wool gloves, a hat with ear coverings and several pairs of wool or polypropylene socks. Thermal underwear will be welcome at night and some Gore-tex rain gear will come in handy if you're visiting during the wet season or hiking in the mountains.

For the heat, two sleeveless shirts, a pair of thongs or sandals and shorts will be about all you'll need. For women who don't want to attract a lot of annoying attention, however, the shorts should be replaced by a light skirt or dress. There is still a prejudice in Bolivia against women wearing shorts but men will encounter no major social restrictions regarding their clothing.

In addition you'll also need two pairs of trousers – one to wash and one to wear; a long-sleeve, lightweight shirt to wear under itchy woollen or alpaca sweaters; underwear and socks; swimming gear – there are lots of waterfalls and hot springs; one pair of sneakers or comfortable walking shoes; and a 'dress up' set of clothes.

If you don't want to carry a pack full of clothing in preparation for all the variables, it's not difficult to find fairly inexpensive clothing in the major Bolivian cities.

Those who wear extreme sizes, however, may run into difficulties. Finding warm pullovers and gloves for children is a

Top: Accounting Bolivian style – La Paz (WH)
Left: Young girl – La Paz (WH)
Right: Aymará women on Calle Graneras – La Paz (WH)

Top: La Paz and the peaks of Illimani (WH)
Bottom: La Paz city (TW)

problem, as is finding larger sizes – especially in shoes. The average Bolivian is simply smaller than the average foreigner.

Books Any novels or guidebooks you'll be needing should also be taken from home. English language books and guides are scarce and extremely expensive in Bolivia. To keep the weight down, many travellers just rip out (no, I won't be offended) or photocopy sections of guidebooks covering areas they plan to visit.

For long plane and boat rides, take along at least one thick paperback. When you're finished, it can be easily traded with other travellers, and those who have resorted to reading *Condorito* comic books will bless you.

You may also want to take a diary to record people and events. I like to carry the 'blank book' variety so I may add sketches as well as descriptions. If you're going to carry an address book, be sure it's not the only copy in existence. This would be a devastating item to lose, as I learned from personal experience.

Photos Lastly, think about taking some photos of your friends and family. Bolivians are always anxious to share their family album with visitors and they will want to see yours too.

Some postcards of your city or country would also be helpful in communicating something about your home to Bolivians and fellow travellers alike. I don't know how many times I've been asked about Alaska, only to be at a loss for words without some pictures to give them an idea of what it looks like. In addition, postcards of wildlife, festivals or sports activities from your home make great gifts for Bolivian children.

Getting There

AIR

Only a limited number of airlines offer service directly into Bolivia and those that do, charge higher fares than those that fly into neighbouring countries. One possible explanation for this is that there are a number of regulations dealing with aircraft operation into and out of La Paz.

The altitude of the La Paz airport means that pilots operating aircraft there need high-altitude certification, and high speed take-offs and landings inflict a lot of wear and tear on equipment. Therefore, it's normally much less expensive to fly into Chile, Peru, Brazil or Argentina and then worry about getting to Bolivia.

It's a relatively simple matter to overland from any of those places and air fares within South America, especially from Peru, are reasonable enough to justify landing there first.

Travelling from Paraguay directly into Bolivia is difficult overland and rather expensive by air, but the situation improves considerably if you take a more roundabout route through Brazil or Argentina.

Border Considerations

If you're flying into Peru, Brazil or Colombia, keep in mind that an onward ticket is required before you'll be admitted to any of those countries. A Miscellaneous Charges Order (MCO), a voucher good for equivalent worth in travel on any IATA-approved carrier, should suffice. If unused, it can be cashed in when you get home.

Student Travel

Worldwide, there are a number of student travel organisations which offer bargain-basement airfares to out-of-the-way destinations the world over including a few in Latin America.

Anyone under 26 years of age who has a YIEE (Youth International Educational

Exchange) card or anyone under 34 with an ISIC (International Student Identity Card) and their travelling companions are eligible for a variety of exceptional travel discounts.

It's a good idea to pick up one of these cards before you leave your home country because it's very difficult to get them in Latin America. Even to renew one of them you're looking at a delay of several months.

Some sample one-way fares, in US dollars, available through the STA Travel, San Francisco (address following) are:

	Los Angeles	*New York*	*Miami*
Caracas	175	170	120
Guayaquil	185	205	135
Rio de Janeiro	440	360	325
São Paulo	460	375	340
Buenos Aires	465	395	340
Montevideo	465	395	340
Santiago	430	445	395

Other organisations which offer similar fares and services, and from whom you can get ISIC cards, are:

Australia
STA Travel, 224 Faraday St, Carlton, Victoria (tel 03-3476911)
STA Travel, 1A Lee St, Railway Square, Sydney, NSW (tel 02-2121255)

Austria
OKISTA * Türkenstrasse 4 1090, Vienna (tel 0222-347526)

Belgium
ACOTRA * Rue de la Montagne 1000, Brussels (tel 02-5128607)

Canada
CHA * 333 River Road, Vanier, Ottawa, Ontario KIL 8H9
Canadian International Student Services, 80 Richmond St W £1202 Toronto, Ontario M5H 2A4 (tel 416-3642738)

Denmark
DIS REJSER * 28 Skindergade 1159, Copenhagen (tel 01-110044)

France
ILT/SSTS * 7 Rue La Michodiere, 75002 Paris (tel 1-42665467)

Ireland
USIT * 7 Anglesea St, Dublin 2 (tel 01-77-8117)

Italy
CTS * Via Piave £49, 00187 Rome (tel 47-9931)

Japan
STA Travel, Sanden Bldg, 5th floor, Room 5A, 3-5-5 Kojimachi Chyoda-ku, Tokyo 102 (tel 03-2211043)

Netherlands
NBBS * Rappenburg 8, Box 11054, 2301 Eb Leiden (tel 071-145044)

New Zealand
STA Travel, 10 High St, Auckland (tel 390458)

Sweden
STF * Vasagatan 48 Box 25 101-20 Stockholm (tel 08-7903100)

Switzerland
SSR Reisen * Bäckerstrasse 52, 8026 Zurich (tel 01-2423000)
International Student Travel Conference, Weinbergstrasse 31, CH 8006 Zurich.

United Kingdom
STA Travel, 74 Old Brompton Rd, London SW7 3LQ (tel 5811022) WST * 38/39 Store St, London WC1E 7BZ (tel 01-5807733)

USA
Whole World Travel, Suite 400, 17 East 45th St, New York, NY 10017 (tel 212-9869470)
Council on International Educational Exchange, 205 East 42nd St, New York, NY 10017
STA Travel, 166 Geary St, San Francisco, CA 94108 (tel 415-3918407)
STA Travel, Suite 507, 2500 Wilshire Blvd, Los Angeles, CA 90057 (tel 213-3802184)
STA Travel, 6609 Hillcrest Ave, Dallas 214 (tel 36000977)

West Germany
STUDIOSUS Reisen * Luissenstrasse 43 8000 Munich (tel 089-52-30-00)

* Those marked with this symbol sell the YIEE card.

From North America

One of the world's greatest official airfare bargains is the current US$362 return fare from Miami to Lima. It is far cheaper than even the best one way fare available. As a matter of fact, the return fare to Lima combined with a Lloyd Aereo Boliviano

(LAB) ticket from Lima to La Paz comes out to only US$503 while the lowest one-way fare from Miami directly to La Paz is US$562 on Eastern or LAB.

The popularity of this fare will probably ensure that similar bargains will be around for quite awhile. If you find that option sold out (as will be likely unless you reserve it far in advance), an alternative is to travel on Faucett for US$462 return on Tuesday or Saturday nights.

If you want to fly directly to La Paz from Miami, the least expensive option is to go on Eastern's thrice-weekly flight for US$659 return or on LAB's daily-except-Tuesday runs for the same price. LAB gives you the additional option of getting off in Santa Crúz for no additional charge. The one-way fare on either of these carriers is US$562.

As should already be obvious, all the good deals from North America are out of Miami. From the west coast to Lima the best fare is on Varig or Eastern, both of which offer return only APEX (Advance Purchase Excursion) fares of US$823. Varig flies on Sunday and Wednesday and Eastern flies on Monday. It would still be less expensive to travel via Miami using a Super Saver ticket from Los Angeles than to fly to South America directly from Los Angeles.

Keep in mind that due to excessive competition between carriers and a lot of governmental red tape in determining fare structures, flights originating in the US are subject to all sorts of restrictions and regulations. This is especially true of bargain tickets. Just about anything that costs less than standard tourist or economy fare will have to be purchased at least 14 days prior to departure and most often 30 days before.

In addition, you'll have to book departure and return dates in advance. What's more, these tickets are normally subject to minimum and maximum stay requirements which will usually be seven days and six months, respectively. Of course, if you're planning to buy a return ticket and trash the second half of it anyway, this won't be a problem.

From the US, open tickets which allow an open return date within a 12-month period are generally not available and serious penalties – up to 50% of some bargain fares – are imposed if you make any changes in the return booking mid-trip.

If you've missed a flight, however, or want to go home early, it's worth going to the airport anyway and trying to get on a flight without calling attention to your schedule change. If the plane isn't full, you should have no problem; the hassles only arise when you try to get an advance reservation.

If all else fails, however, a well-prepared, heart-wrenching hard luck story may do the trick. Something like: 'my travelling companion is in the hospital with haemorrhagic fever and I can't just leave her alone there . . . ' This one worked for me, but unfortunately it was the truth.

From Australia & New Zealand

As far as the travel industry is concerned, trying to get to Bolivia from Australia is akin to trying to travel from Burkina Faso to Fiji. It's not easy and most unfortunately it's not cheap.

Most round-the-world fares, which seem like they should offer the Aussies and Kiwis a little relief, tend to include only the northern hemisphere and massive surcharges are levied if the traveller wants to include Latin America or the South Pacific. Sometimes, however, there are round-the-world tickets that include South America and don't cost an arm and a leg.

One option that should be considered is to take advantage of Qantas or Air New Zealand's APEX fares between Sydney or Auckland and the US west coast which are currently about US$1236 return, with up to three stopovers. Thanks to Paul Hogan's rash of *G'day, come on down* TV commercials and the popularity of

Crocodile Dundee, however, US tour groups have these fares booked up well in advance and you'd be wise to purchase such a ticket at least six months before you plan to travel.

From LA or San Francisco it's only a matter of overlanding or finding a cheap APEX ticket to Miami.

Those who'd rather travel directly to South America really have only one viable option and its currently less expensive than the roundabout route through the US.

You can fly from Sydney via Auckland to Buenos Aires in Argentina or Santiago in Chile, for a one-way fare of A$1305; or all the way through to La Paz for A$1399 one-way, A$2140 return. For information on getting from Santiago or Buenos Aires to Bolivia, see the From Chile and From Argentina sections.

From Britain & Europe

Undoubtedly, the least expensive official way to Latin America from Europe is via Miami. On Virgin Airways, People's Express, or whatever bargain basement trans-Atlantic carrier is currently operating, you can hop over to New York for about US$130 one way.

The APEX fare from New York to Miami return is currently US$99 on a number of carriers, but if you're pressed for time and don't want to sit around in New York for 14 days, Air Canada and Piedmont both offer a US$495 return fare direct from London to Miami.

If you're coming from the Continent, it may be worthwhile checking out what kind of deal Aeroflot can make from East Berlin to South America via Cuba. I lost count of the number of Germans and Swiss I met in Bolivia who'd gone this route for less than US$500.

It would also pay to shop around at bucket shops. A bucket shop, in case you haven't had any experience with them, is a travel/ticket agency which buys unsold tickets directly from the carriers at a considerable discount and passes the savings along to the public.

As a matter of fact, the bucket shops will probably be able to get you all the way to South America – either Bogotá, Caracas, São Paulo, Lima or Buenos Aires – for less than US$350 each way.

From Brazil

LLoyd Aereo Boliviano has flights from São Paulo to La Paz on Monday, Wednesday, Friday and Sunday, stopping in Santa Crúz en route. The fare to La Paz is US$277 one-way and to Santa Crúz costs US$229. Varig flies the same route on Tuesday, Thursday, Friday and Saturday. There is a US$9 departure tax on any international flight originating in Brazil.

Another exit point from Brazil is Cobija, across the river from Brasília. LAB does the milk run from Cobija to La Paz twice weekly, and TAM has three weekly flights. During the rainy season (November to March), however, it's very difficult to get on a flight and weeks go by with no activity at all.

From Argentina

LAB has a service from Buenos Aires via Santa Crúz on Tuesdays, at a cost of US$277 to La Paz and US$229 to Santa Crúz. That flight also lands in Salta so you can buy a ticket from there.

From Chile

LAN Chile flies to La Paz from Santiago and Arica on Fridays and Mondays for US$152 and US$96, respectively. LAB flies the same route on Tuesday, Thursday and Saturday for about 20% less. From Santiago only there is a US$12.50 departure tax.

From Peru

There are LAB flights from Cuzco to La Paz for US$100 one-way on Wednesday and Saturday but they're normally booked up for weeks in advance. If you're planning to go this route, it may be worthwhile to book it before you leave home or well before you ever get to Cuzco.

LAB and Aero Peru both fly between Lima and La Paz. LAB has service on Tuesday, Thursday, Saturday and Sunday and costs US$141 one-way. Aero Peru flies on Wednesday and Friday.

There is a ticket tax of 21% for Peruvian residents and 7% for non-resident tourists.

From Paraguay

There are Eastern flights from Asunción to La Paz on Tuesday, Thursday and Saturday but the fare is rather steep at US$262 one-way.

OVERLAND

It's becoming increasingly popular for travellers to overland to South America from the USA along the Gringo Trail. Anyone experienced in overland travel in developing countries will find few surprises along this stretch which includes six or seven extremely diverse nations between the Río Grande and the Colombian border. There are, however, a couple of catches which you should be aware of before attempting this route.

First of all, Guatemala, Honduras, El Salvador and Nicaragua are all experiencing some well-publicised internal difficulties which are often accompanied by violence, military activities and general paranoia, which all tend to make things uncomfortable.

Very recently, Panama has also been experiencing a great deal of conflict. In the interest of personal safety, El Salvador and the Honduras/Nicaragua border region should be either avoided or put behind you as quickly as possible.

Secondly, Nicaragua has an odd rule which requires foreigners to exchange US$60 at the piss-poor official exchange rate upon entering the country. This rate is so bad that this requirement is akin to charging US$60 admission to Nicaragua.

Finally, since the Pan-American Highway is broken in Eastern Panama, travellers are obliged to either fly into Colombia or overland past the Darien Gap using a combination of methods, all of which include at least a seven to 14-day slog through the jungle.

From Brazil

Via Corumbá Corumbá, opposite the Bolivian border town of Puerto Suarez, has both rail and bus connections from São Paulo, Rio de Janeiro, Cuiabá and southern Brazil. It is the most popular port of entry between Bolivia and Brazil.

From the city, take a bus to the frontier and from there a taxi to the railhead at Quijarro. From Quijarro, a train leaves daily for Santa Crúz during the dry season. During the wet, you may have a wait of several days.

Via Northern Brazil There are three border crossings from northern Brazil into Bolivia but, unfortunately, all of them are dead ends as far as rail or highway connections are concerned.

From Cáceres north of Cuiabá you can cross to San Matías in Bolivia, but from there it will be necessary to fly to Roboré and Santa Crúz in order to connect with terrestrial transport.

A popular crossing is from Guajará-mirim in Brazil by motorboat across the Río Mamoré into Guayaramerín, Bolivia. From there, a road goes to Riberalta and dead-ends.

It's possible to take a 10 to 15-day river trip up the Mamoré to the highway at Puerto Villarroel near Cochabamba, or from Riberalta up the Río Beni to Puerto Linares fairly near La Paz; but conditions are basic so you should be prepared. Alternately, LAB has three flights per week from both Guayaramerín and Riberalta.

From Argentina

Via La Quiaca Several trains leave daily from Retiro station in Buenos Aires going to the current railhead at Tucamán.

A combination bus ticket may be purchased at the same time to get you from Tucumán to Salta or Jujuy.

From either of those cities, there are buses leaving every two hours or so during the day for La Quiaca, which is across the Río Villazón from the Bolivian town of Villazón. Only taxis are available to get you across the border but both the train and bus terminals in Villazón are less than 30 minutes walking distance of the bus terminals in La Quiaca.

A bus leaves daily from Villazón to Tupiza and Potosí at 4 pm and another goes to Tarija. There are trains from there to La Paz on Tuesdays, and only as far as Oruro on Monday and Thursday.

Via Orán This is a minor border crossing, with customs formalities, in the hamlet of Aguas Blancas, which is one hour by bus from Orán and across the Río Bermejo from Bermejo in Bolivia. Access across the river is by ferry. From Bermejo, there are several bus companies that do daily runs to Tarija.

Via Pocitos From Retiro Station in Buenos Aires, take the train to the railhead at Tucamán and from there take a connecting bus to Tartagal. Another bus from Tartagal goes to Pocitos on the frontier.

In Pocitos, you cross the border on foot, about a 10-minute walk, to Pocitos in Bolivia, and then take a taxi into Yacuiba, five km distant. From Yacuiba, there are trains on Tuesday, Thursday and Saturday to Santa Crúz. Buses are available to Tarija, also.

From Chile

Via Arica There is a twice monthly train from Arica to La Paz which costs US$20 and takes at least 24 hours. You have to change trains and go through customs at the border in Charaña and it's a very cold and uncomfortable proposition. Alternately, there's *ferrobus* service on Saturdays at 9 am which takes 11 hours and costs US$51 per person.

By bus, *Flota Litoral* leaves on Monday and Friday at 1 am from Calle Chacabuco in Arica and costs US$18; and *Agencia Martinez* runs a service from Arica to connect with Bolivian trains. The latter goes only as far as Charaña on the frontier. The Bolivian trains have no reliable schedule so the Chilean bus does a run whenever a train is expected to arrive. From Arica to the border costs US$7.20.

Via Antofagasta/Calama Going to La Paz from Antofagasta, you must take a two-hour bus ride to Calama (US$3). One train per week leaves Calama for Ollagüe at midday on Wednesday and takes about eight hours to do the *all* uphill run to the frontier. In Ollagüe, you have to walk across the border to Avaroa in Bolivia, and connect with the Bolivian train to Uyuni, Oruro and La Paz.

At the rail office in Antofagasta you can buy a combination bus and train ticket all the way to La Paz. As on all routes between Chile and Bolivia, warm clothes are absolutely essential!

From Peru

Via Puno There are basically two routes from Puno into Bolivia. The quickest but least interesting is by *micro* from Puno to the frontier at Desaguadero where you can connect with a Bolivian bus to La Paz.

The other route, which is far more interesting is via Copacabana and the Straits of Tiquina. Micros leave Puno before 9 am and enter Bolivia at Copacabana. There you connect with another micro, or a bus company (*Manco Capac* or *Transportes 2 de Febrero*), for the five-hour trip into La Paz, crossing the Straits of Tiquina on an auto ferry. The entire run from Puno to La Paz can be easily done in a day.

There are other very obscure border crossings such as the one from Puerto Acosta north of Lake Titicaca and a couple of ports of entry along the rivers of the north but they require a great deal of effort and there is no public transport available.

From Paraguay

The route overland into Bolivia from Paraguay is very rough and probably isn't worth considering unless you don't mind a long wait at Mariscal Estigarribia, or one of the other remote Grán Chaco outposts, for an infrequent vehicle heading into Bolivia.

Coming from Paraguay, it's much easier to cross into Brazil at Ponta Porã from Pedro Juan Caballero and travel by train from there to Corumbá in Brazil (18 hours with a change at Campo Grande). At Corumbá, you can cross to Quijarro, Bolivia.

Another option is to travel from Asunción to Formosa in Argentina, and from there take a bus to Tartagal and then to Pocitos on the Bolivian/Argentine frontier.

Getting Around

AIR

Travel by air in Bolivia is not expensive and is often the only means of getting to the more out-of-the-way places. During the wet season, it is the only transport method not completely washed-out by the rain. This doesn't mean that the rainy season doesn't disrupt air schedules; it does, and often for weeks at a time. But in times of flood, in theory at least, planes can still get through.

Bolivia's national carrier is Lloyd Aereo Boliviano (LAB). It never, never, never runs on schedule but fares are reasonable – in some cases less than twice the bus fare – and they fly pretty much anywhere in the country you might wish to go. They also have international flights to Miami and all major South American cities except Bogotá.

As might be expected, service is very basic, but throughout its history LAB has maintained a perfect safety record and the pilots are familiar with Bolivia's difficult terrain. LAB has ticket offices in every town it serves and, except around holidays, seats are usually available the day before the flight.

Transportes Aereos Militares (TAM) is the second notable internal carrier. As with most military operations, schedules change frequently, flights are often cancelled and reservations are ignored. They aren't as reliable as LAB (which isn't reliable by any definition), but they do fill in some gaps in LAB's schedule and service a lot of small towns which the other airline doesn't.

TAM operates smaller planes, such as the Fairchild F27 Turbo-prop, which fly closer to the ground than the big jets. If you're interested in the view or aerial photography, this may be worth considering.

Most airports charge an airport tax on internal flights which is not included in the ticket price and is payable at check-in time. In Riberalta, for example, the tax is US$2 per ticket, while in La Paz it's only 75c.

In addition, a departure tax must be paid on all international flights leaving the country. If it's paid in Bolivian currency, it is US$7.50 per person, but if the traveller has wisely disposed of all his or her Bolivianos before leaving for the airport, it's going to cost US$15 in US currency.

LAB and TAM both allow 20 kg of luggage, excluding carry-ons, without additional charges.

BUS

If you're interested in meeting the Bolivians, their children, their luggage and their animals, this is the way to go. Long distance bus lines in Bolivia are called *flotas*. Large buses are called *buses* (BOO-says) and small ones are known as *micros* (MEE-cros).

Just about everyone will use this mode of transport during a trip through Bolivia and the middle-class locals use it almost exclusively. While this form of travel is inexpensive and allows you a down-to-earth experience of the people and landscape, it has a few drawbacks which must be considered.

First of all, most flotas depart in the evening and arrive at their destination early in the morning, often too early to get a hotel without paying for the previous night. It also seems that no matter how many companies service a particular run, they all leave at the same time of day, so schedule options are limited.

Although most buses travel at night, conditions are not optimum for sleeping. If you have a seat, and fortunately most flotas do accept advance seat reservations, you'll soon discover the bus was designed with capacity, rather than comfort, in mind.

The floors, racks and roof will be packed to overflowing with bags, boxes, tins, animals and Bolivians. With a little arithmetic, you can calculate that the locals travel with an average of 16 pieces of luggage per person, which leaves pitifully little room for your feet.

Add to that the obligatory radio or tape player, that invariably blares at concentration-shattering volumes throughout the night; highway police stops and narcotics searches in every town; and the inevitable equipment failure that plagues most runs; and you'll be lucky to even close your eyes, let alone sleep.

In addition, it seems that the highway budget in Bolivia takes very low priority. Frankly, the word 'highway' can be applied to only a handful of routes around La Paz and Cochabamba. Elsewhere, the word 'track', or in some cases 'rut', would be more appropriate. Given the incredibly rugged and steep terrain they've had to work with, however, the Bolivians have done an admirable job of opening up inhospitable territory.

Another concern is the rainy season. From November to March, any or all modes of public transport, including airlines, may suspend service for weeks at a time without explanation. *Mañana*, they'll mutter – 'maybe tomorrow'.

Hillsides come crashing down, bridges collapse into swollen rivers, roads turn into quagmires and mudpits or wash away altogether, and travellers become frustrated as carefully-worked schedules go awry. A good rule of thumb to use is that any bus journey over unsurfaced roads, even under optimum conditions, will take half as long again as scheduled. During the rainy season, plan on double or triple the time.

Equipment must also be reckoned with. Buses in Bolivia range from sagging, sputtering, dilapidated wrecks to large and relatively comfortable coaches with Pullman seats and ample leg room for the average foreigner. Unfortunately, many companies run both types and a few in between so it's difficult to be assured of a good one. Generally, any flota with the name 'Pullman' attached to it will run nicer buses. Some roads in Bolivia, however, are so bad that companies will only run expendable equipment over them.

Another serious problem in Bolivia is

drunken driving. Although it's officially a no-no, don't be surprised to see your driver swill a couple of litres during a single rest stop. All this isn't intentionally meant to put you off; it's just the way things are, so if you're overly nervous it may be better to travel by air or rail.

The good news is that buses are convenient. Between any two cities, you should have no trouble finding at least one bus leaving every day. On the most popular routes like La Paz-Oruro, 20 flotas each do eight to 10 runs daily.

Bus travel is also an excellent way to meet Bolivians and get to know them. They will invariably be interested in what you think of their country, what you're doing there, and how much it's costing you to do it. In addition, if you can manage to travel by daylight, you'll be treated to an eye level view of the spectacular wilderness landscapes and the serene little farms and villages that are the essence of the country.

What to Carry

It's a good idea to take along food and something to drink on long bus journeys, especially if you're travelling in remote areas. Rest stops are unscheduled and depend largely upon the whims and bodily necessities of the driver.

If you'd rather wing it, at some brief stops such as police searches, intermediate stations and toll posts, the bus will probably be invaded by vendors selling everything from parrots to shampoo. Most offer food, however, and you can buy a complete meal or just bread and fruit.

You can also buy *refresco*, a weak, sweet fruit juice with a fuzzy ball of 'something' at the bottom of the glass. It's really not too bad if you tell them to keep the fuzzy ball.

Absolutely essential on any bus trip, day or night, is twice as much warm clothing as you expect to need. At night, even in the jungle areas, it gets surprisingly cold and on the Altiplano it gets bitter! If your alpaca pullover is safely packed away on the roof of the bus you will suffer, and even with it inside, you'll wish you had two pairs of thermal underwear and an Eskimo parka to go with it.

Even during the day changes in altitude will necessitate frequent addition and subtraction of clothing. Once you've done this a few times, you'll understand why the Bolivians were all so overdressed when they boarded the bus in 30° heat.

Major Routes

La Paz – Oruro
: A three hour trip on surfaced roads. Departures every half hour or so; US$2.50.

La Paz – Copacabana
: Takes five hours. Buses leave four times daily. Return buses leave at 7 and 8 am and again around midday; US$4.

La Paz – Cochabamba
: Takes 10 hours. Twenty different flotas leave at around 7 pm. Some buses pass through Oruro, which takes a little longer; US$8.

Cochabamba – Sucre
: This is a rough 12 hour ride. Several flotas depart daily after 7 pm; US$6.

Cochabamba – Santa Crúz
: This trip takes 14 hours. A score of companies all depart between 4 and 6 pm; US$7.

Potosí – Sucre
: A six hour journey. There is one scheduled departure daily at 9 am from the bus terminal but in reality, many buses make this run, leaving when full; US$5.

Villazón – Potosí
: Takes 13 hours and leaves daily at 4 pm; US$7.50.

La Paz – Coroico
: This trip is six hours of white-knuckle terror. Flota Yungueña departs at 9 am on Monday, Wednesday, Friday and Saturday; US$3.50.

Coroico – La Paz
: A six hour trip. Buses depart on Monday, Wednesday, Friday and Sunday at 7 am; US$3.50.

TRAIN

ENFE (*Empresa Nacional de Ferroviarios*) is the Bolivian National Railroad and it is the crown jewel of all that is frustratingly inefficient and disorganised about the

country. In the Oriente (eastern Bolivia), where the train more or less serves as a lifeline, a favourite pastime is to sit around and swap ENFE stories. They're always good for a laugh.

First of all, the trains run on no real schedule. There's an official timetable all right, but it's meaningless. Instead, arrival and departure times are written on a chalkboard at the station as soon as it looks like something may happen.

In small stations, tickets are not sold until the train is actually in the station, thus confirming an arrival, and chaos ensues. Even in larger stations, tickets cannot be reserved until the day the train is expected to depart.

Each station is allotted a certain number of seat reservations (although some smaller stations receive no seats at all) and they go on sale as soon as ENFE employees get around to opening the window and the police arrive to keep order.

Despite signs prohibiting sleeping in the railroad stations, hundreds of people queue up on the previous day – or sooner – to wait for tickets. This sometimes necessitates multiple queues: those waiting for today's tickets, those waiting for tomorrow's, for the next day's, and so on.

It doesn't always work this way though. Police will often herd everyone into the same queue and when the *boletero* (ticket-seller) discovers people not wanting the current day's tickets, he boots them out and they are left to battle among themselves about how to re-form the queue.

When the day's allotment of tickets is sold out, the window is lowered and that's it. The lucky ticket-holders settle in to await their journey and everyone else wanders around muttering that there has to be a better way.

Keep in mind that if you do reach the ticket window, you must present the personal documents of each person for whom you are buying tickets. This is done to prevent scalping which, as you can imagine, would be a very lucrative enterprise under these circumstances.

If you are lucky enough to get a seat reservation and the train does arrive, the trip itself will be more of the same sort of thing experienced in the queue. On one trip from Uyuni to Potosí, I just about reached the limits of my good nature.

The chalkboard announced that the train would depart at 7 pm so I arrived shortly before. I boarded, only to find that my seat was already occupied and it required a shouting match and the help of the conductor to displace the offender. I stowed my luggage on the rack and got comfortable. Then the locals began arriving, each with their usual 16 pieces of luggage.

At around midnight, five hours after the train was scheduled to depart, the temperature in the coach was below zero and ice was forming on the windows. There was no light and everyone was shivering and huddling under piles of blankets.

A family of four occupied the two seats across from me and a 150 kg campesina was sitting beside me. All of her luggage was packed into the floor space between the seats, and a man and his young daughter had settled in on top of it. The campesina was chewing coca leaves and spitting green juice onto the luggage. The family across from us, who had been on a shopping spree in Argentina, were surrounded by all sorts of electronic gadgetry and as there was no room on the floor, they asked us to hold some of it for them.

Finally, at 4 am, the station bell sounded; the train was finally ready to depart! The bell sounded again at 5 am. At 6.15 am, we finally pulled out of Uyuni, but 10 km out of the station we made an unexplained 2½ hour stop in the middle of the Altiplano desert.

People got off the train and set the bush on fire to keep warm. When we finally started up again, the accompanying jolt sent luggage crashing down from overhead racks onto the passengers. The entire 14-hour journey to Potosí was a series of bone crunching jolts and unexplained delays.

Thanks to the incredible piles of luggage and hundreds of unfortunate folk who'd been unable to buy reserved seats, it was impossible to reach the bathroom during the entire trip, making things even more uncomfortable. Just as well though; I can imagine what the toilet must have looked like! I arrived in Potosí that night frazzled, disoriented and feeling as if I'd been passed through a meat-grinder.

The most incredible thing was that the locals were all smiling, chatting and acting as if nothing was amiss. In actual fact nothing was amiss; that was all normal for ENFE.

Fortunately, short of avoiding the train altogether, there are several methods of avoiding experiences like the one I had. Bolivian trains carry 1st and 2nd class coaches, but the only apparent difference is the price. The facilities themselves look just about the same (the trip I recounted was 1st class!) and the distinction is only made to separate the campesinos from the wealthier classes.

In addition to coaches, some trains carry *bodegas*, or boxcars, and 2nd class passengers are permitted to ride in them. On most runs, there is space to spread out and relax, adequate ventilation and, because the doors are left open, a good view of the passing scenery.

The other good news is that 2nd class tickets don't include seat reservations and they may be purchased from the conductor. He will sell you a ticket for a mere 10% to 20% more than it would cost at the window, but without the hassles of queuing.

If you do choose to travel in the bodegas, extreme heat and extreme cold are matters to be reckoned with. Also, be sure to take something to sit on; the bodegas are only cleaned by the bottoms of passengers. In addition, its a good idea to make sure that the boxcar is actually going all the way to your destination to avoid having to shift later.

If you're travelling from the Brazilian or Argentine frontiers, you'll have to be on hand when the cars open in order to stake out a place to sit. These runs are crowded with merchants and their wares, mostly contraband (noodles, wine, flour, etc), being brought unofficially into the country.

Another popular option is to ride on the roof of the train. In warmer climes, this is quite pleasant but it entails obvious risks (remember the jolting starts and stops) and if you fall off, ENFE won't stop to pick you up.

Finally, this brings us to the best option of all; the *ferrobus*. This bus on rails is ENFE's redeeming achievement. It runs on time (give or take an hour or two), is fast and comfortable, and ticket sales are limited to available seats in both 1st and 2nd class. On some runs, tickets are even sold before the day of departure.

This service is a bit more expensive than the normal trains, but that serves to eliminate some of the competition for tickets and consequent queuing problems. Demand for tickets still far exceeds the supply, however, so you'll have to be quick. Often the military reserves large blocks of seats so the general public loses out.

As always, the rainy season presents problems. In most cases a rail washout will be repaired in 24 hours, and flooded tracks will reappear as soon as it hasn't rained for awhile. But, if a bridge washes out the line will be closed indefinitely. At this point, it's time to look for an alternate form of transport.

When travelling internationally by rail to Chile, Brazil or Argentina, you will have to get off, pass through customs of both countries and carry your luggage across the border. In theory, trains connect with each other across borders, but don't count on it.

Major Lines

Scheduled times listed are official only.

La Paz – Villazón

Local train Wednesday & Sunday – 7.15 pm.

Express train Monday, Thursday & Friday – 4.40 pm.

If you're heading for Argentina, you'll need to walk across the border in Villazón (2.5 km) and take a bus to Tucumán via Salta or Jujuy. From there, trains leave for Buenos Aires several times daily.

Villazón – La Paz

Express train Tuesday – 1.45 pm; 1st class US$10.80, 2nd class US$7.25.

When travelling this route, it's much quicker to alight at Oruro and take a bus from there.

Villazón – Oruro

Express train Monday & Thursday – 11.45 am; 1st US$8, 2nd US$5.25.

La Paz – Charaña

Express train Tuesday – 11 pm; 1st US$15.25, 2nd US$10.20. Fares include bus connections to Arica in Chile.

There is also sporadic ferrobus service all the way to Arica, but it changes with demand so ask at either Arica or La Paz for details.

La Paz – Potosí/Sucre

Ferrobus (to Potosí only) Monday, Thursday & Saturday – 7 pm; 1st US$10.60, 2nd US$7.20.

Express train (to Potosí) Wednesday & Saturday – 5.20 pm; 1st US$7.70, 2nd US$5.15.

Express train (to Sucre) Wednesday & Saturday – 5.20 pm; 1st US$10.50, 2nd US$7.

La Paz – Cochabamba

Ferrobus Monday, Wednesday & Friday – 8 am; 1st US$9.50, 2nd US$6.30.

La Paz - Avaroa

Express train Friday - 11.50 am; 2nd class only, US$6.05.

From Avaroa, there are train connections to Calama (Chile) and a bus from Calama to Antofagasta (Chile). It is also possible to buy a straight-through ticket all the way to Antofagasta.

Sucre/Potosí - La Paz

Ferrobus (from Potosí only) Tuesday, Friday & Sunday - 11.30 am; 1st US$9.57, 2nd US$6.35

Express train (from Sucre) Monday & Thursday - 8.50 pm; 1st US$9.29, 2nd US$6.30.

Express train (from Potosí) Monday & Thursday - 8.50 pm; 1st US$6.84, 2nd US$4.55.

Santa Crúz - Quijarro

Ferrobus Monday, Thursday & Saturday; 1st US$14.50, 2nd US$13.50.

Express train daily - 12 noon; 1st US$10, 2nd US$6

Quijarro - Santa Crúz

Ferrobus Wednesday, Friday & Sunday.

Express train daily - 6 am.

Yacuiba - Santa Crúz

Ferrobus Tuesday, Thursday & Saturday - 9.30 pm; 1st US$7.50, 2nd US$10.50.

Express train Tuesday, Thursday & Saturday - 12.35 pm; 1st US$5.50, 2nd US$4.

Mixed train Monday and Friday - 7.20 pm; 1st US$5.50, 2nd US$4.

TAXI

Outside of Beni and Pando departments, taxis are relatively inexpensive in Bolivian cities. There are no meters and the driver and passenger merely agree on the price to a specific destination. The price will usually be the same regardless of the number in your group, although the driver may charge a little more if you have a lot of luggage.

There are, however, a couple of warnings about taxis. Be sure to carry enough small change to cover the fare. Drivers often plead a lack of change and require you to pay more, or they run around trying to break a five or 10 Boliviano note.

When first arriving in a city be sure to ask a merchant, or other local in the transport terminal, what the usual taxi fare is to your destination before agreeing on a price with the driver. Many drivers think that tourists can be taken for a ride, in more ways than one.

Collective taxis in Bolivia are called *trufis* and follow set routes displaying coloured flags which represent their destination. They are always cheaper than taxis and nearly as convenient. A trufi driver will usually deviate from his route in order to get you to your destination.

A taxi may also be chartered to travel longer distances. This method is particularly useful if you want to visit places near major cities, but between or outside the local and long-distance bus networks. An example is the popular return trip to Milluni, near La Paz, which will cost about US$40 for up to four people.

BOAT & SHIP

The most relaxing means of getting around in Bolivia is by water. You can lie in a hammock for days on end and read, sleep, relax and just watch the world go by.

More adventurous types can even buy or hire a dugout canoe and explore jungle rivers under their own steam. For this activity, of course, you'd need a measure of expertise in wilderness survival and would have to be familiar with the hazards of navigation on multi-channelled tropical waterways.

There is no scheduled passenger service in Bolivia's portion of the Amazon Basin and the majority of those travelling there will have to rely on cargo transport. The quality, velocity and price you find will largely depend on the luck of the draw.

Most of the boats are primarily cargo vessels; passenger transport, let alone passenger comfort, was the last thing the boat builders had in mind. Accommodation will probably be tight, but still much better than on some of the 'cattle-boats' that ply the Amazon proper.

Most passages include food and, though on-board cooks tend to show little

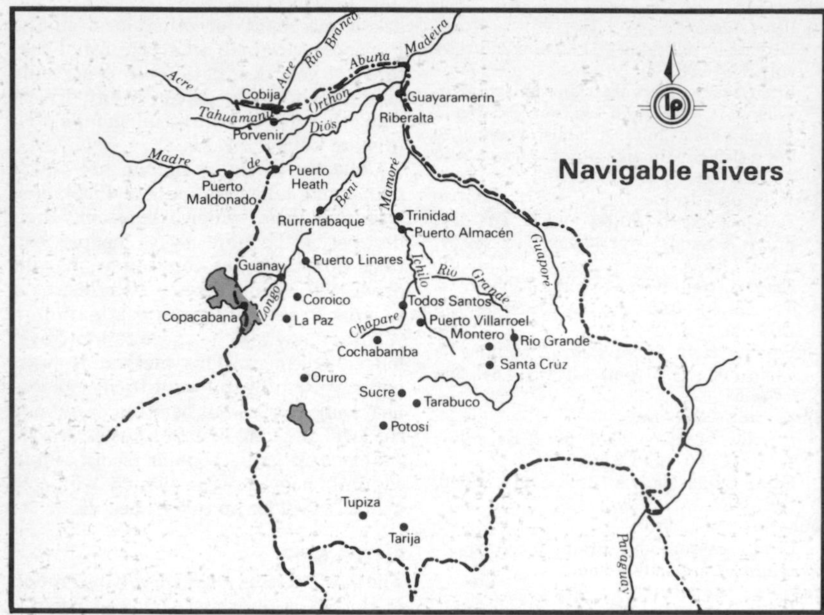

imagination, the fare is life-sustaining. Breakfast will invariably consist of *massaca*, which is a mash of manioc root, plantains, *charqui* (dried meat), oil, maize and salt. You have to acquire a taste for it. Other meals will consist of some kind of rice or noodles, more charqui and fried or steamed plantains. On some runs, passengers are treated to turtle eggs and soup made from turtle meat.

Other boats transport lemons, bananas, grapefruits and oranges, so fruit is plentiful. Coffee is made from river water and sugar is added unsparingly until it reaches a syrupy consistency. One cup is enough to send you into insulin shock. The point of all this is to encourage you to take along a supply of goodies to complement your diet and relieve your taste buds.

The majority of ships are equipped with toilet facilities, but showers and clothes washing facilities are rare. Laundry is done in the river and passengers generally bathe there too. While such creatures as piranhas and alligators don't seem to pose much of a threat (everyone swims in the rivers), check with locals anyway, before jumping in.

The most popular routes are from Puerto Villarroel to Trinidád, Puerto Linares to Riberalta, Río Grande (Puerto Banegas) to Trinidád, and Trinidád to Guayaremerín. All of these trips will require three to five days – if things go well.

While the riverside scenery is interesting, it changes little, so several good long books are highly recommended. Don't expect to be bored, however. On such trips, shipboard friendships develop quickly and the mere fact that the Bolivian passengers have ventured into this frontier region of their country provides them with a sort of kinship with foreign travellers.

Top: La Paz street scene (TM)
Left: Young La Paz merchant (WH)
Right: San Francisco – La Paz (TW)

Top: Market scene – La Paz (WH)
Left: Mercado de Hechiceria (Witches' Market) – La Paz (TM)
Right: Sucre Market, a vegetarian's nightmare (TM)

In addition, I find this area actually more interesting than the Amazon proper. For a start, the rivers are narrower and therefore the boats travel nearer the shore, allowing better observation. Secondly, because the area is little-developed it has a much lower population density so opportunities for viewing wildlife are much better than along the heavily-populated Brazilian rivers.

You will almost certainly have the chance to see sloths, monkeys, capybaras, rheas, turtles, many species of birds and butterflies, and hundreds of pink river dolphins. There is also a good chance of spotting alligators in the water and the possibility of seeing an anaconda or even an anteater.

As this is the main cocaine-refining centre of Bolivia and since relatively few legitimate travellers have passed this way, your motives may be looked upon as suspicious by some. As usual, a friendly conversation about your travels and your home, or your opinions about this frontier part of the country, should put them at ease.

On some boats, passengers may be required to bring a hammock for sleeping, but on others a sleeping bag will suffice. It can get chilly at night and there's always a heavy dew. In every case, some sort of mosquito protection (a net or a good repellent) is essential, and if you're required to spend a lot of time outside, you'll need sunscreen too.

On one trip I took, between Puerto Baradór and Guayaramerín, the decks were full and I was allowed to sleep on the roof of the boat. Words cannot adequately describe the sunset, the stars and the raucous night-long jungle symphony I was witness to; all of which were missed by those sleeping under the roof and nearer to the noisy engines. In fact, I didn't want to sleep at all in case I missed a moment of it.

Water travel is not limited to the rivers, however. Lake Titicaca, shared with Peru on Bolivia's western boundary, is traditionally the highest navigable lake in the world. At an altitude of 3820 metres, it bustles with all sorts of watercraft including the world-famous totora reed boats which Thor Heyerdahl used on his Ra II Expedition in North Africa. These sturdy canoes have plied the waters of Titicaca since pre-Columbian times.

In the more recent past steamers, which were carried piece by piece from the sea to landlocked Bolivia, carried passengers between Guaqui and the Peruvian ports, linking the railroad terminals of the two countries. This service was discontinued in 1985, however, when the port of Guaqui disappeared under the waters of the rising lake.

A ferry service operates between San Pedro and San Pablo, across the narrow Straits of Tiquina. This is along the most well-travelled route between La Paz and Copacabana, Puno and Cuzco (the latter two are in Peru).

To visit the several Bolivian islands of Lake Titicaca, there are launches, sailboats and rowboats for hire in Copacabana and Huatajata. Prices are reasonable, especially if you can muster a group. The cost is the same for one person or 15.

Cruise ship service is provided by Transturín Ltda, of La Paz. It is relatively expensive, however, compared to other modes of transport on the lake. Their bus leaves La Paz at 6.30 am weekdays during the winter; and on Monday, Wednesday and Friday during low season. The trip to Puno in Peru costs US$70 per person, but the actual 'cruise' only goes from Huatajata to Copacabana with a half hour stop at the Isla del Sol (the Island of the Sun).

Crillón Tours, also of La Paz, offers hydrofoil excursions between Huatajata, Copacabana, Isla del Sol and the Peruvian ports of Juli and Puno.

DRIVING

Unless you are extremely adventurous, have a lot of time and money, and just want to 'prove that you can do it', driving in Bolivia as an exclusive means of transport is not recommended.

The advantages of a private vehicle are, of course, schedule flexibility, access to remote areas, and the ability to seize fleeting photographic opportunities. The disadvantages, however, are numerous and should be carefully considered.

As mentioned previously, roads in Bolivia are marginal and few are paved. Those which are surfaced suffer from various states of disrepair and high speed travel is simply not possible. Roads are narrow and they twist and wind, following mountain contours and rocky riverbeds.

In southern Bolivia, I once saw a pretty little stone barn beside a river. After travelling for four hours, I saw the same barn again, but from the other side of the river. Instead of spending money to build a bridge, the highway department had routed the road around the river.

Again, the rainy season must be considered. From November to March, many roads are impassable for weeks. Mud, flooding, washouts, landslides, avalanches and rockfalls are all common and road transport grinds to a halt until repairs can be made. In the Chapare region north of Cochabamba, bridges destroyed in the 1986 flooding still haven't been repaired and vehicles are dragged across some hefty rivers behind tractors.

If you remain undaunted, be sure to carry a set of tools, extra petrol, oil and water, and every spare part that might conceivably give out en route. If you're going to be travelling off major routes, a four-wheel drive, high-clearance vehicle and several spare tyres and wheel rims are also essential. Always carry plenty of food and drinking water.

Driving Regulations

An international driver's licence is required to operate a motor vehicle in Bolivia (motorbikes excluded). They can be obtained from the automobile club in your own country.

When entering Bolivia, a circulation card, called an *hoja de ruta*, must be obtained from the *Servicio Nacional de Transito* at the frontier or in the Bolivian city where the trip begins. These two documents must be presented and stamped at all police posts, that is *trancas* and *controles*, along the routes.

Tolls are sometimes charged at these check points and vehicles and luggage are often searched for contraband. The Bolivian Consulate in Washington, DC, warns against unofficial trancas set up by unauthorised individuals who try to extort money and possessions from unwary motorists.

As in most of the Americas, Bolivians drive on the right hand side of the road and, with only a couple of exceptions, traffic regulations are similar to those in the US and Europe. Speed limits are infrequently posted, but in most cases, road conditions will prevent you from exceeding them anyway.

An unusual driving practice goes on in cities, where you will undoubtedly notice a lot of horn honking going on. This isn't always to get traffic moving or to intimidate pedestrians, so although the constant noise is bothersome, offence should not be taken.

The reason for the cacophony is that when two cars approach an uncontrolled intersection (those with no policeman or functioning signal) from different directions, the driver who honks first has the right-of-way if he intends to pass straight through. Turning vehicles, of course, must wait until the way is clear before doing so. Keep in mind, though, that this system sometimes doesn't work in practice. While timidity may cost some time, it's certainly better for your sanity until you get used to Bolivians' driving habits.

When two vehicles meet on a mountain road not wide enough to allow both to pass, the vehicle headed downhill must back up until there's enough room for the other to overtake. Again, this doesn't always work in practice and loud, animated and violent discussions sometimes occur before one driver finally concedes. In the meantime, traffic is blocked in both directions and tempers flare; though it's all usually part of the game.

Petrol in Bolivia is low-grade, but is available in all major towns.

Car Rental

While rental vehicles are available in Bolivia, they are not regularly serviced and the vehicle insurance you buy from rental agencies often only covers accidental damage. Breakdowns are normally your own problem, but even where they are covered, the logistics of making repairs must be handled by the driver.

Auto parts are a rare commodity, impossible to find in remote areas, and you will invariably find yourself hitching into town to search for a part that may or may not be available. It goes without saying, then, that anyone attempting automobile travel away from major cities ought to have an intimate knowledge of the workings of the internal combustion engine and all its related parts.

Rental agencies will require an international driver's licence, a major credit card or cash deposit and, in most cases, accident insurance. You'll be charged a daily rate and a per km rate (some will allow a set number of free kms, after which the rate will apply). You will also be required to buy petrol and repair any non-accident related vehicle malfunctions which may occur during the rental period.

The following is a list of car rental agencies in major cities:

La Paz

- Imbex, Avenida Arce 2303 (tel 379884)
- Rent-a-car International, Frederico Zuazo 1940 (tel 342506)
- Rent-a-car Oscar Crespo Maurice, Simón Bolívar (tel 35094)
- Kolla Motors, Rosendo Gutiérrez 502 (tel 341660)
- Hertz Rent-a-car, Hotel Sheraton, Avenida Arce (tel 322654)

Cochabamba

- International Rent-a-car, Colombia 3652 (tel 26635)
- Kolla Motors, Avenida Melchor Urquidi (tel 28117)

Sucre

- Rent-a-car Sucre, Avenida Hernando Siles 958 (tel 21963)

Your Own Vehicle

A description of the logistics of outfitting and shipping a private vehicle to South America are beyond the scope of this book, but following is some very basic information for those who'd like to pursue the matter further.

The usual route taken is from North America through Mexico and Central America. The vehicle is then shipped by sea past the Darien Gap, which is the end of the road in Panama, to Colombia or Venezuela. Some travellers suggest, however, that shipping costs may be lower from the US east coast or New Orleans.

It is possible to enter Bolivia by road from Chile, Peru, Argentina and Paraguay. The route from Chile is extremely poor, but the one from Paraguay shouldn't even be considered.

MOTORCYCLE

In the lowland areas of Bolivia where roads are scarce, motorbikes are a popular means of getting around in towns. They can be hired for US$20 to US$25 per day, and are a great way to explore those areas which are not served by public transport.

To hire a bike, head for the motorcycle taxi stands which are usually found on or near the main plaza of most lowland or jungle towns. Motorcycle taxi drivers can make a lot more money by hiring out their bikes than by working, and while you're using their bike they have the day off.

Needless to say, there's a lot of competition, so be sure to negotiate the price – which should be payable upon return of the vehicle. That's all there is to it. All you need is a driver's licence from your home country; no other special licences or permits are required.

HITCHING

Hitching in Bolivia is easy. As a matter of fact the majority of the population, basically the poorer people, use it in one form or another as their primary means of transport.

Private and commercial vehicle owners use it as a means of lowering their costs, and overland travellers who want to get off the main routes will have to use it also.

Carros (autos), *camionetas* (pickups) and *camiones* (open-bed lorries), will all accept paying passengers. Often passengers will be loaded aboard far beyond the practical (and far, far beyond the comfortable) capacity of the vehicle.

For this, the driver usually charges about 75% of the price of standard bus fare on the same run. If no bus does the run, the prices will be much higher in proportion to distance than on the major routes.

Be sure to ask your fellow passengers the correct price before making any agreements with the driver. He will assume you're rich and won't understand that in your country, rich people don't normally climb into the back of rattle-trap trucks loaded with chickens, oil drums, noodles and 92 other passengers.

Hitching in Bolivia doesn't usually mean waiting for hours on a bleak stretch of roadway with your thumb in the wind. This is one thing in the country that is organised. Every town has a market, street or plaza where trucks and pickups looking for passengers wait.

When they are full, by the driver's definition, they leave. It gets to be quite a contest. Once he's got a few passengers, the driver keeps announcing that he will leave *ahorita* – 'right away'. If his passengers, however, feel that he's taking too much time to get 'full', they all shift to another waiting vehicle. At this point, all other passengers in all other waiting vehicles also shift.

The lucky driver of the nearly 'full' vehicle keeps trying to recruit a few more for as long as his passengers will tolerate it. As soon as they begin to climb down, he announces imminent departure. True to his word, the vehicle begins to move. After a quick spin around the block, it returns to the spot where it was waiting before 'departure'. When patiences again begin to wear thin, say after another 15 or 20 minutes, the vehicle actually departs.

Another less trying method is to take a taxi or a micro to the *tranca*, a highway police post outside every entrance to every town. All vehicles must stop there and it's a convenient place to ask drivers where they are headed. The drawback is that at this point you've lost the option of choosing a place to sit.

While most Bolivians ride in the back of trucks and pickups because of the economic benefits, many drivers will give foreigners (especially women) VIP treatment and allow them to ride in the cab. Even if they don't, you can volunteer to pay 30% or so more and ride inside anyway. This isn't nearly as interesting as riding *atrás*, but if it's raining, you'll appreciate the option.

This brings us to another problem: rain damages cargo. For this reason, every *camión* carries a handy piece of tarpaulin called *la carpa*. It covers everything, including passengers, and it's difficult to adequately describe the discomfort caused by this device.

First of all, it's dark underneath and of course, claustrophobic. Secondly, it's heavy and because it rests on your head, it seems heavier. Worst of all, though, it traps the diesel and carbon monoxide fumes emitted by the vehicle and forces the passengers to breathe them in nauseating and health-threatening quantities. More than once I've stood outside on the bumper in freezing rain to avoid this experience.

And speaking of rain, be sure to take out a variety of clothing before riding *atrás* in trucks and pickups. Even if you're sitting atop your luggage, it probably won't be accessible during the trip because it will be wedged tightly beneath cargo, luggag and other passengers.

TOURS

A growing number of foreign and Bolivian tour operators are cashing in on Bolivia's appeal to travellers and you need only take a walk around downtown La Paz to see the impact they've had.

Tour options range from fully-guided, multi-week excursions which include food, transportation, accommodation, transfers, etc, to half-day familiarisation tours in or near major cities. The former are usually bought outside Bolivia from a travel agent and tourists pays handsomely for the luxury.

The typical package tour in Bolivia will include a hydrofoil excursion on Lake Titicaca, a tour of the Tiahuanaco ruins, a drive to Chacaltaya, and museum visits and shopping in La Paz. Some even visit mines in Potosí or Oruro. While this is a comfortable way to 'see the sights', it's also a confining and expensive way to travel and isn't for everyone.

The shorter tours are arranged through hotels, agencies and tourist offices and if you're in a hurry, they're a convenient way to quickly visit a sight you'd otherwise miss. They're also relatively inexpensive, say US$20 to US$30 for a day, less for a half-day trip.

This is an excellent way to visit Tiahuanaco, for instance, because a guide is included, usually English-speaking, and the ruins can become something more than an impressive 'pile of rocks'.

A short tour is also useful if you want to visit the Chacaltaya ski slopes and won't be in La Paz on a weekend to go with the climbing club. A quick guided reconnaissance tour will familiarise you with a city and provide points of reference for solo navigation.

For the more adventurous, who nonetheless don't want to strike out into the wilderness alone, there are a number of outfits which offer trekking, mountain climbing, river running and jungle exploration packages.

Some major tour outfitters in La Paz and the prime destinations are:

Garza Tours
: (tel 322351); La Paz city tours, Lake Titicaca, Chacaltaya, Tiahuanaco.

Turisbus
: Calle Illampú 704 (tel 325348); Tiahuanaco tours, Chacaltaya and transport to Peru.

Balsatour
: Avenida 16 de Julio 1650 (tel 356566); Tiahuanaco and Lake Titicaca for US$10 to US$15.

Transturin
: Avenida Camacho 1321 (tel 363654); Lake Titicaca cruises US$70.

Paititi Tours
: Calle Juan de la Riva, Edificio Alborada £106 (tel 329625); Chacaltaya, jeep tours, jungle expeditions, trekking, La Paz city tours.

Guarachi ANDES
: Edificia Santa Anita £314, PO Box 20886 (tel 320901); climbing expeditions and equipment rentals, climbing information and transport to peaks over 6000 metres.

Crillón Tours
: Avenida Camacho 1223 (tel 374566); hydrofoil tours of Lake Titicaca including Huatajata, Copacabana, the islands and Peruvian ports.

La Paz

A visitor's first view of La Paz will never be forgotten. Although it's never rated up there in the realm of spectacular cities like Rio, Capetown, San Francisco or Hong Kong, it certainly deserves to be.

Anyone arriving from the Altiplano, which includes all air, rail and highway passengers (except those who somehow sneaked past the city into the Yungas), will probably look with distaste and pity upon the poor and littered upper suburbs which flank the approach to La Paz. The muddy roads, which look as if they haven't had any attention since Inca times, are lined with auto repair shops and junkyards; unkempt children play in the muddy potholes; and nearby, Indian women do their laundry in a sewage-choked river.

Then suddenly, there it is. The earth drops away as if all the poverty and ugliness has been obliterated and there, 400 metres below, is La Paz, filling the bowl and climbing the walls of a gaping canyon nearly five km wide from rim to rim.

If you're fortunate enough to arrive on a dark night, La Paz will look like a mirrored reflection of a glittering night sky. On a clear day, you will see above it the towering three peaks of Illimani (6402 metres), and when you remember that the altitude of La Paz is 3636 metres, this looming, snow-crowned sentinel seems unimaginably lofty.

For me, this vision of La Paz is similar to that of the Grand Canyon or Iguaçu Falls; no matter how many times I see it, I always gasp involuntarily at the sudden intensity of the view.

The home of more than a million Bolivians, over half of whom are of Indian heritage, La Paz is the nation's largest city, its *de facto* capital and its centre of commerce, finance and industry.

History

The city was founded by a Spaniard, Captain Alonso de Mendoza, on 20 October, 1548 and named *La Ciudad de Nuestra Señora de La Paz* – 'The City of Our Lady of Peace'. Mendoza was under the orders of Pedro de la Gasca to whom the Spanish king had entrusted rule over the former Inca lands.

Mendoza chose, for the site of his city, a site that was previously occupied by a community of Aymará miners and goldsmiths called the Chuquiago Marka; so although Mendoza is given the credit, the founding fathers of Bolivia's largest city were actually a pair of Indians named Hullustus and Thunupa.

The Spaniards quickly seized the gold mines, of course, and Mendoza became the first mayor of the new city. The conquerors also imposed their religion and lifestyle on the Indians and since most of the colonists' women remained in Spain, the unions between Spanish men and Indian women soon gave rise to the area's mostly *mestizo* population.

The 16th century historian Cieza de León remarked of the new city:

> This is a good place to pass one's life. Here the climate is mild and the view of the mountains inspires one to think of God.

Despite León's rather lofty assessment (and one wonders if he didn't accidentally get off in Cochabamba!), the reason for the existence of La Paz' was much more down to earth. The Spanish never had been able to resist the shiny yellow metal and the Río Choqueyapu, which now flows beneath La Paz, seemed to be full of it.

Although the site of La Paz, at the bottom of a rugged canyon, seemed to indicate an unpromising beginning for a successful metropolis, the protection this very position gave it from the fierce

Altiplano wind and weather and the fact that it was situated along the main trade routes to Lima, offered the city some hope for survival and possible prosperity after the gold was no longer an issue.

Much of the silver from Potosí bound for Peruvian ports on the Pacific, passed through La Paz and by the time the rail lines were built the city was enough of a centre to command attention.

On 1 November 1549, the task of designing the city was given to Juan Gutierrez Panaigua. He was to lay out plazas and public lands and designate sites for public buildings. La Plaza de Españoles, now known as Plaza Murillo, was to be the site of the cathedral, royal homes and government buildings.

Two years after the founding, a lieutenant of the Spanish forces, Hernandez Girón, disappeared (and was never heard from again) while collecting taxes from the population for the king of Spain. Whispers of things to come, perhaps.

The city's coat of arms, commissioned in 1555 by King Carlos V, reads:

> The factions, in concordance on peace and love, joined together and founded communities of peace in order to perpetuate their memory.

Even so, the City of Peace has known precious little of it since those days. Spain controlled the city with a firm grip and the Spanish king had the final say in all matters political. He once denied the job of mayor to a petitioner named Miguel Cervantes de Saavedra, although it was probably just as well. The rejected candidate stayed home and wrote *Don Quixote* instead. Some Bolivians feel, however, that if he'd been given the opportunity, he would have written it anyway, but to the glory of Bolivia rather than Spain.

Twice in 1781, for a total of six months, a group of Aymará Indians under the leadership of Tupac Katari laid siege to La Paz. They also destroyed public buildings and churches before the uprising

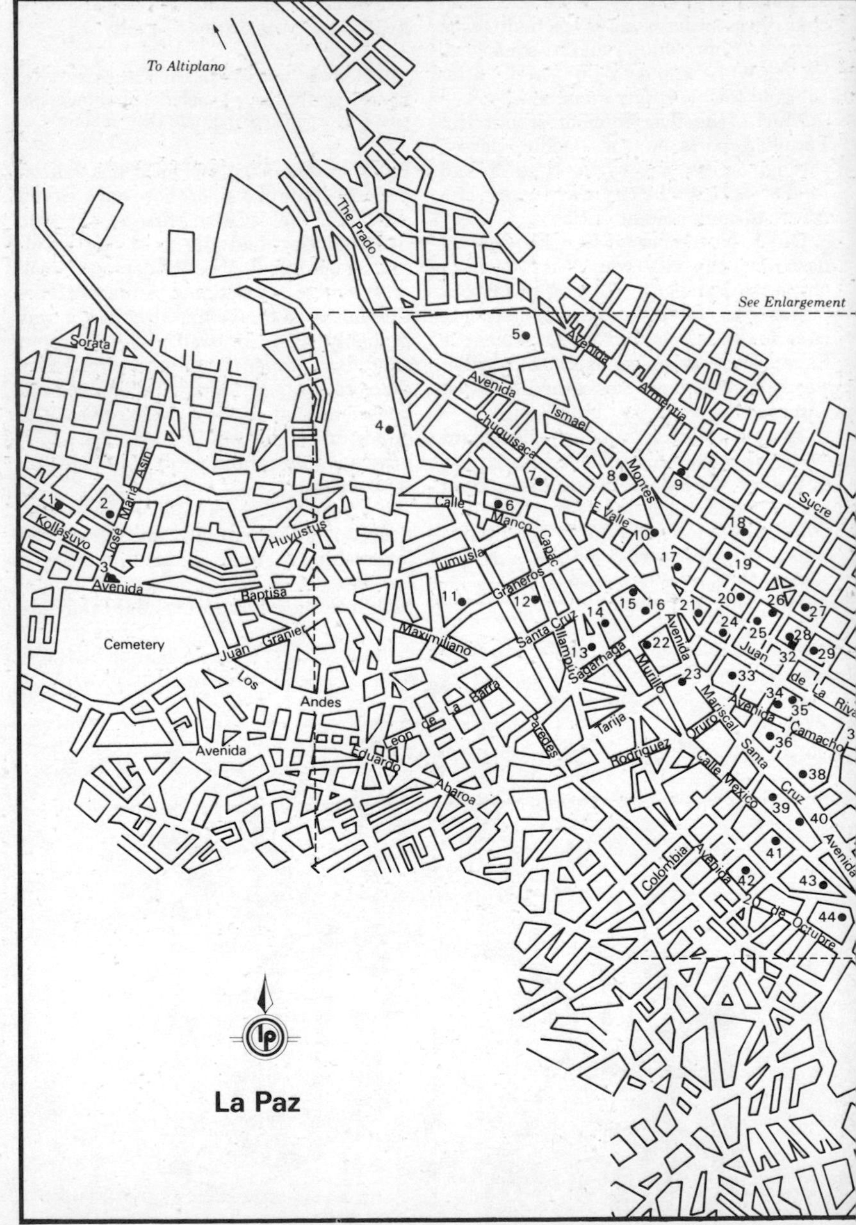
To Altiplano
The Prado
See Enlargement
Sorata
Avenida
Armentia
Avenida
Ismael
Chuquisaca
Montes
Calle
Manco
Capac
E Valle
Sucre
José
María
Asín
Kollasuyo
Huyustus
Tumusla
Graneros
Avenida
Baptisa
Cemetery
Juan
Granier
Maximiliano
Santa Cruz
Illampu
Sagarnaga
Avenida
Murillo
Juan
de
La
Riva
Los
Andes
La
Barra
de
Leon
Avenida
Eduardo
Abaroa
Paredes
Tarija
Rodriguez
Oruro
Mariscal
Santa
Cruz
Camacho
Calle Mexico
Avenida
Colombia
Avenida
20 de Octubre
La Paz

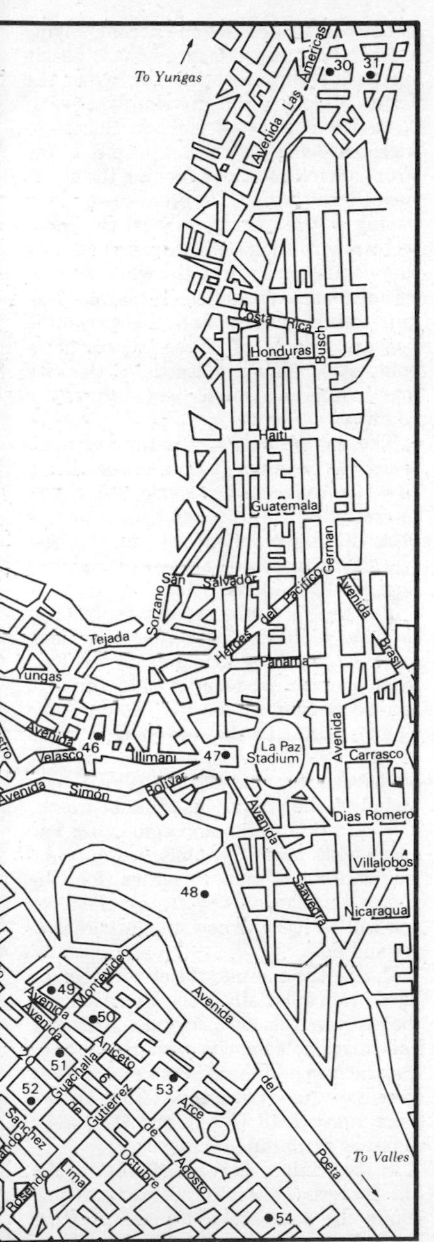

1 Trucks to Sorata
2 Flota Ingavi
3 Trucks to Zongo Valley
4 Train Station
5 Terminal Terrestre
6 Budget hotel area
7 Church
8 Transportes Aéreos Militares
9 Museums
10 Market
11 Black Market
12 Residenciál Rosario
13 Witches' Market
14 Artesan's Market
15 Galeria Artesanal San Francisco
16 Basilica de San Francisco
17 Casa de La Cultura
18 Santo Domingo Church
19 Museum of Ethnography & Folklore
20 National Art Museum & Hotel Torino
21 Shampoo Shop
22 Peña Naira
23 Transit Office
24 Super Salteñas
25 Cathedral Art Museum
26 Palacio de Gobierno
27 Legislature
28 Post Office
29 Manjari Vegetarian Restaurant
30 Flota Yungueña
31 Trucks to the Yungas
32 USA Consulate
33 ENTEL
34 Casa de Cambio Sud Americano
35 Travel Agency & money exchange
36 Lloyd Aéreo Boliviano
37 Public Assistance
38 Government Mapping Office
39 Instituto Boliviano de Turismo
40 American Express
41 Club Andino Boliviano
42 Jail
43 Library
44 Immigration for Extensions
45 Museo Arqueológico de Tiwanaku
46 Residenciál Illimani
47 Templete Arqueológieo Semisubterráneo
48 Lookout
49 Esquina del Bigote Restaurant
50 Sheraton
51 Goethe Institute
52 Brazilian Consulate
53 W German Consulate
54 Immigration

was quelled. Another siege of the city by high plateau Indians 30 years later lasted for two months.

From the time of Bolivia's independence in 1825 onward, the Plaza Murillo in La Paz has been centre stage for revolutions and protests. Bolivian presidents were once placed on the 'endangered species' list owing to the abnormally high mortality rate that accompanied that high office.

In 1946, the then president of Bolivia, Gualberto Villarroel, was publicly hanged in the Plaza Murillo by 'distraught widows'; and the presidential palace on the plaza has come to be known as the *Palacio Quemado*, or the 'Burned Palace', for its turbulent history of being gutted by fire.

La Paz Today

These days political unrest in La Paz is so common it scarcely rates as newsworthy. Every visitor will have the opportunity to see a political demonstration of some description although, thankfully, very few are accompanied by gunfire or tear gas.

In one that I witnessed, a group of angry students were protesting low university expenditures by stopping city buses in the streets and summarily dismantling their engines. In a dozen others protests, traffic was blocked, demands were chanted and the city's activities effectively ground to a halt.

You may wonder how a political demonstration can stop an entire city. Well, La Paz has only one main street; a wide thoroughfare which follows the course of the Choqueyapu River (which you won't see, by the way, because it's underground these days). From top to bottom, although it changes names several times along its length, it is popularly known as *the Prado*.

Away from the Prado everything is uphill, steeply and narrowly uphill, and many of the streets are cobbled or unpaved. Above the downtown skyscrapers, the adobe neighbourhoods and accompanying informal commercial areas climb nearly up to the canyon's rim. So, when the Prado is blocked the city simply stops.

La Paz is the best place in Bolivia to kick back and watch the people go by. From a hotel room overlooking the street near Plaza Murillo, I've often spent hours gazing at the passing crowds: the *chola* women with their obligatory bowler hats and voluminous skirts, the white-shirted businessmen and politicians, the machine-gun toting military and the grovelling beggars. Each of these represent a completely different aspect of the city and, in a sense, a microcosm of the entire country.

The market exists in Latin American society as common ground for socialising as well as a place to buy goods. So if you're interested in meeting the people or just observing the local way of life, the best place to do so would be in one of the city's dozen or so markets.

There's an artisans' market, a witchcraft market, a flower market and a black market. Anything available in La Paz, from phonograph records to toothpaste, can be bought in the market on Calle Buenos Aires. In the hundreds of stalls along Calle Graneros, you can buy just about any type of clothing you'd like, including the ubiquitous chola attire.

In addition to life and colour, La Paz has a wide range of hotels, restaurants, entertainment and activities for the visitor, and the longer you stay, the more you will realise just how much there is to see and do.

During the summer the climate can be harsh, rain falls daily in the afternoon and the canyon fills with clouds. Frequent hailstorms pelt the city with icy golfballs from heaven and the steep streets become torrents of runoff. Daytime temperatures hang around 18°C but the dampness makes is seem much colder.

In the winter, days are slightly cooler but the crisp, clear air is invigorating. While the sun shines, the temperature

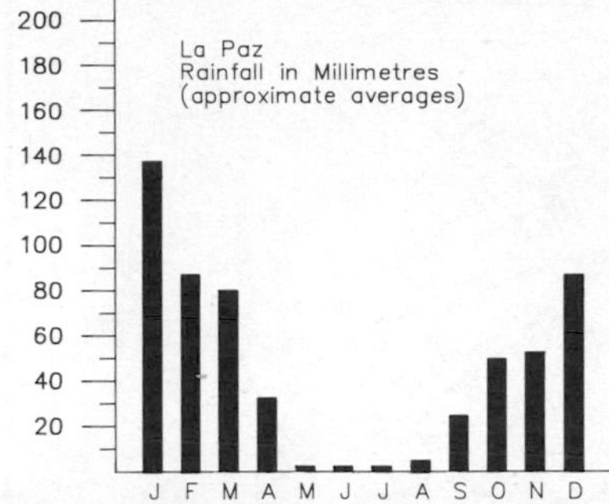

may keep to the mid-teens, but at night it often dips below freezing. In a city where central heating systems are unknown, such cold can be oppressive and debilitating. From time to time, rain and even snow fall during the winter. At all times of the year, warm clothes are essential here nearly four km above the sea.

La Paz is a great city to explore on foot, but don't be in too much of a hurry or the altitude will take its toll, especially when you're walking uphill.

Orientation

It's almost impossible to get lost in La Paz. There's only one major thoroughfare, the Prado, which follows the path of least resistance down the canyon. The rest of the city lies somewhere above it, so if you want to get back to the Prado just head downhill.

The main street changes names several times, so you'd do well to familiarise yourself with all of its appellations. From top to bottom they are Avenida (Ismael) Montes, Mariscal Santa Crúz, Avenida 16 de Julio and Villazón. At the lower end, it splits into Avenida 6 de Agosto and Avenida Arce; the latter continues downward at the lower elevation.

The centre of commerce and finance is found on the north side of the Prado as are many public facilities such as the post and telephone offices. Most of this section extends through the few blocks below Plaza Murillo. The government offices are, of course, centred around Plaza Murillo itself. Most of the travel and tour agencies are located around Calle Loayza and Avenida Camacho.

South of the Prado are various markets, bars and shops, always bustling and crowded with people and bus traffic. The main market area is in the vicinity of Calle Buenos Aires.

The budget hotel area has its focus on Calle Manco Capac, but inexpensive hotels may be found all over the city.

The most well-preserved colonial section of town is near the intersection of Jaen and Sucre where there are four well-visited museums. The narrow cobbled streets, the colonial churches, the early Spanish architecture and the mud neighbourhoods clinging to the hillsides all offer a glimpse of the time when La Paz began.

Contrary to the US and European systems, the wealthier neighbourhoods and social clubs seem to be at lower altitudes. The most prestigious suburbs are found far down the canyon while the 'view lots' near the rim are occupied by poorer adobe or makeshift neighbourhoods.

Information

Tourist Office The *Instituto Boliviano de Tourismo* (tel 367463) operates an information centre on the 4th floor of Edificio Hermann near Plaza Venezuela on the Prado. Their mailing address is IBT, Casilla 1868, La Paz. For 50c, they will provide you with an excellent map of the city which, on the reverse side, includes selected local bus schedules, distances, useful addresses and the altitudes of nearby peaks.

They have a host of other brochures dealing with La Paz and the entire country, some in English and German, but if you speak Spanish even a little, ask for information in that language. I'm not sure about the German, but the English translations are so impossible that they read like nonsense; for example: 'there are

clear vestiges of a civilisation that rose amongst the most prodigious time advances.'

A glance at the Spanish text will reveal that this is trying to say: 'there existed a civilisation that was more advanced than all others of the period'.

The tourist office is officially open from 9 am to noon and 2 to 6 pm.

Other Information There is an information centre at the bus terminal but the purpose of this is primarily to arrange taxis and hotel rooms for arriving visitors.

If you're asking for information on the street, be warned that Bolivians aren't overly concerned with the accuracy of their answers and directions. They're not being malicious, they just want to appear helpful and knowledgeable and will often give you an answer whether they know or not.

So, never take an answer at face value. Ask several people the same question and if one answer seems to stand out above the others, it's probably as close to correct as you'll find.

Maps The best city map available is sold by the tourist office, but larger hotels and travel agencies will often distribute free city maps showing the location of their establishment in relation to points of interest in La Paz.

National maps and topo sheets may be bought at the government mapping office at Avenida 16 de Julio 1471. City and national maps of lower quality may be found at bookshops and in the kiosks at the main post office.

If everyone seems to be out of the map you're looking for, try the *Instituto Geografico Militar* (IGM) office on the corner of Saavedra and Subrieta in Miraflores. In order to avoid a nasty scene, ask the guard at the gate where you'll need to enter to buy a map. The military can be really sticky about formalities, so you'll certainly need your passport to enter this restricted compound. Be prepared for a bit of red tape. Topographic sheets with scales of 1:50000 are available for the area around La Paz.

Post & Communication The main post office is on Calle Ayacucho just above its intersection with Potosí. If you'd like to post a parcel from there, a customs official is on duty upstairs and will be able to inspect it on the spot. Postcards, envelopes, maps, packing materials and greeting cards are available in a dozen or so shops scattered about the main lobby. Hours are 9 am to 6 pm Monday to Saturday and 9 am to noon on Sunday. They have *poste restante* and philatelic services.

If you're sending letters or parcels overseas, you should consider certifying them for 50c apiece. While this won't ensure delivery, it will certainly increase the chances. *Expreso* service is available for domestic mail. It costs 10c extra per piece and in theory is speedier than the regular post.

If you're having anything shipped to you in La Paz, or anywhere in Bolivia for that matter, it's helpful to declare the lowest possible value at the point of origin. When you go to pick up the package, you'll find yourself sinking in a quagmire of muddled red tape and owing an import duty of up to 100% of the item's declared value.

Below the main post office, 1½ blocks down Calle Ayacucho is the ENTEL office where local, national and international calls may be made. Public telephones are also found in hotels, restaurants and street stalls. A local phone call in La Paz will range from 5c at ENTEL to 15c on the street.

ENTEL also offers telegram and TELEX services.

Business Hours Even those restaurants which serve breakfast don't roll up their aluminium doors until 9 or 9.30 am so don't bother wandering the streets searching for a caffeine fix any earlier than that. Shops, travel agencies and financial institutions will likewise open at 9 or 10 am. If you want to eat or shop before those hours, you'll have to go to the street markets where dribbles of activity begin as early as 6 am.

At noon the city virtually closes down, excluding the markets and restaurants which remain open to serve lunch-hour crowds. Things begin to re-open at around 2 pm but some businesses remain out of commission until as late as 4 pm. Commercial businesses then stay open until at least 8 or 9 pm. Many bars and restaurants close at 10 pm although a few serve until midnight, but these should be avoided by lone women!

On Saturdays shops, services and even some eateries close down at noon; and on Sundays, almost everything remains dead until evening. Even on weekends, however, street markets remain open at least until mid-afternoon and more often into the evening.

This schedule holds true for most of Bolivia.

Money Many *casas de cambio* can be

found on Avenida Ayacucho and Calle Colón on the block just above Avenida Camacho. The process of exchanging currency in these establishments involves few hassles.

Casa de Cambio Sudamer on Calle Colón changes travellers' cheques and is open from 9 am to noon and 2 to 5 pm on weekdays. On Saturdays, the *Unitours* travel agency near the corner of Loayza and Mercado will change cash or travellers' cheques for a slightly lower rate than is available during the week, and the staff speak English.

The best place to exchange, however, is at the *Shampoo Shop* on Yanacocha near Mercado. That's not its real name, but it sells shampoo (there's an impressive display of dandruff combatants, hair creams and conditioners in the window) and has been known to travellers for years. The operation reminds me of a bookie joint in an old-time gangster movie. There is a prominent sign posted near the register which reads *Prohibido la entrada de particulares*, which roughly translated means 'employees only'.

Here's how it works. Walk up to the register and whisper *cambios*. A uniformed guard will escort you around the counter to a plush office in a back room where your money will be exchanged. They change cash at a very good rate and travellers' cheques fetch the same rate as the exchange houses offer for cash. For a mere 1.5% commission, they will also change travellers' cheques to cash dollars and certify the legitimacy of each dollar with a rubber stamp.

Along Avenida Camacho *cambistas*, or 'street changers', will change cash for about the same rate given by the casas de cambio, which at the time of writing was about B$2.2 per US$1. Due caution should be exercised in dealing with street changers, (see the Changing Money section in the Facts for the Visitor chapter).

If you don't mind a lot of hassles, one bank in La Paz will change cash or travellers' cheques but only in larger quantities (over US$200 or so). The exchange office in the *Banco Central de Bolivia* on Calle Ayacucho is on the 18th storey and the view over the city is superb. They give about the same rate as the casas de cambio, but there is much more paperwork involved in the transaction.

Bookstores There are quite a few bookstores in La Paz but the majority wouldn't be of much interest to travellers unless you're looking for comics, cheap and trashy novels or Bolivian school texts. A good, complete selection of Spanish language literature and reference books, however, is available at *Gisbert & Cia, SA*, Calle Comercio 1270.

Los Amigos del Libro, near the corner of Mercado and Colón, has a large selection of popular English and German language paperbacks and souvenir books. Dictionaries and Spanish language books are also sold.

Souvenir books and guidebooks, including the South America Handbook, are available at appropriately sky-high prices at Kennedy Airport.

Consulates The addresses and business hours of some of the more useful consular offices in La Paz are:

Argentina
Edif. Banco de la Nación Argentina 2nd floor (tel 353089); 9 am to 2 pm.
Austria
Edif. Petrolero 7th floor (tel 326601); 1.30 to 4 pm.
Belgium
Plaza Abaroa esq. Sanchez Lima 2400 (tel 328942); 3.30 am to 1.30 pm.
Brazil
Fernando Guachalla 494 (tel 35718); 10 am to noon, 2 to 4 pm.
Canada
Edif. Alborada 5th floor 505 (tel 375224); 10 am to 2 pm.
Colombia
6 de Agosto 2528 (tel 351199); 9 am to noon, 2.30 to 6.30 pm.

China People's Republic
Plaza Abaroa 500 (tel 340111); 9 am to noon, 3 to 6 pm.
Chile
Avenida 6 de Agosto final 2932 (tel 322201); 8.30 am to noon.
Denmark
Edif. Castilla 5th floor 508 (tel 322601); 9 am to noon, 2 to 6 pm.
Finland
Edif. Alborada Mezzanine (tel 329625); 9 am to noon, 2.30 to 6 pm.
France
Edif. Banco Industrial (tel 360430); 8.30 am to 1.30 pm.
Israel
Edif. Esperanza 10th floor (tel 358676); 9 am to noon.
Japan
Rosendo Gutierrez 491 (tel 373151); 9 am to 5.30 pm.
Mexico
Calle Clavio 245 (tel 329505); 9 am to 5.30 pm.
Netherlands
Avenida Arce Edif. Victoria 2nd floor (tel 356153); 9 am to 12.15 pm, 3 to 6.30 pm.
Norway
Avenida Mariscal Santa Crúz Edif. Esperanza 11th floor (tel 322528); 9 am to noon, 2 to 6 pm.
Paraguay
Avenida Arce Edif. Montevideo (tel 322018); 8.30 am to 12.30 pm.
Peru
Avenida Mariscal Santa Crúz 1285 (tel 352031); 8.30 am to 1.30 pm.
South Africa
Calle 22 Calacoto 7810 (tel 792101); 9 am to 12.30 pm, 2 to 5 pm.
Spain
Edif. Guanabara 1st floor Calle Cordero esq. Avenida Arce (tel 357203); 9 am to 2 pm.
Sweden
Mercado 1046 5th floor (tel 327535); 9 am to noon.
Switzerland
Edificio Petrolero 6th floor (tel 353091); 9 am to noon, 1 to 4 pm.
UK
Representing New Zealand and Australia
Avenida Arce casi Campos 2732 (tel 329401); 9 am to 12.30 pm, 2 to 6 pm.
USA
Potosí esq. Colón 1285 Edif. Tobias 2nd floor (tel 320494); 9 am to noon.
USSR
Avenida Ballivián 1403 (tel 792048); 8 am to noon, 2 to 6 pm.
West Germany
Avenida Arce 2395 (tel 352389); 9 am to noon.

Airlines Although they do not all service La Paz, a number of airlines have offices and agents in the city.

Aerolineas Argentinas
Avenida 16 de Julio Edif. Alameda planta baja (tel 351711)
Aero Peru
Calle Colón 157 Edif. Barrosquira 1st floor (tel 370002)
Air France
Avenida 16 de Julio Edif. Alameda mezzanine 1-2 (tel 38729)
Alitalia
Avenida Camacho 1280 3rd floor (tel 323494)
American Airlines
Edif. Mariscal de Ayacucho 3rd floor 305-306 (tel 340831)
Avianca
Edif. Mariscal Ballivián 2nd floor 204 (tel 375220)
British Airways
Edif. Mariscal de Ayacucho 3rd floor 305-306 (tel 35541)
Eastern Airlines
Plaza Venezuela, Edif. Hermann planta baja (tel 351360)
El Al
Edif. Mariscal Ballivián 12th floor 1209 (tel 377246)
Faucett Peruvian Airlines
Edif. Mariscal de Ayacucho 3rd floor 305-306) (tel 360637)
Iberia – Airlines of Spain
Avenida 16 de Julio Edif. Petrolero planta baja (tel 360637)
Japan Airlines
Edif. Ballivián 4th floor 407 (tel 3752521)
KLM
Avenida Mariscal Santa Crúz 1297 (tel 324945)
LAN Chile
Edif. Mariscal de Ayacucho planta baja (tel 366563)

Lineas Aereas Paraguayas
Galería Hotel Plaza (tel 378321)
Lloyd Aereo Boliviano
Avenida Camacho 1460 (tel 353606)
Lufthansa
Avenida Mariscal Santa Crúz 1328 (tel 372170)
Pan Am
Edif. Alameda 7 planta baja (tel 341863
Qantas
Edif. Comos mezzanine (tel 352079)
SAS
(tel 377246)
Swissair
Edif. Credinform Penthouse B Ayacucho 378 (tel 375057)
TWA
Plaza Isabel la Católica 2498 2nd floor, Dept 'D' (tel 322047)
Viasa
Edif. Avenida 16 de Julio 1490 (tel 357730)
Varig Cruzeiro
Edif. Cámara de Comercio Avenida Mariscal Santa Crúz esq. Colombia (tel 358754)

Club Andino Boliviano

Founded in 1939, this is an outstanding organisation of climbers, backpackers, skiers and other outdoor enthusiasts. The group is also dedicated to the conservation of Bolivia's wilderness and natural resources. Their office is at Calle Mexico 1638 (tel 324582) and their mailing address is Casilla 1346, La Paz.

This group will provide brochures and answer questions regarding any outdoor activities you may wish to pursue in Bolivia, particularly in the La Paz area. They not only organise weekend ski trips to Chacaltaya, but also do remote ski expeditions to both Condoriri and Mururata, where they plan to eventually create resorts in order to develop Bolivia's potential as a high altitude ski training destination.

If you're interested in backpacking, trekking or technical climbing in the Bolivian Andes, the club organises guided expeditions and hires out climbing or camping equipment. If they don't have the equipment you need, they'll do their best to find it for you.

The club is in great need of quality climbing gear which is difficult to obtain in Bolivia. They have suggested that if you have your own equipment and don't want to carry it around after you've finished climbing, they can arrange your participation in an expedition in exchange for your equipment afterwards.

Club members scale all the major Bolivian peaks at least once a year. For the schedule of climbs, or any other information, write to the President, Leslie McTyre Gutierrez (he speaks English) at the club office address. If you'd like to keep abreast of activities, club membership costs US$4 per month and is open to anyone.

Sport

If you're interested in a round of golf or a game of tennis, you may have to join a club because public facilities do not exist.

La Paz has two tennis clubs: the Club de Tennis La Paz (tel 793930) Avenida Arequipa-La Florida; and the La Paz Sucre Tennis Club (tel 324483) Avenida Busch 1001.

If you just want to get in a couple of games, you may be able to call and arrange a few hours' access to the courts for a reasonable price.

Those who would like to try their skills on the world's highest golf course at Malasilla can expect to pay at least US$10 for a caddy and a round of 18 holes. Private equipment is necessary.

Skiing is possible at Chacaltaya and is described in detail in the Around La Paz section.

Professional football, *futbol*, is very popular with Bolivians as it is all over Latin America. It is played at Hernando Siles Stadium on Sundays year round and also on Thursday nights during the winter. Check the newspapers for times and prices if you're interested in attending.

Hotels and the tourism office also keep abreast of such things.

Cinemas

There are numerous cinemas scattered all over the city. Most films are shown in English with Spanish subtitles, but sound systems are poor and crackly and nobody bothers to keep quiet for the foreign dialogue, anyway, so a knowledge of Spanish will help.

The pictures shown aren't generally top quality. Most of them came and went quickly in other countries several years earlier, but if you happen to enjoy the Girls' Dorm, Ninjas from Space and Rocky Meets Rambo sort of pictures, you can spend a lot of time in La Paz cinemas. In all fairness, I must admit that occasionally a quality film sneaks through and is usually well-attended.

Things to See

La Paz has no shortage of the usual goodies, such as museums, churches, Andean culture and colonial architecture, but it also has a lot of surprises. For the acclimatised, it's one of those cities that invites exploration on foot and, as mentioned in the Orientation section, it's almost impossible to get lost.

Before you set off, keep in mind that attractions such as museums tend to be closed on weekends, Mondays and during lunch hours. So, to get the most out of a walk around La Paz, you need to plan your time accordingly.

In addition, be sure to take some kind of rain protection. A lovely sunny morning, especially in summer, may turn into a torrentially wet nightmare by noon. Also, carry along a warm, long-sleeved sweater for those times when the blazing sun passes behind an innocent white cloud. The temperature difference from moment to moment will seem phenomenal!

Churches

San Francisco The basilica of San Francisco, on the plaza of the same name, stands out above all others in La Paz. Its decor and architecture form an interesting blend of indigenous and Spanish styles.

Construction began in 1549 after its foundation the previous year by Fray Francisco de los Ángeles. Although the original structure collapsed under heavy snowfall around 1610, reconstruction began in 1744. The second building was constructed entirely of stone quarried at nearby Viacha, and the facade is decorated with stone carvings representing natural themes.

Indian weddings are traditionally scheduled for Saturday mornings and the finery of the locals worn on these occasions is both colourful and beautiful to see.

The Cathedral Although it's a fairly recent addition to La Paz' collection of religious structures, the Cathedral on Plaza Murillo, on which work began in 1835, is an impressive structure – mostly because it is built on a steep hillside. Its base at the top on Calle Comercio, is 12 metres higher than its base on Calle Potosí.

The sheer immensity of the building is also overpowering. It has a high dome, hulking columns, thick stone walls and high ceilings. The altar, however, is relatively simple. The real attraction inside is the profusion of stained glass work throughout. The window behind the altar is a particularly interesting depiction of a gathering of Bolivian generals and presidents being blessed from above by a flock of heavenly beings.

Santo Domingo Like the Church of San Francisco, Santo Domingo, on the corner of Yanacocha and Ingavi, displays indigenous influence in its decor and the natural themes on its facade. The rest of the structure if of limited interest, however.

Museums

Museum of Ethnography & Folklore On the corner of Ingavi and Sanjines, this museum is open Monday to Friday from 8.30 to 11.45 am and 2.30 to 6.30 pm. Admission is free. This is a must for anyone interested in anthropology. The museum covers the customs and artistry of some of the more neglected Bolivian ethnic groups living throughout the country.

Especially fascinating is the collection of photos and artefacts of the Chipaya culture, a group that inhabits the Altiplano west of Oruro. Their language, rites and customs differ greatly from those of other Altiplano inhabitants. Some theories place them as descendants of the vanished Tiahuanaco culture.

Mineralogy Museum The Mineralogy Museum houses a complete collection of Bolivian gems, metals and minerals. There are even a few from elsewhere. If you're into the periodic table, you can learn the chemical composition of each specimen. The museum is on the 3rd floor of the *Banco Minero* at Calle Comercio 1290. The attendant is very friendly and happy to answer questions. It's open Monday to Friday from 9 to 11 am and 3 to 5 pm. Admission is free.

Open-Air Museum This museum, also known as the *Templete Arqueológico Semisubterraneo*, is in front of the stadium. It's a replica of the real thing at Tiahuanaco and also contains several statues taken from the ruins. If you aren't planning to visit the actual site, this is worth seeing.

Museo Arqueológico de Tiwanaku The *Museo Nacional de Arqueología*, which is called the *Museo Tiwanaku* (both spellings, 'Tiwanaku' and 'Tiahuanaco' are correct) on most maps, is on Calle Tiwanaku just below the Prado. General admission is 50c, but students get in free with a student card. It's open Tuesday to

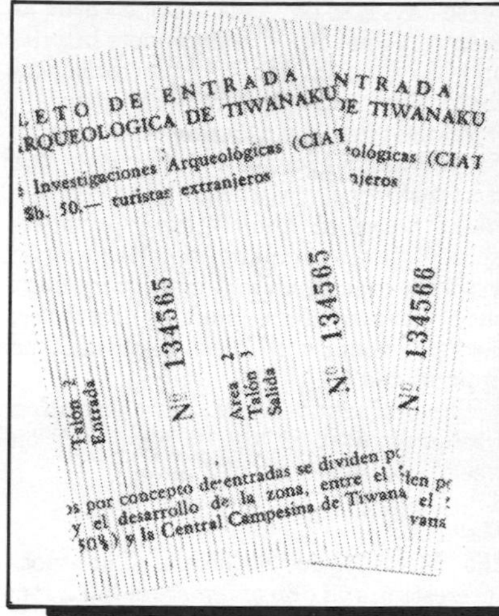

Saturday from 9.30 am to noon and 3 to 6.45 pm.

The museum contains an excellent collection of artefacts displaying and explaining the most interesting aspects of the five stages of Tiahuanaco culture.

Many of Tiahuanaco's treasures were stolen or damaged during the colonial days and much of the ancient stonework went into Spanish construction projects. Golden and other metallic relics and artwork found their way into European museums or treasuries early on and, as usual, Bolivia lost out. Most of what's left in Bolivia – pottery, figurines, trepanned skulls, mummies and a few textiles and metal objects – can be seen in this museum. It's certainly worth visiting even if you normally hate museums because it's not overwhelming and can be easily digested in an hour or so.

Cathedral Museum The Cathedral Museum is open Tuesday and Thursday from 10 am to noon and 3 to 6 pm. Adult admission is 50c. The museum consists mostly of typical religious paraphernalia, but there are two unusual mother-of-pearl coffins and individual portraits of the 12 apostles which are quite well done.

The National Art Museum Housed in the former *Palacio de Los Condes de Arana*, which was constructed of pink Viacha granite in 1775, the art museum is on the corner of Comercio and Socabaya by the Plaza Murillo. Having been restored to its original grandeur by two prestigious architects, the husband and wife team of Teresa Gisbert and José de Mesa, the building itself is actually more impressive than the works of art it contains.

In the centre of a huge courtyard, surrounded by three storeys of pillared corridors, is a lovely alabaster fountain. The 1st floor is dedicated to contemporary artists, and the 2nd floor to the late renaissance works of Melchor Perez de Holguín and students of his school in Potosí. The 3rd floor houses works of other Latin American artists.

There are 14 salons in all, though unfortunately only three of them are currently available for viewing. One of these is a highly worthwhile exhibit of the work of sculptress Marina Nuñez del Prado.

Visiting exhibits are shown in the outer salon and can be seen free of charge. Admission to other areas is US$1 for adults and 50c for students. Those under 18 are admitted free.

The museum is open from Tuesday to Friday between 9.30 am and noon and 3 and 7 pm. On Saturday, opening hours are only until 6.30 pm.

Marina Nuñez Museum A museum exclusively dedicated to the work of Marina Nuñez, at Avenida Ecuador 2034, may be visited from 9 am to noon and 2 to 6 pm Tuesday to Friday and between 9 am and noon on Saturday. It appears, however, that the scheduled opening hours are not strictly followed and you may have to phone ahead (tel 324906) for information and schedules.

Other Museums The four museums located in one of the few remaining colonial sections of town near the intersection of calles Jaen and Sucre can be easily visited and absorbed in one shot. One combination ticket covers entrance to all four and costs US$1.25 for foreigners, US$1 for Bolivians and 25c for students of any nationality. They're open Tuesday to Friday from 9 am to noon and 2.30 to 6.30 pm. On Saturday and Sunday, they're open from 10 am to 1 pm.

The Museo Costumbrista Juan de Vargas This, in my opinion, is the most interesting of the four with art, photos and superb dioramas of old La Paz. One diorama is a representation of *Akulliko*, the hour of coca-chewing; another shows the festival of the Day of San Juan on the 23rd of June. Numerous colourful dolls in traditional costumes, and some colonial artefacts are also displayed.

The Museo del Litoral This is mostly a collection of historical maps which attempt to verify Bolivia's claim to Chile's Segunda Region (the former state of Antofagasta). There are also some relics of the War of the Pacific, during which Bolivia lost this seacoast province.

Casa de Murillo Once the home of Pedro Murillo, a leader of the La Paz Revolution of 16 July 1809, the house now displays some colonial art and furniture, textiles, medicines, musical instruments and household items of glass and silver. Murillo himself was publicly executed by hanging in the plaza named after him on 29 January 1810. One of the paintings on display in the house is entitled *The Execution of Murillo*.

The Museum of Pre-Columbian Precious Metals This museum houses three salons of pre-conquest silver, gold and copper works and the presentation is quite impressive. A fourth salon of various examples of pottery from the same period is located in the basement.

Prison Visits

A very popular activity among travellers these days is to pay a visit to one's own, or even someone else's, compatriots imprisoned in La Paz. Most foreign prisoners there were accused of drug-trafficking.

While it may seem disagreeable to some (travellers have mentioned that, given the circumstances, it is almost like visiting a zoo), most of the foreign prisoners appreciate the company and a word or two in their own language. Items in very short supply around there, such as cigarettes, books and snack goodies, would also be appreciated.

The prison is open for visitation weekends from 9 to 10 am, and on weekdays from noon to 2 pm.

Markets

The Mercado de Hechicería The most interesting and unusual market in La Paz thrives along Calle Linares between Sagárnaga and Santa Crúz. Also known as *Mercado de los Brujos*, or the witches' market, it's a very colourful place. What they're selling here isn't exactly witchcraft, as we would envision it, but it is a means of manipulating and supplicating the various good and bad spirits that populate the Aymará world. In Aymará, it's called *laki'asina catu*.

Photography in the area of this market seems to be a no-no, but quick and gutsy photographers will be able to sneak in a shot or two of the merchandise. The merchants sell herbs and folk remedies as well as a few more unorthodox 'magical'-type ingredients.

Did you know, for instance, that a dead llama foetus buried beneath the cornerstone of a new home or office building is considered a *cha'lla* (toast or offering) to *Pachamama* and will encourage her to bring good luck therein. If you're on a budget, it's possible to buy a colourful plateful of herbs, seeds and various critter parts to remedy any combination of ills or haunts you may be experiencing.

The Mercado Negro The black market is more or less just that, a place where you can pick up duty-free and undocumented merchandise. Most of it isn't stolen, exactly, although some of it is bootlegged.

In the case of music tapes, they make no effort to conceal that fact; the album cover in the case is nothing but a photocopy of the original! The never-say-die Bolivians have come up with this method in response to a prohibitive duty officially placed on all imported goods. It's apparent that officials just look the other way.

The Flower Market Appropriately located right across the street from the cemetery at the top of Avenida Tumusla, this beautiful splash of colour amid one of La Paz' drabber areas unfortunately also sits right beside a festering open sewer and garbage dump. This is confusing to the nostrils, to say the least.

Street Stalls From the Plaza Perez Velasco upward toward the cemetery, the streets are crowded with vendors and market stalls selling practical items from clothing and fast foods to groceries, health care products and cooking pots. This area is always bustling with activity as the chola women rush about gossiping and making purchases.

Festivals

La Paz has quite a few local festivals and holidays during the year, but two seem to stand out as being of particular interest to visitors.

El Grán Poder *La Festividad de Nuestro Señor Jesús el Grán Poder* takes place in La Paz around the beginning of June each year. It began in 1939 as a candle ceremony and procession led by an image of Christ through the indigenous neighbourhoods of La Paz. The following year, a folkloric group was formed by the local union of embroiderers and they participated in the event.

Over the years, the festival attracted more folkloric groups and the celebration

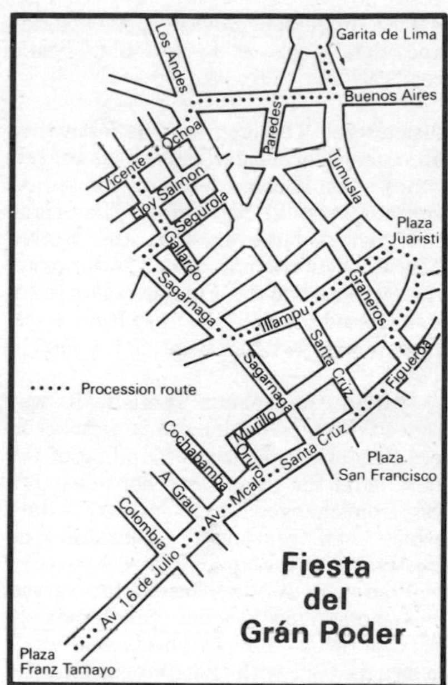

got bigger and more lively. It has developed into a strictly *Paceño* festival and dancers and folkloric groups from all over the city participate. The embroiderers have a lot of work preparing elaborate costumes for the event and the performers practice for weeks in advance.

A number of dances, such as the *suri sikuris* in which the dancers are bedecked in ostrich feathers, the lively *Kullasada*, and the *Inkas* which attempts to duplicate ancient Inca ceremonial dances, have been perpetuated and almost canonised by this growing annual celebration which has developed into one of the three major annual festivals in the country.

El Grán Poder is a glimpse of Aymará culture at its festive finest and it is surely a wild and exciting time in La Paz. If you're in the area at the time and want to catch the procession, go early to stake out a place along the route (see map) and watch for stray or unruly water balloons. The tourist office can provide specific dates and details about a particular year's celebration.

Alasitas Fair The origin of the festival of abundance, or *Alasita*, dates back to Inca times when it coincided with the spring equinox every 21 September. Historians now agree, however, that the festive Alasitas Fair celebrated each 24 January, though based on the original, began in La Paz around the time of Tupac Katari, the Indian who led the siege of La Paz in 1781.

During the colonial period, it was moved from the equinox to 20 October in order to also honour the founding of the city. After the siege, Governor Sebastián Segurola changed it to 24 January, a date which had previously celebrated the Festival of Our Lady of Peace.

Traditionally, the Alasitas fair served to demonstrate and honour the abundance of the fields. The campesinos weren't pleased at all with the changes and the January date imposed by the Spaniards, so they decided to turn the celebration into a corny mockery of its original significance.

They decided that 'abundance' would not only apply to crops, but also to homes, tools, cash, clothing and lately, cars, trucks, aeroplanes and even 12-storey apartment complexes. The little god of abundance, *Ekeko*, made his appearance and the modern Alasitas traditions began.

Ekeko, whose name means 'dwarf' in Aymará, has come to be the household god and the keeper and distributor of material possessions. Needless to say, the locals prefer to remain on the better side of his kindness, and during the Alasitas fair, they buy him miniatures of everything they'd like to get hold of during the course of the year.

A small plaster image of Ekeko is loaded down with household utensils, baskets of coca, wallets, airline tickets, suitcases full of cash (in US$!), lottery tickets, liquor, chocolate and all the other material goods that the people believe constitutes 'abundance' for their families. The more optimistic buy buses, Toyota 4x4's, Volkswagen beetles and three storey suburban homes.

Ekeko, god of abundance

If you won't be able to make it to the Alasitas Fair and would still like to see what Ekeko looks like, there is a statue of him at the intersection of Calle Comercio and Mariscal Santa Crúz.

Places to Stay – bottom end

La Paz has an enormous number of low cost hotels and residenciales. The vast majority of them are in the area between Calle Manco Capac and Avenida Montes (the Prado). By the way, midnight is lockup time for all bottom end hotels in La Paz.

Alojamiento Pullman at 665 Avenida Montes is a bit grimy around the edges but at US$2 per person it's cheap, there's a bar and restaurant attached, and they even have hot water at times.

Also not too clean is *Alojamiento El Pasajero* at Calle Chuquisaca 579. It costs US$2.50 a single for Bolivians and US$3 for foreigners; or US$2/2.50 per person for Bolivians/foreigners, for a double or larger. They make it very clear that only one shower is allowed per person per day.

From the outside, *Hotel Italia* at 303 Manco Capac looks like it should be more expensive than it is. It's clean and is becoming marginally popular with young travellers. There is a peña in the attached restaurant on Friday and Saturday nights at 10 pm. Rooms with shared bath cost US$2.50 per person, a room with private bath is US$3.25, and they have hot water 24 hours a day. Ask for a room in the front – they're nicer, even if they are a little noisier.

Just up the street at 364 Manco Capac is *Hotel Andes*. It's friendly and sometimes has hot water. A room without bath costs US$3 per person or with private bath is US$4.

Practically next door to the Andes is *Alojamiento Central* at 384 Manco Capac. They sometimes have hot water, but no private baths are available. Rooms cost US$3 per person.

The much advertised and ultra-clean *Residenciál Rosario* at 704 Illampú straddles the mid and bottom-range as far as price is concerned, but I'll mention it here because of its enormous popularity with foreign travellers. I'd recommend it to anyone who doesn't mind being a little closer to transportation terminals and little further from the centre of activity in town.

It has been accurately described as trendy and would not be ideal for down and bedraggled budget travellers unless they want to splurge for a taste of relative luxury. There is an excellent restaurant upstairs which is open to non-guests. Tepid showers are available 24 hours a day. Try to get a room away from the noisy echo in the reception area. For shared bath, singles/doubles/triples cost US$5.54/7.15/9.45. Rooms with private baths are US$12.53/14.55/18.55.

In the lobby downstairs is the Turisbus tour office, which will organise transport to Peru and arrange sightseeing excursions to popular attractions around La Paz.

Closer to the centre of town, there are a few nice cheap places to stay. If being central and within walking distance of just about everything is the most important consideration in your choice of a hotel, the *Torino* at 457 Socabaya is your best bet and is by far the most popular ultra low-budget travellers' hotel in La Paz.

It's fairly clean and has nice hot showers from 6 am to 1 pm. There is also a locked baggage room and a free left baggage service for guests. The central courtyard has a rather noisy bar which is frequented by a fairly consistent bunch of semi-conscious regulars, but fortunately, this closes down at 9 pm and things quieten down. They charge US$2.50 per person, but don't have any private baths.

Another pleasant and centrally located place is *Hostal Austria* at 531 Yanococha. They have one, two, three and four-bed rooms and charge US$3.50 per person. Hot water is available at all times.

The most pleasant inexpensive accommodation in La Paz is the *Alojamiento Illimani* on Calle Illimani not far from the stadium. It's a bit further from the centre of things and a fairly long way from transportation terminals, but it's quiet and friendly and is becoming very popular with more laid-back travellers. There's hot water a few hours a day, a laundry sink, a patio sitting area where cooking is also allowed, and the señora will pleasantly admit you if you arrive or return after lock-up time at midnight. Single and double rooms, without bath, are US$2.65 and US$4.25. There's also a nice view over the city from the clothes line area.

A couple of places that are probably best avoided include the *Hotel Sagárnaga*, on the street of the same name, and the *Hotel Metropoly* on Manco Capac. The staff at the former apparently tend to hound tourists about unimportant matters and the whole operation seems disorganised and has been described as 'a little fishy'. The Metropoly is also reported to have some serious problems. Although the owner is friendly, her staff are apparently unbearable. Even travellers who were accustomed to basic accommodation told me that the toilets in this place were unthinkable. Those who know Bolivia at all can imagine what this means.

The only other really disagreeable place I found was the *Alojamiento Illampú* at 635 Illampú. It's run down, very dirty and unfriendly but, admittedly, at US$2 per night it is economical.

Places to Stay – middle

If you take a room with a private bath, the previously described Residenciál Rosario serves as a nice, mid-range hotel.

Another one, centrally located near Plaza Murillo, is *Hostal Yanacocha* at 540 Yanacocha. It's got hot water all hours, private baths, and it's quite clean. A room costs US$7.60 per person.

The *Hotel Panamericano* on the margin of the budget hotel area at 454 Manco Capac is clean and caters to tour groups that don't want to pay for the Sheraton. For groups of 10 or more with reservations, they will charge only US$4.80 per person, which is a bargain. All rooms are clean and have private baths and hot water. For US$1, you can have a continental breakfast of juice, coffee, rolls and condiments.

Non-tour individuals will pay US$13.50 a single, US$15.60 a double or US$22 a triple. Bolivians get about a 15% discount. According to the Bolivian rating system, the Panamericano is a two-star hotel.

Hotel Avenida at 665 Avenida Montes (Upper Prado) is clean and has hot water. The price is US$8.50 per person with private bath or US$7.50 without.

The *Hostal Claudia* is centrally located on the Plaza del Estudiante next to the university. It's clean and has large rooms and hot water, but is a little noisy from the traffic and the university. A single without private bath will cost US$7.25; a double with private bath is US$16.25 and without is US$9.80.

Places to Stay – top end

The Hotel Plaza (tel 378300) bills itself as the highest five-star hotel in the world, which is true since the equally five-star *Sheraton* (tel 356950) is a few metres lower, just down the street on Avenida Aniceto Arce. A double room in either of these will cost around US$75 and a single room only slightly less. If you're after a bit of luxury, these are both bargains considering what similar accommodation in your home town would cost.

The four-star *Libertador* (tel 343263), Calle Obispo Cárdenas 142, will cost less than US$50 for a double and US$40 for a single.

The *Emperador* (tel 340013) which rates three stars is on the stadium plaza and costs slightly less that the Libertador.

If you're planning to stay in any of these nicer hotels, reservations should be made in advance through a travel agent or by writing or phoning ahead to confirm room availability.

There are a number of other nicer hotels to be found in La Paz. A travel agent will be able to provide a complete rundown.

Places to Eat

La Paz has a wealth of restaurants ranging from those that serve poor imitations of edible food to those that successfully aim to please a discriminating palate. The latter aren't all posh and pricey 42nd-storey affairs either; most are quite reasonable, and some of the finest are downright cheap.

My first recommendation is to avoid anything that looks like an American fast food chain, especially *Genie's* (a disgusting imitation of Wendy's) and *McDonal* (you can guess what this is supposed to look like!), both on the Prado.

Don't expect a lot of variety in the fare to be found in La Paz. Nearly all of the restaurants specialise in, or serve exclusively, some kind of beef or chicken. The only variety to be found lies in the quality and price.

Breakfast When you're looking for breakfast in La Paz, keep in mind that most of the restaurants that serve it don't open until 9 or 9.30 am. As I mentioned when describing the business hours, if you're an early riser and need a caffeine fix before you can face the day, the markets always have stalls that sell bearable coffee for about 20c. If you're really desperate, you'll appreciate the high-voltage jolt you'll get from the muddy syrupy coffee concentrate served in such places.

A good place to find the most popular Bolivian breakfast food is *Super Salteñas* on Calle Socabaya. They are disputably billed as the world's best salteñas, although some that I've eaten in the market near the cemetery are certainly in the running too.

If you'd like a good old Yankee-style breakfast, try *California Donuts* on Avenida Camacho. They're a bit overpriced, but the donuts are the real thing and you can eat them with Irish coffee or rich hot cocoa with lots of gooey additives.

For a heftier breakfast, nothing beats the restaurant in the Residenciál Rosario on Illampú. They serve ham, eggs, breads, cheese, pancakes, orange juice and excellent cocoa and cappuccino. Non-guests are welcome.

If you just want to grab a quick coffee and a roll or salteña, I'd recommend *Confiteria Club de La Paz* at the intersection of Camacho and Mariscal Santa Crúz. Another good place is *Cafés Paris* on Ayacucho. *Confiteria Marilín* on the corner of Potosí and Ayacucho is repeatedly recommended but their coffee should be avoided.

Lunch Lunch specials may be found all over town. Every Mom & Pop cubbyhole in the city serves some sort of bulk meal, and chances are you'll find something appealing in these more informal establishments.

If you'd rather eat in a higher class restaurant, the Café Paris on Ayacucho serves a bounteous lunch special – soup, salad, main course, drink, and a dessert for US$1.75. I've never been able to finish one.

Another very pleasant place to eat lunch is *Esquina del Bigote* at Montevideo and Avenida Arce, but go early. Around 12.30 pm the place is crowded to overflowing, which in itself is an indication that the food is worthwhile. The staff are also a friendly lot. A complete lunch similar to the one at the Café Paris costs only US$1.25.

Max Beiber on Avenida 20 de Octubre, *Café Verona* on Colón, and *Coppelia* on Loayza have all been consistently recommended for lunch, but they are a bit more expensive than those previously mentioned.

The cheapest place to eat a quick lunch is in one of the markets. They have takeaway snack stands where they sell such things as *empanadas* and chicken sandwiches, and also restaurant stalls with under cover sitting areas. If you don't expect too much in the way of sanitation, you can get a filling meal of soup, a meat dish, rice, lettuce and *oca* or potato, for about US$1.

If you're travelling on limited funds and are planning to eat this way throughout Bolivia, keep in mind that your internal plumbing will need a little while to get used to the idea. Don't give up on market food just because you get the runs the first time you try it.

There are a couple of reasonable places to find a hamburger. *California Burgers* (in the same building as California Donuts) on Avenida Camacho, and *Hamburgon I & II* on Potosí (look for the hippopotamus), are both possibilities.

The best quick chicken in town can be found at *Pollo Copacabana* where you can get a quarter roast chicken, chips and fried plantain smothered in ketchup, mustard and *ají* for less than US$2. There are two locations, one on Calle Potosí and one on Calle Comercio.

Dinner Most of the places listed under lunch also serve dinner. Again, a particularly nice place to eat is the Residenciál Rosario. They serve such goodies as cream of asparagus and french onion soup, breaded chicken (unheard of elsewhere in Bolivia!), and pasta dishes, all nicely done.

The *Manjari Restaurant* on Potosí near Colón has superb vegetarian dinner specials for just over US$1. The bread they serve is an indescribably delicious concoction of whole wheat and honey. Vegetarian fare is also served at *Lakshmi* on Calle Jimenez two blocks from Plaza San Francisco.

A host of cheap eateries may be found in Evaristo Valle just above Plaza Perez Velasco.

The majority of nicer and higher-priced restaurants in La Paz are concentrated in the lower end of town around 20 de Octubre, 6 de Agosto and 16 de Julio (it must be easy to remember historical dates in La Paz!).

Don Quixote on the Prado serves steak and *parrillada* (mixed grill); and *Churrasqueria Miraflores* at 2029 Saavedra does Argentine steak, *pique macho* and parrillada. Seafoods are the specialty of *Moby Dick* on Batallón Colorados; nice Chinese cuisine may be had at the *Hong Kong Restaurant* on the Plaza del Estudiante; and nearby is the award-winning *La Carreta* which serves parrillada and Argentine beef. *Max Beiber* on 20 de Octubre does good dinners as does the excellent *Los Escudos* on Mariscal Santa Crúz near Avenida Camacho.

For traditional Bolivian cooking, try *Restaurant Monaco* on Avenida Villazón or *Kari Tiahuanaco* on Plaza Ravelo.

Entertainment

Peñas Every visitor to La Paz who wants a taste of Bolivian folk music should try to attend at least one *peña*. A peña is an Andean or highland Bolivian folk music show which may include dancing.

The music is usually played on typical Andean instruments such as the *guena*, a single-reed flute; the *zampoña*, the famous multi-reed flute; and the *charango*, a ukulele-type instrument which often has a sound box made of an armadillo carapace. Shows featuring only guitars, singing, comedy or a combination of these, however, are also common.

In all cases, the music gets better as the bottles get emptier, so to get you started the admission charge will generally include your first drink.

The most popular peña is at the *Naira* on Sagárnaga just above Plaza San Francisco. It plays nightly except Sunday at 10 pm and costs US$5. Other peñas can be found at *Cas del Corregidor, Café Paris* on Ayacucho, and *Los Escudos* on Mariscal Santa Crúz. If you'd like to attend a peña, the best bet is to check the La Paz paper for advertisements and details of what is available while you're there.

Bars Don't expect too much from bars in La Paz. Bolivians go to a bar to drink and get drunk, not to dance or carry on semi-intelligent conversations. In order to avoid trouble and remain intact, most bars close down at midnight or earlier; though even at that hour things are touch and go. Most of their patrons are good and sloshed by 6 pm and the extra six hours doesn't improve their state at all.

So, unless you enjoy being cursed and slobbered on by incoherent drunks, you'll probably want to avoid bars altogether. A lot of these people are also particularly lacking in affection for some foreign governments. They're none too fond of Ronald Reagan for instance, and they all seem to think that Hitler is still in power in Germany, so you may find yourself in an uncomfortable position when natural inhibitions are eliminated by drink. To most people in this state, gringo faces are all North American or German and no amount of argument or explanation seems to put things straight, so be careful.

Some rather offbeat travellers (thanks

Bernard & Bill!), offered me the following advice about a bar that particularly impressed them. For what it's worth:

> The *Regufio Bar* just off the Avenida Americas should be recommended as an interesting cultural experience. It's sleazy. Expect police raids, shady characters and lunatics. Only go to drink beer or *singani* and get roaring drunk. Women shouldn't go alone.

Nicer places to buy drinks are called *wisquerias*. If you'd like the sort of atmosphere found in a slightly more up-market saloon or pub, try *Mateus* in the Alianza Building on Fernando Guachalla, the *Alhambra* at Loayza 115, or the *Coppelia* at Loayza 233.

Things to Buy

Along Calle Sagárnaga between Mariscal Santa Crúz and Isaac Tamayo is the artisans' market where expensive tourist shops compete with street vendors.

As a general rule, the nearer a shop is to the Prado, the higher the prices will tend to be, mostly because a lot of tourists are willing to pay for the luxury of not having to climb so far uphill. In addition, shopkeepers will generally not haggle over prices as much as the street vendors, whose prices are lower to begin with. I suspect that the trendier shops do most of their business with tourists who, for one reason or another, feel uncomfortable with bargaining.

In the artisans' market area, all sorts of clothing, including *ponchos, chompas, chullos*, vests, jackets and mufflers, can be bought in wool, llama and alpaca, or any combination of the three.

Alpaca is the finest and is therefore the most expensive. Some pieces are hand-dyed and woven or knitted, but others are obviously machine-made. Learn to tell the difference and never take an overzealous shopkeeper's word for it. Many would tell you it was made of solid gold if it would result in a sale.

I also beg you not to buy anything represented as *vicuña*. Although it's the finest and softest wool available in the world, finer even than cashmere, the little vicuñas will soon be history if steps are not taken to prevent their demise. As they are strictly wild animals and cannot be domesticated and raised for their valuable wool, it means that every vicuña product represents a dead animal. Please, let's leave them alone.

Some shops sell Andean musical instruments. The most popular are *zampoñas* and *guenas*, as well as drums and armadillo-shell *charangos*. Others specialise in wood-carvings and ceramics from the Oriente and silver items from Potosí. Some deal in rugs, wall-hangings, woven belts and pouches which carry the designs and artistic personality of the craftsperson.

Quite a few shops sell all sorts of tourist kitsch (yes, even in Bolivia!), like ceramic ashtrays with Inca-like decorations, Tiahuanaco design figurines, jewellery and T-shirts.

It's a safe bet to say that any type of handicraft available in Bolivia can be found somewhere in La Paz, although prices will naturally be lower several middlemen down the line at the point of original production. Prices will vary, of course, depending on quality, but you can expect to pay around US$8 for a passable alpaca sweater and up to US$20 for an exceptional one. A chullo will cost around US$2 and a very nice poncho up to US$20 or US$25. Prices for just about everything will be slightly higher in La Paz than in Puno, Cuzco or elsewhere in Peru, but I believe the average quality of what's available justifies it.

Getting There & Away

Air Information on domestic and international LAB services is given in the Getting There and Getting Around chapters. Following, is a complete list of all international airlines which serve La Paz and a brief description of their service. Specific schedules and fares change rapidly so it's best to contact the individual carriers for such details.

Lufthansa
Three flights to and from Frankfurt on Tuesday, Friday and Sunday.
Eastern Airlines
From Asunción on Tuesday, Friday and Sunday.
To Asunción on Tuesday, Thursday and Saturday.
From Miami (USA)/Calí (Colombia) on Monday, Wednesday and Saturday.
To Calí/Miami on Tuesday, Friday and Sunday.
Varig
To and from Rio de Janeiro and São Paulo (Brazil), and Santa Crúz (Bolivia) on Tuesday, Thursday and Saturday.
Aero Peru
To and from Lima on Wednesday and Friday.
LAN Chile
To and from Santiago, Iquique and Arica (all in Chile) on Friday and Monday.

The following is a sample of one-way air fares to or from locations around Bolivia. These include a 4.2% domestic tax. Santa Crúz - US$39; Cochabamba - US$24; Sucre - US$28.30; Tarija - US$35.60; Trinidád - US$31; Yacuiba - US$52.65; Riberalta - US$56.65; Guayaramerín - US$56.65; Camiri - US$45.20; Cobija - US$66; Puerto Suarez - US$86.95.

Bus Most travellers who enter La Paz by bus are coming from Peru. If you buy tour bus packages directly from Puno to La Paz you'll have to change vehicles at the border, but the buses will generally drop you at the hotel of your choice upon arrival in La Paz.

If you're doing the trip on your own you will have to travel with either Transportes 2 de Febrero or Transportes Manco Capac from Copacabana to La Paz. The terminals for these two lines are on Calle José Maria Asin near the cemetery and quite a long way from all the budget hotels. Those planning to walk to a hotel anyway can be consoled by the fact that at least all the hotels are 'downhill' from the terminals.

If you're going to Copacabana in Bolivia, or on to Peru, *Turisbus* (tel 325348) has daily service to Puno (Peru) via Copacabana for less than US$10. The Turisbus office is on the 1st floor of the Residenciál Rosario and you can arrange for the bus to collect you from your hotel.

Also destined for Copacabana, Transportes Manco Capac (tel 350033) leaves from its terminal at 7 am and 1.30 pm; and Transportes 2 de Febrero (tel 377181) departs at 8 pm and 3 pm. One-way fares are around US$3.

Flota Ingavi (tel 328981) provide regular services all along the southern route into Peru. Buses leave frequently during the day, from their terminal on Calle José Maria Asín, and go via Guaqui and Tiahuanaco in Bolivia to Desaguadero in Peru.

Buses to Huatajata and other eastern Lake Titicaca towns and villages, leave about every half hour between 4 am and 5 pm from Avenida Manuel Bustillos and Kollasuyo, also near the cemetery. Coming from these towns, you have to flag the bus down on the highway.

From Calle Angel Babia in the same area, *Transportes Larecaja* goes to Sorata twice daily at 6.30 and 7 am. Tickets go on sale at 2 pm the previous day.

The terminal for *Flota Yungueña* (tel 312344), which serves several Bolivian towns, is in the Villa Fátima suburb steeply uphill from the stadium area. Buses leave for Coroico on Tuesday, Thursday, Friday and Saturday at 9 am; and leave Coroico for La Paz on Wednesday and Friday at 1 pm. To Chulumani, Irupana, Guanay and Caranavi, they leave daily at 9 am and return daily at 7 am, the exception being the Saturday service from Irupana and Chulumani.

Trucks to the Yungas leave from just above the petrol station beside the Flota Yungueña office.

All other bus transport to and from La Paz leaves and arrives at the main bus terminal, the *Terminal Terrestre Cuidád de La Paz*, on Plaza Antofagasta 1½ blocks above Avenida Montes.

To and from Oruro, one flota or another is leaving every few minutes. I recommend *Nobleza* for their comfortable buses and agreeable attitude. The trip takes three hours and costs US$2.50.

To Cochabamba and Santa Crúz, *Bolívar, San Francisco, América, Cóndor, El Dorado, Andino* and a dozen others leave between 7.30 and 8.30 pm. To get to Santa Crúz, you must stop in Cochabamba for eight to 10 hours. You will arrive in Cochabamba the morning after departure and in Santa Crúz in a zombie state the morning of the second day.

To Sucre and Potosí, *Flotas 10 de Noviembre, Trans-Pullman La Paz* and Cóndor all depart between 5.30 and 6.30 pm daily.

To Tarija, *San Lorenzo* and *Velóz del Sud* both leave at 5 pm daily.

Flota Panamericana does sporadic international runs to Lima, Cuzco, Arequipa and Puno in Peru, and to Jujuy and Salta in Argentina.

Flota Litoral leaves on Tuesday and Friday at 6 am for a very, *very* rough 22-hour journey to Arica in Chile. The fare is US$18. Buses from Arica to La Paz leave from Calle Chacabuco in Arica on Monday and Friday at 1 am. *Agencia Martinez* in that same city connects with the Bolivian train at Charaña on the border. That fare is US$7.50.

Refer to the Getting Around chapter for other information on schedules and fares.

Train Three rail lines run out from La Paz. One goes southward to Oruro, Uyuni, Tupiza and Villazón, connecting with Argentine transport to the railhead in Tucamán in Argentina. Branches from this line cut off at Uyuni for Calama (Chile), at Rio Mulato for Potosí/Sucre, and at Oruro for Cochabamba.

Another line goes to Arica in Chile; and the third, which is not currently in use, goes to Guaqui on Lake Titicaca.

Arranging rail travel in Bolivia is normally not easy and La Paz is no exception. Arranging a passage out of La Paz can be nerve-wracking at best and impossible in most cases. For 'official' schedules and fares refer to the Getting Around chapter.

If you're heading south toward Argentina or Antofagasta in Chile, I strongly recommend you take a bus to Oruro and buy your onward passage from there. They add extra coaches to the train at Oruro and the set up there is comparatively well organised. In La Paz it may require some underhanded dealing in the WC or several days of your time just to get hold of a ticket.

The railroad station in La Paz is on upper Manco Capac.

Getting Around

Airport Transport Kennedy International Airport (formerly El Alto) sits on the Altiplano at 4018 metres. It is the world's highest commercial airport, which will be very obvious if you ever arrive or leave from there. The larger planes need several km of runway to take off and must land at higher speeds than usual to compensate for the lower density atmosphere. Stopping distance is much greater too and planes must be equipped with special extra-durable tyres in order to land in La Paz.

The airport doesn't have much in the way of facilities. There's no place to change money and the only eatery is an overpriced coffee shop. There's little else, apart from a few souvenir stores, a bookshop and a duty-free shop which is only available to passengers departing internationally.

The domestic departure airport tax at La Paz is 75c while the international tax is US$7.50 or US$15, depending on the type of currency you use. It's cheaper to pay in Bolivianos than US dollars. All international flights originating in La Paz are also subject to a 13% fare tax. Domestic fare tax is only 4.2%.

There are two roads to the airport, the *autopista* or toll road which costs 15c and the sinuous 'other road', but there is no means of getting there on public transport that is both cheap and easy.

The cheapest method is to take a city bus, for 13c, to *La Ceja* market at the lip of the canyon and then walk the two remaining 'level' km to the airport. The easiest method is to pay US$6 to US$10 and take a taxi.

In between, there is a viable alternative. Along Avenida Camacho and the Prado, *trufis* headed uphill are probably going to La Ceja or El Alto neighbourhoods. The normal fare to these places is US$1, but you can sometimes convince the driver to take you all the way to the airport for as little as US$2.50 for one or two people.

If you're going to town from the airport, there are no buses and collectives are much cheaper than taxis (US$1 as opposed to US$6 to US$10). Taxis wait immediately outside the terminal exit and collectives may be found just across the parking lot.

Bus La Paz city buses, called micros, are grinding sputtering, smoke-spewing wrecks, most of which appear to be rapidly wheezing their way toward the junkyard. The fact is, I suspect, that many of them were driven a hundred thousand km or so in the US before even making their debut in Bolivia. They do, however, fulfil their purpose of providing cheap but slow coronary-free up and down transport for the city's masses.

By the way, a foreigner new to South America may learn the meaning of the word 'masses' on a La Paz city bus. The crowds are much more intense here than at a mere rock concert or football game at home. The buses mock the law of gravity and defy the principles of brake and transmission mechanics as they struggle fully packed up and down the hills of the city.

Since there's only one door, bodies don't circulate from front to rear. Instead, they push, shove, curse and climb over each other when their stop comes up. If you feel uncomfortable about being aggressive, you could be on the bus all day. Obviously, it's probably not a good idea to transport a lot of luggage on city buses; it also follows that a little caution should be taken with jewellery or valuables.

In addition to a route number or letter, micros plainly display their destination on a signboard posted in the front window. This eliminates the hassle of sorting out and memorising a whole lot of numbers.

Bus stops are not very well marked, but most people don't bother to use them anyway. Doors are usually left open, either for ventilation or because the entryway is blocked with passengers. Traffic is normally such that the bus is stationary more often than it's moving, anyway, so you can hop (or squeeze) on just about anywhere.

The price for most buses is 10c although a couple of private lines charge 13c.

Taxi Although just about everything in La Paz that is worth seeing is within fairly easy walking distance of the hotels, most people will definitely not want to do much walking while burdened by a lot of luggage. Both the rail and bus terminals are near to, but rather steep climbs from, the main hotel areas and considering the altitude of La Paz, hoofing it with a heavy pack through the traffic is not fun at all.

Fortunately, taxis in town aren't very expensive. One should expect to pay about 50c for up to four passengers around the main section of town, which includes nearly everything shown on the main city map in this book.

Be warned that taxi drivers are not always very well-versed in the geography of the city, so have a map handy and be able to explain roughly where you want to go. The name of a budget hotel normally isn't good enough. They'll know where the Sheraton is but the Residenciál Rosario will usually draw a blank. If you can tell them it's near the intersection of Graneros and Illampú, it will give them a better idea, and if you can direct them you'll have an even greater chance of arriving quickly at your destination.

To get a taxi, just flag one down. If all of them appear to be full or occupied, try anyway. Often drivers will fill up with passengers and drop them off in the order in which they climbed aboard. While this may seem slow, it's actually much faster than waiting for a vacant taxi during the busiest times of day.

Be sure to arrange a fare with the driver in advance and always carry enough change to pay close to the correct fare.

If you'd like to hire a long distance taxi, they gather at the *Centro de Taxis* on Manco Capac and Viacha. Prices are also negotiable.

Around La Paz

VALLEY OF THE MOON

The Valley of the Moon, or *Valle de la Luna*, isn't really a valley at all but a bizarre and ominously eroded hillside maze of miniature canyons and pinnacles, technically known as badlands, which inspires the imagination and invites exploration.

In the same canyon as La Paz, but about 11 km below the city in an area called Río Abajo, the valley may be visited easily in just a morning or be combined with a hike to the nearby Muela del Diablo to fill an entire day.

The valley offers a quiet break from urban La Paz which is only physically near to this peaceful place. For those who'd like to camp, there are some

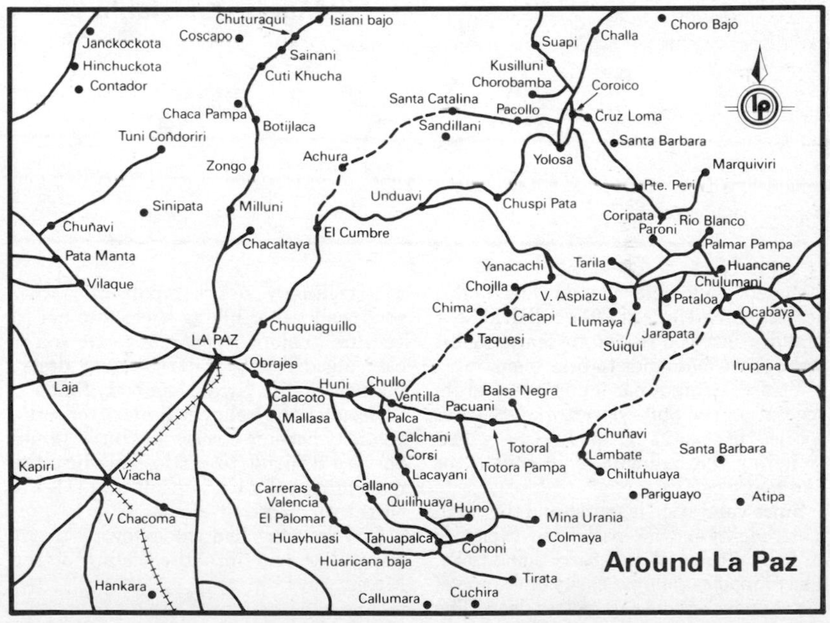

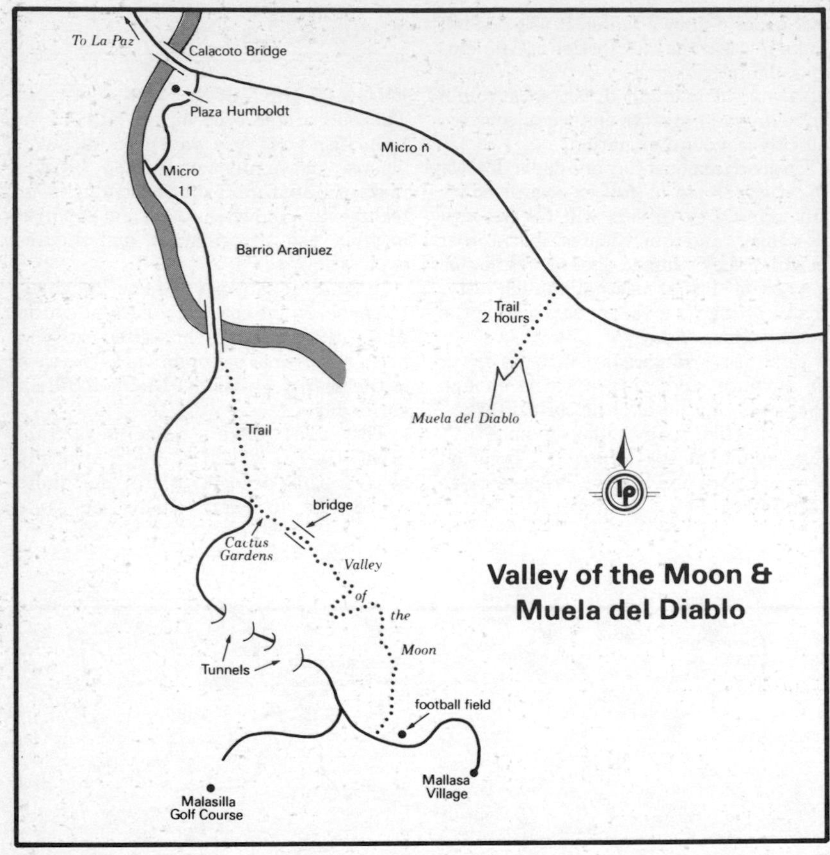

secluded and undeveloped level sites across the road from the football field near Mallasa but you've got to search a bit through the badlands to find them.

This amazing lunar landscape and its vegetation are quite desert-like. Several species of cactus grow in the valley including the hallucinogenic *choma*, or San Pedro cactus.

Since vegetation is sparse and the earth material silty and unconsolidated, exploring on foot in the area can carry some risks. The pinnacles collapse easily and some of the canyons are over 10 metres deep. The soil is slippery, so it's important to wear good walking or hiking shoes and not to venture in alone. Also, make sure you're carrying drinking water because desert hiking can quickly deplete body fluids.

Because the valley is a maze, of sorts, you may become disoriented but it would be very difficult to get lost because the road practically encircles it and a fairly clear trail crosses it.

One traveller had the following to say about her trip into the Valley of the Moon.

Top: Valle de La Luna, near La Paz (TM)
Bottom: Valle de La Luna, near La Paz (WH)

Top: Isla de La Luna – Lake Titicaca (DS)
Bottom: Flooded farmland after early 1986 flood – Copacabana (DS)

We were dropped off at the bizarre but quite beautiful Valley of the Moon which stands in striking contrast to urban La Paz. Our 'guide' took us trekking through this lunar-like maze of canyons, amongst strange clay 'stalagmites' which unexpectedly, but often, crumble under foot.

To the un-acclimatised, rock climbing at this altitude is no fun. Finally we scrambled from yet another weird canyon, puffing like steam trains, to the highlight of our trek – the cactus garden and a bridge suspended some 30 feet over a small canyon, looking like someting right out of 'Raiders of the Lost Ark'.

Crossing the bridge was certainly a highlight (stunt routines in the Bolivian desert no less!), but it was not for those with weak hearts or footwear. Our guide was an Englishman, the locals are probably more sensible – and hopefully the bridge has been fixed.

Getting There & Away

To get there from La Paz, take any micro marked Calacoto, get off at the Plaza Humboldt and wait near the corner to catch micro 11 to its final stop at Barrio Aranjuez. Cross the bridge to your right at this point and follow a rather non-descript trail across a ditch and up the hill to your left. You can also walk up the road but it's quite a bit further.

After about 10 minutes, you should arrive at the cactus gardens, which are not marked as such but are easily identifiable because they resemble a slightly artificial stand of cactus. Across the garden there is a very poor, and a little frightening, foot bridge across a gully. This trail will lead through the Valley of the Moon and end up at the football field near the village of Mallasa where you can find several stores which sell snacks, beer and soda pop.

If you turn right on this road, away from the village, you'll eventually find the Malasilla Golf Course. It's on a turnoff from the main road not far above the cactus garden.

Since the rains drastically alter this fragile landscape, it's possible that portions of the trail will wash out in years to come and may change this route. Still, if you enter the valley at the cactus garden and keep walking uphill, you'll eventually arrive at the road.

EL CUMBRE TO COROICO

North-east of La Paz and also known as the *Choro trail*, this is the premier hike with young travellers in all of Bolivia. It begins at El Cumbre, the highest point on the La Paz-Coroico highway, and climbs to 4859 metres at Apacheta Pass before descending 3250 metres into the steaming Yungas to the village of Chairo.

Strong hikers can finish the walk in two days but most people prefer to take more time to enjoy the incredible variety of landforms and vegetation to be found throughout the different levels of altitude. The trip can be done quite comfortably in three days but those unused to long distance hiking should allow at least four.

The cultural aspects of this trip are also interesting as there are distinct differences in dress, dwellings, crops and herds as you pass through the various stages of the walk.

If you're interested in experiencing pure Andean cultures, however, this is not the hike to take. It will soon be obvious to you, especially on the upper trail, that many well-meaning gringos have passed before and bestowed upon the locals gifts of candy, cigarettes and money, thus giving the people a taste for things not locally available to them.

All along this route, I kept hoping for pleasant interaction and conversation with the people and instead was met with demands for material goods from both adults and children.

What we, in our high-technology, fast-paced society fail to realise is that a lack of money, television, automobiles and expensive playthings does not necessarily constitute poverty. The people of the Yungas valleys have crops, animals and homes which provide sufficient food, clothing and shelter. They live out their lives in a peaceful environment amid the mountains, free from most of the threats of world conflict. They work hard with the land and in turn, it takes care of them.

While it would be difficult for us to get used to this lifestyle, the highland Bolivians have known nothing else for well over a thousand years and they are as comfortable with it as we are in our own element. When we condescendingly hand out candy or cigarettes, we cause dental and health problems which they cannot remedy; and when we give money, we impose on them a foreign system of values and upset a well-established balance.

The slums which ring La Paz are evidence of the number of campesinos who have migrated to the city in search of money, and in doing so have traded a relatively prosperous life for real poverty.

While there may be many that disagree, try to consider the long-term consequences of your actions. If you share a conversation, a smile, a photograph or perhaps some coca leaves as a sign of your friendship, the people will accept you as a friend rather than as Santa Claus.

El Cumbre to Coroico Hike The *Choro trail* itself is not too difficult to access or to follow. From La Paz, take any micro marked Villa Fátima. Ask to be let off at the service station just below the *Flota Yungueña* office. The flota leaves at 9 am daily and charges US$1 to the high point of the Yungas road where this hike begins.

Just up the road, behind the service station next door to the Flota Yungueña office, you can find trucks which leave for the Yungas every few minutes between about 7 am and early afternoon. They charge 50c per person to the pass.

The road climbs steeply out of Villa Fátima and less than an hour out of La Paz is the summit. Get off at the statue of Christ which marks the crest of the highway and follow a well-defined track to your left for about one km. There, a smaller track turns right and passes between two small ponds. Follow this up the hill until it curves to the left and begins to lose altitude, at which point you take the light track which leads uphill to the right and through a notch in the barren brown hill before you. This is Apacheta Pass.

At the pass is a curious pile of stones called Apacheta Chucura where travellers for centuries have marked their passing by tossing a stone atop it. From there, the trail trends downhill all the way to its end at Chairo.

Good first night campsites may be found on the football field at Achura (sometimes known as Chucura) and along the river an hour's walk below the town.

Some tentless travellers we met stayed with a family in town for 50c per person, but that evening the mayor showed up at the home and demanded a tribute of US$5 each to stay in the village. Similarly, in the same area some woodcutters blocked our path and told us permission to pass would cost us candy and cigarettes.

In both instances, treating the situation as a joke saved the day. Even if what they ask may seem a pittance to you, giving in to their demands will perpetuate the practice and it will become quite a nuisance to travellers that follow.

The good suspension bridge at Choro was destroyed in flooding several years ago and has been replaced by two weak twig-and-vine structures which don't appear to be very permanent either. The first one, however, is the better and is also the more convenient.

Above the village of Choro, many stretches consist of pre-Columbian paving which are both beautiful and at times annoyingly difficult to negotiate due to their state of disrepair.

From the crossing, the trail climbs steeply to the ridge above town and enters dense trail-swallowing vegetation. Campsites are plentiful between this point and Chairo, but in most cases it's necessary to bring water from elsewhere. Be sure to bring water purification tablets because while good surface water is plentiful, human and animal life exist throughout

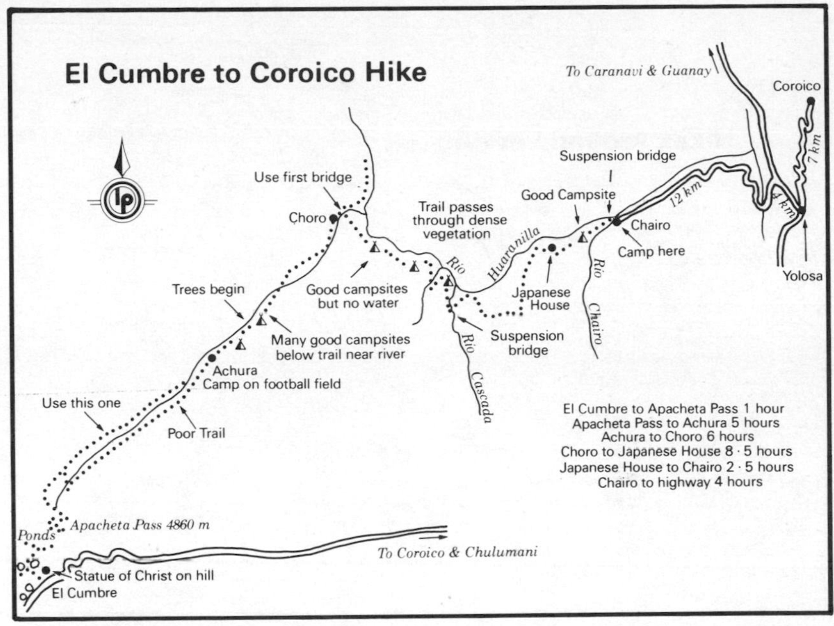

the length of this trail and some contamination does occur.

From the ridge above Choro, the trail plunges and climbs alternately from sunny hillsides to jungle-choked valleys. It crosses streams and passes waterfalls. At one point, it crosses a deep gorge with the help of a crude but effective suspension bridge.

Near the trail's end, about 2½ hours from Chairo, you will encounter a curious and unexpected sight; an oriental home surrounded by beautifully-manicured gardens. The Japanese owner is friendly and enjoys visitors who stop by to chat and sign his guest book. He's also happy to let you camp in his garden.

From there, it is seven easy downhill km to Chairo from where, on Monday, Wednesday or Friday mornings, you can find trucks to Yolosa or Coroico. There's also other light, intermittent traffic.

If you need to stay over in Chairo, it's possible to camp near the trail on the other side of the suspension bridge. Meals and supplies are available from the small shop on the main street. Prices are low and the owners are some of the friendliest people you're likely to meet.

It's possible to walk the relatively level 12 km from Chairo to the highway, but it includes a rather hairy river-fording and due caution should be exercised, especially during times of heavy rain. Plan on four to 4½ hours for the walk and carry water.

From the intersection, it's easy to find a truck going to Yolosa, four km away, from where you can find another to take you the remaining seven km uphill to Coroico. If you're in a hurry, it's also easy in Yolosa to find transport to La Paz.

HIKES AROUND VENTILLA

There are several other places of interest near La Paz that can be visited in a day, or two with an overnight stay. Around Ventilla,

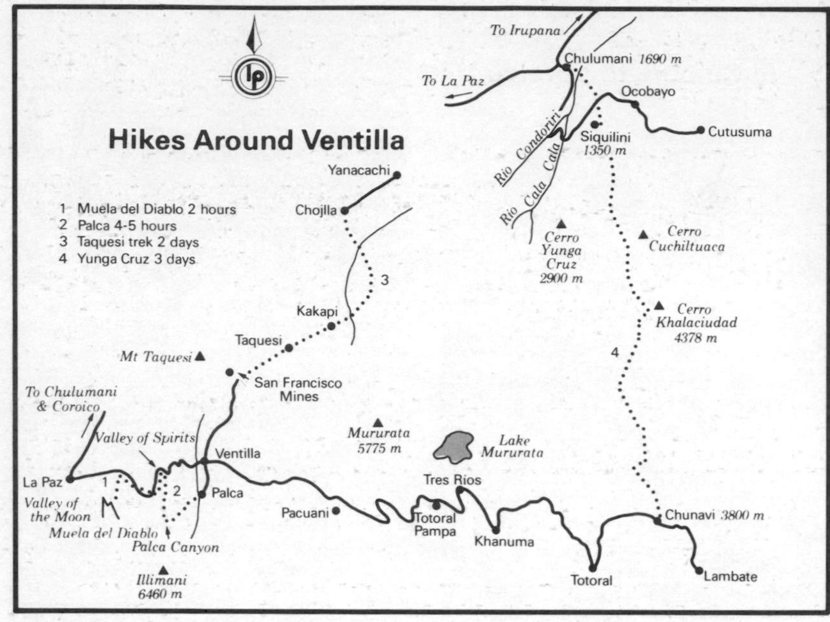

east of La Paz, there are some interesting and fairly easy walks and hikes.

Muela del Diablo

The Muela del Diablo or Devil's Molar, a prominent rock outcropping which is actually an extinct volcano, is on the north side of the Río Choqueyapu Valley.

To get there, take micro Ñ past Calacoto and Plaza Humboldt. Ask the driver to let you off at the trail to Muela del Diablo. In two hours, it's possible to walk to the point where technical expertise and equipment are necessary to ascend any further. The view of La Paz and the Cordillera is quite good and this hike can be easily done in conjunction with a trip to Valley of the Moon.

Palca Trail

This hike is definitely worthwhile for the fantastically eroded scenery along the way and the close-up views of 6322-metre Illimani.

Getting back to La Paz from Palca is not particularly easy, so you should go prepared to spend the night, if necessary. An early start will increase your chances of finding transport back to the city.

To get there, take micro Ñ to Chasquipampa near the Muela del Diablo. The trail leaves from Chasquipampa and passes through the *Valle de Animas*, or Valley of Spirits, a hillside of eroded spires similar to Valley of the Moon. It then follows the Río Uni into Palca Canyon and finally ends in the village of Palca. The hike takes between four and five hours.

From Palca there is occasional transport back to La Paz, but don't count on it in the late afternoon. You can opt to walk back to Ventilla, about an hour away, and try to catch a ride from there or ask around Palca for a place to sleep. If you have camping gear of course there's no problem, but ask permission before setting up a tent in a field or pasture.

If transportation back to La Paz is difficult to find, in a pinch you can always walk the trail back to Chasquipampa and take micro Ñ back to town.

Taquesi Trek

Popularly known as the Inca Trail or Inca Road, this is rapidly becoming one of the most popular walks in the Andes. The route was used as a highway not only by the early Aymará but also by the Incas and the Spanish, and it's still a major thoroughfare for the Indians of today. It serves as a route to the humid Yungas over a relatively low pass in the Cordillera Real.

Nearly half of the trail's 40 km consists of expert pre-Inca paving and today's visitors can marvel at the quality of the engineering that was employed in the road's construction.

The walk itself will take only 12 to 14 hours, but it's best to plan several days for the excursion because transport to and from the trailheads can be unreliable.

In addition, it's best not to attempt this trip in the rainy months unless you enjoy staying cold and wet while slogging through ankle-deep mud. Since the end of the trail is in the Yungas, however, you can plan on some rain at any time of year.

To get to the upper trailhead from La Paz, you'll need to get to Ventilla, which is sometimes called Ventanilla. The easiest way is to hire a long-distance taxi at the *Centro de Taxis* on Calle Manco Capac. If you have a larger group, four or five people, this can be quite economical as it should only cost about US$20 for the one-way trip.

Another method is to take micro Ñ to its final stop at Cotacota and then walk up the road to the tranca at Ovejuyo. All transportation must stop there and, if you arrive in the morning, there should be no problem finding a truck to Ventilla.

It's quite difficult to find transport from Ventilla to San Francisco mine, which is the start of the Inca Trail, so you'll probably have to walk. About 150 metres past the town, take a left and walk up the rather poor road which leads to the mine. It should take about four hours to reach the trailhead on foot, but you may be able to flag down a passing vehicle for a lift – if one comes by.

The trail turns off to the right just past the mine and begins by climbing a series of switchbacks (hairpin bends) towards the pass at 4650 metres. There's a mine tunnel at the top which may be explored with a torch. The trail trends downhill from there all the way to Lower Chojlla where it begins to climb towards the road at the end of the hike.

From Upper Chojlla, at 2280 metres, a crowded bus leaves for La Paz early in the morning. If you'd rather not spend a night in that drab village, you can walk five km to the more pleasant town of Yanacachi or even out to the main Yungas road (about three km from Yanacachi) where you'll find lots of traffic headed back to La Paz.

Yunga Crúz

This little-known trail, which consists almost exclusively of pre-Hispanic paving, leads from the village of Chunavi to the south Yungas provincial capital of Chulumani.

The walk will require three or four days and transport from La Paz to Chunavi is via Ventilla (see the Taquesi Trek description). You'll have to find a truck heading towards Lambate and ask to be dropped at Chunavi. To return to La Paz, catch one of many daily trucks from the tranca at Chulumani or go with Flota Yunguña, at 7 am daily except Saturday.

The tourist office in La Paz distributes a free map of this route and the Club Andino Boliviano can help you with further details.

Other Treks

Detailed information on other hikes and treks in the Yungas and the Cordillera Real is available from Club Andino Boliviano.

Serious hikers and trekkers will want to pick up a copy of *Backpacking and Trekking in Peru and Bolivia* by Hilary and George Bradt. It's full of background information on the culture, geography, vegetation and wildlife of the Andes as well as general backpacking tips and suggestions pertinent to the mountain areas. It also includes detailed descriptions of trips varying in length from one hour to several weeks. It's highly recommended.

CHACALTAYA

The world's highest developed ski area lies atop a glacier on the slopes of Mt Chacaltaya, just a 1½ hour ride from downtown La Paz. The run lies between 5200 and 5400 metres elevation and the easily accessible summit of the mountain is 5600 metres above sea level.

Needless to say, if you're coming from the lowlands, you'll have to wait a few days in La Paz before attempting a visit to this altitude. Also essential are warm (preferably windproof) clothing, sunglasses and sunscreen.

See the Health section in the Facts for the Visitor chapter for information on ways to avoid or cope with soroche (altitude sickness). *Acetominophen* and *micoren* tablets, available in La Paz pharmacies, will adequately relieve discomfort during short-term visits to high altitudes.

The Club Andino Boliviano (tel 324682) takes groups to Chacaltaya for skiing on Saturdays and Sundays. To reserve a spot, give them a call or drop by their office at Calle Mexico 1638. The office is open weekdays from 9 am to noon and 2 to 7 pm.

If you arrive in La Paz late on Friday or Saturday evening after the office closes and would like to attend the following day, call Cristina Portocarrero (tel 791277), and she'll do her best to secure a place for you.

Ski trips leave from the club office at 8 am and arrive at Chacaltaya sometime before 10 am. You ski until 5 pm and are back in La Paz by 6.30 pm. The cost of transport is US$10; equipment rental costs US$10; and the rope tow is US$4.

The club is currently working on replacing the utterly confounding cable-tow now in operation at Chacaltaya and they have plans to build some luxury cabins at the slope, just down the hill from their present lodge.

If you're going skiing, make sure you eat well the previous day, but go easy during the trip because digestion at this altitude requires a great deal of the energy you'll be needing for other activities. Snacks and hot drinks are available at the lodge but if you want anything more you'll have to bring it from town. Watch out for the gringo pricing at the lodge; the concessionaires will try to charge you almost double the Bolivian price.

When you're choosing your ski equipment, be sure to get a good tow hook with a complete U-shaped curl to it, or you won't be able to negotiate the tow. Also, wear

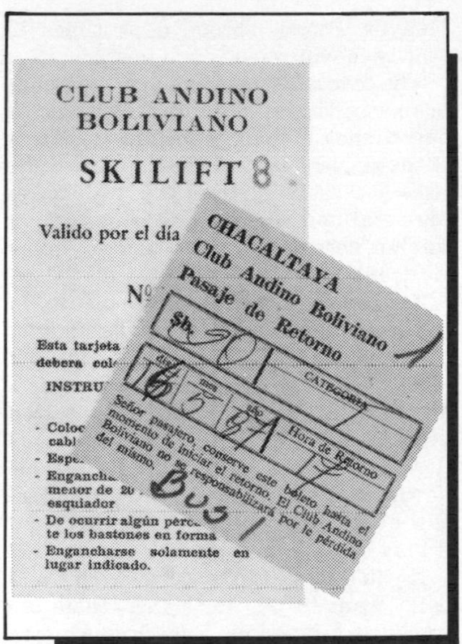

expendable clothing as it tends to get ripped up on the cable.

On Saturdays, the equipment is supplied by Club Andino and on Sundays by the ski shop in the lodge. If you go on Sunday and they don't have the right size boots, ask them to get some from the club. If you don't insist, you'll have to accept boots that don't fit, which will prove to be not only extremely uncomfortable but probably quite dangerous. This may take some coaxing, however, because the ski shop owner is very disagreeable when it comes to sharing business with the club.

The Chacaltaya slope itself is a bit steep and during the dry season can be extremely icy. There's no 'bunny hill', but even beginners can have a good time if they're not afraid of a few bumps.

If you're not interested in skiing, a trip to Chacaltaya can still be a rewarding experience. The views of La Paz, Illimani, Murarata and Huayna Potosí are spectacular. It is also an easy climb from the lodge to the summit of Mt Chacaltaya.

Carry warm clothing and water on this climb, which is just over one km. Take plenty of rests, say a 30-second stop every 10 steps or so and longer stops if needed, even if you don't feel tired. If you begin to feel light-headed, sit down, place your head between your knees and don't continue up or down until the feeling passes.

If you won't be in La Paz on a weekend, several tour agencies offer day trips to Chacaltaya during the week.

Places To Stay

If you'd like to spend the night at Chacaltaya, you can either sleep in Club Andino's lodge or ask the club equipment dispenser if there might be room to sleep in the laboratory just below the ski lodge. The latter is heated, and the scientific personnel there are friendly and they welcome visitors.

A warm sleeping bag, food, and *acetominophen* and *micoren* tablets are absolutely necessary for an overnight stay in either location.

If you've spent Saturday night on the slope and want to catch the Sunday bus back to La Paz, you may have to buy another ticket or stand in the queue on the way down. If the bus isn't full, there should be no problem using the second half of your Saturday ticket. At any rate, don't offer to pay again if they don't ask you to.

ZONGO VALLEY ICE CAVES

The beautiful Zongo Valley between Mt Chacaltaya and Huayna Potosí drops from 4624 metres to 1480 metres within 33 km. It contains the mining village of Milluni and the Bolivian Power Company's hydro-electric generating station. The ice caves below the glacier of Huayna Potosí, however, are the most visited attraction.

The best access to the caves from La Paz is by taxi from the *Centro de Taxis* which costs about US$40 for an all-day trip, for up to five people. Be sure that the driver understands that you want to go to Zongo

Valley via Milluni. Many taxi drivers expect you to ask for Chacaltaya, and may try to take you there anyway.

To reach the trail to the caves, you will pass the *Companía Minera del Sur* (the Southern Mining Company), near Milluni, where you must pass through a gate. The trip from the gate to the trailhead takes about 30 minutes by vehicle.

At about 4600 metres, you will find a trail off to the right. The taxi should leave you there at the entrance to Zongo park, but make sure the driver realises that he needs to wait for you while you ascend to the caves. The walk there and back will require a minimum of three hours.

From the entrance to the park the road continues winding downward into Zongo Valley, but you want to follow the trail upward. To the north is Huayna Potosí and at its foot is a man-made lake with milky blue-green water.

From there, follow the aqueduct along a ledge of the steep hillside for about 50 minutes. After you cross a bridge, walk 20 metres and cut off up the hill to the right, following the cairns which mark the trail. There are beautiful green pools in this area and an impressive view of Huayna Potosí, shrouded at times in swiftly-moving clouds and mist.

The cave is 100 metres above the bridge or about a 35-minute climb. Its entrance is easy to spot. It's a large opening at the foot of the glacier. The cave itself is also quite big – at least 50 metres deep, two metres high and four metres wide. A lantern or torch is necessary if you'd like to explore its deeper recesses.

At the entrance there's plenty of headroom. The walls capture the sunlight and you can see the layers of clear and cloudy blue ice inside. The ice is smooth and rounded into unusual shapes. As you proceed into the cave, it quickly gets darker, narrows and begins to slope downward. At this point, watch your feet as the cave is formed by running water and it may be wet or slippery.

If you'd like to go to Zongo Valley and don't want to pay for a taxi, there are trucks that sometimes leave from Avenida Baptista, near the cemetery in La Paz, very early in the morning. Return transport can be a problem, however, and you may have to spend the night in Milluni.

Lake Titicaca

Traditionally, this deep sapphire-blue lake which straddles the Peru-Bolivia border has been regarded as the highest navigable body of water in the world. It sits at an elevation of 3810 metres amid rolling, scrub-covered hills in the heart of the Altiplano north-west of La Paz.

While there are, in fact, higher lakes in both Peru and Chile which are navigable to smaller watercraft, Titicaca is still the highest lake which is actually serviced by scheduled commercial passenger vessels.

Its current dimensions are 233 km long, measured from north-west to south-east, and 97 km wide, from north-east to south-west. With a surface area of over 9000 square km, it is South America's second largest lake, after Venezuela's Lake

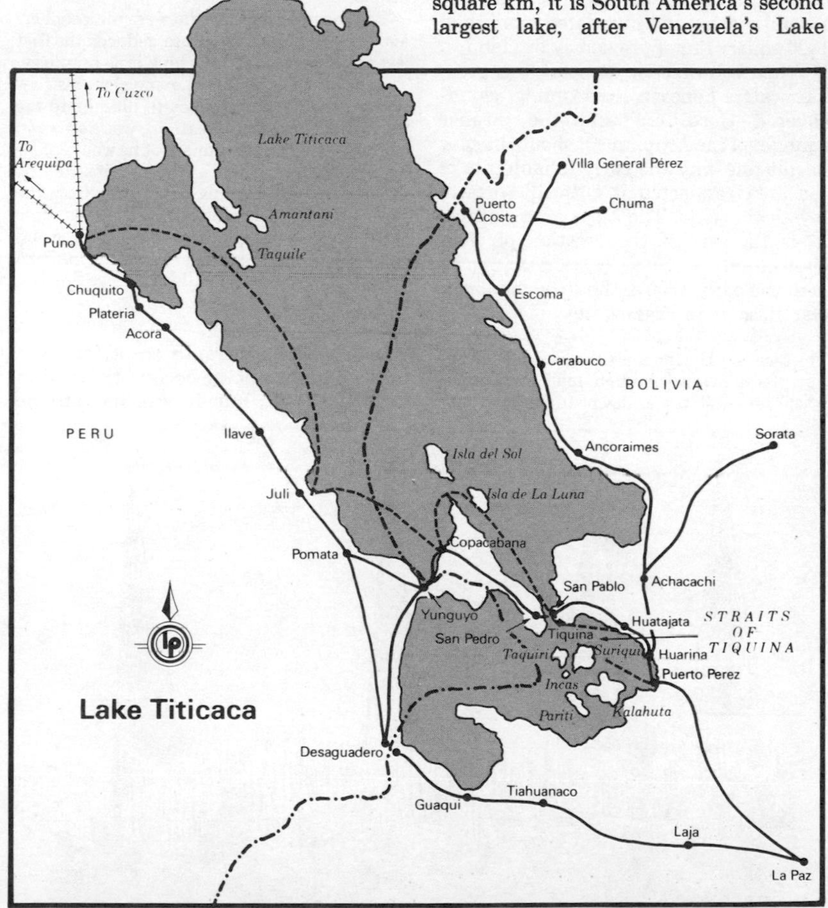

Maracaibo. It was only recently proved that Titicaca is not 'bottomless', as has long been rumoured, although its greatest depth has been measured at a staggering 457 metres.

Historically, the lake was much larger than it is today. In pre-Inca times the ceremonial centre of Tiahuanaco flourished on its shores. The ruins of that ancient city, however, are now 20 km away from the nearest contact with the lake.

More recently, during the flooding of 1985-86, the waters of Titicaca rose several metres and inundated more than 1000 square km of previously dry land.

When you first see its sparkling, gem-like waters beneath the looming, cloud-covered Cordillera and the intense sunlight of the Altiplano, it should be easy to imagine why the early inhabitants of the area connected it with all sorts of mystical events. The Incas even claimed it as the site of the creation of their civilisation.

In the early 1600's, the Inca chronicler Garcilaso de la Vega wrote:

> The Incas say that on this (Titicaca) Island, the Sun placed his two children, male and female, when he sent them down to instruct the barbarous people who dwelt on the Earth . . . They say that after the deluge, the rays of the Sun were seen on this island, and over the great lake, before they appeared in any other part.
>
> The first Inca, Manco Capac, taking advantage of the ancient legend and assisted by his own genius and wisdom, seeing that the Indians venerated the lake and the islands as sacred things, composed another legend saying that he and his wife (Mama Ocllo (Huaca] were children of the Sun and that their father had placed them on that island that they might thence pass through the country, teaching the people.
>
> The Incas Amautas, who were philosophers and learned men of the State, reduced the first legend to the second, teaching it as prophecy. They said that the Sun, having shed his first rays on that Island whence to illuminate the world (in the original Creation), was a sign and a promise that on the same spot he would place his own children, whence to go forth instructing the natives and drawing them away from the savage condition in which they lived, as those (Inca) kings actually did later. With those and similar legends the Incas made the Indians believe that they were children of the Sun.

Garcilaso was apparently sceptical of the Inca's claim to being born of the Sun in Lake Titicaca, but it was only to be

expected that such a legend would surface. The pre-Inca peoples of the Altiplano believed that the Sun itself and also their bearded, white supreme being *Viracocha* had both risen out of its brilliant and mysterious depths.

Titicaca Island, where it all took place, is near the village of Copacabana in Bolivian waters. It was renamed *Island of the Sun* by the Spaniards.

The lake is still revered by the people who live on its shores and islands. They fish its depths, gather its reeds to make canoes, farm its ancient terraces and normally lead peaceful lives beside the waters, all the while remembering that the Sun, which makes all things possible, was born there.

The floods of 1985-86, however, illustrated graphically another aspect of the control the lake has over the lives of its inhabitants. Highways, docks, fields, pastures and city streets disappeared beneath the rising waters. Adobe homes turned to mud and collapsed and 200,000 people in both Peru and Bolivia were displaced. The lake's only outlet, the Río Desaguadero, is still draining off the surplus rain that fell during those few months.

If you're visiting the area you can travel across the lake to ruin-strewn islands, see the remnants of Bolivia's most important archaeological site, join in a fiesta in the sacred village of Copacabana, or watch the reed canoes and sailboats plying these waters as they have done for over a millennium.

You can also just wander the heights overlooking the lake and realise that life hasn't really changed much in these parts since the days when the Incas were capturing the imaginations, and the lands, of the Aymará inhabitants with dazzling tales of their origins.

Visiting Titicaca's Peruvian islands or lakeside settlements is also interesting and as easy as just crossing the border.

LAJA

The tiny village of Laja, formerly known as Llaxa and Laxa, lies between La Paz and Tiahuanaco. When the Spanish captain Alonso de Mendoza was charged with locating a new rest stop and founding a city along the route from Potosí to the coast at Callao in Peru, he set out towards the north-west.

On 20 October 1548, he arrived in Laxa and declared it to be the chosen location. He soon changed his mind, however, and the site was quickly shifted to the nearby gold-bearing canyon where La Paz is today, so Laxa missed out.

In the Laja plaza there's a lovely alabaster sundial and an impressive church which was built in commemoration of Spanish victories over the Incas. The interior of the church is ornamented with gold, silver, wooden carvings and colonial artwork.

TIAHUANACO

Little is actually known about the Tiahuanaco people who constructed the great ceremonial centre on the southern shore of Lake Titicaca over a thousand years ago. Evidence of their civilisation has been found throughout the vast area that later became the Inca Empire. It's also apparent that the Tiahuanacans profoundly influenced the Incas, particularly in the area of religion.

Archaeologists generally agree that the civilisation that spawned Tiahuanaco rose around 600 BC. The ceremonial site was under construction around 700 AD, but after about 1200 AD the group had melted into obscurity, becoming another 'lost' civilisation.

The civilisation's development has been divided by researchers into five distinct periods, numbered Tiahuanaco I through V, each with its own outstanding attributes.

Tiahuanaco I is placed between the advent of the civilisation and the middle of the 5th century BC. Significant finds from this period include multicoloured

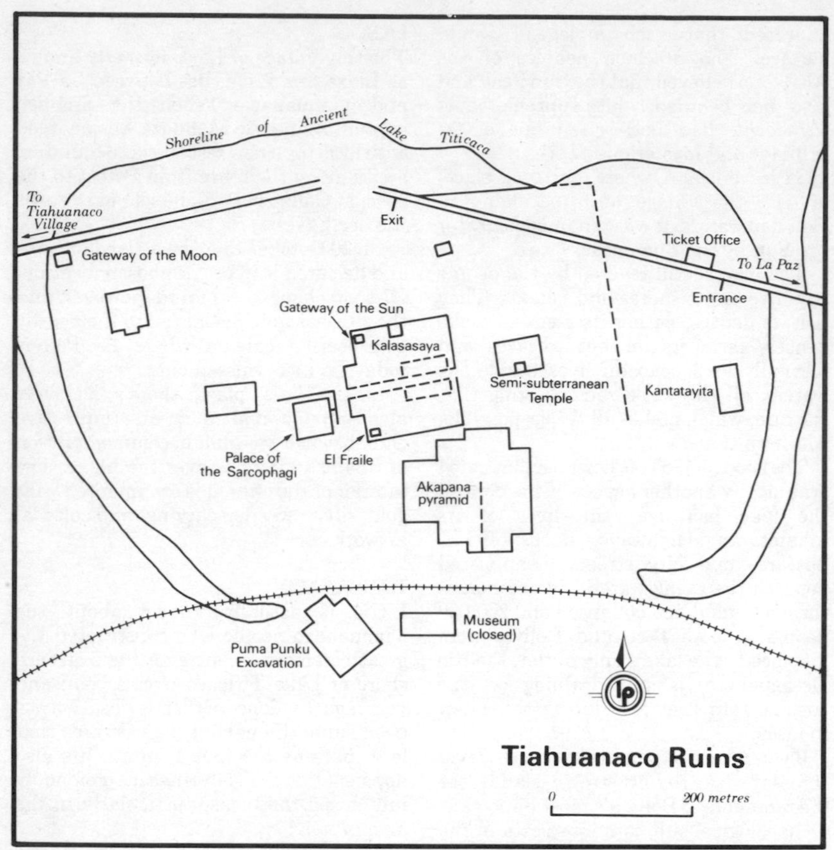

pottery and human or animal effigies in painted clay.

Ceramic vessels with horizontal handles were the hallmark of Tiahuanaco II which ended around the beginning of the Christian Era.

For the next 300 years, the third period produced geometrically-designed tri-colour pottery, sometimes decorated with images of stylised animals.

From 300 to 700 AD Tiahuanaco IV, also known as the Classic Period, developed. The large stone structures which may be seen at the site today were constructed during this period. Use of bronze and gold at this time is evidence of contact with groups further east in the Cochabamba Valley and to the west on the coast of Peru. Pottery representing human heads and faces with bulging cheeks indicate that the coca leaf had, at least that far back, come into use.

Tiahuanaco V, or the Expansive Period, lasted until the disappearance of the entire culture around 1200 AD. The quality of pottery produced declined significantly and large-scale monuments were no longer being constructed. There is some evidence that the construction of Tiahuanaco itself was halted, for some mysterious reason in the middle of the project, near the beginning of this period.

Pieces from Tiahuanaco I and II are no longer available for viewing since the on-site museum housing them is currently closed. Pieces from the three later epochs may be seen in museums all over the country, but especially in La Paz and Cochabamba.

When the Spanish arrived in South America, local Indian legends stated that Tiahuanaco had been the capital of the bearded white god *Viracocha*, and from his city he had reigned over the civilisation.

Whether it was a capital or not, Tiahuanaco was certainly a great ceremonial centre. At its height it was a city of possibly 20,000 inhabitants, encompassing approximately 2.6 square km.

Although only a very small percentage of the original site has been excavated, and what's left of it is less than overwhelming, Tiahuanaco does include the most imposing megalithic architecture of pre-Inca South America.

There are stone slabs weighing 175,000 kg, or more, strewn about the site in jumbled heaps. Oddly enough there are no quarries in the near vicinity which could have produced these stones. The nearest place that the basalt megaliths could have been brought from is on the Copacabana Peninsula, 40 km away across the lake.

Even the sandstone blocks had to be transported from a site over five km away. It's no wonder then that when the Spaniards asked local Indians how the buildings were constructed, they replied that it was with the aid of the god/leader *Viracocha*. They could conceive of no other plausible explanation.

The treasures of this ancient civilisation have literally been scattered to the four corners of the earth. Early stone and pottery finds were sometimes destroyed by religious zealots who considered them to be pagan idols and the gold was looted by the Spanish. Some of the work found its way to European museums; farmers destroyed pieces of it as they turned the surrounding area into pasture and cropland; the church kept some of the statues or sold them as curios; and the larger stonework went into Spanish construction projects, and even into the bed of the La Paz-Guaqui railroad line which passes just south of the site.

Fortunately, a portion of the treasure was preserved and left in Bolivia. A few of the larger anthropomorphic stone statues have been left on the site, or are displayed in the Open-Air museum in La Paz. The ruins themselves were so badly looted and disturbed, however, that much of the information they could have revealed about their builders is lost forever.

The most outstanding structure on the site is the semi-artificial pyramid of *Akapana*; a roughly square hill, over 16 metres high, the base of which covers a surface area of about 200 square metres.

There is an oval-shaped sunken area in the centre which some sources attribute to early, haphazard Spanish excavation; and others, because of the presence of a stone drain at one end, believe was used for water storage.

Much of its original construction material, however, went to build nearby homes and churches and these days, apart from what's left of a couple of monoliths, the pyramid is in a rather sorry state.

The walls of the nearly square ritual platform compound of the *Kalasasaya*, north of the pyramid, are constructed of huge blocks of red sandstone and andesite, and measure 130 metres long by 120 metres wide. The blocks are precisely fitted, to form the three metre high platform base.

Monolithic uprights flank the massive entrance steps up to the restored portico of the enclosure, beyond which is an interior courtyard and the ruins of priests' quarters. Other stairways lead up to secondary platforms on which there are

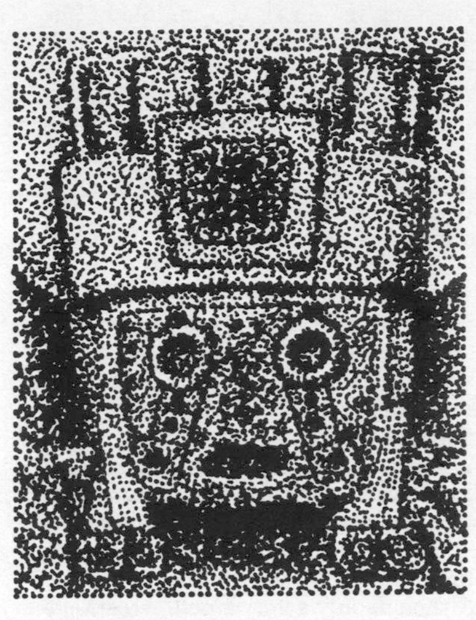

other monoliths and the famed Gateway of the Sun.

Standing at the north-west corner of the Kalasasaya, the most well-known structure at Tiahuanaco is the *Gateway of the Sun*. This megalithic gateway was carved from a single block of andesite and archaeologists assume that it was associated in some way with the Sun deity.

The surface of this fine-grained, grey volcanic rock is ornamented with low-relief designs on one side and a row of four deep niches on the other. Some believe that these may have been used for offerings to the Sun, while others maintain that the stone served as some kind of a calendar. The structure is believed to weigh over 44,000 kg.

There's a smaller, similar gateway carved with zoomorphic designs near the western end of the site, which is informally called the *Gateway of the Moon*.

Near the main entrance to the Kalasasaya, a stairway leads down into the *Semi-subterranean Temple*. A red sandstone structure, measuring 26 by 28 metres, the temple has a rectangular sunken courtyard whose walls are adorned with small carved stone faces.

To the west of the Kalasasaya is another rectangular area known as the *Palace of the Sarcophagi*. With dimensions of 55 by 60 metres, it is still in the process of excavation. It is surrounded by double walls and you can see the foundations of several houses.

The heap of rubble at the eastern end of the site is known as *Kantatayita*. Archaeologists are still trying to piece together the well-carved slabs and deduce some sort of meaning from them but they appear to be the huge design plans for a building.

Not far from the Tiahuanaco site is the excavation of *Puma Punku*, where megaliths of over 440,000 kg have been discovered. As in the case of Kalasasaya and Akapana, there is evidence that Puma Punku was begun with one type of material and finished with another. Part of it was constructed of enormous pieces of sandstone and the rest was of notched and jointed basalt blocks.

Admission to the Tiahuanaco site costs US$2 for foreigners and US$1 for Bolivians. Guides are available for about US$2.50 but you will have to bargain them down to this price. They'll initially ask up to US$20 just to see if someone will pay it.

There are good restaurants and an incredibly colourful Sunday market in the village of Tiahuanaco, which is just one km beyond the ruins.

Getting There & Away

Taxis may be hired from the *Centro de Taxis* for US$20 to US$[illegible] return, but try to bargain them down. A dozen or more tour agencies offer reasonably-priced guided full day and half-day tours to Tiahuanaco from La Paz.

Flota Ingavi leaves about eight times per day from Calle Jose Maria Asín near the La Paz cemetery. (Take any micro marked 'Cementerio' to get there.) From the corner above the flower market, the office is one block uphill and two blocks to the right. The trip costs US$1 each way.

Buses are crowded far beyond comfortable capacity, so plan on waiting an hour or two at the office for a seat reservation or the trip will be rather disagreeable. Even when people are hanging out the windows and doors, the drivers are still calling for more passengers.

In order to return to La Paz, you'll either have to flag down a passing micro, which will probably already be filled to overflowing before it reaches the ruins, or walk into town and catch one along the main street.

Micros going on to Guaqui, or to Desaguadero in Peru, leave from the main plaza in town or may be stopped as they're leaving the village. Again, expect crowds.

GUAQUI

Three hours by bus from La Paz, Guaqui sits beside and partially under Lake Huanamarka. Also known as Lake Wiñaymarka, or any of a half dozen other correct spellings, it is the southern extension of Lake Titicaca. Guaqui is only 20 minutes by micro beyond Tiahuanaco and not far from the Peruvian frontier at Desaguadero.

A tranquil little Altiplano town, it has a truly beautiful church with an altar of silver and some colonial artwork inside.

In Guaqui, evidence of the damage done in the '86 floods is still apparent. Half the town is in ruin and much of it is still under the waters of Lake Titicaca. There is no longer a train service from La Paz, and the famous lake steamer which ran between here and Puno was discontinued when the Guaqui port disappeared under rising flood waters.

Places to Stay

Residencial Guaqui is the nicest place to stay, but it was damaged in the flooding and is undergoing very slow repairs.

Alojamiento Herrera at 407 Avenida Arce is cheap but dirty and also closes for long periods of time when business is slow, which is quite often these days. The best bet is to ask around for sleeping quarters in a local home.

Getting There & Away

You can get to Guaqui from La Paz on the same bus that stops at Tiahuanaco. From Guaqui, you can catch a micro to Desaguadero in Peru for 25c, or a camión to the border.

From Desaguadero, you can go on to Puno or the border town of Yunguyo, both in Peru, or back into Bolivia to the sacred town of Copacabana.

The last bus to La Paz from Guaqui leaves from the main avenue in the lower part of town near the lake between 4 and 5 pm. The fare is US$1.75.

HUATAJATA

The tiny community of Huatajata lies on the shore of Lake Titicaca, in the Lake Huanamarka section, about midway between Copacabana and La Paz.

The only yacht club on the lake is headquartered in Huatajata. If you're interested in taking a spin around that part of the lake then ask the club for information, as the members sometimes hire out boats.

There's really not much to see in the town itself, it mainly serves as a base for trips to the islands in the southern section of Lake Titicaca, but it is a pleasant place to experience day-to-day life in a typical lakeside community. You'll soon realise that very little ever changes in Huatajata.

Each morning the fishermen take their boats out on their daily run and each afternoon they return to clean or sell the day's haul, while the women spend the days repairing nets, caring for children, weaving, cooking and cleaning fish.

In late spring or early summer, depending on the year, a small nearby community called Compi stages a folk festival with dancing, feasting and bicycle racing. The tourist office in La Paz will be able to provide more information about this popular event.

Places to Stay

The *Catari Brothers* run a very pleasant alojamiento where you can stay for US$2.50 per person. It's right on the shore and has magnificent views of the lake, especially at sunset. There's a sign for it on the main highway but not near the building itself; just look for a three-storey white house on the waterfront. If you have trouble finding it, just ask anyone in town for directions.

Another alojamiento is the *Wiñay Marka*, half a block from the highway. It's easy to find because it's the most imposing building in town. Rates there are also S$2.50 per person.

Places to Eat

Apart from the yacht club, the only places to eat in town are at the two alojamientos. Their specialties are – you guessed it – fish.

Getting There & Away

The buses which go through to Copacabana will not sell you an advance ticket if you're only going to Huatajata so you have to catch a bus from the corner of Manuel Bustillos and Kollasuyo near the cemetery in La Paz. They leave about every half hour between 4 am and 5 pm and also service other lakeside communities as far as Achacachi.

To return to La Paz, just flag down any bus going that direction along the main highway. The last one runs at about 6 pm.

HUANAMARKA ISLANDS

The three most visited islands in Lake Huanamarka are Suriqui, Pariti and Kalahuta, which can be easily seen in a few hours. It is also possible to camp overnight, especially on the more sparsely populated islands of Pariti and Kalahuta.

Kalahuta

Kalahuta, which in Aymará means 'stone houses', served as a cemetery for the Incas. The entire island is dotted with stone tombs several metres high.

Superstitious locals are afraid to live outside the island's one town of Quequaya and are also reluctant to venture anywhere at night due to legends of horrible fates befalling those who so desecrate the cemetery. If you choose to camp there, you'll have the island largely to yourself.

Along the shore of Kalahuta, you'll be able to see the ubiquitous *totora* reed for which this section of the lake is famous. Fishermen and farmers travel to the island's main bay during the day in totora reed boats, while others come to gather the reed which will be used in the construction of these vessels.

Top: Guaqui, Lake Titicaca before flood (TM)
Left: Puya Raimondi (VN)
Right: Totora reed boat, Huatajata – Lake Titicaca (WH)

Top: Entrance to Moorish Cathedral – Copacabana (DS)
Left: Moorish Cathedral – Copacabana (DS)
Right: Children's coffins – La Paz (TW)

Pariti

Like Kalahuta, much of Pariti is surrounded by marshes of totora reed. It is a small friendly island with little to offer but a view of the tranquil lifestyle of those who live there. The Indians there trade cheese, fish and woollen goods in Huatajata for items from the Yungas and La Paz. Their sailboats, used for fishing, are beautiful to watch as they slice through the Titicaca waters in search of fish.

Suriqui

Suriqui, the best known island in the southern portion of Lake Titicaca, is famous for its totora reed boats, which continue to be used in the daily lives of the inhabitants.

The process of construction is quite simple. The green reeds are gathered from the shallows of the lake and left in the sun to dry. Once they are free of all moisture, they are gathered into four fat bundles and lashed together with grass. Sometimes a sail of reeds is added. These bloated little canoes don't last very long as far as watercraft go. After six months or so, they get waterlogged and begin to sink and rot, so in order to increase their life span they're often stored on the lakeshore.

In the early 1970s Dr Thor Heyerdahl, the rather unconventional Norwegian explorer and scientist, solicited the help of the master Aymará shipbuilders of Suriqui Island to design and construct his vessel the *Ra II*.

Heyerdahl hoped to prove his theory that there was early contact and migration between the ancient peoples of North Africa and those of the Americas by demonstrating it was possible to travel great ocean distances using the boats of the time.

Four of the Aymará shipbuilders accompanied him on the expedition and one of them, Paulo Esteban, now operates a small museum near the dock in Suriqui.

Esteban's *Museo San Pablo* has all sorts of paraphernalia about the *Ra II* and the other Heyerdahl expeditions which also employed the use of ancient design boats, such as the *Ra I*, *Tigris* and the *Kon Tiki*. He also displays the various types of boats he has built himself and he sells small meticulously-constructed models. He's an interesting and humble person and is very happy to chat with visitors who are interested in his work.

Incas

This is a small, uninhabited island near Suriqui. Legend has it that this tiny island was part of the Inca system of underground passageways reputed to link many parts of the Inca Empire with the capital at Cuzco.

Getting There & Away

Any of the Aymará fishermen in Huatajata will probably be glad to take a day off to shuttle tourists out to the islands for a reasonable rate.

The most knowledgeable and economical guides, however, seem to be the Catari Brothers. Ramon Catari will take up to 15 people to Kalahuta, Pariti and Suriqui for about US$30 and will provide a running commentary on the legends, customs, people, history and natural features of the lake. He'll give you as much time as you'd like on each island and introduce you to many of his friends living on them, who will in turn provide insights into the Aymará way of life around Lake Titicaca.

If you'd like to spend the night on one of the islands, you can negotiate to be fetched the following day.

Copacabana

A sunny town of red tile and adobe on the southern shore of Lake Titicaca, Copacabana was established around a splendid bay between two hills, Cerro Calvario and Cerro Sancollani.

The Sanctuary of Copacabana, as it is also known, has been a religious haven for

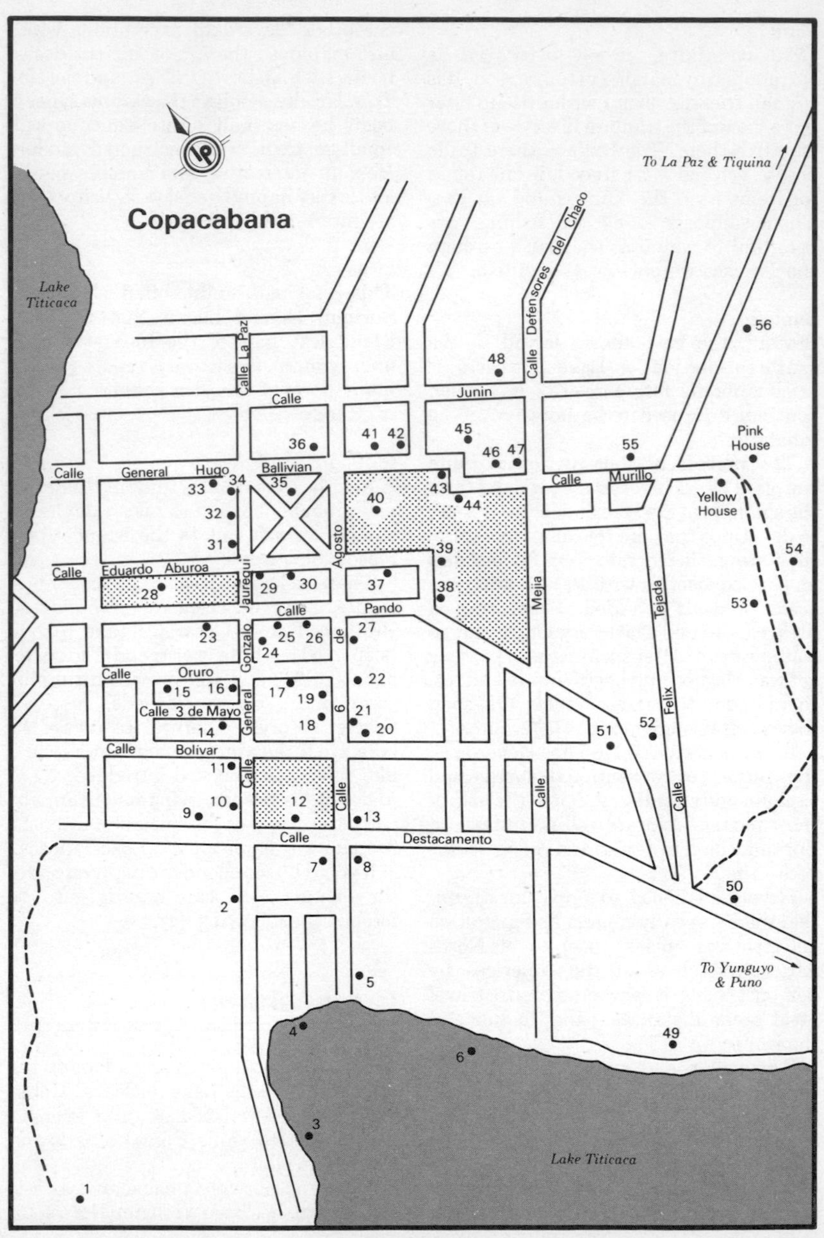
Copacabana
Lake Titicaca
To La Paz & Tiquina
Calle La Paz
Calle Defensores del Chaco
Calle Junin
Calle General Ballivian
Hugo
Calle Murillo
Pink House
Yellow House
Calle Eduardo Abaroa
Calle Gonzalo Jauregui
Calle 6 de Agosto
Calle Pando
Calle Oruro
Calle 3 de Mayo
Calle General
Calle Bolivar
Calle Mejia
Calle Felix Tejada
Calle Destacamento
To Yunguyo & Puno
Lake Titicaca

1	Cerro Calvario & Mountain Shrines	30	Transportes Manco Capac Bus Terminal
2	Alojamiento Bolívar	31	Transtur 2 de Febrero Bus Terminal
3	Armada Boliviana (Naval Base)	32	City Hall
4	Boat Launch	33	Post Office
5	Alojamiento Las Playas	34	Police & Court House
6	Beach	35	Plaza 2 de Febrero
7	Alojamiento Kota Kahuaña	36	Residenciál Patria
8	Prefectural Hotel & Grounds	37	Pension El Turista
9	Alojamiento Urinsaya	38	Hospederia
10	Alojamiento San José	39	Alojamiento Imperio
11	Ambassador Hotel	40	Cathedral
12	Bus park	41	Alojamiento Illimani
13	Hospital	42	Alojamiento Cochabamba
14	Alojamiento Panamericano	43	Plazuela Tito Yupanqui
15	Residenciál Copacabana	44	Church Dispensary
16	Alojamiento 2 de Febrero	45	Library & ENTEL Office
17	Residenciál Casa Blanca	46	Alojamiento Manco Capac
18	Playa Azul	47	Alojamiento Tunari
19	Banco del Estado Bolivia	48	Alojamiento Sucre
20	Food Market/Money Exchange	49	Beach Camping Area
21	Pensión Aransaya	50	Customs
22	Paso del Inca	51	Plazuela Manco Capac
23	Alojamiento Primavera	52	Alojamiento Titicaca
24	Residenciál La Porteñita	53	Inca Road to Niño Calvario/Cerro Sancollani
25	Alojamiento El Turista	54	Ancient Aqueduct
26	Alojamiento Antofagasta	55	Alojamiento Emperador
27	Café 6 de Agosta	56	Cemetery
28	Mercado & food stalls		
29	Restaurant Puerta del Sol		

centuries, ever since the Incas established it in honour of the Sun and his children Manco Capac and Mama Huaca. When the Spanish Christians arrived, the town fell into the hands of the Dominicans and the Augustinians and a pagan-Christian relationship developed in the religious life of the townspeople.

In the 16th century miracles began happening in the Sanctuary of Copacabana, after the presentation to the town of a carved, black wooden statue of the Virgin Mary. The Moorish cathedral was built then, to accommodate the huge number of Indian pilgrims.

Copacabana serves as a pleasant stopover on the Straits of Tiquina route from La Paz to Puno and Cuzco in Peru. The best time to visit is during a fiesta when the otherwise sleepy little town springs to life with pilgrims and visitors from all over Bolivia.

There is a small fiesta every Saturday, complete with music and market activities, but the three main annual events are Good Friday, Independence Day (August) and the Festival of the Virgin (February).

The climate of Copacabana is generally pleasant and sunny with most of the annual rain falling in mid-summer (December and January). At an altitude of over 3800 metres, however, it is subject to bitterly cold nights and water-cooled winds from the lake. This is immediately obvious the moment the sun sets, when the temperature drops 5°C within a few seconds.

Since the air is so thin, it also conducts

scorchingly high levels of ultraviolet radiation. So remember to use a reliable sunscreen, especially when you're near the lake receiving reflected rays off the water, and you should wear some sort of hat if you're outside for any length of time.

Information

Post & Communications The post office is on Ballivián, near the corner of La Paz, just off the Plaza 2 de Febrero. It is open whenever its employee is available to be there, which isn't too often.

ENTEL is next door to the library on Plazuela Tito Yupanqui. It's closed on Sundays.

Changing Money The bank, Banco del Estado Bolivia, is next to the Playa Azul Hotel on Calle 6 de Agosto. It is reportedly open Wednesday through Sunday mornings, but I found this to be a gross generalisation. Their fanciful display of travellers' cheque stickers, plastered on the tellers' windows, are apparently only decorative – they will not exchange travellers' cheques. Be sure to carry a supply of cash from either La Paz or Peru.

Do not under any circumstances try to change Peruvian intis at the bank or you'll lose up to 50% of the value.

The Hotel Playa Azul will exchange Peruvian *intis* as will the small food market on Calle Bolivar, near the Pensión Aransaya.

The best rates, however, can be found in the small store next to Transportes Manco Capac on the Plaza 2 de Febrero. The staff are also happy to exchange US$ cash.

In Peru, rates comparable to these are available around the plaza in Yunguyo, just beyond the Peruvian frontier.

Things to See

Apart from the huge cathedral, and the small Manco Capac monument in the *plazuela* (little plaza) of the same name, most of the area's attractions are in the surrounding hills and countryside.

The Cathedral

The sparkling white Moorish cathedral, built between 1610 and 1620, dominates the town. The building itself is, typically, a repository for both European and local religious art, including the famous *Virgin of Candelaria*. The black statue was carved in the late 1570s by the Indian artist Francisco Yupanqui, grandson of the Inca Tupac Yupanqui. The Virgin, encased in glass above the main altar, is never moved from the cathedral as the locals believe that its disturbance will cause a devastating flood of Lake Titicaca.

The beautiful church courtyard, just outside the main cathedral, is usually ablaze with the colours of wild and domestic flowers. There's a small museum just off the courtyard but it's only open on Sundays, and even then it's only accessible to prearranged tours, so individual travellers have little chance of getting in.

Cerro Calvario

A trail to the summit of Cerro Calvario, the hill to the north-west of town, begins near the church at the end of Calle Destacamento. It climbs past the *Stations of the Cross* to the shrines of the *Sorrows of Mary*.

The summit, which provides a superb view of both the lake and the town, can be reached in about half an hour, taking frequent altitude rests into account.

Cerros Sancollani & Copacate

To the south-east of town, the slopes of Cerro Sancollani and Cerro Copacate are dotted with Inca *asientos* (seats), and ancient agricultural terraces. These hills offer unrestored and little-known ruins, within an hour's walk of town.

To get there, follow Calle Murillo to its end where, between two brightly-coloured houses, it turns into a cobbled Inca road.

Fifty metres or so beyond this point, a stone aqueduct leads off to the left. The entrance is a metre or so above the road level, so look carefully. The easiest access to the mountains is from the saddle at the top of the aqueduct.

The hill just to the north of the saddle is called Niño Calvario, or 'Little Calvary', and its weirdly rugged rock formations and oddly-arranged piles of boulders are worth exploration. A trail leads from the end of Calle Murillo to the *Horca del Inca*, or Inca Gallows, a trilithic gate perched oddly on the hillside.

If you're going walking in these hills, beware of a particularly insidious variety of thorn bush which grows there and creates ribbons of skin at the slightest contact. Watch what you're brushing against!

Tribunal del Inca

On the other side of town, just below the La Paz road near the cemetery, is the site known as the Tribunal del Inca. The original purpose of this place is unknown, but there are about seven carved stones with *asientos* (seats) and basins. It's not overly impressive but the place is simply hopping with thousands of small frogs, if you're interested in such things.

From the Tribunal, a short walk down the road toward La Paz will bring you to the *Baños del Inca*, or Inca baths, which are more stone basins of unknown purpose.

Market

Like most Bolivian markets, the one in Copacabana, between Calles Pando and Eduardo Abaroa, opens at around 6 am and continues until well after dark.

Local specialties include handmade miniatures of Lake Titicaca reed boats; huge mutant peanuts; a wide variety of Andean potatoes; and puffed *choclo*, a South American version of popcorn which, if crispy, can be quite delicious. You can also find the dark-coloured felt derby hats worn by local women. The hat-making process can be seen at several shops around town. Ask at the market for present locations.

Fiestas

Copacabana hosts three major fiestas during the year.

On *Good Friday* the town is full of pious *peregrinos*, or pilgrims, who have travelled to Copacabana to do penance at the Stations of the Cross on Cerro Calvario. Many of them journey on foot from La Paz, 158 km away.

Once on the hill's summit, they light incense and buy miniature homes, buses, automobiles, shovels, boxes of food, and suitcases full of phony US dollars in the hope that they will be blessed with the real thing during the year of their pilgrimage. In this respect, the festival bears a resemblance to the famous Alasitas Fair celebrated in La Paz in January.

In the evening, starting at dusk from the cathedral, the pilgrims join a solemn candlelit procession through the town. Before them, go a statue of Christ in a glass coffin and a copy of the Virgin of Candelaria, the patron saint of Bolivia. A local priest relates the significance of the holiday through a microphone, a military band plays dirges and city hall's audio system blares *Ave Maria* for all to hear.

From Good Friday through Easter, the cars and trucks that carry the pilgrims home are decorated with bright plastic garlands and blessed with alcohol for the journey ahead.

The *Independence Day Fiesta* lasts for an entire week (3 to 10 August) and is far more animated than the Good Friday celebration.

It is characterised by around the clock music, parades, fireworks and an amazingly high, and continuous, consumption of alcohol. Although Copacabana is relatively free of petty thievery during the remainder of the year, this is a time to beware of light-fingered lifters who may prey on careless celebrants.

On the first two days of February,

Copacabana celebrates the *Fiesta de la Virgen de Candelaria* in honour of the black wooden statue housed above the altar in the church. Although this fiesta is celebrated to varying degrees around the entire country, Copacabana - which is never slow to find an excuse to party - puts on an extra-big bash.

Indians and dancers from both the Peruvian and Bolivian shores and islands of Lake Titicaca show up and perform traditional Aymará dances, and there's much music, drinking and feasting.

Places to Stay

For a town of its size, Copacabana is well-endowed with hotels, *residenciales* and *alojamientos* so, unless you arrive at the height of a fiesta, you should have no trouble finding acceptable, inexpensive accommodation.

Two fairly nice hotels dominate the higher end of the exclusively low-priced selection of hotels in Copacabana.

The *Playa Azul* on Calle 6 de Agosto offers clean rooms and hot water for US$3.50 per person with/without private bath. For a little extra (a total of US$7.50) you can also have three meals a day, but this is not recommended as the food offered is meagre and marginal.

The *Hotel Prefectural*, near the beach, affords a lovely view of the lake and surrounding mountains. It also has a nice restaurant, pool tables, sundecks, clean rooms, and live entertainment on weekends, for US$10.50 per person with the meal plan and US$4.50 without.

Most of the other lodgings in town fall within the 75c to US$2 range with prices doubling during fiestas.

I highly recommend the *Alojamiento Urinsaya* at 390 Calle Destacamento. It has super-clean airy rooms, hot showers for several hours a day, and only costs US$1.25 per person. There is a laundry sink and a sun deck. The proprietor, Señor Gaspar Baltazar, is a veritable fount of information on the history and location of Inca ruins in the area and he is happy to provide detailed directions to some of the more obscure sites.

Nearby is the *Alojamiento San Jose* with equally clean rooms and hot showers for US$1 per night. The *Alojamiento Las Playas*, on Calle 6 de Agosto near the beach, offers hot water, a nice view of the lake and a restaurant. The rooms cost 75c per person and it's probably the best bargain in town.

A new hotel called *Alojamiento Kota Kahuaña*, at 15 Avenida Busch, is becoming very popular with travellers. It's friendly and costs only US$1.50 per person. One drawback is that, although they advertise a lake view, some of the rooms lack windows; so check your room first.

Near the Plaza 2 de Febrero are the *Residencial Patria*, which is very friendly, the *Alojamiento Illimani* and the *Alojamiento Cochabamba*, all of which are clean and have restaurants and hot showers and cost US$1 to US$1.50 per night.

Residencial Copacabana on Calle Oruro, *Residencial La Porteñita* on Calle General Gonzalo Jaurequi, and *Alojamiento Imperio* on Calle Conde de Lemus (off Pando), offer similar amenities in the same price range - about US$1.50 per person.

The *Alojamiento El Turista*, on Calle Pando, was gaining a reputation as the travellers' hotel in Copacabana but at this point, I wouldn't recommend it due to reports of theft on the part of the staff.

The *Ambassador Hotel*, on Calle General Gonzalo Jaurequi, has private baths, sundecks, a nice courtyard and the rooms cost US$2. *Paso del Inca*, at 115 Calle 5 de Agosto, has gaudy Inca-like decorations, hot water sometimes and a pleasant courtyard area. It costs 50c per night.

If possible, avoid *Alojamiento Antofagasta* on Calle Pando, as it is quite dirty. *Alojamientos 2 de Febrero* and *Panamericano* (see the map) offer no amenities and the proprietors are

unfriendly, so they are not recommended unless accommodation is tight.

Both the water and electric utilities in Copacabana are highly unreliable and can be expected to fail for at least several hours per day. When hotels claim to have hot showers, that means they have hot water available when the water and electric services coincide.

Camping

Although the slopes around Copacabana are generally steep and rocky, there are several excellent campsites in the area. Refer to the Around Copacabana map.

The field across the dirt road from the beach is fairly private and comfortable. The summits of Cerro Sancollani and Niño Calvario both have smooth, grassy saddle areas suitable for tent camping. They also provide magnificent views of the lake, the surrounding farms and villages, and even the distant Andean Cordillera. Another pleasant campsite is the high point of the Inca road toward Yunguyo, less than a km beyond the southern end of Calle Murillo.

Places to Eat

Standard fare in Copacabana includes *asado de cordero*, char-broiled lamb; *churrasco*, barbecued steak; *lomo* and *brazuelo* back and shoulder of beef; and *trucha*, trout from Lake Titicaca.

The trout were introduced in 1939 by foreign pisciculturists in order to improve the protein content in the diet of the local people. For many years the trout were also tinned and exported, but that came to an end when the number of fish was severely depleted. Today, however, the lake produces the largest rainbow trout in the world and definitely some of the most delicious.

There is little originality in the methods of preparation of any dish; all are served with dry rice, fried potatoes and lettuce.

The *Pensión Aransaya* on Calle 6 de Agosto is the best restaurant in town but, surprisingly, not the most expensive. The staff are friendly and offer excellent food, service and variety. Expect to pay about US$2.50 for a meal of trout with coffee, tea, cocoa or beer.

Café 6 de Agosto, just up the street, is relatively expensive for the quality and has a very limited menu, but it is a clean and friendly place.

Alojamiento Titicaca, on Calle Felix Tejada, also has reasonably-priced meals with good soup and average dinners. It is immensely popular with locals.

On the plaza, the *Restaurant Puerto del Sol* offers drinks, television and superior service, but the food doesn't live up to expectations.

If you're looking for a quick snack, there's a sweet little old lady who sells coffee, cocoa and bread near the *Alojamiento Bolivar*, on Calle General Gonzalo Jaurequi.

As usual, the bargain basement of the food scene is found in the market food stalls where numerous small operations compete fiercely for your business. You can eat a generous meal of trout or beef for a pittance, while a contingency of the town's canine population patiently awaits a handout.

Getting There & Away

To/From La Paz The journey from La Paz to Copacabana is quite wonderful as it follows a magnificent route across the Altiplano to the Straits of Tiquina, where you and your bus are ferried between San Pablo and San Pedro separately. (This is because the bus ferries have been known to turn over in the water).

The tourist buses that are actually small micros provide the best and least crowded viewing opportunities along the way. Two major companies operate between La Paz and Copacabana daily.

Transportes 2 de Febrero (La Paz tel 377181) leaves La Paz at 8 am and 3 pm daily and arrives in Copacabana five hours later. Most locals use this and the other line, *Transportes Manco Capac* (La Paz tel 350033), which leaves at 7 am and 1.30 pm daily.

The former charges US$2.25 and the latter US$2.50 for the journey; but neither of these prices covers the cost of the ferry across the Straits of Tiquina, which is about 20c.

Numerous tourist buses, slightly more expensive at US$4 to US$5 each way, are also available. The tourist office on Avenida 16 de Julio (the Prado) will book it for you and arrange hotel pickup. I recommend *Turisbus* whose office is in the Residenciál Rosario in La Paz.

If you're heading to La Paz from Copacabana, Transportes Manco Capac departs Monday through Saturday at 7 am and 1 and 3 pm; and on Sundays at 4 pm. Transportes 2 de Febrero leaves at 8 am daily. The trip takes about five hours, provided the Tiquina ferry is readily available.

Vicuña Tours leaves daily, except Monday, at 1 pm from Pensión Aransaya where advance tickets may be purchased for US$4. If you don't have an advance ticket, numerous micros gather around the plaza between noon and 2 pm and you can buy a ticket from the driver at the time of departure.

To/From Peru There's an abundance of tourist bus companies that operate between Puno, in Peru, and Copacabana. You need only walk down the main street in Puno to be deluged with offers of cheap transportation to Copacabana and beyond. The average rate is about I/120 (intis) or US$3 each way. The trip takes two hours, excluding customs which can become quite involved. All transport from Puno to Bolivia leaves between 8 and 9 am.

Avoid *Profian Tours* on this or any other route as travellers report they are notorious for taking your money and not delivering the transportation.

If you're coming from Peru and need a visa, there is a Bolivian consulate in Yunguyo. Micro drivers from Puno will stop and wait while you get a visa to enter Bolivia. Some nationalities, mostly Latin Americans, must register with the police before entering Bolivia through Copacabana. Drivers will also wait while you take care of this formality, if necessary.

Heading towards Puno from Copacabana, you should wait at the plaza or at the Pensión Aransaya around midday. Any minibus with Peruvian license plates will be going to Puno and there is no shortage of them! The trip takes about two hours excluding customs and costs US$3.

Tours

A number of guided excursions of Lake Titicaca which originate in La Paz include a stop in Copacabana, usually around lunch time. You have a choice of hydrofoils, cruise ships and land transport of all descriptions. For those with limited time and unlimited funds, this is a quick way to 'do' Titicaca.

For some suggestions, see the listing of companies under Tours in the Getting Around chapter. A reasonable price estimate for any type of water transport tour of the lake is US$50 to US$100 per day. Some multi-day tours which include Lake Titicaca can also include Cuzco and Machu Picchu or other Peruvian destinations.

ISLANDS OF THE SUN & MOON

Isla del Sol

The Island of the Sun, was known to early inhabitants as Titicaca, or 'Rock of the Puma', the name which was eventually given to the entire lake. The island lies two hours by slow launch from the beach at the end of Calle 6 de Agosto in Copacabana.

The Isla del Sol has been credited as the birthplace of all sorts of important entities, including the Sun itself. It was

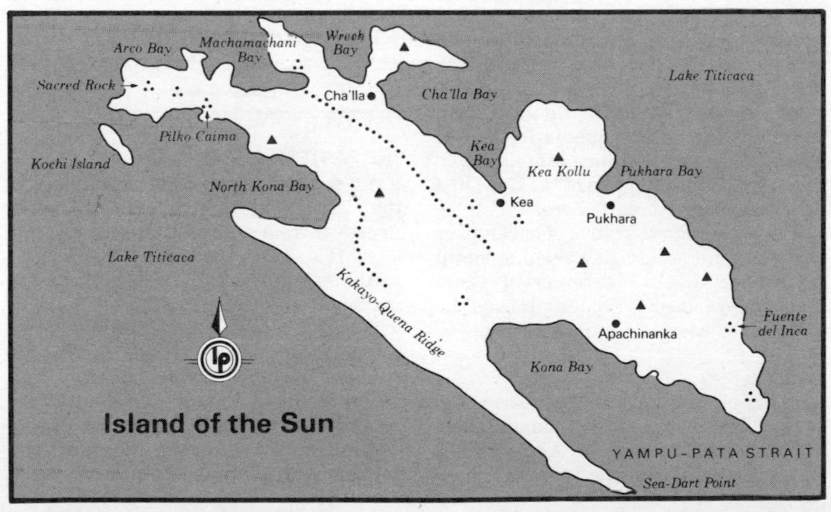

there also that the bearded white god *Viracocha* and the first Incas, Manco Capac and his sister/wife Mama Huaca, all mystically made their first appearance, under direct orders of the Sun. Modern-day Aymará and Quechua inhabitants of Peru and Bolivia still accept these legends as fact, so the island holds a very sacred place in local folklore.

The sacred rock where the Inca creation legend began is on the north-west corner of the island. On the shore nearby, a set of Inca steps lead up from the boat landing site and a trail follows an ancient route to the main ruins of *Pilco Caima*, which include the two storey *Inca's Palace*.

The ruins are worth a good look but it's also pleasant to visit the tiny traditional villages; explore the island's dry slopes, which are covered with sweet smelling *koa* (incense) brush; or hike over the ancient terraces, which are still planted in potatoes and tomatoes by the families that live there.

To the north-east are the ruins of the *Temple of the Sun* and near the eastern shore is the *Fuente del Inca*, or the Inca's Fountain.

Isla de la Luna

The Island of the Moon, formerly known as *Koati*, was the place where *Viracocha* commanded the moon to rise into the sky.

It's a very peaceful little island surrounded by clear aquamarine water. There are ruins of an Inca temple and a 'nunnery', for the Virgins of the Sun, in a valley on the north-east shore.

The walk up to the grove of eucalyptus on the summit, where a few shepherds still graze their flocks, is rewarded by a spectacular vista of Cerro Illampú and the entire snow-covered Cordillera Real.

Places to Stay

It is possible to camp just about anywhere on the hills or shores of both islands, away from the populated areas. An overnight stay will also allow time for much more serious exploration of these fascinating islands than is possible in a brief day trip from Copacabana.

Getting There & Away

There are numerous launches and sailboats available for the journey to one or both islands. You should arrange in advance with the pilot how long you want to spend at each island or you may find yourself very short on time.

Be sure to carry food and water since it's not possible to visit the ruins *and* the villages in a half-day trip. A good sunscreen will also prove invaluable; remember the Sun was born here, and he's still going strong.

To hire a boat, show up at the beach in Copacabana between 6.30 and 8 am. A sail-boat, for six people, will cost about US$20 for a visit to Isla del Sol. The trip can be done in six hours but allow a bit longer as the wind can be fickle.

A launch will cost about US$50, for up to 12 people, and you can visit both islands in an easy eight-hour trip. If you only want to visit the Isla del Sol then a launch will cost from US$20 to US$30. The amount of competition for passengers at the time you arrive will determine the bargain you can strike.

If you plan to spend the night on the islands, remember to arrange return transport before you go.

THE EASTERN SHORE

If you're heading north from Huatajata to the Peru-Bolivia border area at Puerto Acosta there are a few places of interest along this side of the lake.

About 90 km north of La Paz is the large market town of Achacachi, just north of which is the turn off to the delightful colonial town of Sorata (see the Yungas chapter), about 50 km further on.

The church in Ancoraimes, about 20 km north of Achacachi, features a lovely ornamental screen above the altar; the colonial township of Carabuco has a colourful Sunday market; and from Escoma (165 km north of La Paz) you can visit some nearby valleys.

It may be possible to cross into Peru from Puerto Acosta near the border, but it will require some effort as there is no public transport.

PERUVIAN LAKE TITICACA

Half of Lake Titicaca lies within Peru and there are many worthwhile places to visit on that side too.

The principal settlement on the Peruvian shore is Puno and most excursions begin there. In the vicinity of Puno, you can visit the *chullpas* (towers) of Sillustani, which were burial chambers used for the storage of mummies.

The floating islands of the *Urus* are another extremely popular attraction. Although the pure Urus tribe is gone now, their descendants, of mixed blood, continue to live on artificial totora reed islands in the middle of the lake.

Two larger natural islands, Taquile and Amántani, are also frequently visited as they're communities of relatively pristine Indian culture.

From Puno rail lines head north to Cuzco and Machu Picchu, and south-west to Arequipa where connections can be made to Lima and the rest of coastal Peru. If you're after more information on this fascinating country, pick up a copy of Lonely Planet's *Peru – a travel survival kit* by Rob Rachowiecki. It describes in detail anything you'll need to know about travelling in this ancient land.

The Yungas

The Yungas, where steep jungle covered cliffs loom above humid cloud-filled gorges, form a distinct natural division between the cold and barren Altiplano and the level Amazon rainforests which cover all of northern Bolivia. The word Yungas means simply 'valleys' and valleys they are.

Above the Yungas stand the lofty Cordillera Real, while the minor transition zone between the valleys and the flat lowlands is called the Alto Beni Region. A trip from the 4600-metre El Cumbre pass into the Alto Beni entails a loss of 4343 metres elevation in 80 km.

Despite the extreme humidity and precipitation, which can be tiresome, settlers have long been attracted to the Yungas for a number of reasons. While the climate overall is much more agreeable than on the Altiplano and the physical beauty of the place is astonishing, to say the least, such things don't tend to motivate Bolivians as much as pure economic considerations.

The first major draw to the Yungas, in the early days of the Inca Empire, was the discovery of gold in the valley of the Río Tipuani. Naturally the gold-crazed Spanish got in on the deal as soon as they appeared on the scene, and forced the local population into labour along the Yungas streams. The Spaniards received a fortune from this incredibly productive area, and even today there are still a few prospectors haphazardly making a living there.

Most of the inhabitants involved in agricultural activities live in the intermediate altitudes, roughly between 600

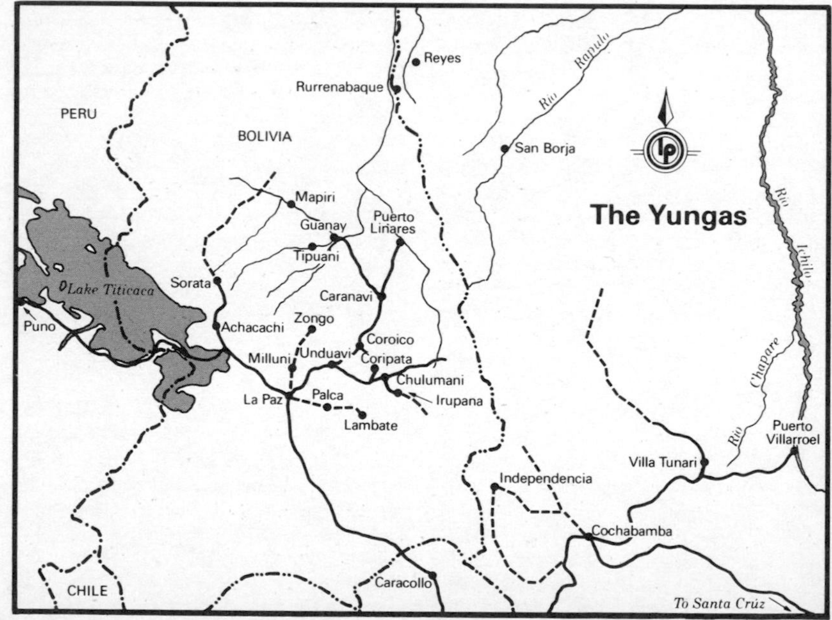

and 1800 metres. Sugar, citrus fruits, bananas and coffee are grown in large enough quantities to adequately supply the highlands with these products and transportation is plentiful even if the route is difficult between the valleys and the heavily-populated areas higher up.

The Yungas are also the primary area of coca production in Bolivia. This activity is centred on the village of Coripata and extends towards the South Yungas capital of Chulumani.

The climate of the region is humid and rainy throughout most of the year. The bulk of the heavy precipitation falls between November and March and winter rains are much gentler. The average temperature year round is about 18°C, but daytime temperatures in the 30s, accompanied by motivation-stifling humidity, are common.

The Yungas consist of two political provinces of the La Paz Department, North and South Yungas, with their seats of government in Coroico and Chulumani. The area serves as a lowland resort for the residents of the chilly highlands and the area is growing in popularity as a destination for heat-hungry Altiplano-dwelling Bolivians and foreign travellers.

Coroico and Chulumani are the principal centres of transportation and commerce. The smaller villages of Guanay and Sorata are also of interest, and numerous similar agricultural villages dot the countryside all across the region. The larger, equally uninteresting towns of Caranavi, Coripata and Irupana have little to offer the visitor but a quiet place to relax and enjoy the tropical heat and lush vegetation.

Most of the popular hikes and treks in Bolivia begin near La Paz and end in the Yungas. For descriptions of some of these, see the Around La Paz section.

COROICO

Coroico, which serves as the North Yungas capital is a very serene little village perched atop Cerro Uchumachi at an altitude of only 1500 metres. Its vantage point, nevertheless, commands a far-reaching view of steaming jungled canyons, cloud-wreathed mountain tops, patchwork agricultural lands and dozens of small settlements. When it's clear, you can see the snow-covered summits of the Cordillera Real.

It's a quiet place and conducive to relaxation, especially if you need to slowly return to reality in stages after several glorious days walking from El Cumbre.

The weather in Coroico is warm year-round with rain almost daily in the afternoon and powerful downpours during summer. Fog is common at any time, but especially in the afternoon when it rises from the deep valleys and obscures the town's spectacular view.

The main crops grown in the Coroico area are citrus fruits and coffee.

Information

Changing Money The *Lluvia de Oro Hotel* changes cash dollars. The pharmacy across the street will change cash and when there's a demand for dollars they'll also exchange travellers' cheques.

To be on the safe side though, bring what cash you'll be needing in the Yungas with you, especially if you plan to travel further north into the Amazon Basin.

Things to See & Do

Coroico is good for relaxing, swimming, lying in the sun, or walking in the surrounding hills. The town itself and its tranquillity are the prime attractions. For a good panoramic view of Coroico and its countryside, walk up to the little church on the hill.

Three of the hotels in town have swimming pools. You'll have to ignore the colour of the water, however, if you really want to enjoy them as they're not exactly the brilliant chlorine blue you're probably accustomed to.

The *Mothers of Clarissa Convent*, on the other side of the steps from the La Casa Restaurant below the plaza, is an

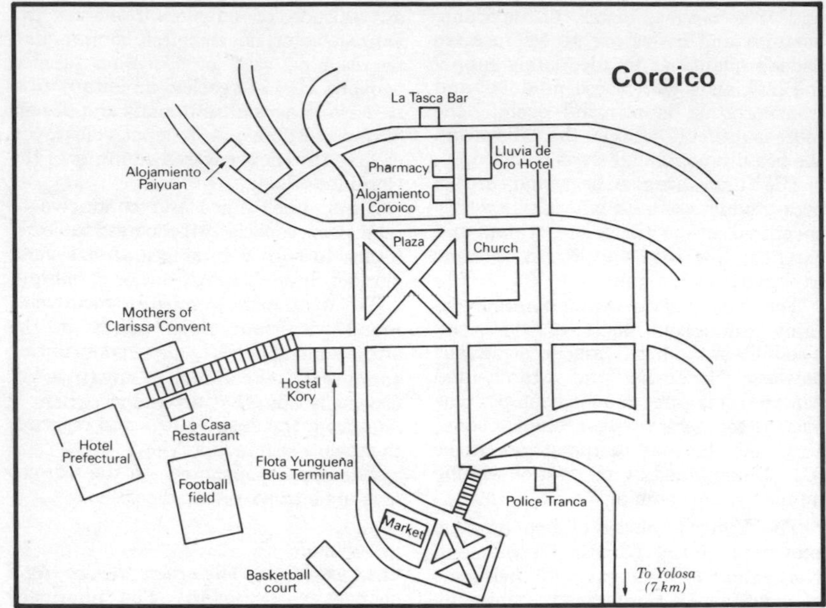

interesting place to visit. The nuns there make and sell delicious peanut butter, biscuits and local wines.

There are also quite a few small carpentry shops around town which sell practical handmade wooden items.

Places to Stay

The all-round best budget hotel in Coroico is the *Lluvia de Oro*. It's got a good restaurant, a swimming pool and sun deck, a patio and garden areas. A room with a window costs US$2.50 per person, while one without a window, on the ground floor, costs only US$1.50. It's clean but only cold showers and shared baths are available.

The *Alojamiento Coroico* is nothing but basic accommodation with cold showers and shared baths only. It costs US$1.75 per person.

The *Hostal Kory* ('kory' means 'gold' in Quechua) costs US$1.50 per person with good views of the surrounding mountains and valleys. Again only cold showers are available and there are no rooms with private baths. There is a swimming pool which may be used by non-guests for US$3.

The *Alojamiento Paiyuan* has a good view and costs US$1.25 per person but it's very basic.

The *Hotel Prefectural* gets two stars under the Bolivian rating system. Just down hill from town near the football field, it offers a very nice view down into the Yungas. All rooms have private baths and there's a good dining room. They charge US$6 per person.

Camping

A few secluded spots may be found near the church on the hill above town.

Places to Eat

The best restaurant in town is the friendly *La Casa* down the stairs from the main plaza. It is run by a German woman and her Bolivian husband who are both very friendly and enjoy talking with foreign visitors.

They serve great fondues, coffee, chocolate, pancakes and some local dishes. Excellent continental or American breakfasts are available for very reasonable prices. If you'd like to eat fondue you'll need at least two people and it helps to make a booking. A wonderful *raclette* costs only US$5 per person!

The dining room at the *Lluvia de Oro Hotel* offers typical Bolivian fare with daily lunch and dinner specials for US$1.75. They serve very good soups and chicken dishes.

Pensión Bolivar near the market has nice, inexpensive lunch specials.

Getting There & Away

Flota Yungueña does the run from La Paz to Coroico, from its Villa Fátima office, on Tuesdays, Thursday, Fridays and Saturdays at 9 am.

If you'd want to go to Coroico by bus on any other day of the week you'll need to take the Guanay bus, get off at Yolosa and catch a ride the seven km uphill to Coroico.

Trucks from La Paz leave regularly until mid-afternoon every day from up the street behind the Flota Yungueña office.

Many people walk to Coroico from El Cumbre. For details, see the El Cumbre to Coroico description in the Around La Paz section.

Because Coroico is so popular, it's a notorious place for getting stuck. If you're not planning to use truck transport back to La Paz, then make flota reservations out as soon as you arrive. Flota Yungueña goes to La Paz on Monday, Wednesday, Friday and Sunday at 7.30 am. The trip costs US$3.50 and takes about six hours, if things go well.

If you want to go to Caranavi, Guanay, Puerto Linares, Chulumani or even La Paz by truck, then wait at the transit office in Coroico for a vehicle to Yolosa seven km down the hill.

You'll have no trouble finding transport from Yolosa to Caranavi, Guanay or La Paz, but to get to Puerto Linares you'll probably first have to go to Caranavi and then find another vehicle going to Puerto Linares. To get to Chulumani, you have to change vehicles at Chuspipata.

If you'd like to travel through the main coca growing region of Bolivia, then take a truck from Yolosa to Arapata, another from Arapata to Coripata, and then another to Chulumani, but expect to wait awhile in each place for a truck going in the right direction.

The La Paz to Coroico Road

I've heard rumours that a road more terrifying than the one from La Paz to Coroico exists somewhere in Zanskar or Bhutan, but I won't believe it until I see it.

If you're nervous about unsurfaced roads just wide enough for one vehicle, sheer 1000-metre dropoffs, hulking rock overhangs, or waterfalls which spill across and erode away the highway, then your best bet is to either skip Coroico altogether, walk both ways, or take the flota, bury your head somewhere and don't look until it's over.

Truck drivers along this stretch seem to travel at unreasonable breakneck speeds given the conditions, with horns blaring, brakes squealing and loads lurching out over the Great Abyss. I also wonder if many of the drivers are completely sober. A number of crosses, which have been accurately described as 'Bolivian caution signs', line the way in testimony of the fact that this is not an easy trip.

Those who do dare to travel in an open truck and keep their eyes open, however, will be rewarded with some of the most stunning vertical scenery South America has to offer. Take raingear as the mists and waterfalls can be drenching and since this road drops over 4000 metres in 80 km, an arctic-to-tropical range of clothing is also necessary.

CHULUMANI

The road to Chulumani, which extends on to Irupana, is quite beautiful and is much wider and less unnerving than the one to Coroico.

The capital of South Yungas, Chulumani is another relaxing town with a view. It is a centre for growing coca, coffee and bananas, and it sees very few tourists except during the week following 24 August when the town stages the *Fiesta of San Bartolomé*. Visitors from all over show up then to join in the fun.

Legend says that the town's name, derived from *Cholo-Umanya* which means 'tiger's drink', was decided on when a jaguar came to drink at the town well.

Rebels during the 1781 La Paz Revolution escaped to the Yungas and hid out in the valleys around Chulumani until things calmed down.

Places to Stay

The *Hotel Bolivar* just up from the main plaza is clean and costs US$2.50 per person. They have cold showers but often there's no water at all.

At US$5 per person, the *Hotel Prefectural* below the market is a fairly good deal but it's seriously lacking in character and reminds me of a sterile military barracks. Make reservations at a La Paz tourist agency to ensure room availability.

The *Hotel García* is a very friendly place and has a nice restaurant on the terrace overlooking the surrounding countryside. Rooms with/without private bath cost US$4.50 per person.

The friendly *Residencial El Milagro* is very nice with a beautiful garden, antique-furnished reception area and a great view. A two-bed double here costs US$11 with a private bath; a one-bed

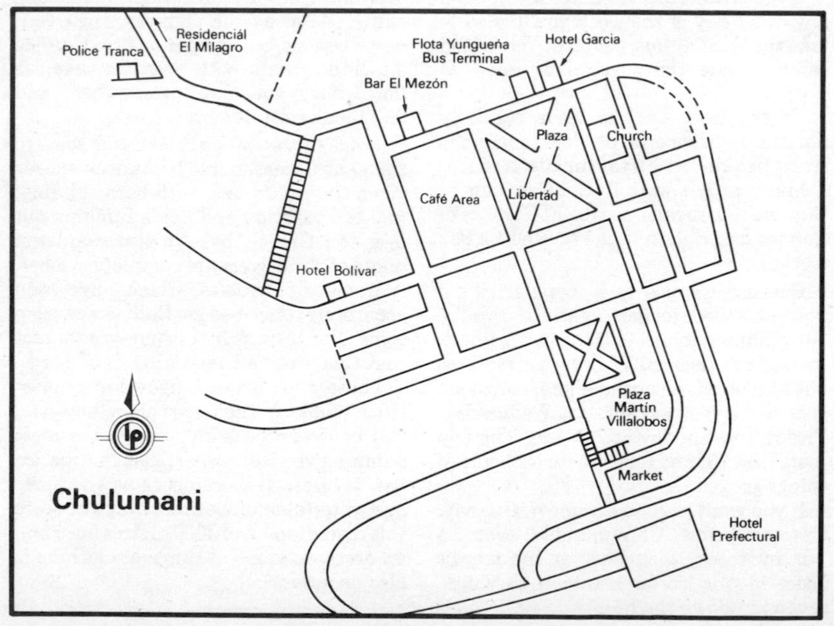

double is US$12.50, also with private bath; and a room with six beds and a bath goes for US$30. Since it's primarily for couples, there are no single rooms.

Places to Eat

The market in Chulumani may well be the cleanest in Bolivia and it serves good, inexpensive meals. It's especially great for breakfast because local coffee is served. If you're not a coffee fan, try their delicious cocoa.

The restaurant at the *Hotel García* is probably the nicest in town. They serve typical Bolivian meals on a patio overlooking the never-never and prices are reasonable for the quality.

There are many small cafés scattered around and just above the Plaza Libertád. *Bar El Mezón* is good for drinks and music.

Señora Hilda Ricardo's shop, which is near the church on the main plaza, has been recommended for great local coffee.

The dining room at the *Hotel Prefectural* is reserved for guests only.

Getting There & Away

There's a Flota Yungueña bus from La Paz every day at 9 am and trucks leave from the parking area behind there every few minutes until mid-afternoon.

If you're going to Chulumani from Coroico or Guanay, you have to get off in Chuspipata or Unduavi and change vehicles. If you're travelling by truck, the same clothing suggestions mentioned in the La Paz to Coroico Road description apply for this trip too.

Along the route to Chulumani from the south, look for Bridal Veil Falls on the left side of the road and El Chaco castle 60 km beyond the junction at Unduavi.

To return to La Paz, the ENTA government bus leaves roughly three times per week but with no set schedule. Flota Yungueña leaves every morning except Saturday at 7.30 am and costs US$3.50.

Trucks to La Paz and to other Yungas towns can be boarded at the transit office. By truck, the trip to La Paz takes approximately eight to nine hours. Again, make sure you have the proper clothing for the trip or you will suffer.

GUANAY

Guanay serves as a base for interesting excursions into some of the remote coöperative or private gold mining operations along the Río Mapiri and Río Tipuani. The miners and panners along the way are friendly and enjoy explaining and demonstrating their operations to visitors.

The miners come in to Guanay to buy their supplies, paying with the gold they've found. The numerous saloons and eating establishments in the town reflect the frontier atmosphere of the area.

Access to the gold-mining areas is by dugout canoes, which may be hired in Guanay. The trip to Mapiri takes one day each way and costs US$10 per person upstream and US$7.50 downstream. The river passes through dense jungle and some sort of insect repellent is necessary.

Places to Stay

The best inexpensive hotel in town is *Hotel Santos*, but *Hotel México* has also been recommended.

Getting There & Away

Bus Flota Yungueña serves both Caranavi and Guanay, leaving at 9 am daily from La Paz, but truck traffic is plentiful and less expensive. If you're going to Puerto Linares, you'll have to get off in Caranavi and take a truck from there. Buses return to La Paz from Guanay at 7 am daily.

A road to link Puerto Linares and Guanay with Trinidad and Cobija is currently in the planning stages. There's already a track of sorts, but it can only be negotiated with extreme difficulty.

Walking Another method of accessing this area is on foot. A six to eight-day hike from Sorata to Guanay along the Río Tipuani is described in detail in the Bradt guide *Backpacking and Trekking in Peru and Bolivia*.

Boat From Guanay and nearby Puerto Linares, which is accessible via Caranavi, it is possible to travel by boat down the Río Beni to Rurrenabaque and Riberalta. It takes three to four days depending on the depth of the river.

From Riberalta there are buses to the Brazilian border at Guayaramerín. If you're interested in this trip, read the section on river travel in the Getting Around chapter. To find a boat in Guanay or Puerto Linares, you only need to ask around the port area in either town. There is normally at least one leaving each week.

SORATA

Sorata has often been described as having the most beautiful setting in Bolivia and this is by no means a gross exaggeration.

It sits in a valley, at an elevation of 2695 metres, beneath the towering snow-capped peaks of Illampú (6362 metres) and Ancohuma. The trees and flowers in this lush green valley are so bountiful that local inhabitants believe that it must have been the site of the Garden of Eden. The huge palm trees in the plaza are also rather impressive.

In colonial days, Sorata served as a link to the goldfields of the Río Tipuani and a gateway to the Alto Beni and points north. Today, however, the road from La Paz to Guanay handles all the transport and movement between the Altiplano and the Yungas so Sorata has slipped into a comfortably stagnant obscurity.

Sunday is market day in the town, and in September riotous fiestas are held in both Sorata and nearby Achacachi.

Things to See & Do

Most visitors to the town make the 12 km hike to San Pedro Cave, which is about three or four hours away near the village of San Pedro.

To get there, walk downhill from Sorata's main plaza. The street becomes a rocky trail which takes you all the way to San Pedro. The cave will be on your right about 500 metres beyond the village. You'll need a torch if you want to explore it, so either bring one along or ask to borrow one from the guard who lives nearby.

After entering the cave, you'll be able to walk several hundred metres before reaching a cold underground lake which impedes further exploration. Watch out for the hundreds of bats.

Although this hike can be done in one day, such a schedule would leave little time for exploration so you may want to take along food and camping equipment and spend the night.

Sorata is also the base to use if you're setting out to scale Mt Illampú or Ancohuma. Technical expertise and professional climbing equipment are necessary, however.

An interesting note about Ancohuma: although its altitude is listed officially at 6427 metres, it seems there might have been a mistake made in its original measurements because most atlases and maps published after 1983 record its elevation as a whopping 7014 metres! This makes it clearly the highest peak in the western hemisphere, 54 metres higher than Argentina's Aconcagua!

Places to Stay

The best place to stay in town is the *Residencial Sorata*. The owner is friendly and helpful and can explain various excursions and points of interest in and around town. The residencial has a nice garden and a great view of the surrounding Cordillera Real. It costs US$2.50 per person.

Getting There & Away

Sorata is a long way from the other Yungas towns because there's no road connecting it directly with Coroico or Chulumani. There is a trail to Guanay, however, which can be hiked in about a week if you're feeling energetic. It follows the Río Tipuani which is the gold prospecting centre of the Yungas.

From La Paz, buses for Sorata leave daily at 7 am from near the cemetery and cost US$2.50 per person. Alternatively you can try going to Achacachi near Lake Titicaca on the same bus that goes to Huatajata and catch a truck or another bus from there. The trip takes about 4½ hours.

Southern Altiplano

Stretching southward from La Paz all the way to the Chilean and Argentine frontiers and beyond is a harsh, sparsely-populated wilderness of scrubby windswept basins, lonely peaks, and glaring, nearly lifeless salt deserts. This is the archetypal Altiplano, a land of lonely mirages and indeterminable distances. Though the air retains no warmth, the land and sky meet in waves of shimmering reflected heat and the horizon disappears. Stark mountains seem to hover somewhere beyond reality and the sense of solitude is overwhelming. Even North America's desolate Great Basin seems cosy by comparison.

The nights are just as haunting. Even in the Arctic, I've never seen blacker night skies or icier stars. As soon as the sun sets, you'll learn very quickly that this air has teeth. The cold is so intense that it chills through and through in a matter of seconds and there is little available, it seems, can conquer it.

Geologically, the vast plateau was a deep intermontane valley in the days of the tyrannosaurus rex. When the Andes were much newer than today, during the Cretaceous period some 100,000,000 years ago, erosion in those mountains filled the valley with a 15,000-metre-deep deposit of sediment. Thus was the Altiplano born. With such porous alluvial soil, the fertility of the basin is predictable, but especially in the south, the presence of salts, lack of adequate moisture, and a rocky surface character make agriculture here a challenging venture.

The few people that inhabit this region live at the ragged edge of human endurance. They are among the hardiest living anywhere on earth. They contend with wind, drought, bitter cold, and high altitude with none of the modern conveniences which make such things bearable in the harsher climates elsewhere. These people labour unceasingly throughout their lives to wrest an existence from this land. Miners, farmers, and herders; the campesinos of the Altiplano deserve a great deal of respect for their accomplishments.

Even given the opportunity of relative prosperity in the developing lowlands, the Aymará have chosen not to leave their ancestral home. This is the same hardy group of people that managed to resist efforts of the Incas to assimilate them, body and soul, into the Empire. They refused to accept the Quechua language and the culture of the conquerors from the West and were the only major conquered tribe to get away with it.

Understandably, the locals tend to look with suspicion and sometimes disdain upon outsiders who live comfortably and come to gawk at their sorry lot. Fiercely proud and stubborn, these Aymará and others will at first seem as harsh and cold as the land they inhabit. Most of the coldness is spawned by a deep suspicion of the motives of foreigners who venture into town with what seems to be a lot of money and no visible means of support. People who work hard at meagre survival can't fathom why you'd be trotting around the globe instead of staying home and attending to work, religious, and family responsibilities (some of your own relatives may feel the same way!). With patience and diplomacy, however, the icy barrier can sometimes be broken and you can enter into a world and a lifestyle difficult beyond imagining.

The Southern Altiplano, rich in mineral deposits, produces a goodly portion of Bolivia's non-illicit exports. Oruro and Llallagua are the centres of tin production and an enormous tin smelter is in operation in Vinto, near Oruro. Further south are more primitive and less accessible ventures. Throughout southern Potosí Department there are rich concentrations of antimony, bismuth, silver, lead, zinc,

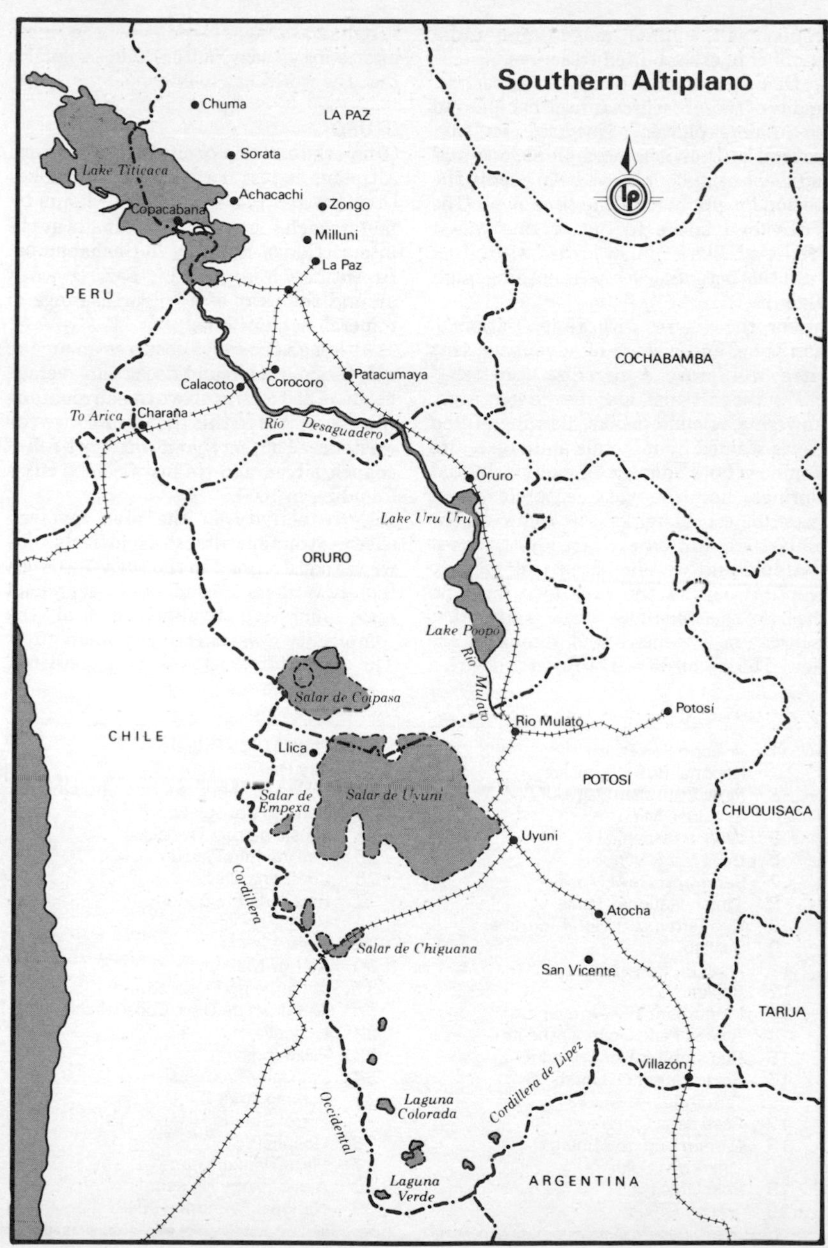
Southern Altiplano
Chuma
LA PAZ
Sorata
Lake Titicaca
Achacachi
Zongo
Copacabana
Milluni
La Paz
PERU
COCHABAMBA
Calacoto
Corocoro
Patacumaya
To Arica
Charaña
Río
Desaguadero
Oruro
Lake Uru Uru
ORURO
Lake Poopó
Río
Mulato
Salar de Coipasa
Potosí
CHILE
Rio Mulato
Llica
POTOSÍ
Salar de Empexa
Salar de Uyuni
CHUQUISACA
Uyuni
Cordillera
Atocha
Salar de Chiguana
San Vicente
TARIJA
Cordillera de Lipez
Villazón
Occidental
Laguna Colorada
Laguna Verde
ARGENTINA

copper, salt, sulphur, magnesium, and a number of other buried treasures.

Due to lack of capital and expertise, many of these resources are either ignored or underexploited. Needless to say, several of Bolivia's more ambitious and efficient neighbours have been eyeing the region longingly for some time now. One Bolivian I spoke to put it this way : 'Bolivia is like a donkey loaded with silver – all this potential wealth is nothing but a liability'.

For the visitor with time, patience, fortitude, and a sense of adventure, this area will prove a paradise. Scattered about the surreal landscape are steaming, towering volcanic peaks, flamingo-filled lakes stained by minerals and algae into rainbow hues, dozens of hot pools and springs, and the vast featureless salt deserts, considered to be some of the flattest terrain on earth. Only the most intrepid and well-prepared will want to venture beyond the rail lines into the heart of this loneliness where transport is scarce and expensive and amenities are few. Those who do will be rewarded with a first-hand view of some of the most interesting geology, culture, and economics that the world has to offer.

ORURO

Oruro, the only major city of the Southern Altiplano is just north of the salty lakes Uru Uru and Poopó, and three hours by motorcoach south of La Paz. It sits at the intersection of rail lines to Cochabamba, Argentina/Chile, and La Paz, crowded around the skirt of a colourful range of mineral-rich low hills.

Although the range occupies an area of only 10 square km and rises to an average height of 350 metres above the surrounding Altiplano, it is to this that Oruro owes its existence. The fact that it was chock full of copper, silver, and tin justified the city's founding in 1606.

Early activity in the area involved silver extraction almost exclusively, but when that declined in the early 1800s the Indian workers moved on in search of more lucrative livelihoods, and the community was effectively abandoned. The importance of the area returned

1 Volcano San Pedro
2 National Road Service
3 Plaza Sebastian Pagador
4 San José Mine
5 Workers Hospital
6 Devil Mask Vendors
7 Carnival & Devil Masks
8 'Union National' Park
9 Bus Terminal & Hotel Termināl
10 Serrato
11 Plaza de Raneheria
12 Bookstore
13 Monument & view over city
14 Avaroa Park, Open-air theatre
15 Bus stop for Hot Springs
16 Santo Domingo Church & Termín Lopez Market
17 Case de la Cultura
18 Monuments to Miners & Unknown Soldiers
19 Post Office
20 Tourist Office
21 Plaza 10 de Febrero & City Hall
22 ENTEL & San Francisco Church
23 German Consulate
24 Iglesia de San Francisco
25 Alojamiento Pagador
26 Confiteria Chic
27 Heladeria El Cóndor
28 Hotel Repostero
29 Main Market
30 Bolívar Market
31 Alojamiento Ferrocarril, San Juan de Diós, Copacabana
32 La Tetilla
33 Plaza Ingavi
34 PIL Dairy Products
35 Parking Area & Petrol Station
36 Hospital
37 Plaza Walter Khon
38 Archaeology Museum
39 National Foundries (ENAF)

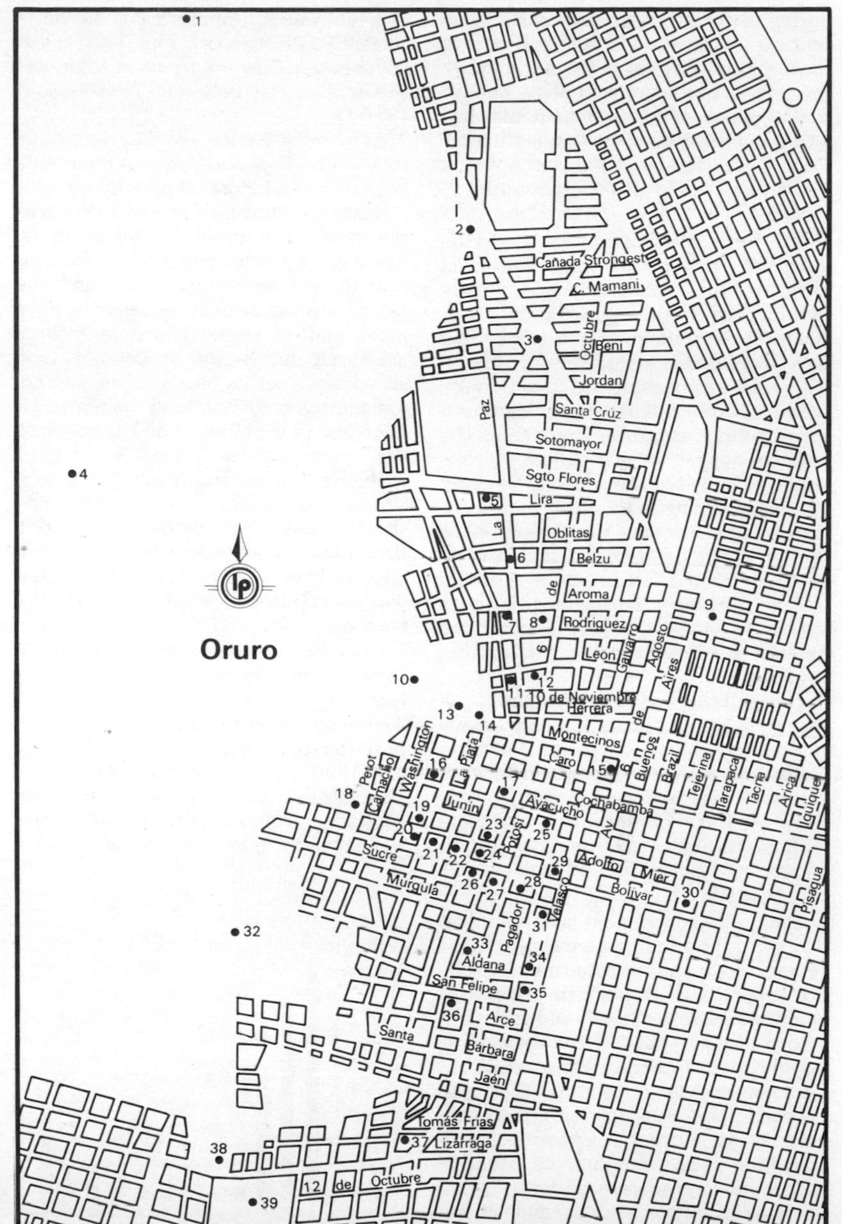
Oruro
1
2
Cañada Strongest
C. Mamani
3
Octubre
Beni
Jordan
Paz
Santa Crúz
Sotomayor
4
Sgto Flores
5
Lira
La
Oblitas
6
Belzu
de
Aroma
9
7
8
Rodriguez
6
Leon
Galvarro
Agosto
10
12
11
10 de Noviembre
Herrera
Aires
13
14
Washington
Montecinos
de
La Plata
Petot
Camacho
16
Caro
15
Buenos
Brazil
17
Tejerina
Tarapaca
Tacna
Arica
Iquique
18
19
Junín
Ayacucho
Cochabamba
20
23
25
Potosí
Av
21
22
24
Sucre
29
Adolfo
Mier
Murguía
26
27
28
Bolívar
30
Pisagua
Velasco
Pagador
31
32
33
Aldana
34
San Felipe
35
36
Arce
Santa
Bárbara
Jaén
Tomás Frías
38
37
Lizarraga
12
de
Octubre
39

during the late 19th and early 20th centuries when tin and copper began to figure prominently in world markets. By the 1920s three major capitalists were in control of Bolivia's exploding tin industry. The most powerful of these was Simon I Patiño, the Indian from Cochabamba Valley who would become (disputably) the wealthiest man in the world.

A tin mine called La Salvadora near the village of Uncia east of Oruro, had been purchased by Patiño in 1897 and quickly became the world's most productive. Patiño's success here sent him snowballing into a capitalistic mania, and by 1924 he had taken ownership of the equally productive mines at nearby Llallagua and thereby gained control of about 50% of the nation's output in that industry. Now secure in his wealth, he moved to England and began buying up European and North American smelters and tin interests. With the tin, the profits were exported abroad. This launched Bolivia into a series of labour uprisings and public outcries which set the stage for Victor Paz Estenssoro's nationalisation of the mines in 1952.

The two other successful 'tin barons', as they were known, Carlos Victor Aramayo from far southern Bolivia and Mauricio Hothschild, a Jew of European extraction, kept their centre of operations in Bolivia. Even so, the 1952 revolution left them without holdings and Aramayo fled to Europe to escape the ill will of his countrymen.

Today, the government is in the midst of turning the mining interests over to the private sector and the resulting turmoil – accompanied by low world tin prices, stiff competition from abroad, and turbulent labour unrest – has left the fluctuating population of Oruro in a state of uncertainty. Many people I talked with believed that Oruro is dying. Others said that it is currently experiencing a transition period but that the situation will improve as things settle down. Due to unstable conditions, high unemployment, and low wages, the city's population is currently decreasing. The best guess anyone can offer in terms of numbers these days is between 150,000 and 170,000.

At a quick glance you can determine that Oruro's population is about 90% Indian. It is therefore one of Bolivia's most culturally colourful cities and is known as the 'Folkloric Capital of Bolivia'. It is, however, by our standards neither a friendly nor welcoming place and the recent mining difficulties seem to have made matters worse. Therefore, visitors are rarely indifferent to Oruro – they either love it or they hate it. Those who are fortunate enough to attend the famed *La Diablada* (a wild fiesta which takes place during carnival each year) are almost exclusively numbered among the former. This is not to say, however, that one should arrive expecting the worst during the remainder of the year. If you're able to effectively demonstrate to the locals that you pose no threat, many will eventually open up.

Once upon a time it was necessary to register with the police upon arrival in Oruro if you planned to stay overnight. This is no longer required, but hotels still have to recommend it.

Climatically, the best time for a visit is between the months of April and July. The city sits at an altitude of 3702 metres and experiences an arid climate, but as in

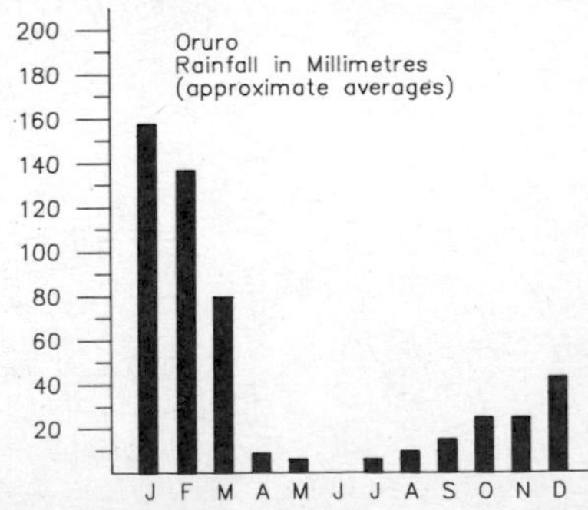

most of Bolivia, the greater part of what rain they do get falls between November and March. Winds blow year-round but seem to be the most violent in the late winter and early spring. Whenever you visit be sure to bring protection against both sun and wind, which may be present at any time. For winter nights, dress as you would for Outer Mongolia or Alaska's North Slope and you can't go wrong. A good stiff Altiplano wind can, when the chill factor is considered, produce temperatures of –40° or lower.

Information

The tourist office is at the top of Plaza 10 de Febrero near the corner of Adolfo Mier and Presidente Montes. They are very helpful and will happily answer specific questions. They also distribute literature and a complete street plan of the city which includes residencial neighbourhoods.

The office is one of the few places in Oruro which has a heater and the staff doesn't mind if you stop by to warm up now and again. It's open weekdays from 9 am to noon and 2 to 6 pm.

Changing Money This can be tricky. There is no place in Oruro to change travellers' cheques so be sure to bring some cash dollars or bolivianos. Dollars can be changed at several shops along Adolfo Mier which display signs reading *Compro Dolares*. Street changers can be found on the corner of 6 de Octubre and Aldana near Plaza Ingavi.

Post & Communications The ENTEL office, one of the nicest modern buildings in Oruro, is near the corner of Sorla Galvarro and Bolívar, just below the main plaza.

The post office is just north of the tourist office near the main plaza. If you're planning to post a package, have it inspected at the customs office (*Aduana Nacionál*) on Velasco Galvarro between Ayacucho and Junín before taking it to the post office.

Laundry Laundry service is available at 497 Adolfo Mier.

Consulate For some unfathomable reason, there is a West German consulate on Adolfo Mier just below the main plaza. It's open weekday mornings until 11 am.

Things to Do

Most travellers who end up in Oruro seem to be passing through en route to someplace else, but for those on a more flexible schedule, there's actually quite a lot to see and do in the area, but most attractions are outside of the city itself.

Several mines in the hills behind the city may be visited by tourists although this is subject to change at any time. When the private sector takes over, it will be up to each individual cooperative whether or not outsiders will be admitted. The most popular mine is *San José*, high on the mountain behind the city, which claims to have been in operation as a silver or tin mine for over 4½ centuries. You can get there on Micro 'D' (marked 'San José') which leaves from the north-west corner of Plaza 10 de Febrero near the tourist office. *Itos*, another mine south-west of town, is reached by Micro 'C' (marked 'Sud').

The cathedral ½ block below the main plaza has nice stained glass work above the altar but *Iglesia San Francisco* is rather ordinary and uninteresting. The *Iglesia del Socavón* above the town offers a view over the city. It figures prominently during the carnival as the site where good ultimately defeats evil in the struggle of La Diablada. For the energetic, there is also a good view from the chapel of Serrato, accessible from the end of Calle Washington. Much easier to reach for a photo of the town is *Conchupata* at the top of Avenida Presidente Montes.

The *Casa de la Cultura* for the Department of Oruro is on Sorla Galvarro north of Ayacucho. It is housed in an old Patiño mansion and now serves as a museum, administered by the university.

It's open weekdays from 10 am to noon and 2 to 4 pm (if the local political situation is calm). Admission is free. Downstairs from the museum, they feature visiting exhibits.

The museum of Mineralogy and Geology at the university is certainly worth a visit of several hours. To get there, catch Micro 'A' in front of YPFB across from the railroad station and stay on until its terminus at the university south of town. The museum is upstairs in the large multi-storey building on the hill. They have minerals, precious stones, fossils, and crystals from all over the world. If it's locked when you arrive, knock on the door and the janitor will let you in. There's no entry fee. From the patio outside is a nice view of Lake Uru Uru to the south, several km distant.

Both the zoo and the Archaeology Museum are in a park, of sorts, on the south end of town. Take Micro 'C' (marked 'Sud') from the north-west corner of the main plaza or across the street from the railway station and get off just beyond the tin foundry compound. The museum is just behind the police station – it's small, but worth a half hour or so. The zoo is just across the children's playground near the museum. It's marginally interesting but nauseatingly unkempt. Its only redemption is a large aviary where Andean condors may be seen close-up, but even this feature pales when one realises that such large and stately birds should be out soaring over some remote Andean crag, rather than being trapped in a pitiful cage. The zoo and the museum each cost 25c for adults and 10c for children. The zoo is open from 8.30 to noon and 2 to 5 pm Monday to Friday. Museum hours are from 9 am to noon and 2 to 5 pm on the same days.

La Diablada

The *Diablada* or 'Dance of the Devils' has come to be the most famous and largest celebration held anywhere in Bolivia. It takes place each year, beginning the first

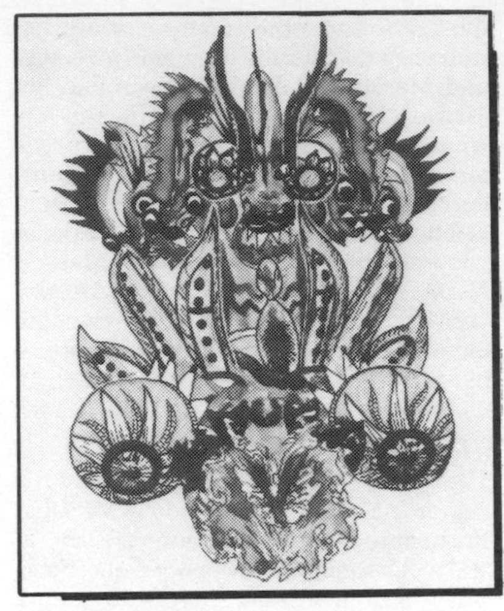

Saturday before Ash Wednesday with a glorious *entrada* or opening parade led by the Michael the archangel character in a bright costume. Behind him, dancing and marching, come the famous devils and a host of bears and condors. The chief devil, Lucifer, wears the most extravagant costume complete with a velvet cape and an ornate mask. He is flanked by Supay, the Andean goddess of evil, believed to be Lucifer's woman.

The procession is followed by vehicles adorned with silver service, in commemoration of the *Achura* festival in which miners offered the highest quality mineral the mines had produced during the year to the saints and gods of the mines.

In the broad sense, the carnival festivities can be described as the triumph of good over evil but it is so interlaced with threads of both Christian and Indian myths, fables, deities, and traditions that to oversimplify it detracts from its uniqueness. The origins of a similar festival may be traced back to 12th century Catalonia, although the locals profess that the celebration commemorates an event that occurred during the early days of Oruro.

Legend has it that a thief living in Oruro, named Chiruchiru, was seriously wounded during a night-time robbery. The Virgin of Candelaria helped him to reach his home near the 'Pie de Gallo' mine before he died. When the miners found him there, they saw hanging over his head an image of the Dark Virgin of Candelaria.

Today, the mine is called *Socavón de la Virgen* or 'Cave of the Virgin' and in the Saturday procession, she is honoured when the archangel and the fierce-looking devilish dancers arrive at the football stadium. Various dances are performed there representing the battle between good and evil. When it becomes apparent that the good has triumphed, the dancers retire to the Chapel of the Socavón and the Virgin pronounces the winner.

If you're interested, another Diablada legend translated into something by the *Instituto Boliviano de Turismo* appears below. If you can make any sense of it, you're better than I.

Huari, a semi God of the Plateau mythology, symbol of strength, zealous guardians of the cult, requested that the town of Uru Uru released the Sun, he perpetrated his vengeance on the sons of Inti, the Sun God, sawing evil and inamisty and discordance. One day a beautiful Ñusta (Goddess) appeared and incited the Urus to return to the rightful ways. Huari, mocked in his intentions, sent a serpent from the soth, a frog from the north, a giant lizard from the northeast and a plague of ants from the east in order to extinguish the Urus farms. This punishment, was conjured by the Goddess who turned the monsters into stones and the ants, into sand.

It is said, that the beautiful Goddess, was the Maddonna of the Pit and she reappeared when the conquistadors arrived back to render protection to the miners.

The design and creation of Diablada costumes has turned into an art form in Oruro. Several Diablada clubs, which consist of members from all levels of Oruro society, are sponsored by local businesses. They own their own costumes, which may cost several hundred dollars each, and rehearse the diabolical dances for months in advance of the carnival.

After the initial entrada, other groups perform at locations throughout the city for the remainder of the celebration. Each group performs its specific dance and has its specific costume and tradition. The most famous and recognisable is *La Morenada*, which re-enacts the dance of the negro slaves brought to the courts of Viceroy Felipe III. The costumes consist of hooped skirts and shoulder mantles and dark-faced masks adorned with plumes.

Another dance with African origins is *Los Negritos*. Performers beat on drums and the rhythm is reminiscent of the music of the Caribbean.

The *Los Llameros* dancers represent Andean llama herders and the *Waca Takoris* satire Spanish bullfighters. The *Waca Tintis* represent the *picadores* used in the bullfights. The *Los Incas* commemorates the original contact between the Incan and South European cultures. The *Las Tobas* dance is performed in honour of the Indian groups of the tropical lowlands which were conquered by the Incas and taken into the Empire.

If you plan to be on hand for carnival, it would be wise to write in advance and secure accommodation or plan to camp. Beware of 'gringo' pricing at this time of year.

Places to Stay - Bottom End

Most of the accommodation available in Oruro falls into this range. The cleanest and most pleasant is probably *Alojamiento Pagador* on Ayacucho near Pagador. It's only US$2 per person but hot water, as in most of Oruro, is unheard of and blankets are jealously rationed.

Alojamientos Ayacucho and *Scala*, both on Ayacucho don't deserve even a passing thought. Both offer only cold showers and cost US$2 per person, but they are very unfriendly and it seems that they dislike foreigners very much.

On Calle Sucre near the railroad station is *Alojamiento El Expresso*. It's dirty but relatively friendly. It costs US$2 per person and has only cold showers. The same goes for *Alojamiento Central* at 5917 Potosí.

Alojamiento Copacabana costs US$2.50 per person, but really has nothing over the others to justify the extra cost. Actually, it's quite a bit dirtier than the cheaper places. It's found at 6352 V Galvarro. Similarly, the *Alojamiento Ferrocarríl* at 6278 V Galvarro costs US$3 per person but provides no extra value for the money.

Alojamiento San Juan de Diós at 6344 V Galvarro is cleaner and friendlier than most. At US$2.50 per person it's fairly nice.

Places to Stay – Middle

The *Hotel Terminal* above the bus terminal is probably the nicest place to stay in Oruro as far as amenities are concerned, but the price structure is a scam if I ever saw one. Bolivians pay US$9.90 for a single and US$14.25 for a double. Foreigners pay nearly twice that – US$17 for a single and US$26.50 for a double. It is as far as I know the only hotel with both private baths and hot showers, which explains why they get away with the vast difference in prices.

The *Hotel Repostero* at 370 Sucre is by far the most pleasant and friendly lodging in town. A private bath costs US$6.50 per person and shared bath costs US$4.50 per person. They don't have hot water, but if you'd like a bath, they'll boil some water for you and bring it to your room.

Camping

There aren't any organised sites, but the best place to camp seems to be in the low hills immediately behind the university. There are a number of quiet and secluded places to pitch a tent, with views of Lake Uru Uru and the city of Oruro. If you don't mind being a little further from town, the lakeshore itself offers some marginal camping but it's not as private as in the hills.

Places to Eat

If you're looking for breakfast in Oruro, you're more or less out of luck. Most places don't open until 11 am or later and those that open earlier don't seem to have anything. *Confiteria Alemana* which opens at 9 am, for example, serves salteñas and Pepsi and absolutely nothing else, not even coffee, until lunch hour. *Confiteria Chic* on Calle Bolivar near 6 de Octubre serves good hot drinks and snacks, but most days, it doesn't bother to open at all. There are a few nicer restaurants on the south side of the main plaza which offer lunch and dinner specials. The best of these is probably *Pigalle* which is popular with foreigners.

For bargain specials check out some of the eateries across the street from the railroad station, such as *Beirut*, *El Turista*, and *San Juan de Diós* which serve typical Bolivian meat dishes: *lomo*, chicken, *churrasco*, and the like.

The railroad station has a passable bar and the bus terminal confiteria serves the best coffee in town.

If you're looking for ice cream try *Heladeria Suiza* on Calle Bolívar or *Heladeria Cóndor*. The Suiza also serves salteñas, hot drinks, and pastries.

Market food stalls in both the main market near the railroad station and *Mercado Fermin Lopez* on Calle Washington are of course the cheapest places to eat. They feature noodles in all forms (imported from Argentina!), *falso conejo*, mutton soup, beef dishes, and *thimpu de cordero*, boiled potatoes, oca, rice, and carrots over mutton and covered with *picante llajhua* sauce.

Whatever you do, avoid *Snack Maggi* and its lousy synthetic gristleburgers. I honestly don't know how they can stay in business serving such awful stuff, even in Oruro.

Things to Buy

The most unique items available in Oruro relate to La Diablada. Along Avenida La Paz there are many small shops where craftsmen sell devil masks and costumes of all descriptions for anywhere from US$3 to US$300 and embroidered wall hangings.

Typical Altiplano llama, wool, and alpaca bags and clothing are available at artesania shops in the centre like *Galeria Bolivar* on the corner of Bolivar and Pagador. Similar but less expensive articles can be bought inside the north-east corner of the main market.

Zampoñas, *charangos*, and other indigenous musical instruments are sold from sidewalk kiosks in front of the train station.

Getting There & Away

Bus Oruro serves as somewhat of a transportation hub in Bolivia. Due to the appalling state of rail travel to or from La Paz, many people choose to use bus transport to Oruro. From here they board trains to points south and east of Oruro with relatively little difficulty. Since it is the nearest large city to La Paz, there is quite a lot of traffic between the two and the highway connecting them is without question the finest in the country.

At least 20 companies running clean, modern coaches each make the trip to and from La Paz six to eight times daily. From terminal to terminal, the run takes three hours and costs US$2.50.

About midway along the journey from Oruro to La Paz, look for a shallow lake about 100 metres off the highway to the left of the bus. It's normally teeming with flamingos and would make an excellent campsite for someone hoping to take some nice close-up photos of the birds.

Buses to and from Cochabamba are just as easy to find as to La Paz. The trip costs US$2.50 and takes six hours. All service beyond, toward Santa Crúz, requires a layover of several hours in Cochabamba, even on those flotas which offer 'direct' service.

To Potosí and Sucre, Flotas *Alianza* and *Universo* leave at 7 pm daily for the rather rough overnight trip. Sucre is six hours beyond Potosí.

Seven times daily, *Flota Bustillo* goes to Llallagua and Huari.

Getting There & Away

Train Oruro is a railroad centre, thanks to it's importance as a mining community. It also has one of the most organised and efficient railroad stations in Bolivia. This, and the fact that train travel is the least expensive method of getting around in the country makes it appealing to anyone heading towards Chile or Argentina or eastward to Potosí, Sucre, or Cochabamba from La Paz.

Rail service between La Paz and Oruro is slow and difficult to arrange while the buses are frequent and cheap. Most people travel by bus from La Paz to Oruro and begin their rail journey there.

If you're travelling towards La Paz by rail, you'd likewise do well to get off in Oruro and take a bus on into La Paz. It could save you the better part of a day.

Official rail schedules and fares out of Oruro are listed below.

Oruro to Sucre
  Express Train Wednesday & Sunday 10.15 pm; 1st US$7.90, 2nd US$5.35
Oruro to Potosí
  Express Train Wednesday & Sunday 10.15 pm; 1st US$5.15, 2nd US$3.50
  Ferrobus Monday, Thursday, Saturday 10.30 pm; 1st US$7.20, 2nd US$4.80
Oruro to Villazón
  Express Train Daily 9.20 pm; 1st US$9.10, 2nd US$6.15
Oruro to Uyuni
  Express Train Daily 9.20 pm; 1st US$3.70, 2nd US$2.65
Oruro to Cochabamba
  Ferrobus Daily 8.00 am; 1st US$5.10, 2nd US$3.40
  Slow Train. Check schedule in station; 2nd class only US$2.45
Oruro to La Paz
  Express Train Tuesday, Wednesday,

Thursday, Saturday, Sunday between 10 & 11 am; 1st US$3.35
Ferrobus Tuesday, Friday, Sunday 6.30 pm; 1st US$4.70, 2nd US$3.15
Slow Train Sunday 9.45 am; 2nd class only US$2.25

Oruro to Antofagasta
Express Train Friday 6.40 pm; 1st class only US$17.10
Tickets go on sale at 2 pm on Thursday but arrive early to ensure a seat reservation.

To Chile The trip from Oruro to Antofagasta will take 30 or more hours. The train actually only goes as far as Calama (Chile) and from there, a bus connects to the coast.

There is some interesting and spectacular scenery along this route and it's a highly worthwhile journey if you come prepared for the uncomfortable conditions. It is essential to carry plenty of warm clothing and a sleeping bag or woollen blanket. Temperatures in the coaches fall well below zero at night and you will be dreadfully uncomfortable, if not suffering, without these things.

At the border settlements of Abaroa/Ollagüe you must change from the Bolivian to the Chilean train. Surprisingly, the Chilean coaches are actually worse than their Bolivian counterparts. Windows are broken and there is no heat or light. Some coaches have wooden benches along the side instead of seats. Cold winds whistle through loose boards and the toilets are actually outside, exposed to the elements.

The customs procedures at Ollagüe are also a bit trying. The settlement lies on an open plain unprotected from the fierce desert winds that howl through this pass in the Andes. Here you have to queue up once to get your entrance stamp and again for a luggage search. The catch is that all of this takes place outside. At night it's a miserable exercise in survival. Bolivian exit stamps, however, are given on the train as soon as it leaves Uyuni: passports are collected in bulk, stamped, and returned coach by coach in the last coach of the train.

It's sometimes possible to change money in Uyuni or Ollagüe but it's best not to count on it. *Casa de Cambio Sudamer* in La Paz gives a better and more reliable rate than anyone in these places.

You can't carry fruit, meat, or cheese across the border into Chile so try to eat up any food you're carrying before reaching the customs search at Ollagüe.

Between Uyuni and the border, this line passes through vast salt pans, featureless deserts, and rugged barren mountains. Flamingos, guanacos, vicuñas, and wild burros are common, and thanks to a startling mirage effect, so are a host of other assorted objects.

Remolinos (known to us as dust devils or willy-nillys) whirl across the near lifeless landscape and scores of snow-capped volcanoes tower over it. The only type of vegetation that flourishes here is *yareta*, a kind of combustible salt-tolerant moss that oozes a turpentine-like-jelly and is used by the locals as fuel. While it appears soft and spongy from a distance, it's actually rock-hard. It grows very slowly and a large clump of it may be several hundred years old. The plant is now an officially protected species in Chile.

To Argentina If you're headed toward Argentina, you'll have to go to Villazón, walk across the border, and take buses from there to the current Argentine railhead at Tucamán. Be prepared for a lengthy stop in Uyuni en route. The cold weather warnings given in the discussion of the route to Chile apply here, too. For more information on the border crossing, see the section dealing with Villazón.

Getting Around

Oruro city micros and mini-buses cost 10c and connect the centre of the city with outlying areas and points of interest. They are lettered A,B,C,D, etc, but this can be confusing because each micro may do several different runs. One Micro 'D', for example, goes to the Vinto smelter and is marked 'Vinto ENAF'. Another Micro 'D' goes to San José Mine and is marked as such. Oruro micros are small and crowded so don't try to carry large luggage aboard.

Taxis cost 25c from the transportation terminals to the centre, or between the terminals. Many will charge 50c, however, if you have a lot of luggage. In this particular city, these prices aren't really negotiable and are accepted as standard cab fare by the locals. Unless you learn that they've risen for one reason or another, don't let the drivers talk you out of more money, which they will surely try to do.

AROUND ORURO

Vinto Tin Smelter

This US$12,000,000 structure was constructed in the early '70s during the presidency of General Hugo Banzer Suarez but by the time it was put into operation the Bolivian tin industry was already experiencing a steady decline. Even so, the *Orureños* are extremely proud of the modern operation and are happy to show it off to tourists.

Only seven km from the centre of town, it can be visited between 9 am and noon on weekdays. To get there, take Micro 'D' (marked 'Vinto ENAF') from the northwest corner of Plaza 10 de Noviembre.

Lake Uru Uru

To visit this large shallow lake just outside town to the south, take Micro 'A' marked 'Sud' to its terminus at the university. From there, walk three km or so along the highway to the lake. There is good fishing for *pejerrey* and it's also possible to see flamingos in the shallow water.

Hot Springs

The nearest hot springs to town are *Capachos* and *Obrajes* along the road to Cochabamba. Take the micro which leaves every few minutes from Avenida 6 de Agosto, between Caro and Montecinos. Capachos is about 16 km from the city and has a covered hot pool. Admission is 50c. If you'd like a private hot bath, however, you must go on to Obrajes, about 23 km distant, which also has a pool. Along the road to Potosí, about 80 km from Oruro, there are other hot springs, *Urmiri* and *Pazña*. You need to get there in a *camión*.

LLALLAGUA

Originally a company town of the Chilean Llallagua Company, Llallagua was bought out by tin baron Simon Patiño in 1924 after he gained a little capital with his success in nearby Uncia. The area's most famous mine, the Siglo XX grew into one of the most productive mines in Bolivia and is currently the largest tin mine in the country, with 800 km of underground passages.

With nationalisation of mining interests in 1952, control of Llallagua passed into the hands of COMIBOL (*Corporación Minera de Bolivia*). It was then operated by the federal government until the mid-1980s when Victor Paz Estenssoro (the president who had initiated the 1952 mining reform) decided during his fourth non-consecutive term of office to return the project to private, miner-owned cooperatives.

A large sign posted outside the Siglo XX mine states that foreigners must obtain permission from COMIBOL headquarters in La Paz before they will be admitted to the mine as visitors. With COMIBOL no longer in control, however, such permission is not available. Given the confusion resulting from the transition-related strife, catering to curious tourists is the least of the miners' concerns these days. Strikes and massive layoffs have turned Llallagua into a near ghost town. Often, promised severance pay hasn't materialised and destitute, out-of-work miners have taken to emigrating from the region en masse.

The miners that remain in Llallagua, though mostly illiterate and largely ignorant of world affairs, passionately try to keep abreast of the Bolivian political situation that so dominates their lives. They will happily engage anyone willing to listen in a lengthy discussion of their favourite topic.

At present, any kind of permission to visit inside the mine is highly unlikely. Things are in such a state of disorganisation that no one really knows who has the authority to sanction such a visit. While I was in the area, even a North American journalist with Associated Press credentials was refused. If you really have your heart set on seeing Siglo XX however, you can give it a shot anyway. There is little that is certain in Bolivia!

Getting There & Away

Llallagua lies 95 km by road to the south-east of Oruro. *Flota Bustillo* has service from Oruro seven times daily. Llallagua is also served daily at 6 pm by *Flota Minera* from Cochabamba.

COROCORO

Corocoro, just east of the Río Desaguadero near the La Paz-Arica rail line, is another major mining town of the Southern Altiplano. The mines of Corocoro produce nearly all of the copper mined in Bolivia and is one of the two major sources of native copper in the world today, the other being on Michigan's Upper Peninsula on the US shore of Lake Superior. Since the copper here is found in nugget form and not in ore which must be smelted, the early native peoples of the Altiplano were able to make use of it long before anyone knew what to do with ore copper. The Museum of Pre-Columbian Precious Metals, in La Paz, displays some fine examples of their work.

SAJAMA NATIONAL PARK

The loosely-defined and undeveloped Sajama National Park occupies a vast area of Western Oruro Department, near the Chilean border. The world's highest forest covers the foothills flanking the impressive Sajama Volcano which may be Bolivia's highest peak at 6542 metres. This 'highest forest' consists of dwarf *queñoa* trees, a species unique to the Altiplano. Unless you're into seeing the highest, lowest, biggest and best of things, you probably won't be too impressed. These 'trees' have the size and appearance of creosote bushes.

The real attractions of the region are the volcano itself – its glaciers, and its wildly eroded slopes – and the surrounding nearly uninhabited wilderness. There are no trails per se and hiking is strictly backcountry. Drinking water is scarce, and an ample supply should be carried on all hikes. The only stores available in the area are at the tiny village of Sajama just a few km from the volcano. If you'd like to warm up, there are some hot springs five km from the village. The locals can point you in the right direction.

A rich variety of wildlife inhabits the area. Look for the wild cameloids, vicuña and guanaco, which are frequently seen. Flamingos, rheas, and viscachas also inhabit the park.

Places to Stay

If you're not camping you may be able to find lodging in a private home in the village of Sajama, but even so, a warm sleeping bag and many layers of clothing will be appreciated during the cold and often windy nights.

With a tent, you can camp just about anywhere in this sparsely-populated region. The nicest place to stay is five to 10 km from the village of Sajama along the road to La Paz.

Just across the Chilean frontier on Lake Chungara in spectacular Lauca National Park is a ranger's headquarters with a couple of beds and a warm stove. Further into Chile at the tiny villages of Parinacota and Putre rough accommodation may be found but transportation from Bolivia can be a problem.

Top: View of Copacabana from Cerro Sancollani (DS)
Bottom: 'Bolivians – The sea belongs to us. To recover it is our duty'
– sign on customs office – Copacabana (DS)

Top: Salar de Uyuni – salt flats (VN)
Left: Laguna Colorada, south-western Bolivia (VN)
Right: Desert landscape around the Salar de Uyuni – Potosí (VN)

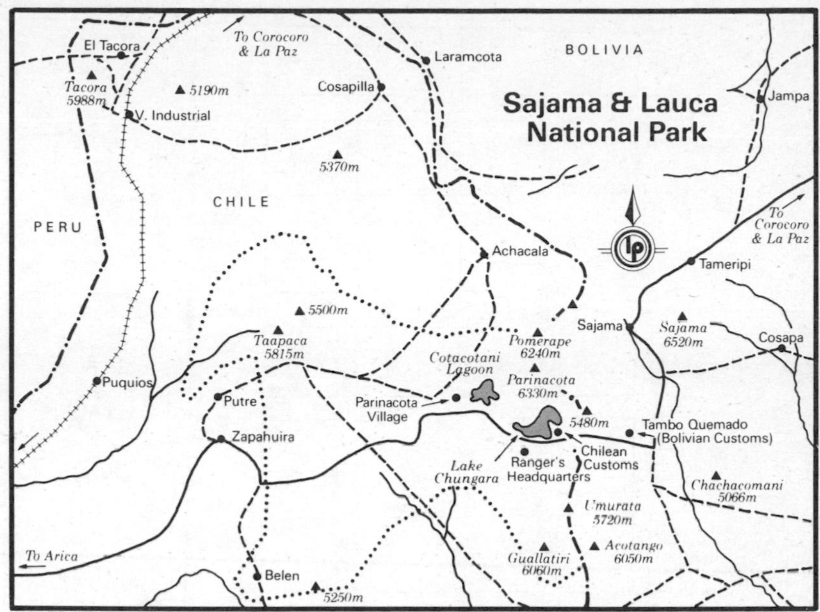

Getting There & Away

Flota Litoral buses leave from La Paz on Tuesday and Friday at 6 am and pass over an excruciatingly rough road which connects the city with Arica, Chile, via the village of Patacamaya. The trip to Sajama will take at least eight to 12 hours and during the rainy season the road may not be passable at all. If the bus is crowded, you may have to pay the full Arica fare of US$18.

To travel onwards into Chile, flag down a bus on a Tuesday or Friday evening. Returning to La Paz, the flota passes in the early afternoon on Monday and Friday, but there may not be space. Trucks do pass infrequently and will accept paying passengers.

After you've come this far, a visit to Lauca National Park is highly recommended before you return to La Paz .

UYUNI

Whenever a Bolivian learns that I'm from Alaska, inevitably the first words he or she can be expected to utter are *mucho frío* or 'very cold'. I get a similar response whenever I mention Uyuni.

Yes, it's bloody cold here in this unattractive desert community and there seems to be no escape from it. The wind bites through any number of clothing layers, buildings are drafty, and nobody has indoor heating. Well, almost nobody. The *jefe* at the railroad station does have a portable space heater but he quickly shoos away any member of the general public trying to warm up in his office.

Even though the town itself looks like a setting in a post nuclear holocaust movie (it's really only the second ugliest spot in the Western Hemisphere – see Puerto Suarez!), it is not without interest.

The local population is around 5,000. Those who are employed in Uyuni are

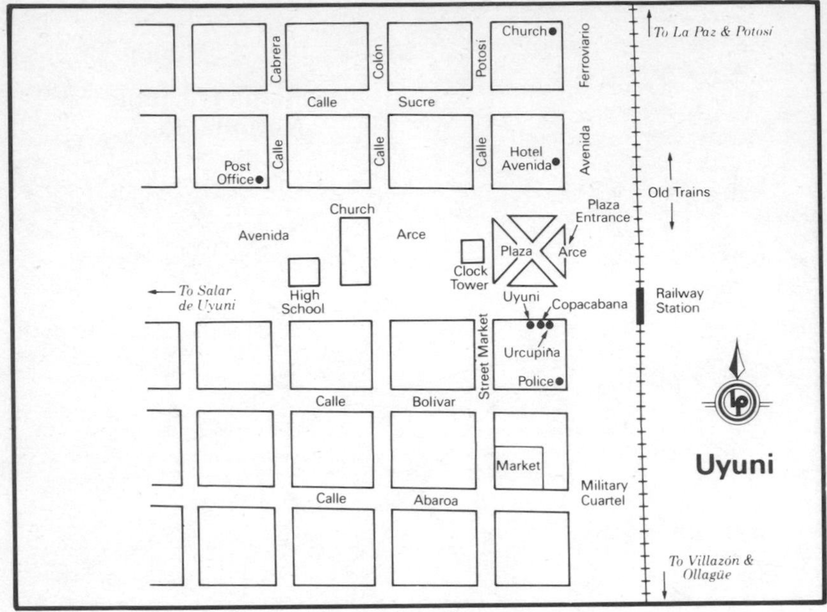

involved in one of two major enterprises: government and mining. The former includes railroad workers, military and police personnel, and city officials. The latter are almost exclusively concerned with the extraction of salt from the nearby *Salar de Uyuni*, one of Bolivia's most unique and impressive sights.

Places to Stay

Unfortunately, not a single hotel in Uyuni welcomes visitors with much better than an unpleasant scowl - maybe it's the climate. Whatever the case, the least disagreeable of the lot is the *Hotel Avenida* across from the railroad station. It's also the cleanest and the best value. At US$2.50, it even offers warm showers (sometimes) and rather overpriced but interesting excursions to the Salar. There are no private baths available.

None of the other available lodgings are worth even a sideward glance unless the Avenida is full, as is frequently the case. The *Residenciál Uyuni* costs US$2 per night with no amenities. The *Residenciál Urcupiña* charges US$2.50 per person for similarly bare-bones accommodation.

The *Residenciál Copacabana* should be avoided even if it means having to bed down in a sleeping bag outdoors. The owners of this establishment are as sour a bunch of characters as I've met anywhere in the world. Maybe there's some truth in the philosophy that a person is the product of their environment but even so, theirs is no way to run a successful business.

Another option is to sleep in the *salón de espera* at the train station. It's free and with all the bodies that usually crash out there, it's probably the warmest accessible place in town. It's also next door to the jefe's heated office and some of the warmth from that room leaks through the wall. The major problem is that people wander in and out of the room all night long and forget to shut the door. The Bolivians seem to be more or less immune to the cold and you may find yourself up and down all night trying to keep the heat in.

If you'd like a quieter and more private spot to sleep, the officials at the *alcaldía* are quite friendly and may allow you to spread out on the floor there if you appear to be reputable.

Places to Eat

There is a decent restaurant at the Hotel Avenida and a few food stalls in the market but that's about the extent of what Uyuni has to offer.

Getting There & Away

Without an all-terrain vehicle, there's no easy way to get to Uyuni save on the railroad. It sits at the junction of the lines to Antofagasta, Villazón, and La Paz and is just south of Rio Mulatos where the Potosí and Sucre line branches off the main route. Thus, all trains travelling between Villazón or Antofagasta and La Paz or Potosí/Sucre must pass through Uyuni.

Trains which serve Uyuni are without exception chronically late and although the official timetable schedules stops of only 20 minutes, I've never spent less than four hours waiting here. Railroad officials and experience tell me that the trains typically run six to 12 hours behind schedule, so don't be too surprised if you're delayed considerably. While you're stuck, walk around the railroad yard and see the old steam locomotives which are decomposing there.

Trains to Antofagasta are scheduled to leave at 4 or 5 am on Wednesday and Saturday.

Also early on Saturday morning, any time after midnight, the *tren tortuga* (turtle train), – as it's locally known – is supposed to depart for Potosí. This route is slow but it crosses the well-known El Cóndor Pass, which at 4786 metres above sea level is the highest point on Bolivian rail lines and also one of the highest in the world.

To Villazón, there is a service on Monday and Wednesday at 2 am and on Friday and Saturday at 4 am.

Trains to La Paz and Oruro leave on Tuesday, Friday, and Saturday around 10 pm. Another train which only goes as far as Oruro leaves early Friday morning, sometime between midnight and dawn.

For more specific schedules, check the chalkboard at the station the day you want to depart.

By air, *TAM* serves Uyuni from the military airport in La Paz.

SALAR DE UYUNI

The Salar de Uyuni which covers nearly all of Daniel Campos province is Bolivia's largest salt lake with an area of 12,106 square km.

In relatively recent geological history, this part of the Altiplano has been covered by two successive large lakes. From 40,000 to 25,000 years ago, Lago Minchín occupied much of South-western Bolivia. The area lay dry for 14,000 years before the appearance of short-lived Lake Tauca, which lasted for only about 1000 years. When Lake Tauca dried up, it left a couple of puddles, Lakes Poopó and Uru Uru, and two major salt concentrations, the Salares de Uyuni and Coipasa. The salt is the result of the leeching of minerals from the mountains. It was deposited because this part of the Altiplano is drained internally, with no outlet to the sea.

The highest level reached by Lake Minchín was 3760 metres. Lake Tauca rose to 3720 metres. For this reason, two distinctive levels of terraces are visible along the shoreline at those elevations. Below the lowest level are fossils of coral in limestone.

These days, the Salar de Uyuni is a centre of salt extraction and processing. The principal area of exploitation is in the small settlement of Colchani, about 20 km up the rail line from Uyuni. There is a salt treatment plant near the Colchani railroad station and vendors board the train there selling small parcels of salt for domestic use. The estimated annual capacity of the Colchani operation is 19,700 tons, 18,000 tons of which is used for human consumption while the remaining 2700 tons is consumed by livestock. There remains at least 2,000,000,000 tons of salt in the Salar de Uyuni.

When there's a little water on the flats, it reflects perfectly the blue Altiplano sky and the effect is positively eerie. When they're dry, the Salar becomes a blinding white expanse of the greatest nothing imaginable.

Getting There & Away

From Uyuni, trucks occasionally go to Colchani near the shore of the Salar, but as usual, return transportation can be a problem. Colchani is a scheduled stop on the rail line from Uyuni to Potosí or Oruro/La Paz, and the salt can be seen from the train, however, to fully appreciate the wondrous immensity of the place, you need to get out onto the salt flats.

It also is possible to hire a taxi in Uyuni for a day trip to Colchani and back. It will cost about US$10 for up to five people. In addition, the Hotel Avenida sometimes arranges tours but you will probably have to muster a group. A day tour may cost up to US$50 per person.

Some Uyuni residents involved in salt extraction commute daily to Colchani and back in private vehicles or on motorbikes and for a small fee you may be able to catch a ride with one of them.

Getting Around

It's possible to cross the Salar to the village of Llica which is the unlikely site of a teachers' college. There are infrequent unscheduled trucks and buses which make the trip in a couple of hours. From Llica, however, they continue further into the South-west carrying supplies to sulphur mines. You may have a long wait before someone passes through to take you back to Uyuni. In Llica you can sleep at the college.

In Uyuni, it's possible to hire a jeep and driver for a week at a time but expect to pay around US$300 per person. Keep in mind, however, that a breakdown in this forsaken place could prove disastrous if you're unprepared.

If you will be driving on the Salar, remember to carry a compass, food, water, extra fuel, tools, spare parts, and a means of warming up. Many drivers have become lost on the white expanse and without reference points to follow, they tend to drive in circles until the vehicle runs out of gas. For anyone lost on the Salar, chances of rescue and survival are slim indeed.

Although the South America Handbook describes a boat which crosses the Salar to Llica, long time locals assure me that there has never been enough liquid there in recent history to support a boat of any description.

SALAR DE COIPASA

Much more remote than the Salar de Uyuni is the other great salt desert of Coipasa which lies to the north-west of the Salar de Uyuni. Both were part of the same prehistoric lakes which covered most of this area over 10,000 years ago.

The road into this area is extremely poor and vehicles are subject to bogging down in deep sand, so don't attempt to get there with anything less than a 4WD.

The village of Coipasa sits on an island in the middle of the Salar. Just to the north on the delta of the Río Sabaya is the amazing village of the Chipaya Indians. This group, which is conjectured to be the remnant of the lost Tiahuanaco civilisation, occupies but a single desert village of circular mud huts.

The Chipaya language, vastly different from either Quechua or Aymará, closely resembles Mayan but some anthropologists note similarities to Arabic and North African tribal languages, also.

Chipaya tradition states that they

descend from the builders of the *chullpas* (stone burial towers) found scattered around Lake Titicaca. Their religion deifies phallic images, stones, rivers, mountains, and animal carcasses, to name but a few. Their most revered god is the phallic church tower in the village.

Nine whitewashed cones of sod, which serve as altars, are placed within a radius of 15 km of the settlement. They are used as receptacles for appeasement offerings to evil spirits. The people offer prayers to the Sajama Volcano, too, because they believe that a revered spirit dwells within.

In general, tourists are not particularly welcome here, although I did talk with some extremely mellow and open-minded individuals who visited and developed a minimal rapport with the people. If you don't go to gawk or take photos, you'll have a better chance of being accepted. Cameras are more or less forbidden by the Indians, who are very superstitious about such things.

SOUTH-WESTERN BOLIVIA

The South-western corner of Bolivia is the most remote highland area in the country. With few roads or inhabitants, unpredictable weather conditions, only a few scattered settlements, and unreliable transport, travel into and around the region becomes an exercise in patience and creativity. The area is more or less sectioned off from the rest of the country by rail lines from Villazón to Uyuni and Ollagüe and by the minor ranges of hills called the Cordillera de Lipez and Cordillera de Chichas.

The prehistoric lakes Minchín and Tauca – that evaporated some 10,000 years ago and left behind a parched landscape of brackish puddles and salt flats – once covered most of this high plateau country. Nearly treeless, the region south of the Salar de Uyuni is inhabited only by a few miners and military personnel, and some very determined Aymará who occupy small villages along the Antofagasta rail line.

The almost perfectly flat landscape is interrupted by numerous volcanoes which rise abruptly near the Chilean border. Bleached deposits of brine provide an occasional splash of white amid the prevailing of browns, and several algae-stained lakes add blues, yellows, greens, and reds to the palette. *Laguna Colorada* and *Laguna Verde*, Red Lake and Green Lake respectively, are the best known of these.

Historically, this lonely country hasn't seen much activity. Sometime during the mid-1400s, the reigning Inca Pachacuti sent his son Tupa Inca Yupanqui to conquer lands southward. He was apparently a clever PR man because the south-western extremes of Bolivia and the desert areas of northern Chile were taken bloodlessly. The conquerors marched onward across the wastelands to the northern bank of Chile's Maule River where a fierce tribe of Araucanian Indians forced them to stake out the southern boundary of the Inca Empire and sent them packing back to Cuzco.

Due to the undeniably harsh conditions encountered in these deserts, the Incas never effectively colonised the area. These days, little has changed and the landscape is dotted with only mining camps, health and military posts, and geothermal projects. Recently, uranium was discovered at Polulos and projects to exploit it should be getting underway soon.

Ollagüe Volcano

The easiest way to catch a glimpse of South-western Bolivia is to ride on the Uyuni-Antofagasta railway. On Ollagüe Volcano, which straddles the Bolivian/Chilean border, there is a high density of geothermal activity – including fumeroles and sulphur lakes. You can catch a ride up the active smoking volcano to the 5000-metre level, with miners who work at sulphur camps on its slopes.

Laguna Colorada

As its name implies, Laguna Colorada is a

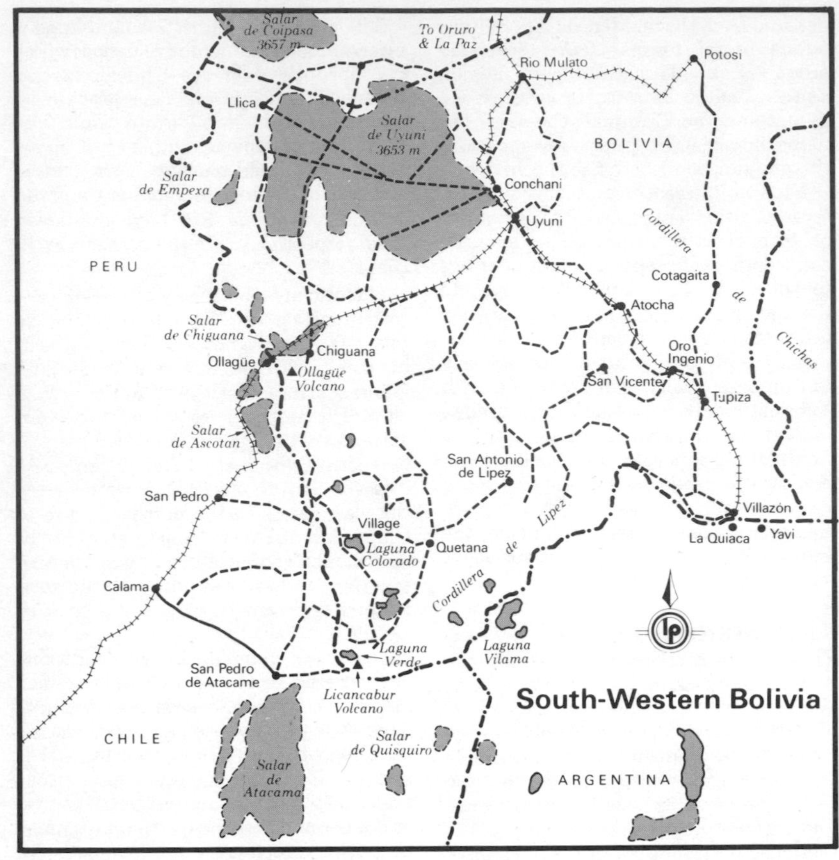

fiery red lake - about 25 km from the Chilean border. It is inhabited by several unique species of flamingos. On the Western shore of Laguna Colorada there is a camp where visitors without tents can probably find a place to crash for the night. About 15 km south-west of here is an impressive geyser basin which may be accessed by any robust vehicle.

Near Laguna Colorada there is a sulphur mining camp called *Campamento Susana*. Most transport you find along the tracks around Laguna Colorada will be supplying or servicing this camp or the developing geothermal project 25 km or so south of the lake which is known as *Sol de Mañana*.

Laguna Verde

Laguna Verde is a small blue-green body of water at the corner of the south-west extremity of Bolivian territory. It is flanked by two sulphur mines and a military base where the army will usually welcome overnight guests who may wander in.

Atop Licancábur Volcano, just to the west of Laguna Verde, is an Inca crypt. On this and many other peaks in the vicinity, young men were marched to the summit – exposed to the cruel elements – and forced to freeze to death as a sacrifice to the gods, in commemoration of significant events within the Empire.

Sud Lipez

The province of Sud Lipez was once a booming place with 18,000 people involved in mining and grazing, however the current labour strife in the mining industry is having a serious effect on the area and much of the population has recently moved away. There is still a relatively excellent road from Tupiza to San Pedro de Lipez and traffic between the two remains constant throughout most of the year. If you end up here, it's possible to lay out a sleeping bag in the school.

Rosa de Oro Mine

This operation, which is 100 km or so from Tupiza, is the most profitable and efficient antimony mine in Bolivia because they process and refine the antimony in the area and ship the finished product to market instead of the raw ore, as its competitors do. If you're passing through here, ask about a tour of the site. The owners, the Bernales, are friendly and may be willing to show you around if they have time.

San Vicente

This little place wouldn't even rate a mention were it not the village where the legendary outlaws Butch Cassidy and the Sundance Kid supposedly met their untimely demise at the hands of the Bolivian Army. Butch's sister, however, claims that he returned from South America to Utah years afterward and that the entire Bolivian encounter was more or less a fabrication embellished over the years into a popular folk legend.

San Vicente may be most easily accessed from Tupiza via Oro Ingenio but I really can't think of any reason to go there.

Getting There & Around

Before you set out on an adventure through this undeveloped corner of the Andes, it's important to realise that getting around is not easy and that you will be depending a great deal on luck and the hospitality of the people who live here. It's therefore a good idea to bring along some sort of gifts for stranded officials and workers who may prove helpful. Life in these outposts can be very lonely for them and such luxuries as coffee, alcohol, coca, cigarettes, and sweets are unavailable, so they would be greatly appreciated. If you're opposed to distributing such health hazards you could bring reading materials, vegetables, or fruit which are also in short supply.

Flexibility is the key if you're relying on finding rides in private trucks or jeeps. Be prepared to wait considerable periods of time for transportation going your way. Often days and weeks pass without a sign of activity. The safest bet would therefore be to hire a 4WD and driver in Uyuni or Tupiza. These will cost as much as US$300 to 400 per person per week if you plan to venture this far into the never-never.

Coming from Tupiza, which lies on the Villazón rail line, you can flag down one of the cargo trucks, fuel trucks, or ambulances that sometimes service the mines, foundries, geothermal camps, and health stations from that city. Historically, the roads in the south-west have been so poor that they were only passable a few months of the year (late March to October) but now the army goes year-round to Laguna Colorada and Laguna Verde and visitors can catch a lift with them. For more info on the Tupiza area, refer to the chapter dealing with Southern Bolivia.

Many travellers visiting here are entering Bolivia from Chile, but this is by no means a straightforward proposition unless they're travelling on the rail line.

Though difficult, it is possible to travel from San Pedro, Chile (not to be confused with San Pedro de Atacama which is a little further south), into South-western Bolivia through a place called Lito on the frontier to Laguna Colorada and Laguna Verde. With a bit of luck, rides may be arranged from San Pedro to the border. Once at Lito, (nothing more than a few deserted stone huts), you may be able to flag down a camión servicing Campamento Susana. More likely, however, you will be forced to walk the 25 km to the mining camp.

At Campamento Susana there is a military post where you will be checked into Bolivia, but no official entry stamps are available. For these, you'll have to go to the federal police in either Uyuni or Tupiza or to the border post at Ollagüe/Abaroa. From Susana, it's relatively easy to find a ride northward to the rail line at Chigüana from where one may board the train toward Uyuni.

For anyone just passing into Chile to buy fuel (the nearest filling station is at San Pedro de Atacama), a Bolivian military stamp from Laguna Verde should suffice to get you out and in again.

The remoteness and difficulty of travel in this area cannot be overstressed. Anyone attempting to visit South-western Bolivia on their own must be equipped with a tent, a warm sleeping bag, fuel, a reliable stove, a compass, water, topographical sheets of the area, twice as much food as you expect to need, and clothing sufficient for sub-zero temperatures. Soroche is also a very real problem, especially for hikers, and snow can be expected during the winter. Even though the locals will do what they can, no reliable help can be expected should you run into trouble. *Peustos sanitarios* (health posts) are dispersed around the area for the benefit of local miners, military, and campesinos, but their medical supplies and expertise are generally very basic and shouldn't be counted on.

The best time for travellers to be wandering around South-western Bolivia is between late March and October when the days are cold but dry. During the remainder of the year, the roads turn into quagmires and transportation is sparse. Unless you're one for considerable adventure and/or punishment it's actually risky and not recommended to visit during this time.

If you've got a bit of spare cash and would like to take a sightseeing tour through the region, American Express in Sucre and Potosí offer five or six-day excursions out of those cities between the months of May and September. A tour for up to five people will cost US$900 on the five-day itinerary and US$125 more for the extra day.

For up to five people the price includes transport by jeep, three meals daily, lodging, and a guide. Not bad considering the effort saved by going this route.

Many thanks to Clare Best (England), Terry Terrill (Canada), David McGuire (England), and Vincent Neussl (Austria) for their help in writing this section.

Typical tour schedules are:

Typical tour schedules are:

	5-day	*6-day*
Day 1	Potosí to Salar de Uyuni	Same
Day 2	Salar to Laguna Colorada	Same
Day 3	Laguna Colorada	Same
Day 4	Laguna Colorada to Salar	To Laguna Verde
Day 5	Salar to Potosí	Laguna Verde to Salar de Uyuni
Day 6		Salar de Uyuni to Potosí

VILLAZÓN

Most travellers entering Bolivia from Argentina or vice versa, pass through Villazón. The twin village of La Quiaca lies just across the Río Villazón in Northern Argentina. In addition to being a port of entry, Villazón serves as a warehousing and marketing centre for contraband – food products, electronics goods, and alcohol – which is smuggled into Bolivia from Argentina. This business is known locally as the 'ant trade' because thousands of kg of goods are carried across the bridge daily on the backs of peasants who form a continuous human cargo train across the frontier.

All this activity takes place under the noses of customs officials who seem to do a lot of looking the other way. Only selectively do they enforce the law, especially when they notice a passing item that strikes their fancy. A lot of Argentine wine is confiscated this way!

The contrast between the Bolivian and Argentine sides is rather striking. La Quiaca is a neatly-groomed little place with tree-lined avenues, surfaced streets, nice restaurants, and well-stocked shops. Across the frontier, however, you enter the real Andes. Villazón is a dusty, unkempt and haphazard-looking settlement which is of very little interest except as a point of entry or exit.

Many Bolivians have settled on the Argentine side of the border and most of Jujuy province seems to be populated by Bolivian ex-pats. Migration into Argentina continues at a significant rate and gives Villazón the distinction of being the 'Tijuana' of Bolivia.

For tourists, crossing the border should be no problem at all, but don't get caught up in the contrabandist's procession or you'll be hours getting through. Immigration offices and federal police are found on either side of the bridge and formalities here are normally minimal and friendly. This is one of two ports of entry in Bolivia where they'll grant you permission to remain in the country for 90 days, but you have to request it. If you're entering Argentina here and need a visa for that country, get it in either Tarija or one of the other Argentine consulates around Bolivia because there is none in Villazón.

British citizens are now almost universally admitted to Argentina and some are even given visas on the spot at the consulates but most are required to wait 14 days. Everyone should be prepared for thorough and exhaustive customs searches about 20 km into Argentina. Entering Bolivia, the searches are casual – if conducted at all. Bolivian Immigration is open from 7 am to 7 pm and doesn't close for lunch.

If you're heading south from La Quiaca, a visit to Yavi – where there is a beautiful little church with onyx windows – is highly recommended. It's only a few minutes on a good road from La Quiaca.

Climate-wise, this border region has typical Altiplano weather patterns. High winds blow across the unprotected plain almost constantly and nights are cold, but the majority of days are clear.

Warning

Plain-clothes police stop foreigners in the streets of Villazón and say that they must confiscate any 'illegal' US dollar notes you may be carrying. Of course, dollars are not illicit items anywhere in Bolivia; this is just another racket game in the endless repertoire of Bolivian officialdom, but since few foreigners want to stay in town long enough to raise much of a fuss about it, it's a difficult one to eliminate. Any problems you have should be reported to the officer's superiors but the best bet is to avoid the situation in the first place. Hide your cash well, leave it in your room, or tell the offender that you only carry traveller's cheques (this worked for me) and hope for the best. If they do find cash, it may help to let them know that you can and will cause them serious repercussions should they insist on carrying out such highway robbery.

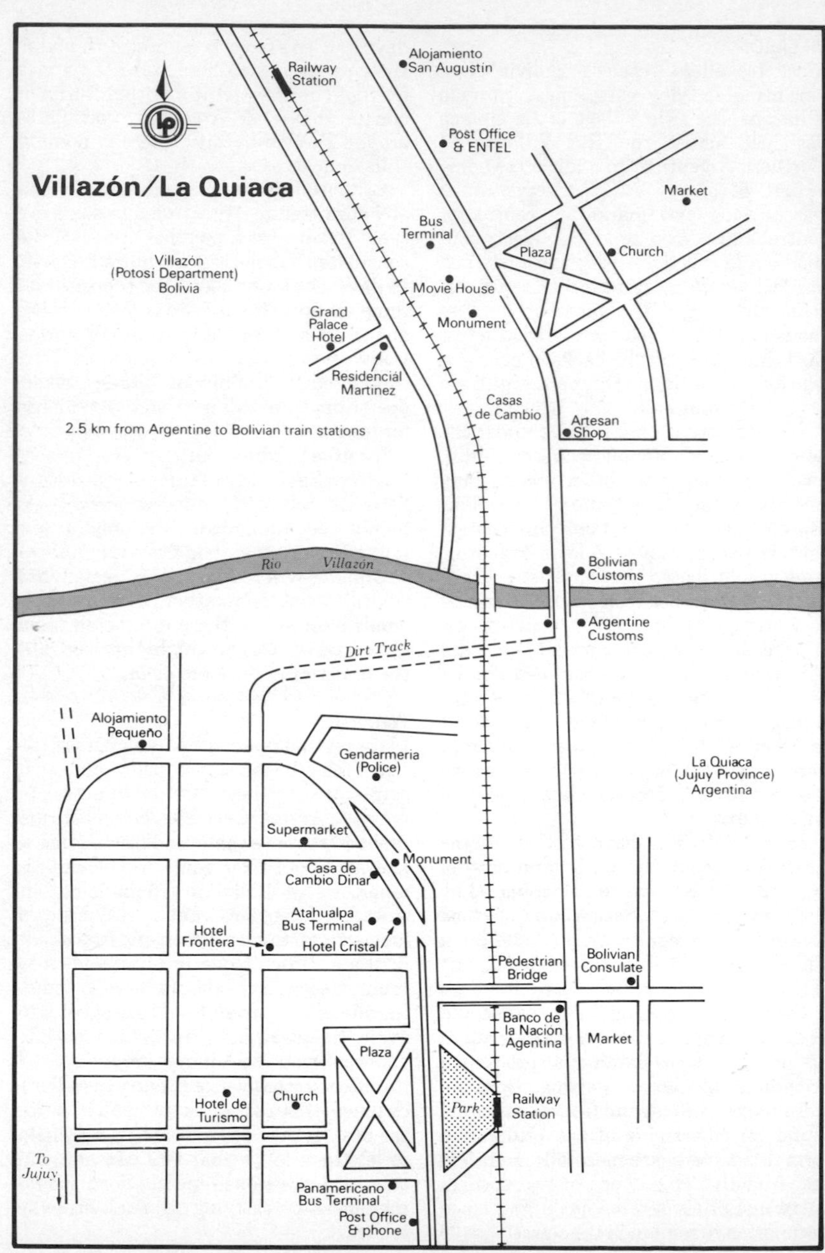
Villazón/La Quiaca
Railway Station
Alojamiento San Augustin
Post Office & ENTEL
Market
Bus Terminal
Plaza
Church
Villazón (Potosi Department) Bolivia
Movie House
Monument
Grand Palace Hotel
Residenciál Martinez
Casas de Cambio
Artesan Shop
2.5 km from Argentine to Bolivian train stations
Rio Villazón
Bolivian Customs
Argentine Customs
Dirt Track
Alojamiento Pequeño
Gendarmeria (Police)
La Quiaca (Jujuy Province) Argentina
Supermarket
Monument
Casa de Cambio Dinar
Atahualpa Bus Terminal
Hotel Frontera
Hotel Cristal
Pedestrian Bridge
Bolivian Consulate
Banco de la Nación Agentina
Market
Plaza
Hotel de Turismo
Church
Park
Railway Station
To Jujuy
Panamericano Bus Terminal
Post Office & phone

Additional Warning
There is another popular scam surfacing these days that involves foreigners. A packet of money is 'accidentally dropped' onto the pavement in front of a traveller. When he or she picks it up, the person who 'dropped' it immediately accuses the foreigner of robbery and the foreigner is arrested, caught red-handed with the 'stolen' goods. Only after a substantial 'fine' is paid is the 'offender' allowed to go free. In Villazón, it's probably best not to 'find' anything or even try to be helpful by picking up a dropped item.

Information
Post & Communications There are post and telephone offices on both sides of the border (see map for locations) but Argentine service seems to be superior on both counts. The post is generally more reliable than in Bolivia and reverse charge phone calls are accepted to limited areas.

Time change There is a one-hour time difference between Bolivia and Argentina. Noon in Villazón is 1 pm in La Quiaca.

Consulate There is a Bolivian consulate in La Quiaca, which is open from 8 am to 1 pm Monday to Saturday.

Changing Money If you're changing cash dollars or Argentine australes into bolivianos, you can get the best rate at one of the numerous casas de cambio along Villazón's main street just above the international bridge. Not all places offer the same rates, however, so it pays to shop around and even bargain with them. *Casa de Cambio Dinar* in La Quiaca gives a slightly lower rate when you buy bolivianos, but it's a good place to buy australes. They don't accept travellers' cheques, however. If you're entering Argentina here, it's a good idea to just exchange enough cash to get you to Salta or Jujuy where rates are considerably better.

Banco de la Provincia de Juyuy does not exchange money at all. *Banco de la Nación Argentina* does but it's quite a ripoff. On cash dollars they pay 15% less than the going rate in Jujuy. They exchange travellers' cheques (not Citicorp or Visa) for 25% less.

Places to Stay - bottom end
In La Quiaca, the only inexpensive hotel is *Alojamiento Pequeño* - not far from the frontier. It's very basic, but friendly and clean. There are no private baths or hot water, but it costs only US$2.40 per person.

Quite a few economical alojamientos and hotels can be found in Villazón. The *Grand Palace* across from the bus terminal is clean with a restaurant and hot showers. A room with private bath is US$4.50 per person, US$3 per person without bath.

Near the train station at 860 Antofagasta is the rather marginal *Alojamiento San Agustín*. No private baths or hot water are available but it only costs US$1.75 per person. The *Hotel Central* has similar amenities but the staff seems to be more agreeable. They ask for US$2 per person but the price is negotiable.

The cleanest, friendliest place to stay in Villazón is the *Residencial Martinez* across the railroad tracks from the bus terminal. There are no private baths but there is an attached restaurant and it costs only US$3.

Places to Stay - Middle
Villazón doesn't have any mid-range accommodation but La Quiaca does have a couple of nicer places. The *Hotel Crystal* at Avenida Sarmiento 539 is clean and offers hot water and private baths for US$9 single, US$14 double, and US$18 for a triple room. On the corner of Arabe Siria and San Martín is the extremely clean *Hotel de Turismo* which charges the same prices as the Crystal but seems to be slightly higher quality. They have a lovely dining room with a stone fireplace and a rather cosy atmosphere.

Places to Eat

Food is much nicer and better value on the Argentine side of the border. A beautiful large steak with chips goes for less than a tiny, tough, overcooked *churrasco* in Villazón. I'd highly recommend the restaurant at the Hotel de Turismo.

On the Bolivian side there are quite a few restaurants which offer reasonable lunch specials for US$1.25 or so, but *Quinta Ingoyen* at 269 Avenida Republica Argentina stands out as one of the best. There are also many inexpensive restaurants near the transportation terminals. As usual, the food stalls in the market are cheap but they don't offer much variety.

Getting There & Away

The vast majority of those visitors passing through Villazón arrive or depart by rail. If you're coming from the South and want to take the train on towards La Paz it will be necessary to walk or take a cab across the border. The distance from bus terminals in La Quiaca and the railroad station in Villazón is between two and three km. To the Bolivian bus terminal is slightly less.

Regarding the train schedule, the station chief laughed when I asked about it. Typically ENFE, the official timetable isn't even a vague representation of reality, but for what it's worth, here it is anyway. Trains are supposed to go to La Paz at 1.45 pm on Tuesday and to Oruro on Monday and Thursday at 11.45 am. First class fare to La Paz is US$10.80 and to Oruro is US$8. Second class will set you back US$7.45 and US$5.45 to La Paz and Oruro, respectively.

The ticket window is supposed to open at 8 am the day of departure but the station chief says it's impossible to get tickets unless you spend the night in the queue at the station.

Those going the other direction who'd like to connect with an Argentine train to Buenos Aires will have to travel by bus to Tucumán via Salta or Jujuy and then arrange a rail passage there. From La Quiaca to Salta and Jujuy, both *Atahuallpa* and *Panamericano* leave at least every two hours from their respective terminals.

Going north from Villazón, all buses depart from the central terminal. The bus to Potosí leaves at 4 pm daily and the 13-hour trip costs US$7.50. To Sucre there is one departure daily, also at 4 pm. The fare is US$12. On Monday, Tuesday, Thursday, Friday, and Sunday at 11 am there are departures to Tarija – a six-hour journey. Service to Tupiza leaves at 2.45 and 3.15 pm daily. This quick trip of 2½ hours passes through some very nice scenery. The fare is US$1.75.

Cochabamba

Chicha quiero, chicha busco,
Por chicha mis paseos.
Señora, deme un vasito
Para cumplir mis deseos.

Roughly translated from an old Bolivian poem, the verse means ' I want *chicha*, I search for *chicha*, for *chicha* are my wanderings. Lady, give me a glass to satisfy my longing'.

To most Bolivians, Cochabamba is known for one of two things. One sort of Bolivian will dreamily remark on its luscious climate. Another sort, such as the author of the above poem, will identify Cochabamba with its luscious chicha. It happens that both images of the city are well-founded.

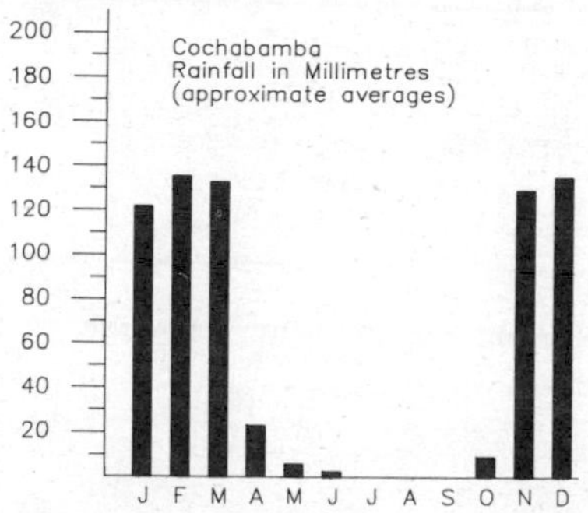

Cochabamba has a warm, dry, sunny climate similar to that found in Mediterranean lands and it physically resembles parts of Spain or Southern California. The Cochabamba Valley is also the production centre of the famous maize brew that keeps so many Cochabambinos in a comfortable stupor. In front of homes throughout the valley and around much of the entire southern Cochabamba department you will notice white cloth or plastic flags flying on long poles. These serve to indicate that chicha is available in that home and you'll soon realise how much of the stuff there is around.

Most visitors will want to try it, of course, but they should be warned that it's highly 'leaded' and at Cochabamba's 2570-metre elevation, it probably packs more of a punch than the majority of outsiders are expecting.

The population of the city is currently around 300,000 and steadily growing. It long held the status of being Bolivia's second largest city but due to the recent push for economic development of the lowlands, those honours have been passed to Santa Crúz.

The name 'Cochabamba' is derived by joining the Quechua words 'cocha' and 'pampa' which together mean 'swampy plain'. The city occupies a fertile green bowl, 25 km long by 10 km wide, set amid a landscape of low hills. To the north-west rises 5035-metre Cerro Tunari, the highest peak in Bolivia east of the Altiplano region. The rich soil of the area yields abundant crops of maize, barley, wheat, alfalfa and orchard and citrus fruits. A large European population inhabits Cochabamba and environs and only a small percentage of the people are of pure Indian extraction.

The city was founded in January of 1574 by Sebastián Barba de Padilla. It was named the Village of Oropeza in honour of the Count and Countess of Oropeza, parents of Viceroy Francisco de Toledo who chartered and promoted the settlement of the place.

During the heyday of Potosí's silver boom, the Cochabamba Valley developed into the primary source of food for the miners in that agriculturally unproductive area. Cochabamba came to be known as the 'breadbasket' of Bolivia due to its high volume of maize and wheat production.

When Potosí declined in importance

Avenida America
Buenos Aires
Pedro Blanco
Beni
Capriles
Stadium
Avenida Uyuni
Ayacucho
Arce
Aniceto
México
My Rocha
Ecuador
Colombia
Chaco
del
Benemeritos
Avenida
Avenida Heroinas
Acho
General
Santivañes
Jordán
Calama
L Cabrera
Nataniel
San Martin
Lanza
Antezana
16 de Julio
Avenida
Oquendo
Avenida Sucre
Avenida Aroma
Aguirre
Cochabamba

1	Palacio de Portales	25	Plaza Busch
2	Estadio departamental	26	Plaza Principal
3	Monumento Abaroa	27	Galeria de Arte Gildaro Antezana
4	Tennis club Cochabamba	28	Iglesia de San Francisco
5	Parque Arqueológico	29	Plaza Sucre
6	Plaza Quintanilla	30	Universidad Mayor de San Simon
7	Paseo El Prado	31	Iglesia de Santo Domingo
8	Parque Zoologico	32	Cathedral
9	Casa Solariega	33	Gram Hotel Las Vegas
10	La Casona	34	Alojamiento Imperial
11	Valencia Restaurant	35	Market
12	Plaza Colon	36	City Hall
13	Plaza Toledo	37	Alcaldia
14	Plaza Cobija	38	Residenciál Florida
15	Convent of Santa Teresa	39	Residenciál San Severino
16	Residenciál Ideal	40	Plaza Esteban Arze
17	Iglesia Hospicio	41	Bus Terminals
18	Museo Arqueológico	42	Mercado Calatayud
19	Casa de la Cultura	43	Trucks to Torotoro
20	Plaza Guzman Quiton	44	Trucks & Bus Parking to Chapare
21	Tourism Kiosk	45	Plaza Rivero
22	Compañia de Jesus	46	Colina de San Sebastian
23	Prefectura & National Police	47	Estacion Central de Ferrocarril
24	Instituto Boliviano de Turismo	48	Mercado de Ferias

during the early 18th century, so did Cochabamba. Grain production in the area of Chuquisaca (Sucre), much nearer Potosí, was sufficient to supply the decreasing demand. By the mid-1800s, however, the economic crisis subsided and the city again assumed its position as the nation's granary. Elite landowners in the valley grew wealthy and began to invest in mining ventures in western Bolivia.

Before long, the focus in Bolivian mining shifted from Potosí to the Altiplano and those mines began to attract international capital. As a result, Cochabamba thrived and the relatively cosmopolitan European/Quechua population gained the reputation of being a prosperous lot.

Economically active and growing, the area today offers a host of historical and archaeological attractions, a progressive atmosphere, and a vitality that is visibly absent in the more traditional cities of the Altiplano and Southern Highlands.

Information

On the rare occasion when the tourist office is open, it's quite helpful. The kiosk can be found on General Acha in front of the ENTEL building. It's officially supposed to be open from 9 am to noon and 2 to 6 pm but you'd be lucky to find someone there by 11 am and I've never seen signs of life in the afternoon.

If you do catch someone in, they will sell you a fairly accurate city plan for 25c, but be warned that it's a little outdated and some significant street names are missing.

Post & Communications The post and telephone offices are both in the large complex between General Acha and Avenida Heroínas near Junín. Postal service from here is quite reliable and the facilities are among the best in Bolivia. A special express post office is downstairs from the main lobby. For mail sent to destinations within Bolivia, this is the way to go.

Changing Money *American Exchange* on the main plaza and *Cambios Universo* on Calle España (just off the plaza) will both exchange travellers' cheques, but American is a more professional operation and gives a better rate. American Exchange will also change your travellers' cheques into US dollars cash for a three percent commission.

Street changers hang out on the corner of Heroínas and 25 de Mayo and among themselves their rates are competitive, but you won't get much over the official rate available at casas de cambio. They will only accept dollars cash.

Consulates Several consular representatives are present in Cochabamba. A few which may be useful to you are:

Argentina
- Avenida Pando 1329 2nd Floor (tel 48268)
- Open 9 am to 1 pm weekdays

Brazil
- Calle Potosí 14455 (tel 45702)
- Open 2 to 6 pm weekdays

Peru
- Avenida Pando 1143 (tel 43276)
- Open 9 am to noon and 2 to 5 pm weekdays

West Germany
- Calle España 149 (tel 25529)
- Open 5 to 6 pm weekdays

USA
- Avenida Heroínas 464 4th Floor, No 115 (tel 25896)
- Open 9 am to noon weekdays

Books & Maps The best place to buy both books and maps in Cochabamba is at one of the two representatives of *Los Amigos del Libro* on Heroínas near España and on General Acha diagonally across the street from the tourist office kiosk. They sell English and German language paperbacks, reference books, and souvenir publications.

A range of thematic maps are also available from street vendors who set up in front of the LAB office in the post office/ENTEL complex.

Churches

Constructed in 1581, the *Iglesia de San Francisco* on 25 de Mayo and Bolívar is the second oldest church in Cochabamba. Major revisions and renovation took place in both 1782 and 1925, however, and very little of the original structure remains. Attached is a convent and cloister which were added during the 1600s. In consideration of the climate, the cloister is constructed of wood rather than stone as would have been customary at the time.

The cathedral was built in Neoclassic style in 1571 making it the oldest religious structure in the valley and the original church of Oropeza. With a myriad of architectural styles added to it over the years the composition doesn't hang together too well, but the frescoes and paintings inside are worth a look. It is found on Plaza 14 de Septiembre.

The *Convent of Santa Teresa* on Calle Baptista and Plaza Granado is quite beautiful inside if you can ignore the Christmas lights over the altar. It is the result of the combination of two churches, one built on top of the other. Work on the first church was begun in 1753 by Jesuits.

El Hospicio on Plaza Colón is composed of a blend of Baroque, Byzantine, and Neoclassic architectural styles. It was started in 1875 and is the newest major church in Cochabamba.

The *Iglesia de Santo Domingo* is a rather interesting structure for several reasons. Although it was founded in 1612, actual construction wasn't begun until 1778 and was still underway in 1795 when its chief promoter, Francisco Claros García died. The ornamentation is Rococo in style and the main doorway, which is flanked by two anthropomorphic columns, is quite artistic.

The *Iglesia de la Recoleta* north of the river is a baroque structure begun in 1654. The attraction here is a wooden carving called *Cristo de la Recoleta*, accurately carved out of only one piece of wood by Diego Ortiz de Guzmán.

Top: Near Laguna Colorada – south-western Bolivia (VN)
Bottom: Flamingos at Laguna Colorada – south-western Bolivia (VN)

Top: Shepherd – south-western Bolivia near Sajama (TM)
Bottom: Travel by Camion in the Cordillera Real (TM)

Parks

Plaza Colón is a pleasant little park with well-kept gardens, fountains, bridges, and ponds. Nearby to the north, the street called Avenida Ballivián, also known as the Prado, is a palm-lined avenue that will carry you directly to southern California.

The *Parque arqueológico* between the disgusting Río Rocha and Avenida Ramón Rivero is full of numerous gruesome stone heads which are reproductions of originals housed in the *archaeological Museum* in the centre of Cochabamba. Beside this park is a very unusual children's playground.

Not far along the river to the west is the zoo, which is not worth the trouble of a visit.

San Sebastián Hill which lies at the western end of Avenida Aroma towers over the airport and is a good place to relax and read or watch the planes. There is quite a nice view over the entire city from this vantage point.

From San Sebastián, a trail leads along a ridge to another nearby hill, *La Coronilla* where there is a monument dedicated to the women, children, and elderly persons who courageously defended the city of Cochabamba from the Spanish forces of Jose Manuel Goyeneche in 1812.

Museums

The *Archaeological Museum* of Cochabamba is probably the nicest and most complete one in Bolivia. They display artefacts dating from as early as 15,000 BC and as late as the Colonial Period. Admission is US$1.50 and the excellent guided tour, conducted in English or Spanish, takes about an hour and a half. The museum is on 25 de Mayo between Heroínas and Colombia. It's open weekdays 8.30 am to noon and 2 to 6 pm.

The *Natural History Museum* and the *Art Museum* are both on the 4th floor of the *Casa de la Cultura* on the corner of Heroínas and 25 de Mayo. They're open 8.30 am to noon and 2 to 6.30 pm Monday to Friday. Admission is free. The Art Museum is small and rather bland, but the Natural History Museum is certainly worth a little time. They have the most fascinating collection of moths, butterflies, spiders, beetles, and bugs that I've ever seen. Even the insect-squeamish will be impressed.

The *Placio de Portales* north of the river offers free guided tours from 5 to 6 pm Monday to Friday. This must be seen in its elegance and the obvious wealth of its builder, tin baron Simon Patiño, cannot be adequately described. To give you some idea, the fireplaces are of flawless Carrera marble, the furniture and woodwork were carved in wood imported from France, the walls are covered with brocaded silk, and one very intricate 'painting' is actually a tapestry. The gardens and exterior are equally representative of inconceivable affluence and extravagance. The house was completed in 1927 but was never occupied and today is used as a sort of hostel for visiting artists and entertainers.

To get there, take Micro G from near the corner of Calle San Martín and Avenida Heroínas.

Markets

Cochabamba has quite a few markets which occupy former plazas (called *canchas* in Quechua) around the southern part of the city. The one most easily accessible is the *Cancha Calatayud* which occupies a large wide spot in the middle of Avenida Aroma. *Cancha Francisco Rivas* and the *Mercado Central de Ferias* are both near the train station. Several other minor market areas are found scattered around the city, but the larger ones are by far the most well-stocked, crowded, and nerve-shattering places you're likely to find in all of Bolivia.

Fiestas

The major annual festival in Cochabamba is celebrated in honour of the *Heroínas de la Coronilla* on 27 May. It's more of a solemn commemoration than a fiesta, actually, so don't attend expecting a lot of raging, drunken activity.

The fiesta of *Santa Veracruz Tatala* is celebrated on 2 May each year, in and around a chapel seven km along the highway to Santa Crúz. Farmers from around Cochabamba Valley gather to pray for fertility of the soil during the coming growing season. The celebration itself is a bit more animated than the Coronillas and there is folk music, dancing, and drinking to accompany it.

Places to Stay – bottom end

There are quite a few very nice and inexpensive residenciales and alojamientos around Cochabamba. The best and most friendly place to stay in the city is the *Residencial Florida* at S583 25 de Mayo. It's sparkling clean and they have a nice patio with lawn furniture on the main floor, and a sunny deck upstairs. Hot water is available until 1 pm. Its location midway between the town centre and the bus terminals is another plus and it's a good place to go if you're looking to meet other travellers.

The only negative thing I can think of to say about it is that they charge foreigners *less* than Bolivians (that's a switch) and I detest such discriminatory practices no matter which way they go. The owner, a very nice lady who cooks a mean breakfast for her guests, explained to me that she enjoys talking with young backpacking travellers and she designed her price structure hoping to encourage more to stay there. Per person a room costs US$5 for Bolivians and US$4 for travellers.

There are a few other nice places to be found in the same general vicinity as the Florida. The closest is *Residencial San Severino* at S621 25 de Mayo. It costs US$3.50 per person with shared bath. In addition, there are a whole string of cheap alojamientos along Avenida Aroma near the bus terminals. The most popular is probably *Alojamiento Pullman* at E370 Aroma which costs US$3 per person with a cold shower. Hot showers cost an additional 50c. It's clean but the staff is not too amiable.

At S834 Agustín Lopez (just off Avenida Aroma) is the *Residencial Elisa* which costs US$4 per person single, US$3.75 per person double with common bath or US$5 per person with private bath. All rooms include a breakfast of juice, yoghurt, bread, jam, milk, and coffee.

In this same vicinity, it's probably best to avoid the *Alojamiento Sucre* at E256 Aroma which is absolutely filthy. It costs US$3 per person and hot showers are an extra 50c if you're staying here. If not and you just need a shower, they'll charge 75c. Another marginal value is *Alojamiento Aroma* at O-136 on the same avenue. It costs US$2.50 per person but there is no hot water available and often there's no water at all. Also, steer clear of *Alojamiento Miraflores*, an unwelcoming place at E-140 Aroma. It costs US$2.50 per person and has nothing to recommend it but miserable cold showers.

There is also some acceptable accommodation in other parts of the city. The *Residencial Ideal* is on Calle España a few blocks north of the plaza and costs US$5 per person for a room with common bath. It's clean and recommended but in my opinion it's a little overpriced. Hot showers are available and there's a restaurant downstairs. If you're staying here, note the interesting stained-glass windows above the stairwells portraying Bolivian scenes.

The centrally-located *Residencial Imperial* costs US$3.50 single, US$6 double with common baths and hot showers. It's both friendly and clean and they'll watch your luggage while you're out travelling around.

The *Residencial Familiar* is US$4.50 per person with shared baths and hot showers and is at N-234 25 de Mayo. It's fairly popular with travellers.

Places to Stay – middle

Residencial Beunos Aires at N-239 25 de Mayo is clean, but a little dark and gloomy. There is a convenient snack restaurant downstairs. A single room without bath costs US$4.25 while a double is US$7. With private bath a single and double will cost US$6.25 and US$10.50 respectively.

At the *Residencial Ollantay* at N-219 Baptista there is a beautiful courtyard. It's very clean, and tasteful artwork is displayed around the lobby. A room with a private bath and phone costs US$8 single, US$14 double, and US$18 triple. Without bath or phone it's US$6 single, US$10 double, and US$14 triple.

The *Gran Hotel La Vegas* near the main plaza costs US$10 single and US$17.50 double. They offer clean private baths, but the atmosphere is nothing special. Likewise is the nearby *City Hotel* whose prices and amenities are similar.

Near the bus terminals, *Residenciales 2 de Octubre* at E121 Aroma offers hot showers and private baths for US$6.25 single and US$10 double. For US$1.50 extra you can use their sauna. It's more of a live-in sort of place than a lodging for transient travellers.

Places to Eat

You're likely to be pleased with Cochabamba's selection of eating establishments, especially if you're coming from Potosí and Oruro which are anything but epicurean centres.

For breakfast, *Dulce Ilusión* at N-132 España offers a wide variety of sweets and pastries if such things interest you. *Confiteria Cecy* on Heroínas has great orange juice, Irish coffee, eggs, toast, and chocolate. *California Burgers* and *California Donuts* offer pretty much the same for breakfast as the Cecy, but I don't think it quite measures up quality-wise.

The market is the cheapest place to find coffee and a roll and the quality is surprisingly very good. Cochabamba is known for its fruit production and you can find a nice selection of orchard and citrus varieties in the market, too.

For lunch, there are a wide range of choices. The most economical I found was at the *Bar Pensión Familiar* at O-176 Aroma. For US$1.25 you get a complete meal of salad, soup, a main course, and a dessert. Beer at this place costs only 90c, the cheapest I've seen anywhere in Bolivia.

If you like chicken, *Kim's Chicken* on 25 de Mayo near Calle Ecuador offers typical snack meals of chicken and chips for US$1.75. As its name implies, *Las Tablitas Burger House* on the main plaza does burgers and they also serve very nice chicken. If you want a good ol' USA fast-food type restaurant, *California Burgers* qualifies here as it does in La Paz. Be sure to try their excellent and strong Irish coffee which competes directly with that at Confiteria Cecy, which also serves nice lunches.

Confiteria Palermo at N-172 España does standard Bolivian fare – lomo, churrasco, etc – as well as chicken, snacks, and drinks. Similar is *Snack Boulevar* on Bolívar half a block from the main plaza.

El Pahuichi Salón de Té is a pleasant tea house on 25 de Mayo.

Those interested in a quick snack could try *Confiteria Dallas* at the corner of 25 de Mayo and Colombia or across the street at *Fuente de Soda* which serves beer, cocktails, and light meals. *Kivón Helados* at 352 Avenida Heroínas is across the street from the *Bustillo Cinema*. They serve snack meals, pastries, flan, and a variety of ice cream concoctions.

Moving up the price scale, you'll find a whole string of sidewalk cafes along Avenida Ballivián which offer European, Bolivian, North American, and even Japanese fare in a very pleasant environment.

For pizza, go to *Pizza Don Corleone* on Calle España where they also serve good Chilean wine. It's all a bit high-priced but quite welcome after a steady diet of rice, potatoes, beef, and beer.

Reasonable Chinese cooking is available at the *Restaurant Shanghai* at N-160 Calle España.

Another interesting and unique place to check out is *Honey and Pollen Products* on Calle Ecuador between España and Calle Ecuador where they sell foods and cosmetics made from bee products.

There are a couple of night clubs in town. Try the *Aladino* at Avenida Ballivián and La Paz or *Arlequín* in Edificio Recoleta.

Getting There & Away

Air The *José Wilsterman Airport* is at the south-west end of town below San Sebastián Hill. It is served by both LAB and TAM, each of which connect Cochabamba with La Paz and Santa Crúz. In addition, LAB serves Trinidad, Oruro, Sucre, Tarija, and Camiri. TAM goes to Vallegrande.

The airfare to La Paz is US$25 one way. To Santa Crúz it will be about US$21.

Bus Bus terminals are strung out along Avenida Aroma in numbers that keep you wondering how so many companies can survive such competition. Fortunately for travellers, fares reflect this state of affairs and bus travel to or from Cochabamba is quite economical.

Since it is so central, it's fairly easy to get to Cochabamba from just about anywhere in the country that is served by terrestrial transport. Likewise, it's no problem to go from here to any other city. Naturally, a great many buses do the run to La Paz, and well over a score depart between 7 and 9 pm daily. The cost is US$6 for the 11 to 12-hour trip.

Some of the La Paz buses stop in Oruro, but in addition Oruro is served by *Unificado*, *Flota Oruro*, *Danubio*, and others many times per day, at least every half hour in the morning and every hour in the afternoon.

A host of flotas leave for Santa Crúz between 4 and 6 pm. To Potosí, *Flota Panamericana* departs at 5 pm and *Flota San Francisco* at 6.30 pm, both daily. Service to Sucre is available on *Minera* at 5.30 pm, *Unificado* at 6.30 pm, and *San Francisco* at 6.30 pm. Again, all depart daily.

You can go to Llallagua on *Flota Minera* at 6 pm daily or to Vallegrande on *Flota Bolívar* Thursdays and on *Flota Unifacado* Fridays at 7.30 pm.

To Villa Tunari and Puerto Villarroel (Chapare), go to the corner of 9 de Abril and Oquendo near the lake. The first bus leaves at 6.30 am. After that, they leave as soon as all seats are sold. The fare to Chapare is US$2.50.

Train Cochabamba is served almost exclusively by ferrobus which eliminates a few of the major problems normally associated with Bolivian rail travel, specifically trains.

The ferrobus to La Paz leaves on Tuesday, Thursday, and Sunday at 8.30 am. Fares are US$9.50 first class and US$6.30 second. There is a service to Oruro daily at 2 pm which costs US$5.10 first class and US$3.40 second. All ferrobus tickets go on sale the day before scheduled departure at 6 am.

The only non-ferrobus route passing through Cochabamba is a slow local train which connects the little burgs of Aiquile, Mizque, and Angostura to the east with Oruro to the west. If for some reason you'd like to take this route, service to Oruro is on Monday, Wednesday, and Friday. There is no timetable so you'll have to inquire at the station about the anticipated hour of departure. First class fare is US$2.45 and second is US$1.70.

Getting Around

Unless you're travelling to the outskirts of town, the best way to get around in Cochabamba is to hoof it. The climate is certainly conducive to walking and since the city sits on a level valley floor, there are no hills to climb. In addition, despite its population, the central area of the city is rather compact and well laid-out so most everything you'll want to see, with the exception of the *Palacio de Portales*, is within easy walking distance.

Those arriving with luggage will be pleased to learn that the cab fare from the terrestrial transportation terminals to anywhere in town, south and east of the river or north and west of the lake, is only 50c. Beyond those limits it doubles.

Addresses in the city are measured from the Plaza 14 de Septiembre and are preceded by 'N' (*norte*), 'S' (*sul*), 'E' (*este*), or 'O' (*oeste* – to avoid alphanumeric confusion, they often use a 'W' here instead). You should be able to figure out that these stand for 'north', 'south', 'east', and 'west', respectively.

Micro buses are lettered and are rather difficult to use since they do not display their destination. In addition, bus stops in Cochabamba are not marked. The locals know where they stop and to hell with anyone else! Fortunately, help is easy to find and the majority of Cochabambinos will be happy to direct you in the use of their micros, which run to all corners of the city.

QUILLACOLLO

Besides Cochabamba itself, Quillacollo, only 13 km from the main city, is the largest and commercially the most important community of the Cochabamba Valley. Apart from the *feria dominical*, the Sunday market, there is little of interest to be found here most of the year. If, however, you're fortunate enough to be in the area around the middle of August, you can catch the *Fiesta de la Virgen de Urcupiña*, the largest annual celebration in the Cochabamba Department.

Folkloric musicians and dancers come from all over Bolivia to perform at this event. Needless to say, the chicha flows and for three days, 15 to 18 August, many of the participants are only semi-conscious of what's going on.

To reach Quillacollo from Cochabamba catch a micro from the corner of Ayacucho and Aroma. The trip costs 15c and takes about half an hour. You'll be let off beside the main plaza.

INCA-RAKAY

The ruins of Inca-Rakay are mostly crumbling stone walls these days but with a little imagination you can conjure up images of what they once must have looked like. There seems to have been very little research done on them and I've never been able to find much in the way of interpretation of what's there.

The site consists of the remains of several hefty buildings and a large open plaza area overlooking the Cochabamba Valley. There's also a strange rock outcrop that resembles the head of a cóndor, inside of which is a natural passageway leading to the top. Just off the plaza area is a cave which can be explored with a flashlight. Legend says that this cave is the remnant of another of those ubiquitous Inca passageways – this one linking Inca-Rakay with Cuzco – but such a thing is, of course, highly unlikely.

The plaza, which affords a spectacular view of the entire valley on a clear, smog-free day, is an excellent place to set up a tent – a night spent amid these secluded and unattended ruins is quite a haunting experience. If you're staying, remember to bring water as none is available.

Getting There & Away

If you're not planning to spend the night at the site it's a good idea to get an early start out of Cochabamba since the trip will require the better part of a day and you'll want to leave some time for exploring once you reach the ruins.

From the corner of Ayacucho and Aroma in Cochabamba, take a micro to Quillacollo's main square. From there, take a trufi or taxi (50c) or a micro (15c) to the main plaza in the village of Sipe-Sipe. Sometimes, you'll be able to find a micro direct from Cochabamba to Sipe-Sipe for 25c.

On Mondays between 8 and 8.30 am and occasionally at other times (unscheduled)

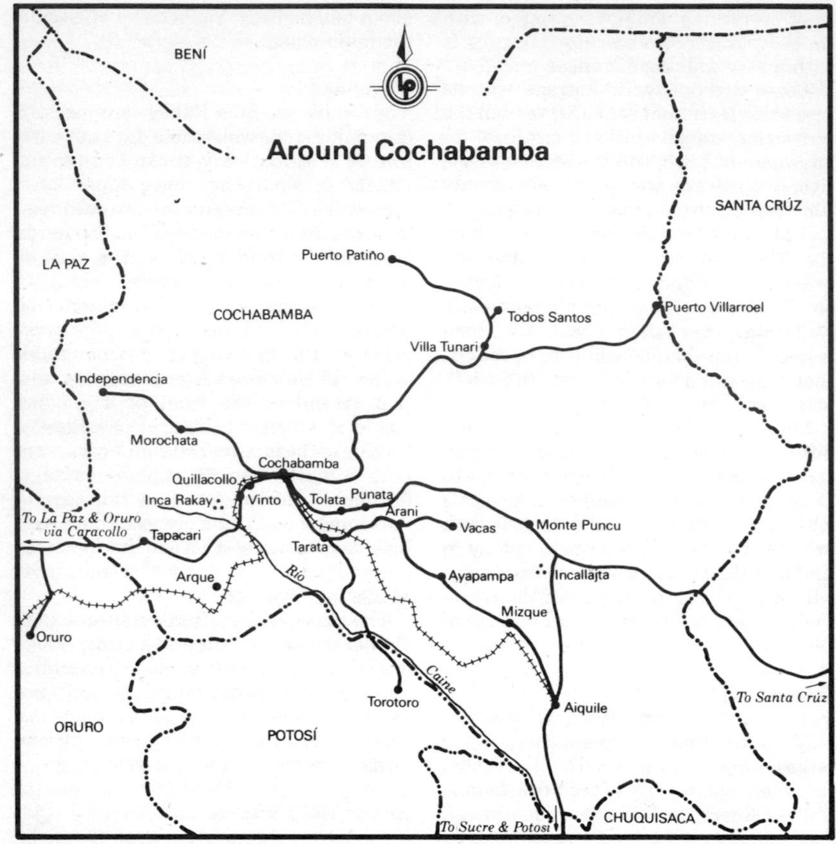

trucks climb up the hill to within several hundred metres of the ruins. If transport isn't available, however, you'll have to walk. Those coming from the lowlands to Cochabamba should stay in town for a couple of days in order to acclimatise to the altitude before attempting this uphill hike.

From the main plaza in Sipe-Sipe, take the road which passes the *colegio* (secondary school). It will narrow into a path and then cross a small ditch. Across the ditch, turn right onto the wider road. At this point, you have a choice. If you stay on the road, it's a relatively easy uphill climb that will take about three hours. If you opt to follow the more direct route, straight up the mountain, it's a tiring two-hour grunt which at times gets very steep.

Those following the road will have to look carefully to find the ruins because they're hidden downhill from the road amid a clump of *molle* (willow-like) trees and rock outcroppings. Keep watching for a place that fits this description.

If you're going the quicker way, the route is not quite so straightforward.

From several hundred metres up the road from town, follow a water pipeline up the hill to the first major ridge. There'll be a large ravine on your left. From there, bear to the right, following the ridge until you see a smaller ravine to the right. At this point, you'll be able to see Inca-Rakay on top of a reddish hill in the distance, but from so far away it won't be obvious what you're looking at.

Cross the small ravine and follow it until you can look across it and see two small houses. In front of you will be a little hill with some minor ruins at the top. Climb the hill and cross the large flat area on top, then climb up two more false ridges and you'll see the ruins.

INCALLAJTA

The ruins of Incallajta, on the easternmost outpost of the Inca Empire are probably the second most important known archaeological site in Bolivia. Lying 144 km east of Cochabamba toward Santa Crúz, it was believed to have been founded by the Inca Emperor Tupa Inca Yupanqui, the son of Pachacuti, who had previously wandered southward to define the southernmost limits of the Empire in present-day Chile (see the Southern Altiplano Chapter). The date of his arrival at Incallajta is estimated to have been some time during the 1460s. In 1525, the last year of the rule of Emperor Huayna Capac, the place was invaded and ruined by hordes of Guaranies from the southeast.

Getting There & Away

Without your own transport it will prove quite difficult to get to Incallajta. If you want to have a go anyway, at visiting this impressive and little-visited site, go to *Cancha Calatayud* in Cochabamba on a Monday or Thursday morning. From here, you should find a truck leaving for Pocona and ask the driver to let you off in Kollpa.

You'll probably have to spend the night in Kollpa, but since there are no hotels there it will either be necessary to camp or make arrangements to stay with a local family. From Kollpa, it's at least a three-hour walk (reportedly 12 km) to Incallajta. The return trip to Cochabamba will probably not be easy, so by all means carry plenty of water, food, and warm clothing for this excursion.

A couple of travel agencies in Cochabamba will occasionally do tours to Incallajta but only if they have a group large enough to make it worth their while. Inquire at the tourist kiosk which agencies are currently offering this.

Those with access to a private vehicle may still have trouble reaching the site. Follow the highway towards Siberia Pass and Santa Crúz 119 km to the turnoff to Pocona. There, turn right and follow the dirt road. At about 18 km the road splits. Follow the left fork to the ruins about five km further on. Don't attempt this road with anything but a 4WD.

PAIRUMANI

Those who haven't already seen enough of Patiño's legacy in Oruro and Cochabamba will want to go to Pairumani. Here one can tour the Tin Baron's estate, *Villa Albina* (named after his wife), the home he actually occupied. The elegant French decor of the main house and the Carrera marble mausoleum nearby are pretty typical of royalty, mineral or otherwise, anywhere in the world. In 1964, the entire estate was donated to the Salesian Congregation (a non-profit organisation) by the Simon I. Patiño University Memorial fund, representative of his heirs. Today it operates as a museum and tourist attraction.

Getting to Pairumani will involve a bit of effort. First take a micro to Quillacollo (see details under Quillacollo). From the plaza there, another micro goes to Vinto. At Vinto, you'll find *colectivos* that will take you to the mansion. The estate is open to tourists only between 5 and 6 pm so you'll have to plan carefully in order to get there at the right time. Although it's only 22 km from Cochabamba, the trip will probably require about two hours.

VINTO

Not to be confused with the smelter of the same name located near Oruro, the village of Vinto in the Cochabamba Valley is noted for two annual fiestas which take place there. On 19 March is the *Fiesta de San José* (or Saint Joseph), who is the patron saint of carpenters. The other, *Fiesta del Virgen del Carmen*, on 16 July is celebrated with folkloric groups, masses, parades, and military bands.

Transport to Vinto is by micro via Quillacollo.

TOROTORO

Torotoro is an absolute jewel, but like Incallajta it is practically inaccessible without private transport.

Paleontology buffs and spelunkers who make the effort to get here will not be disappointed. The town, which sits in a wide spot of a 20-km-long valley at 2600 metres elevation, is flanked on two sides by enormous tilted and layered sedimentary rock formations. On the side of the valley adjacent to the village are numerous incidences of biped and quadruped dinosaur tracks. As the road flattens out beside the stream to the northwest of Torotoro, it actually crosses the path of a group of three-toed tracks which are medium-sized at about 25 cm long each.

Nearer to town, a few metres before the stream crossing, the largest tracks in the area can be seen just above the waterline. Their size is impressive – 35 cm wide, 50 cm long, and 20 cm deep with a stride of nearly two metres!

Several hundred metres upstream from the road, a group of small three-toed tracks climb out of the water and under a layer of rocks. Five km up the stream are more tracks, and dinosaur bone fragments

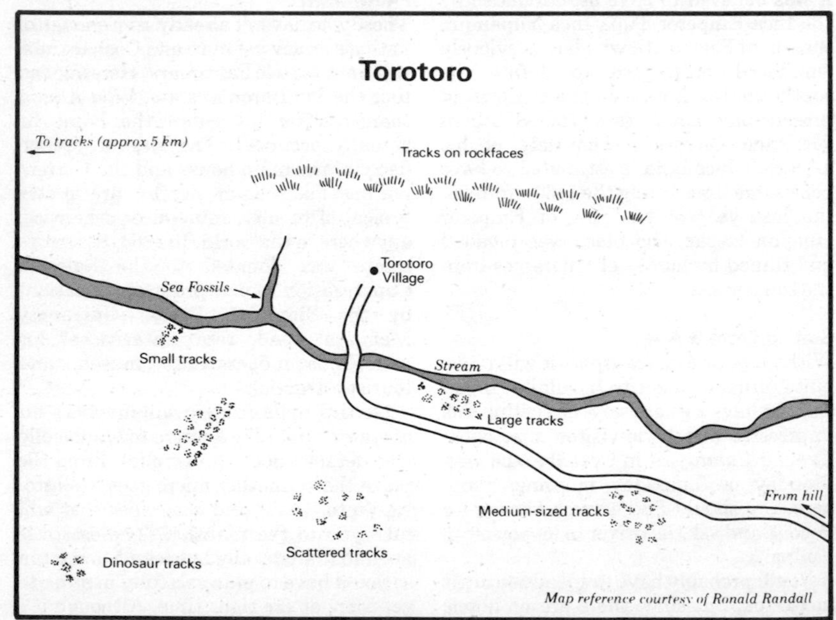

can be found in layers of red earth. When you visit these sites, you will notice that, strangely, nearly all the tracks in the area seem to lead uphill.

In a little side gully just upstream from the village there is a deposit of sea fossils. To confuse matters even further limestone and volcanic layers of rock are both present in addition to the sedimentary layers in which the tracks are found, and a little way downstream more tracks can be seen inside of a limestone cave. Anyone familiar with traditional geologic principles and palaeontological epochs will understand how perplexing all this is!

Six km or so to the northwest of town the stream disappears under a layer of limestone about 22 metres thick and forms the Umajalanta cave which is nearly two km long. Inside, there are numerous stalagmite and stalactite formations, an underground lake with blind catfish, the Umajalanta waterfall, and most surprising of all, more dinosaur tracks. This cave is undeveloped and you'll need a torch if you plan to explore it at all.

To switch gears for a moment, on 25 July each year the village of Torotoro stages the *Fiesta de Santiago* which features sheep sacrifices and *Tinku* fights in which the participants literally beat the hell out of each other with their fists or worse. This may be a good time to look for transportation to Torotoro but certainly not the best in which to visit the natural attractions.

The treasures of Torotoro remain largely pristine and unprotected as a result of the area being so little-known and difficult to access. Though I'm a little hesitant to publicise it so favourably, I realise that the majority of travellers who use these guides are environmentally conscientious and can appreciate the need to preserve a good thing *in situ*. In other words, please take care to leave the area as it is.

If you make any significant discoveries not marked on the accompanying map of the Torotoro area, please report them to Ronald Randall (a palaeontologist from New Zealand who has been living in Bolivia for over 40 years) at Casilla 92, Tarija, Bolivia, so he can investigate further.

Getting There & Away

Torotoro lies in Potosí Department 7½ hours and 130 km by road, south-east of Cochabamba. In a private vehicle, follow the Santa Crúz highway for 31 km. There, you'll want to turn to the right and drive seven km to the village of Cliza. Make sure you have enough petrol at Cliza for the return trip to Torotoro – about 200 km – since none is available beyond there. Keep following the main road towards Oruro for 29 km beyond Cliza. At that point, you need to turn left onto the Torotoro road.

This trip should not be attempted in anything but a 4WD or a large truck and even then not during the rainy season. At one point you'll have to cross the River Caine. Be sure to remove the fan belt before entering the water. The last report I received was that the Bolivians were discussing construction of a bridge at this crossing, but realising the state of affairs in Bolivian public works, I'm sure that the above advice will stand good for many years to come.

For those without private transport, there are a couple of possibilities, but both require a bit of luck to arrange. From Cochabamba, there's a cargo truck which makes unscheduled runs to Torotoro about once a week, leaving from the corner of Arce and Montes. In addition, the *Free Swedish Mission* of Cochabamba flies into Torotoro from time to time and they may have room for a passenger. To inquire, contact Captain Arvindson (tel 46289) in Cochabamba.

CHAPARE

For details on the Chapare region of northern Cochabamba Department, refer to the chapter dealing with the Amazon Basin.

Potosí

I am rich Potosí,
The treasure of the world
And the envy of kings.

Thus reads the slogan on the city's first coat of arms and it wasn't far off the mark. But then, any city with a mountain of silver in its backyard is sure to cop some attention. As a matter of fact, anything that is incredibly lucrative has come to be known in Spanish as *un Potosí*.

A good example is the city of San Luís Potosí in central Mexico where silver was discovered in the 1600s. San Luís, however, never did live up to its Bolivian namesake. Even as far away as China, the name signified wealth and the mythical city of riches in Chinese legend came to be known as *Bei Du Xi* after the real city of riches in Bolivia. That one probably didn't measure up either.

No-one really knows how much silver was extracted from the mountain and carted off to Spain but a popular boast of the day was that they could have built a silver bridge to Spain and had some left to carry across on it. It goes without saying then that quite a lot of the shiny stuff saw its way across the ocean and that the Spanish monarch, who personally received 20% of the booty, was worth more than a few *pesetas*.

I'm sure the story about how all this fuss got started has been embellished into what might be called a 'whopper' but it's still an interesting tale to recount . . . In 1544, it's said, the mountain's riches were discovered by a Peruvian Indian named Diego Huallpa who was tending his llamas in the area. When he realised that two of the beasts were missing, he immediately set off in search of them. While he was still in hot pursuit, night came – and with it, cold – so he stopped to build a fire. The fire got so hot that the earth beneath it began to melt and a shiny liquid oozed out. Huallpa, of course, realised that this was silver, one of the items that the Spanish got so excited about, so he decided not to inform them of his discovery. Instead, he told another Indian, a friend named Huanca, and together they decided to get rich.

The newly discovered vein proved productive and soon a quarrel ensued between the partners about the division of profits. Huanca, who was fed up with the whole mess, went to the Spanish with the news of the mine and needless to say, they were interested.

It wasn't long before the conquerors determined that the magnitude of the discovery was such that it warranted immediate attention. On 1 April (some say it was 10 April), 1545, the Villa Imperial de Carlos V, Potosí, was founded. After that, there was no need to wait around. In the time it takes to say 'Get down there and dig', the first of the silver was on its way to Spain thanks to thousands of Indian slaves impressed into service in the mines.

The work was so dangerous, however, and so many Indian slaves were dying of accidents and silicosis pneumonia that the Spanish began importing literally millions of African slaves to extract the silver. It's difficult not to be shocked when you learn that during the three centuries of the Colonial Period, 1545 to 1825, it's estimated that eight million Africans and Indians died from the appalling working conditions in the Potosí mines. In light of such cruelty, these figures certainly do diminish the appeal of Potosí's colonial ambience.

In 1572, in order to increase the productivity of the slaves, the Viceroy Toledo instituted the *Ley de la Mita*, a law which stated that all Indians and blacks in Potosí over the age of 18 were required to work in the mines in shifts of 12 hours, and remain inside the mines without seeing light of day for four months at a shot, eating, sleeping, and working underground. When they emerged after a 'shift' the Spanish had to bandage their eyes to prevent damage in the bright sunlight. These miners didn't last long either.

Inside the mines, silver was smelted in small ovens known as *huayrachinas* which were fueled with wood and a local plant called *pacha brava*. The silver was then sent by llama train to Arica or Callao (Lima) on the Pacific coast and from there by ship to Spain. Many English, Dutch, and French pirates anxiously awaited in the Atlantic to plunder the riches of Potosí.

During this era, a mint was constructed to coin the silver. Reservoirs were built to provide water for the growing population, and exotic European consumer goods found their way up the llama trails from the coast. The population grew to nearly 200,000 and 80 churches were constructed. Amidst this mania, Potosí became the largest city in Latin America and one of the largest in the world. 'It was raised' said one politician of the period 'in the pandemonium of greed at the foot of riches discovered by accident'.

As with most boom town situations the glory was not to last because the Cerro Rico, the seemingly inexhaustible mountain of silver, began to play out. By the time of Bolivian independence in 1825, the mines were already in decline and in the late 1800s, a severe drop in silver prices dealt a blow from which Potosí has never completely recovered. Tin took over as the major metallic export of the country and Potosinos began mining their tailings for lead, zinc, and tin which had previously been discarded. Silver extraction did continue, however, but on a much smaller scale than it had done previously.

Victor Paz Estenssoro's mining reform of 1952 brought the Pailaviri mine into government control and mining conditions were improved immensely. Miner-owned coöperatives, however, still controlled most of the operations on Cerro Rico and the revolution had little effect upon them. These days, the government mine is plagued by strikes, protests, and general unrest while the coöperatives are plagued by the same appalling conditions and mortality rates that existed during the Colonial Period.

A visitor to Potosí will find remnants of a grand colonial city – ornate churches, monuments, and colonial architecture – in a most unlikely setting. Potosí, at 4070 metres, is the highest city in the world, a fact which you'll soon realise when climbing some of the steeper streets. Set beneath the colourful Cerro Rico and surrounded by barren hills, it's partially protected from many of the disagreeable climatic factors inherent at lower altitudes on the Altiplano. Temperatures, however, reflect its lofty situation and central heating is unheard of so you will be aware of the cold. Autumn and winter bring snow and bitter temperatures but there are quite a few days when the sun provides the place with a weak but welcome warmth. Summers are normally just cold and rainy and the atmosphere is a bit dreary for it, but don't let the weather prevent you from visiting and absorbing some of this tragic and fascinating city.

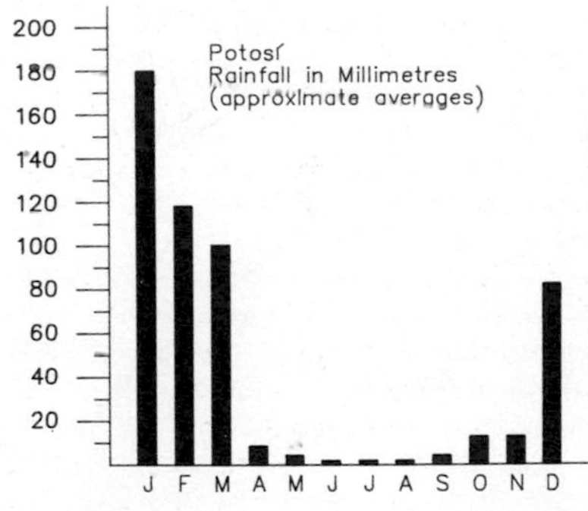

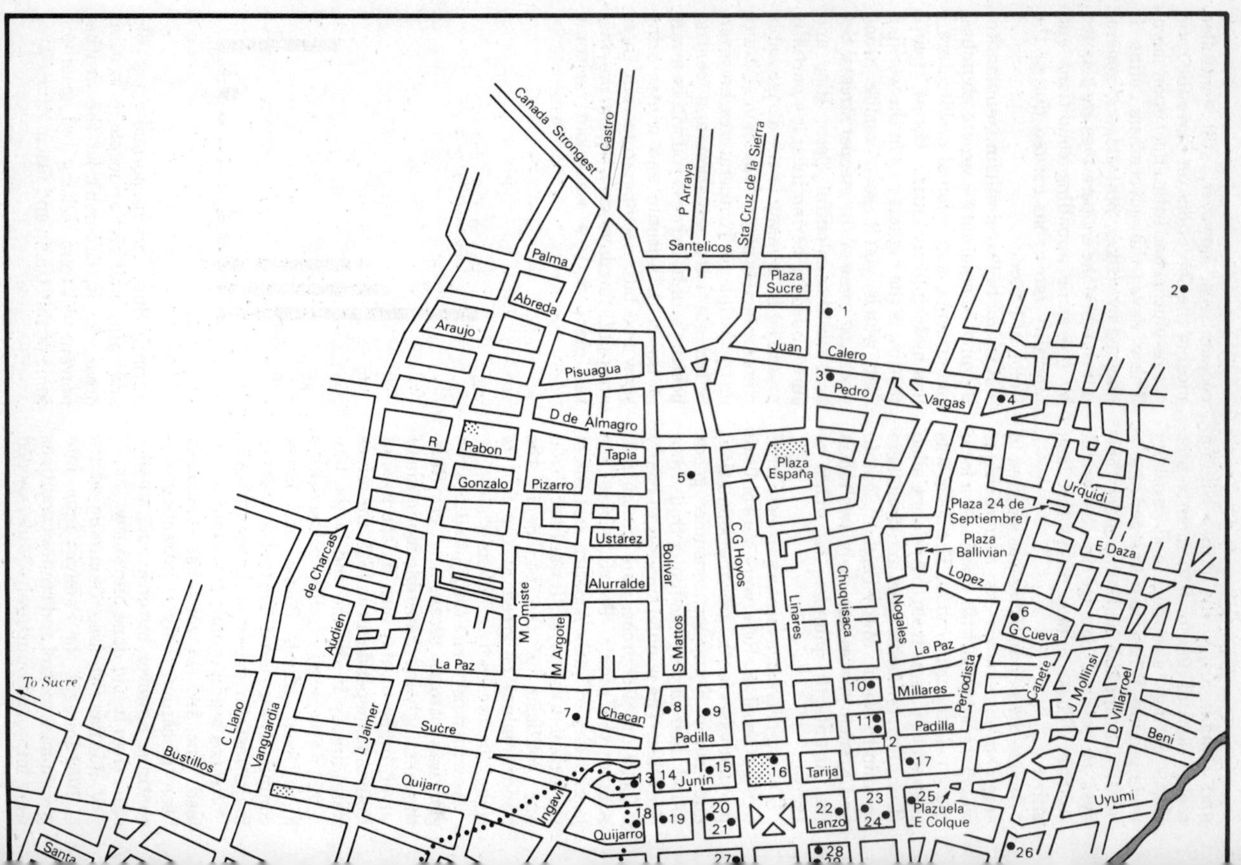
Cañada Strongest
Castro
P Arraya
Sta Cruz de la Sierra
Santelicos
Plaza Sucre
Palma
Abreda
Araujo
Juan
Calero
Pisuagua
Pedro
Vargas
D de Almagro
R
Pabon
Tapia
Plaza España
Gonzalo
Pizarro
Urquidi
Plaza 24 de Septiembre
Plaza Ballivian
E Daza
Ustarez
Bolivar
C G Hoyos
de Charcas
Alurralde
Lopez
Linares
Chuquisaca
Nogales
G Cueva
Audien
M Omiste
M Argote
S Mattos
La Paz
La Paz
Cañete
J Mollinsi
D Villarroel
Periodista
Millares
To Sucre
Chacan
C Llano
Vanguardia
L Jaimer
Sucre
Padilla
Padilla
Beni
Bustillos
Quijarro
Ingavi
Junin
Tarija
Uyumi
Lanzo
Plazuela E Colque
Quijarro
Santa

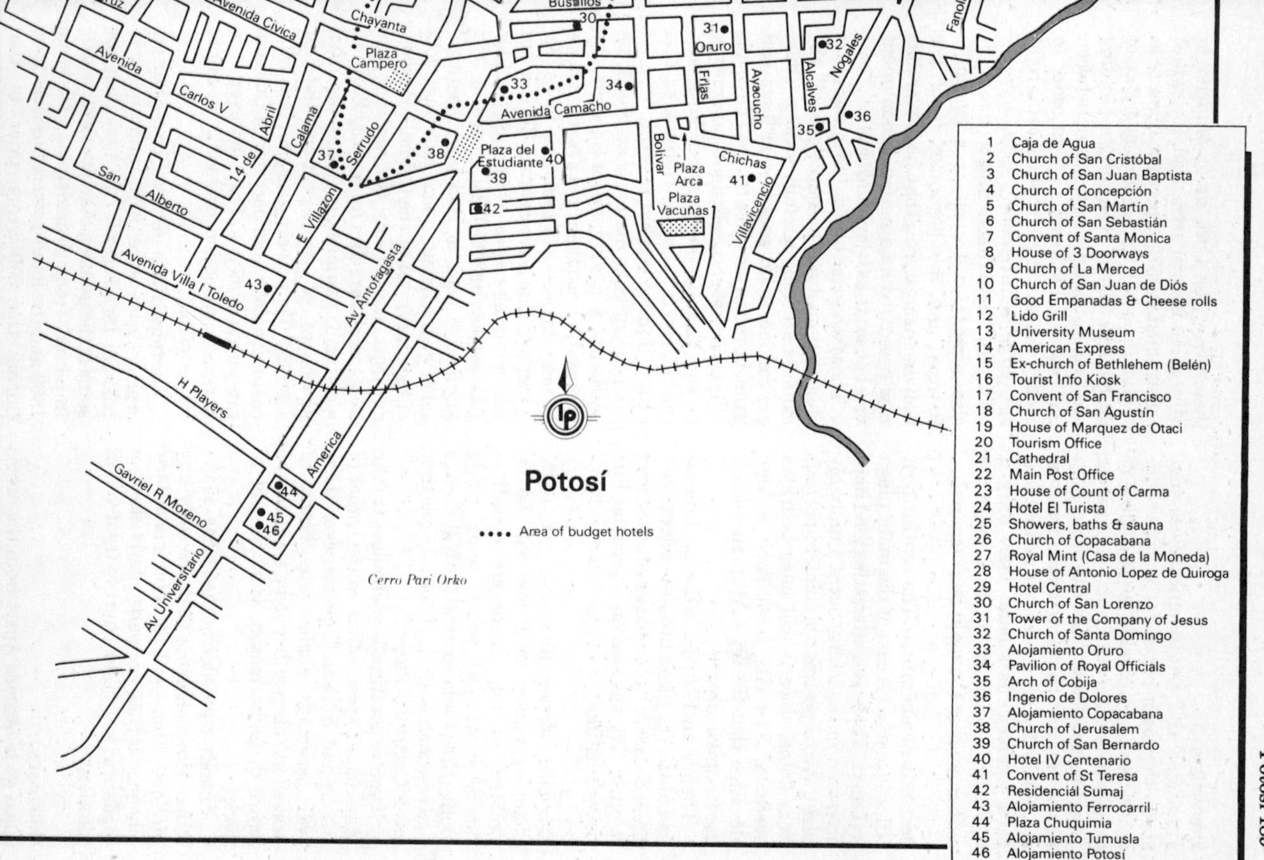
Potosí
Area of budget hotels
1 Caja de Agua
2 Church of San Cristóbal
3 Church of San Juan Baptista
4 Church of Concepción
5 Church of San Martín
6 Church of San Sebastián
7 Convent of Santa Monica
8 House of 3 Doorways
9 Church of La Merced
10 Church of San Juan de Diós
11 Good Empanadas & Cheese rolls
12 Lido Grill
13 University Museum
14 American Express
15 Ex-church of Bethlehem (Belén)
16 Tourist Info Kiosk
17 Convent of San Francisco
18 Church of San Agustín
19 House of Marquez de Otaci
20 Tourism Office
21 Cathedral
22 Main Post Office
23 House of Count of Carma
24 Hotel El Turista
25 Showers, baths & sauna
26 Church of Copacabana
27 Royal Mint (Casa de la Moneda)
28 House of Antonio Lopez de Quiroga
29 Hotel Central
30 Church of San Lorenzo
31 Tower of the Company of Jesus
32 Church of Santa Domingo
33 Alojamiento Oruro
34 Pavilion of Royal Officials
35 Arch of Cobija
36 Ingenio de Dolores
37 Alojamiento Copacabana
38 Church of Jerusalem
39 Church of San Bernardo
40 Hotel IV Centenario
41 Convent of St Teresa
42 Residenciál Sumaj
43 Alojamiento Ferrocarril
44 Plaza Chuquimia
45 Alojamiento Tumusla
46 Alojamiento Potosí
Fanola
Nogales
Alcalves
Ayacucho
Oruro
Frías
Chichas
Villavicencio
Plaza Arca
Plaza Vacuñas
Bolivar
Bustillos
Avenida Camacho
Plaza del Estudiante
Chayanta
Plaza Campero
Serrudo
Av Antofagasta
E Villazon
Calama
Abril
14 de
Avenida Civica
Carlos V
Alberto
San
Avenida
Avenida Villa I Toledo
H Players
America
Gavriel R Moreno
Av Universitario
Cerro Pari Orko

Information
There's an IBT tourist office kiosk just above the main plaza but a visit there would be an unmitigated waste of time in a city where there are a number of better things to do. These folks are of no help whatsoever and the same brochures that are distributed free elsewhere will set you back several dollars here. They have a similarly poor subsidiary office out in the nether lands at the main bus terminal.

Post & Communications The central post office is one block east of the main plaza on Lanza. There's an interesting gift shop/*artesanía* in the lobby, but it's probably best to avoid posting anything important from Potosí since it will have to travel overland. The city is at such a high elevation that the big LAB planes can't use its small airport.

There's an ENTEL office on Linares just above the plaza but I've walked past there dozens of times and have never seen it open. Try the one on Ayacucho just below Bustillo.

Changing Money If you've got cash, changing money in Potosí will be no problem at all. There are countless business establishments along Calle Bolívar and Calle Sucre which will change at a reasonable rate . . . Look for signs that read '*Compro Dólares*'.

If you've got travellers' cheques, try the American Express office on the corner of Junín and Bolívar. The manager there will personally change any brand of travellers' cheque but if he's not in the office for some reason, you'll be out of luck.

There's a possibility that some of the other establishments that normally buy dollars cash will accept travellers' cheques if they are particularly short of dollars so it wouldn't hurt to try if you're desperate.

Museums
Casa de la Moneda Apart from the mines themselves, the *Casa de la Moneda* or Mint is Potosís star attraction. It was first constructed in 1572, where the *Casa de la Justicia* now stands, under the orders of the Viceroy Toledo. The current building was subsequently constructed between the years of 1753 and 1773 in order to control the minting of colonial coins right at their material source.

In addition to functioning as a mint, it also served for a spell as a prison, a fortress, and the headquarters of the Bolivian Army during the Chaco War. It is now preserved as a national monument and houses the Colonial Museum.

Those who wish to visit the museum are obligated to take a tour since all the exhibits are kept carefully locked. Tours are conducted on weekdays at 9 am and 2 pm, both lasting three hours. The cost is US$1. Whatever the outside temperature, be sure to wear thermal underwear and several layers of warm clothing or this visit will prove very unpleasant.

Upon entering the museum, you'll be greeted by a gaudy mask of Bacchus, the wine god, placed there by a Frenchman for a reason known only to him. It looks like something that belongs in a children's fun fair, but don't be put off because the tour gets better. Inside, they have the first locomotive used in Bolivia, a beautiful salon with religious theme paintings (lots of blood, typical of the Colonial Period), carriages, silver coins, two amazing safe boxes, and war relics from many Bolivian wars and skirmishes. There are also collections of seashells from the lost seacoast, Tiahuanaco artefacts, minerals, costumed dolls, and portraits of Bolivian presidents (only a few, however – a complete collection could fill an entire museum!).

Upstairs there are jail-like quarters where slaves were kept, and rooms of colonial furniture. In the basement are some of the minting machines which were imported from Philadelphia, USA, in 1869 and the hand-powered devices used during the 300 years prior to that

MUSEO CASA NL. DE LA MONEDA
POTOSI — BOLIVIA
$b 2'000.000.- | 2 Bs.

purchase. You'll also find several very interesting horse-powered laminating machines on which horses were worked for three days and nights without a break. The average life span for a horse under these conditions was about eight days so, horses were continuously imported from Argentina.

The current Casa de la Moneda is found on the corner of Ayacucho and Quijarro near the Plaza 10 de Noviembre.

Convent of San Francisco This museum of typical religious art is on Nogales above Tarija. Although it's supposed to be open from 2 to 4 pm Monday to Saturday, more often than not, there's no one around even then.

The *Iglesia of San Francisco*, just next door, is fairly interesting. The building was originally constructed in the 1500s but it was rebuilt in 1707. Inside are the remains and a portrait of Antonio Lopez de Quiroga, a wealthy 17th century philanthropist who gave a lot of money to the Church. A gold-covered altar from this building is now housed in the Casa de la Moneda.

Museo Universitario The University Museum on Calle Bolívar between Junín and Sucre is open Monday to Saturday from 10 am to noon and 2 to 4 pm. It has on display various paintings, pottery, and artefacts from the area. The 50c admission charge goes towards the upkeep of the University.

Convento de Santa Teresa This convent, on the corner of Chichas and Ayacucho, is open weekdays from 4 to 5 pm. On display is more religious art, but it is reportedly quite good as such things go. The US$1.50 admission is used to sustain the convent, but buying the ticket can be a little tricky. The church itself is closed and the nuns are cloistered so you've got to go to a wooden shutter at the back of a courtyard just uphill from the church. Attract the attendant's attention by pulling a rope hanging from the wall there. Once you've bought the ticket enter the building by knocking on a big metal door on the street above the church gate. The tour of the museum lasts a little over an hour.

Other A couple of other homes and monuments of note which you may want to visit are the old town hall (*Cabildo*), the home of Antonio Lopez de Quiroga on Calle Lanza, the *Casa de las Tres Portadas* at Calle Bolívar 19-21, the *Crystal Palace* at Calle Sucre 148-156, and the *Arco de Cobija* on the street of the same name.

A couple of interesting statues in Potosí are the *Miner's Monument* on Avenida Villazón, the *Revolutionary Miner's Monument* on Plaza del Minero, and the *Monument to Mothers* on Avenida del Estudiante.

Churches

Belén This former church and convent is now occupied by a movie theatre, but its baroque style architecture and ornamented entrance are impressive. The building was constructed in 1735 and originally served a dual purpose as both a church and a hospital.

La Compañia This Jesuit church, one block below the main plaza on Ayacucho, is renowned for its beautiful and unique bell-tower which was completed in 1707 after the original church, built in 1590, collapsed. Both the tower and the doorway of the present structure are of Andean or *mestizo* style architecture.

San Benito The *Church of San Benito* was begun in 1711 and was completed in 16 years. Its byzantine domes and mestizo, or natural-theme doorway, are probably the most interesting things about it. The entire building is laid out in the shape of a Latin cross.

Cathedral
The main religious structure in Potosí is on the Plaza 10 de Noviembre. It was founded in 1572 but in the early 1800s it was rebuilt in Greek and Spanish baroque styles. Its interior is, in my opinion, the nicest in the entire city.

San Martín This church on Calle Hoyos near Plaza Cervantes was built in the 1600s and is today run by the French Redemptionist Fathers. Inside is a veritable art museum, but I question whether it's worth the climb up there to see it since it's often closed.

San Lorenzo The portal of *San Lorenzo* is one of the most photographed subjects in Bolivia due to its ornate mestizo design. It was carved in stone by master Indian artisans in the 16th century, but the main structure wasn't completed until the mid-1700s when the bell towers were added. The main attractions inside are two Holguín paintings and hand-crafted silver work on the altar.

Unfortunately, in mid-1987 the church was undergoing renovation and it doesn't look like things are going to change in the near future. It is possible to see the portal through the construction fence but photography is difficult and the interior is closed off altogether.

Others Other churches of note in Potosí include *San Bernardo*, *Jerusalén* with its golden ornamentation, *San Juan de Diós* which has stood since the 1600s despite its adobe construction, and *La Mercéd* on Calle Hoyos.

Mines
Coöperative Mines A visit to the coöperative mines is an experience which should not be missed, if for no other reason than to awaken yourself to the fact that there exist today working conditions that most of the world thinks went out with the middle ages. It's difficult to imagine such things without actually witnessing them, and even then you're left in a state of shock.

Contrary to popular rumour, women are admitted to many coöperative mines although a few hang on to the tradition that allowing women underground invites bad luck for the miners. For this reason, local women are usually consigned to picking through the tailings searching for bits of minerals that may have been missed. These women are known as *pailiris* which means 'those who choose' in Quechua.

Quite a few young men in town hire themselves out as tour guides through these mines but the guide that is almost universally recommended is Eduardo Garnica Fajardo whose experience and background well qualify him for the job. Having descended from a family of miners and having been a miner himself, he's closely acquainted with the traditions and the men that labour in the Potosí mines. Over the years, he's picked up enough English and Hebrew to conduct tours in those languages. The four to five-hour tour leaves at 8 am from the main plaza

Top: Condor over the Andes (TM)
Bottom: The summit of Huayna Potosí (TM)

Top: Aymará shepherds on the Altiplano (WH)
Bottom: Campesina on the Altiplano (WH)

and costs US$3. If you'd like to go, contact Eduardo on tel 23138 in Potosí.

Be warned, though, that these visits are not easy. The ceilings are low, passageways are steep and muddy, temperatures reach 45°, and the altitude of nearly 4500 metres is taxing. In addition, you'll be exposed to all sorts of noxious chemicals and gases including silica dust (the cause of silicosis), arsenic gas, acetylene vapors, and other trapped mine gases and by-products of combustion and detonation of mining equipment. Anyone with doubts or medical problems should avoid the coöperative mines and visit the more readily accessible government mine, *Pailaviri*.

The plus side of a mine tour is that you'll have the opportunity to speak with the very friendly and open miners who will be happy to share with you some of their insights and opinions about their difficult lot. Surprisingly, most of them are miners by choice, carrying on a family tradition by working there.

Since the coöperatives are owned by the miners themselves they must produce in order to make a living. All work is done by hand with tools they must purchase themselves. They buy and use weak acetylene lamps which emit a choking gas. In addition, each miner must buy his own explosives, and shops near the Cerro Rico sell such things as dynamite, fuses, detonators, ammonium nitrate, and acetylene (as well as such goodies as black tobacco, coca, *legía*, and cigarettes that make it all bearable). What's significant about this is that anyone who wishes to do so may purchase any of these things, whether they work in the mines or not.

Inside, each miner has a personal work area where he carries out the operation from start to finish. Upon locating a vein he chisels out wells in which to place the dynamite, which he detonates himself, paying dearly for any carelessness. The spoils and tailings must be carried up on his back as many levels as necessary in order to deposit them in an area accessible to the outside by ore cart, to a 'mailbox' for later collection, or to a tailings dump. As compensation, he is paid according to his production.

In most coöperative operations, there is a minimal medical plan in case of accident or silicosis (which is inevitable after seven to 10 years working underground) and a pension of about US$20 per month for those so incapacitated. In case of death, a miner's widow and children collect this pension.

In an average coöperative, the miners will begin work at 10 am after several hours of social coca-chewing in preparation for the day. They work until lunch at 2 pm when they rest and chew more coca. The day normally ends at 7 pm for those who don't spend the night working in order to pick up extra money.

Pailaviri A visit to *Pailaviri*, the state-owned mine that owns the most imposing structure on Cerro Rico above Potosí, will contrast sharply with one to the coöperatives. Here, the government provides electric lamps, jackhammers, lifts, higher wages, and superior medical and pension plans. If you visit only the state mine, therefore, you will get a largely artificial picture of what mining in Bolivia is all about. The most interesting reason to see this one at all is to realise the contrast between the two.

To reach Pailaviri, catch the ENTE No 100 bus between 7 and 8 am across the main plaza from the cathedral. The trip to Pailaviri costs 5c. Since frequent strikes of the government miners' syndicate disrupt the operation of Pailaviri, the powers that be are a little uneasy at the slightest indication of labour unrest. It's not unusual to find the scheduled tours cancelled for indefinite periods of time so ask around town whether or not they're operating before you make the trip up.

El Tío As a visitor in any of the mines, you'll undoubtedly notice a small devilish-looking figure occupying a small niche somewhere along the passageways. Around him will be strewn cigarette butts, coca leaves, glasses of alcohol, and other small tokens. The explanation of all this will be proudly provided to visitors who are curious about it, and who wouldn't be?

As most of the miners believe in a God in Heaven, they say there must of course be a devil beneath the earth in a place where it's hot and uncomfortable. The miners reason that Hell must not be too far from the environment in which they work, so the devil himself must be the owner of the minerals they're digging and dynamiting out of the earth. In order to appease this character – they call him *El Tío* meaning 'uncle' (never *diablo*) – they set up a little statue in a place of honour in the mine and make offerings of cigarettes which they actually place in his mouth and light.

On Friday nights, they celebrate *cha'lla*, which means 'toast' or 'salute'. In order to bring luck and protection from the 'owner' of the minerals they pour a little alcohol on the ground in front of the statue and place coca leaves within easy reach. Then, as in most Bolivian celebrations, they smoke, chew coca, and proceed to drink themselves unconscious. While this is all taken very seriously, it also serves as a bit of diversion from an extremely difficult existence.

Fiestas

The most unusual fiesta celebrated in Potosí is called the *Fiesta del Espíritu* which takes place on the last three Saturdays of June and the first Saturday of August. It is dedicated to the honour of Pachamama, the earth mother, who the miners consider to be the mother of all Bolivians.

At the foot of Cerro Rico, campesinos from the surrounding countryside bring llamas to sell to the miners for use in the festival. Every aspect of this fiesta is conducted according to a very rigid time schedule. At 10 am, one miner from each mine buys a llama after which the families arrive from town to join in the celebration. At 11 am they go to the entrances of their respective mines. From 11 to 11.45, they chew coca and drink alcohol. At precisely 11.45, they prepare the llama for sacrifice to Pachamama by tying its feet and offering it coca and alcohol, and as might be expected, the llama meets its maker at high noon. As the throat is slit, the miners petition the earth mother for luck, protection, and an abundance of minerals. The llama's blood is caught in glasses and thrown around the mouth of the mine in order to ensure that Pachamama will listen to their wishes.

For the next three hours, the men chew and drink while the women prepare the meat of the llama in a *parillada*. It is traditionally served with potatoes baked in a small adobe oven with *aba* and *oca*. When the oven gets hot, it is smashed on top of the vegetables and they bake thus. The stomach, feet, and head, are buried in a three-metre-deep hole as a further offering to Pachamama.

At this point, the music and dancing begins. Later in the evening, truckloads of miners ride down the hill in transport provided by the miner who bought the llama for his respective mine.

What to Buy

Obviously, the most typical articles available in Potosí will be made of silver. The difficulty is in determining exactly how much silver they contain because there is unfortunately no quick and easy way of doing so. There are some silver items for sale in the market, but the more expensive artesanías are generally also more reliable.

The artisans' market is between Calle Junín and Calle Sucre at Omiste. Here they sell a wide variety of local crafts but also a lot of touristy junk, so it pays to be careful when buying.

Places to Stay – bottom end

There are several budget hotels popular with travellers but the unquestionable favourite these days is the *Residencial Sumaj*, not far from the Plaza del Estudiante. The rooms are small and dark but their overall atmosphere seems to be a growing legend among travellers. The hotel itself is quite clean, with two central meeting areas where cooking is permitted. There's even a television for those who want to catch up on a bit of 'culture'.

A single room here will cost US$3, a double will run US$5.40, and a triple US$8. There are no private baths available but they do offer hot showers. Its only drawback is that it's such a long uphill walk to the centre of town. On the other hand, it's convenient to both the bus and train terminals.

In the same range, the *Residencial Copacabana* is clean and costs US$3.15 per person. There are no private baths, but hot water is available. If you request it, they'll arrange a shared room at a lower price.

The *Hotel Central* is only a block from the main plaza, but is relatively far from the transportation terminals. The owners are very nice folks and they provide as many blankets as you'd like. Hot water is available if you request it an hour in advance of your shower. The hotel is in a pleasant and quiet old area of town and they only charge US$3.15 per person.

If you're looking for something close to the railroad station to avoid lugging a heavy pack uphill to the centre, try the *Alojamiento Ferrocarríl* on Villazón just above the station. This is getting to be very popular with foreigners these days, so it's a good place to connect with other travellers. It's both friendly and clean, has hot water, and may be the least expensive nice place in town. They charge US$2.50 for a single room but only US$2 per person for doubles and triples.

In the same area, *Alojamientos Tumusla* and *Potosí* offer similar accommodation for US$2.70 single, US$4.50 double, and US$6.75 triple.

A cheap but rather seedy place frequented by travellers on the lowest of budgets is *Alojamiento Oruro* just above the Plaza del Estudiante. It's very basic with only cold showers which seem all that much colder in this climate. A single will cost US$2.25, a double room is US$3.60, and a triple costs US$5.40.

Places to Stay – middle range

Appearance-wise, the nicest hotel in Potosí is the *Colonial*, which is also the one most frequented by guided tours. It's centrally located near the main plaza and offers (of course) hot showers and private baths exclusively. Singles are US$18 while two and three-bed rooms go for US$24 and US$30. Nearly as popular is *El Solar* which charges the same rates as the Colonial.

The most personable hotel, however, is the *El Turista* at 19 Lanza on a quiet side street near the centre. The LAB ticket desk is here and the very friendly Señor Luksic who runs the whole operation provides the most reliable tourist information in town. In addition, the rooms are clean and all have private baths with hot showers. A double room will cost US$15 while singles are US$9 and triples are a bargain at US$18.

The *Hotel IV Centenario* is the imposing structure on the Plaza del Estudiante near the university. Like all the other mid-range hotels in town, they have a private dining room which is certainly a plus in a city which is not exactly known for its *haute cuisine*. Prices here are the same as at El Turista.

All hotel prices in Potosí are regulated by the government, so if you feel that a price is too high or that you're being cheated, ask to see the list of prices that all of them are required to keep on hand. It's called *la tarifa oficial*.

Places to Eat

There seems to be no eatery in Potosí that really stands out as both good and inexpensive.

The best I found was *Don Lucho* which serves a pretty good lunch for US$1.25, including soup, salad, a main course, and dessert. They must make their money on the beverages which are a bit overpriced. During the high tourist season, they also have a peña on Fridays beginning at 10 pm.

The best food in town can be found at the *Las Vegas* and the *Colonial* but it's quite expensive and both of these places cater more to higher budget tourists than to the locals and *mochileros* (backpackers).

The *Scaramush*, an interesting little place on Calle Bolívar below Junín, offers reasonably-priced if ordinary meals, and it is often recommended as one of the better places to eat in town. Likewise is the *Sumac Orko* which offers filling specials of soup, potatoes, rice, and a meat dish for only about 75c. If you're a fish fan, however, and they happen to be serving lemon trout, forget about the special.

For snacks, there's a small, dark, and nameless place just above the *Dayquiri* on Calle Linares that serves excellent cheese rolls and empanadas. In the morning, meatless salteñas *Potosinas* are available on the streets for 25c to 50c. Meat empanadas are sold around the market until early afternoon and in the evening street vendors in the same area sell corn meal humintas.

Pie, pizza, and reasonable coffee can be had at the *Coffee Shop* on Calle Sucre. The *Lido Grill* up from the plaza on Linares is also good for coffee or chocolate.

The market *comedor* (dining room) is probably the best inexpensive place in town to eat breakfast since most everything else is locked up tight until well into the morning. There are a few *panaderías* which open up at 8.00 am or so, but they don't have a lot to recommend them but several-day-old pastries and coffee from the same era.

Getting There & Away

Air Although I've heard rumours that service by LAB has arrived in Potosí, the route isn't listed on any of their schedules and the LAB office didn't seem to know anything about it, so I'm assuming that the information was mistaken. A smaller airline, *Lineas Aereas Imperiales* (tel 26431), has an office at Calle Ayacucho 30. They do quick runs to Cochabamba where you can catch LAB to La Paz, Santa Crúz, or another larger city.

The LAB office in Potosí (tel 22361) is in the *Hotel El Turista* at Calle Lanza 19.

Bus

Getting to Potosí by bus is fairly easy provided you don't try to do it during the rainy season when, thanks to a couple of hairy river crossings and waterlogged slopes, the trip becomes a little tricky.

There are basically three highway routes into Potosí, all of which pass through rugged mountains and some very impressive scenery, but they are also rough going in places and lots of bumps and bounces are included in the price of the ticket.

To Sucre, there is only one daily Sucre-bound bus that leaves from the main terminal. It departs at 9.30 am. *Soltrans* and *American Express*, whose terminals are near the centre, both offer very comfortable service twice daily for US$6.50. The trip takes six hours if you go this route. The cheapest way to go is by camión or micro which costs only US$4. They leave from Plaza Uyuni as soon as they are full, but since this is such a popular route, that means every few minutes until early afternoon. Between Sucre and Potosí, watch for the picturesque old Río Pilcomayo crossing with its castle-like buttresses just a km or so from the new bridge.

Going to Oruro and La Paz, several lines leave from the main terminal between 6 and 6.30 pm. The trip to La Paz requires about 12 hours. To Oruro, it takes nine.

Buses to Tupiza and Villazón leave between 5 and 5.30 pm from the bus station. To Villazón on the Argentine border takes about 13 hours and costs US$7.50. If you'd like to break the long trip to Argentina in Camargo, trucks leave from Plaza Chuquimia near the bus terminal as soon as they are full.

Keep in mind that the main bus terminal is quite a long way from town so if you're walking, be sure to leave yourself plenty of time to get there . . . at least half an hour from the centre.

Train

On Tuesday, Friday, and Sunday there is a ferrobus service to Oruro and La Paz at 11.30 am. First class fare to Oruro is US$6.35 and second class is US$4.26. First and second class to La Paz cost US$9.57 and US$6.35.

There is an express train to Oruro and La Paz leaving on Monday and Thursday at 8.50 pm. First class to Oruro and La Paz, respectively, is US$4.55 and US$6.84. Second class is US$4.55 and US$3.04.

The express train to Sucre leaves at 7.20 am on Monday and Thursday and costs US$2.45 first class and US$1.75 second class. There is a slow train to Sucre leaving at 8.20 am on Saturdays.

Service to Rio Mulatos, Uyuni, and Villazón is on Sundays at 2 am.

The railroad station in Potosí is at the bottom of Avenida Villazón below the University.

Getting Around

Taxis in Potosí are thin on the ground when compared with other major Bolivian cities, so you can expect to pay about US$1.50 from the centre to either the mines or the transportation terminals.

Most of the local micros provide transport back and forth to the mines on Cerro Rico but there is one that goes to the rail and bus terminals from the cathedral side of the main plaza, stopping at the university en route. All micros in town are a bargain at 5c per ride.

BETANZOS

With its landscape of jagged mountains and its quaint small-town atmosphere, the village of Betanzos is only two hours by bus from Potosí along the road to Sucre. It makes an excellent day trip, especially on Sundays when the market there is in full swing and erupting with colour and activity. Many campesinos in local dress come from the countryside bringing their harvests and handicrafts to sell, and unlike the market in nearby Tarabuco this isn't staged primarily for the benefit of tourists. If you're lucky, you may be able to catch one of the unscheduled fiestas that sometimes occur during the Sunday market.

On 4 and 5 April annually, Betanzos celebrates the *Fiesta de la Papa* and while it isn't well-known, all reports indicate that it's a real winner. Major musical groups travel to Betanzos from all over Bolivia to dance and play Andean folk music and as yet, it hasn't been discovered and altered by tourism.

Trucks and micros leave for Betanzos from Plaza Uyuni in Potosí early Sunday mornings. In addition, any Sucre-bound bus will drop you there.

HOT SPRINGS

Of the various hot springs in the vicinity of Potosí, the nicest and most unusual is at Tarapaya, which was originally used by the Incas and is believed to have curative powers. The locals warned me that all bathing should be done in the morning since *remolinos* or whirlpools often develop early in the afternoon and have caused drownings. The lake is in a volcanic crater on top of a small hill. Below the crater, across the river, is a *balneario* (resort) with a warm pool that uses water from the lake. Another resort, Miraflores, is just a km or so downstream from there.

To reach Tarapaya, go to Plaza Chuquimia near the main bus terminal in Potosí and look for a truck or car going toward Oruro. The 25 km trip along the asphalted highway to Tarapaya costs 50c. Ask the driver to let you off at the bridge where the gravel road begins. To get to the pool and resort, walk along the paved road

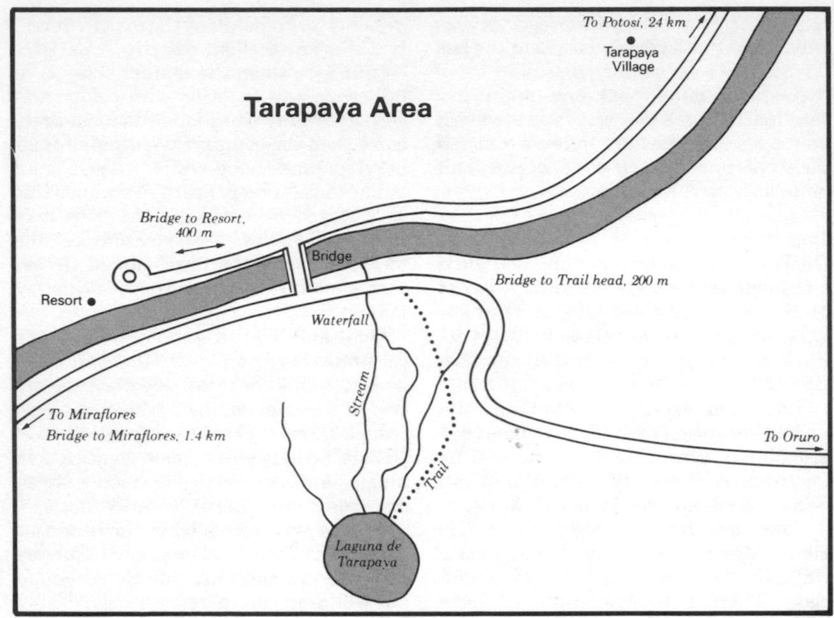

for 400 metres and it will lead you into the parking lot. If you're going to the Lake itself, cross the bridge, turn left, and walk about 200 metres. Just past the waterfall on the right, a trail that looks like a washed out roadbed leads uphill. Follow it about 400 metres to the lake. It may disappear at times into eroded gullies, but if you keep walking uphill or along the streams that flow out of the lake, you'll find it easily.

If you'd like to spend the night in this scenic area, there are a number of level and secluded places to pitch a tent. Plenty of water is available from the river but some sort of purification is necessary.

The other major hot springs in the region are at Chaqui and Don Diego. Chaqui is accessible from Plaza Uyuni by truck or micro. It has a very basic hotel which may be used as a base for exploring the interesting countryside around nearby Puna and Belén. Potosinos frequently venture in this direction on Sundays carrying loads of sugar, flour, rice and bread which they will exchange in the markets for potatoes, cheese, and local farm products. The climate here is much more agreeable than in Potosí and superior quality handicrafts, such as weavings and blankets, are available in small villages.

The hot springs at Don Diego are along the Sucre road and may be reached by truck, also from Plaza Uyuni. The resort has a hostel which costs US$3 per person.

Sucre

It wouldn't be going out on a limb to say that all Bolivians who know Sucre will agree that it is their nation's most beautiful city. Reverently, they've bestowed upon it romantic-sounding nicknames – The Athens of America, The City of Four Names, The Cradle of Liberty, The White City of the Americas. At an altitude of 2790 metres, its residents enjoy a mild and comfortable climate which is nearly as appealing as that of Cochabamba.

The city, which is set in a valley and surrounded by low mountains, remains the official or legal capital of the country. Like the Netherlands, Libya, and South Africa, Bolivia divides its bureaucracy between multiple capitals. Despite the fact that La Paz has usurped most of the governmental power, the Supreme Court still convenes in Sucre and with some kind of twisted pride, the Sureñas maintain that their city remains the real centre of Bolivian government.

Prior to Spanish domination, the indigenous capital of the valley of Choque-Chaca, where Sucre now stands, was known as Charcas. It served as the residence of the religious, military, and executive leaders of the early tribes and its jurisdiction encompassed several thousand inhabitants. When the Spanish arrived, the entire area from Southern Peru to Río de la Plata in present-day Argentina came to be known as Charcas.

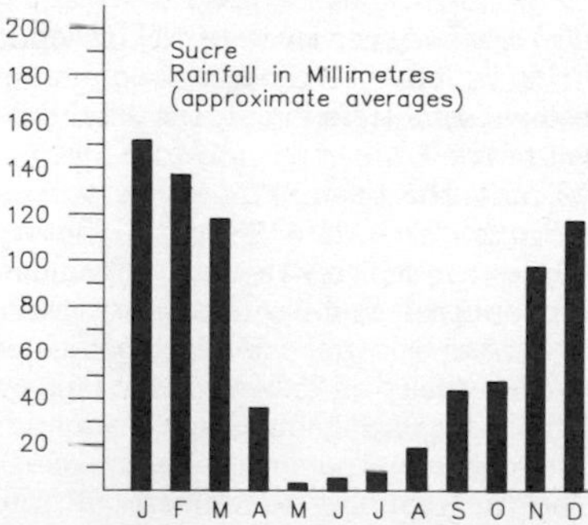

Sucre
Rainfall in Millimetres
(approximate averages)
200 180 160 140 120 100 80 60 40 20
J F M A M J J A S O N D

In the early 1530s, Francisco Pizarro, the *conquistador* who destroyed the Inca Empire, sent his brother Gonzalo to the Charcas region to keep an eye on Indian mining interests and activities which were considered potentially valuable to the Spanish realm. Uninterested in the Altiplano, he concentrated his attention on the highlands to the east of the main Andean Cordilleras. Thanks to his activities there, the city of La Plata was founded in 1538 as the Spanish capital of the Charcas by the Marquéz de Campo Redondo, Pedro de Anzures. He chose as its site the warm, well-watered, and fertile valley of Choque-Chaca, much as the Indians before him had done.

In 1559, within the Viceroyalty of Lima (which governed all Spanish territories in central and eastern South America), King Phillip II created the *Audiencia* or Royal Court of Charcas with its headquarters in the city of La Plata.

The Audiencia was unique in the New World in that it held both judicial authority and executive powers. The president of the Audiencia, a judge, also served as the chief executive officer of the region. Smaller subdivisions within the area were governed by royal officers known as *corregidores*.

Until 1776, the Audiencia presided over most of Bolivia, all of Paraguay, northern Argentina and Chile, and south-eastern Peru. When, however, the Portuguese in Brazil threatened the easternmost reaches of Spanish domination in South America, the new Viceroyalty of La Plata was established there to govern and ensure continued control. At this point, the city of La Plata lost jurisdiction over all but Chuquisaca (a corruption of Choque-Chaca), one of the four provinces of Upper

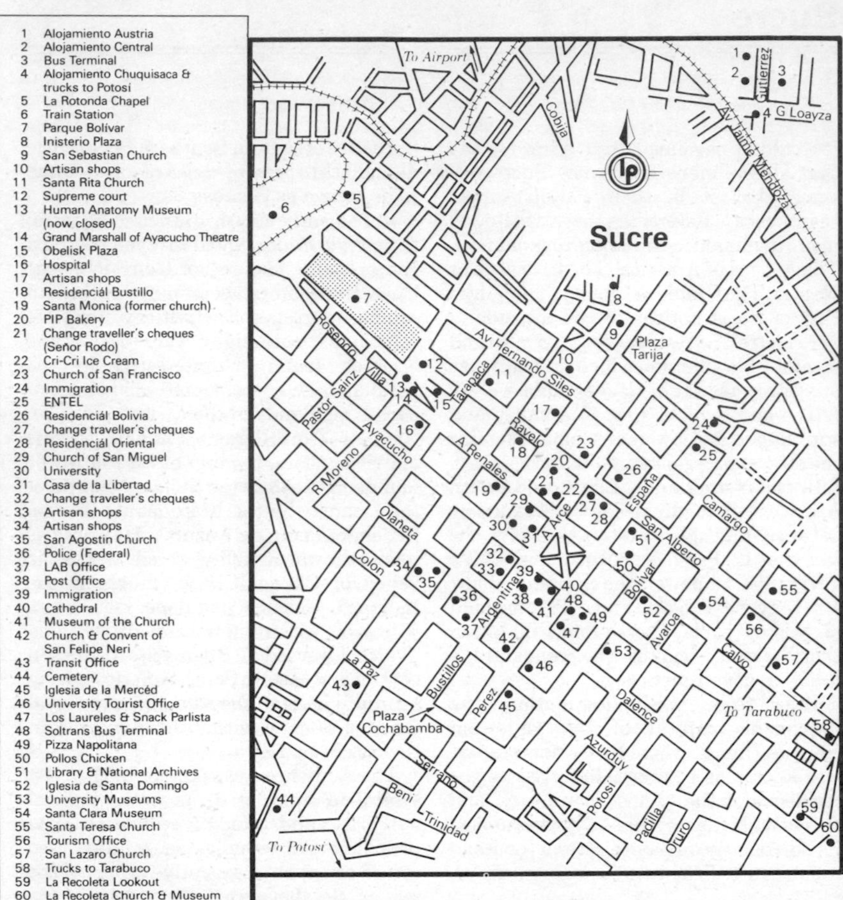

Peru, as all the leftover territory between the Viceroyalties of Lima and La Plata came to be known.

I assume that it was to avoid confusion that the city's name was again changed, this time to Chuquisaca after the province which was created around it. Throughout its history, La Plata/Chuquisaca had the reputation of being the administrative, legal, religious, cultural, and educational centre of all the eastern Spanish territories and it came to be known as the Athens of America.

The city had been given an archbishopric in 1609, which left it fairly autonomous in theological matters. That, the establishment of the *University of San Xavier* in 1622, and the opening of a law school, *Academía Carolina* in 1681 paved the way for the continued growth and development of the liberal and revolutionary ideas which led to 'the first cry of Independence in the Americas' on 25 May, 1809. This set off the alarm throughout Spanish America and one by one, the north-western South American Republics were liberated from

Spain by the military genius of Simón Bolívar and his armies.

After the definitive liberation of Peru at the battles of Junín and Tumusla on 6 August and 9 December 1824, Upper Peru was technically free of Spanish rule, having been traditionally accepted as part of the Lima government. Historically, however, it was more closely tied to the Buenos Aires government to the east and disputes arose about what to do with the territory.

Bolívar's second-in-command, General Antonio José de Sucre, advocated independence for the region and on 9 February, 1825, he drafted and delivered a declaration which stated in part:

> the ... Viceroyalty of Buenos Aires to which these provinces pertained at the time of the revolution of America lacks a general government which represents completely, legally, and legitimately the authority of all the provinces ... Their political future must therefore result from the deliberation of the provinces themselves and from an agreement between the congress of Perú and that ... in the Río de la Plata.

Bolívar, unhappy with this unauthorised act of sovereignty, criticised and rejected the idea but Sucre stood his ground, convinced that there was sufficient separatist sentiment in Upper Peru to back him up. As he expected, the people of the region rejected subsequent invitations to join the Buenos Aires government or to wait for a decision until after the installation of a new congress in Lima the following year. On 6 August, the first anniversary of the Battle of Junín, independence was declared in the *Casa de la Libertad* at Chuquisaca and the new republic was called 'Bolivia' after its liberator. On 11 August, the city's name was changed for the final time to Sucre in honour of the general who promoted the independence movement.

Today, Sucre struggles to retain the flavour of its colonial heritage. All buildings within the central core of the city must be either painted white or whitewashed. In order to house the art and relics of the Pre-Columbian, Colonial, and Post-Colonial eras, numerous museums have been established and churches have been renovated or simply maintained. The city remains a centre of learning and both Sucre and its university still enjoy their reputations as focal points of liberal and progressive thought within the country. Most visitors find themselves wanting to spend at least a few days enjoying and absorbing the pleasant atmosphere, attractions, and pace of life to be found here.

Information

It's apparent that Bolivia is proud of Sucre because it seems that at least 50% of IBT's operating budget went to the tourist office there. It would be a valuable first stop for every visitor arriving in town. The office is well-staffed, friendly, knowledgeable, and it keeps abreast of day-to-day political activities that may affect tourism or tourist attractions.

In addition to maps and brochures, they've got current bus, airline, and rail schedules as well as up-to-date information on hotels, fiestas, and church/museum renovations and closures. You'll find the office in the *Caserón de la Capellanía* (the old vichary) on Potosí, just south-west of San Alberto. It's open from 9 am to noon and 2 to 6 pm.

In addition to the government tourist office, there's a university tourist information centre a bit closer to the plaza on Bolívar near Dalence. It's staffed mostly by giggly female students who consider their time there as more or less a social event, however, they can help you with university-related queries.

For Germans and others who are interested, there's a German/Bolivian Cultural Centre (*Goethe Institut*) which can keep you abreast of what's going on overseas. They also have a selection of current German-language books and newspapers.

Post & Communications The ultra-modern new ENTEL office on the corner of España and Urcillo opens at 8 am. Since all international calls must go through La Paz, you can settle in for a long wait here if you're phoning home. You may get lucky, but I've never waited less than an hour to get through here.

The central post office is on Argentina less than a block from Plaza 25 de Mayo (main plaza) and service from there is normally reliable.

Changing Money If you have travellers' cheques, the best person to see is Señor Rodo on Calle Arenales near the plaza. His sign says '*Compramos Oro y Antigüedades*'. He will also buy and sell dollars cash for a good rate.

The *Hostal Colonial*, near Casa de la Libertad, and several travel agencies in town exchange both cash and travellers' cheques.

Those with cash will also find numerous agencies and businesses displaying '*Compro dólares*' signs. Some of them give excellent (above official) rates so shop around to find out who is offering the most.

Churches

The *Cathedral* on the southern corner of the Plaza 25 de Mayo was begun in 1551. The original structure was completed ten years later, but between 1580 and 1633 major additions were constructed. Of the most interest on the main building is the bell tower, which serves as a Sucre landmark. The interior of this church seems to be less overloaded with kitsch than in most other churches in Sucre.

Around the corner in an appendage of the Cathedral is the *Capilla de la Virgen de Guadelupe* which was completed in 1625. Encased in the altar is the *Virgin of Guadelupe of the Extremadura*, named after a similar one in that region of Spain. She was originally painted by Fray Diego de Ocaña in 1601 but the work was subsequently coated with highlights of gold and silver and adorned in robes encrusted with diamonds, amethysts, pearls, rubies, and emeralds. The jewels alone are said to be worth millions of dollars. Some may find the set up a bit tasteless though, because the priceless virgin's head is ringed by those cheap Christmas lights found over so many Bolivian altars.

The chapel and Cathedral are open from 7.30 to 9.30 am daily. Inside the Cathedral there is also a museum which will be described in the 'Museums' section.

The *Church of San Francisco* at 1 Calle Ravelo was begun in 1538 soon after the founding of La Plata. It started as a makeshift structure built by its founder, Francisco de Aroca, but in the late 1500s, the current church was completed. Inside, the mudejar ceiling is probably the most interesting aspect of the church's architecture. In the belfry is the *Campana de la Libertad*, Bolivia's Liberty Bell, which called to patriots during the revolution. San Francisco is open 7.30 to 9.30 am and 6 to 7 pm weekdays and 4 to 7 pm on weekends.

The best available view of the white Colonial nature of Sucre is to be had from the rooftop of the church of *San Felipe Neri* at 165 Nicolas Ortíz. In the courtyard are gardens of poinsettias and roses, and a nice painting of the Last Supper hangs in the stairwell. Originally the church was built of stone but it was later covered over with the stucco you see today. The stone seats on the rooftop terraces were used by monks for meditation during the days when this church served as a monastery. These days it's used as a parochial school. It's open to visitors from 4.30 to 5.30 pm and if you want to go up to the roof they'll charge 50c admission.

The church of *Santa Monica* on the corner of Arenales and Junín was begun in 1565 and is the best example of mestizo architecture in the city, decorated as it is with seashells, animals, and human figures. Inside, the woodwork on the ceiling is impressive and the courtyard is the nicest in the city with lawns and a variety of semi-tropical plants.

The whole thing has recently been converted into a multi-purpose civic auditorium.

Originally, the *Church of San Miguél* was a Jesuit church, but when the order was kicked out of the area it was rededicated. Built between 1612 and 1621, its architecture reflects Moorish influence. The church contains some very nice period paintings and sculpture. The interior is open from 6 to 7 pm daily.

The *Iglesia de la Mercéd* on Azurduy, diagonally across from San Felipe Neri, contains the most beautiful interior of any church in Sucre and possibly in Bolivia. The baroque-style altar and carved mestizo pulpit are decorated with filigree and gold inlay. Several paintings by the master Holguín – notably *The Birth of Jesus*, *The Birth of Mary*, and a self-portrait of the artist rising from the depths of Purgatory – are on display, as well as several sculptures by other artists. It may prove a little tricky to get into this one. The best way is to knock on the door at 1 Azurduy between 4 and 5 pm weekdays and ask for a quick look around.

At 101 Calvo is the *Iglesia de Santo Domingo*, which was constructed in the middle of the 16th century by the Dominican Order. The only item of real interest is a wooden carving of Christ.

San Lázaro is the oldest church in the Audiencia de Charcas, having been constructed in 1544. The silverwork on the altar and the several paintings attributed to the school of Polanco are the only notable features, since most of the original building has been reworked. It's on Calle Calvo between Potosí and Padilla.

Cemetery

The enthusiasm that surrounds this cemetery is completely disproportionate to what's there. Total strangers will rush up to tourists on the street and anxiously ask whether they've yet seen the cemetery. 'See it,' they urge. 'It's wonderful.' The tourist office will remind you not to miss it. Restaurant owners will sing its praises. I went expecting a Bolivian version of LA's Forest Lawn and found nothing that could remotely inspire any of the emotions the locals seemed to experience. What you have are some poplar trees trimmed into ho-hum arches and some unkempt gardens and mausoleums of wealthy Colonial familes. I don't rate it even worth the price of the taxi to get there but don't take my word for it or a lot of proud locals may be very disappointed.

Museums

The *Casa de la Libertad* has been designated a National Memorial in commemoration of the many events of historical importance that have taken place there, particularly the signing of the Bolivian Declaration of Independence on 6 August 1825. The actual document is on display as are numerous other historical mementoes of the era.

The first score of Bolivian congresses were held and doctoral candidates were examined in the *Salon*, that was originally a Jesuit chapel. Behind the pulpit hang portraits of Simón Bolívar, Hugo Ballivián, and Antonio José de Sucre. General Bolívar said that this portrait of himself, painted by Peruvian artist José Gil de Castro, was the most lifelike representation ever done of him.

This museum also houses portraits of presidents, military decorations, old governmental documents, and war and independence-related art and relics. Most memorable of all is a huge wooden bust of Bolívar carved by artist/musician Mauro Nuñez.

The Casa de la Libertad is open Monday to Friday from 10 am to noon and 3 to 5 pm. Admission is 50c but if you want to take photos, they charge US$1 extra.

The *Recoleta* which was established by the Franciscan Order in 1601, and overlooks the city of Sucre from the top of Calle Polanco, has served not only as a convent and museum but also as a barracks and a prison. In one of the stairwells is a plaque marking the spot where in 1828 President D Pedro Blanco was assassinated/executed. Outside there are courtyard gardens brimming with colour and nearby is the renowned *Cedro Milenario* – the ancient cedar – a huge tree that they claim was once even larger. It is the only remnant of the cedars, which at one time grew here in abundance.

The museum is worth a look, too. It contains quite a few anonymous paintings and sculptures from the 16th to 20th centuries, including numerous interpretations of St Francis of Assisi. One particularly nice wooden carving of St Francis and another work called *Christ Bound to the Column*, by Diego Quispe Curo, are the most well-known items to be found here. In addition, you can see all sorts of odds and ends, such as native arrows used in the Bolivian Oriente, crosses from funeral masses, and a complete collection of Bolivian currency. Note the denominations from bolivianos to pesos back to bolivianos again – they illustrate well the massive inflation that has plagued Bolivia over the years.

Don't miss the inside of the church. In its choir are the magnificent wooden carvings which represent the Franciscan monks who were crucified in Nagasaki, Japan, in 1595.

The Recoleta is open from 9 am to noon and 2 to 5 pm. Admission is 50c.

The old monastery of *Santa Clara* which was founded in 1639 is now a museum. In 1985, this museum was robbed and several paintings and some gold ornaments from the chapel disappeared. The most talked-about item that remains is a canvas that was too big to carry off. The robbers sliced a big chunk out of the centre of it and left the rest hanging. And it's still hanging just that way. The most beautiful and interesting thing to be seen here is the old pipe organ that was built and used in the 1600s. It still works and the guide will demonstrate it if you ask.

Admission to the museum is 50c. It's open from 8 am to noon and from 2 to 5.30 pm.

The three museums at the university on Bolívar and Dalence are all worthwhile and should be seen if they're not closed by political strife as is unfortunately often the case. When all is well in Sucre, they're open from 9 am to noon and 2 to 5 pm. There is no admission charge.

The first of the three, the *Charcas Colonial Museum*, was founded in 1939 and occupies 21 large rooms. It houses the best-known works of art in Bolivia, including some by Holguín, Padilla, Gamarra, and Villavicencio. You'll also see ornate furniture which was handcrafted by Indians of the Jesuit missions.

The *Museum of Anthropology* which was started in 1943 has separate sections dealing with Folklore, Archaeology, and Ethnography. Highlights include mummies, skulls, and artefacts from the eastern jungles of Bolivia. There are also the usual collections of pottery, tools, and textiles.

The most unique of the three university museums is the *Museum of Modern Art*. Paintings and sculptures from all over Latin America are exhibited here. Be sure to see the handcrafted charangos by Bolivian artist/musician Mauro Nuñez and the section devoted to native art.

The *Cathedral Museum* next door to the Capilla de la Virgen de Guadalupe contains a remarkable collection of religious relics, certainly the best church museum in all of Bolivia. In addition to paintings and carvings, they have some priceless gold and silver articles set with rubies, emeralds, and other precious stones. This museum was closed for renovation in early 1987 but it should be open again by the time you read this. Opening hours will probably change so ask at the tourist office for current information.

La Glorieta

After an extended tour of Europe, the

wealthy businessman Don Francisco Argandoña decided he'd like to build a home in Sucre that reflected the impressive architectural styles he'd seen overseas. He commissioned the architect Antonio Camponovo to design a castle that incorporated a blend of European styles to be built on the outskirts of Sucre. The result was *La Glorieta*, an imposing structure that is difficult to discuss without passing judgement on it. Decide for yourself whether you like it or not.

You can visit it Monday to Friday from 9 am to noon and 2 to 6 pm or on Saturdays from 9 am to noon. It's seven km from Sucre along the highway to Potosí and must be reached by taxi.

Parque Bolívar

The *Parque Bolívar* between the train station and the Supreme Court is the cleanest and most pleasant city park you're likely to find in Bolivia. It's full of shady trees, green lawns, and benches. There is also a public tennis court, a swimming pool, and a childrens' playground. For homesick Frenchmen, they even have a miniature replica of the Eiffel Tower. The top of the stairway inside it affords a nice view of the park, anyway.

What to Buy

Those who want to take home a souvenir typical of Sucre should consider shopping around for a *charango*, a small ukelele-like stringed instrument with a sound box which is often made from an armadillo carapace. Learning to play one is another matter altogether but if you already play the guitar, you should be able to figure out how to get some pleasant sound out of it. The salesperson may even give you a quick lesson or two.

While charangos are sold all over Bolivia, some of the best artisans are found right here in Sucre or the surrounding countryside and many shops in town specialise in them.

Also created out in the remote environs of Sucre at Potolo are the famous and magnificent weavings of red animals on black backgrounds. Prices for these are steep even by Western standards, but the degree of skill, artistry, and quality going into them justifies it. Although they are woven in small villages which may only be visited with a maximum of effort, these weavings may be purchased from street vendors in Sucre or Tarabuco.

If you failed to pick up silver goods and jewellery in Potosí, there are street vendors who hang out on Calle Ravelo near the market who'll give you another chance to buy these things at negotiable prices.

Places to Stay – bottom end

The city is so popular that finding inexpensive accommodation should be quite easy because there is a lot of it. The main area of budget hotels has its focus on the market and spreads out for several blocks along Calles Ravelo and San Alberto.

The nicest and most popular place to stay is *Residencial Bustillos* at Ravelo 158, just one block from the market. It's sparkling clean and comfortable and although the shower heads are the most frightening I've seen in Bolivia, they do have hot water all day long. No private baths are available here. They charge US$4 per person no matter how many occupy a room.

Another place that's growing in popularity is the *Residencial Oriental*, which is clean but a bit expensive for what you get. There are no private baths, hot water only occasionally, and no single rooms available, but it does have a TV room which always seems to be crowded. They also charge US$4 per person.

In the same area, *Alojamiento El Turista* is a very average place, but for those on a strict budget it's probably the best bargain around. They have hot showers and charge only US$2.50 per person.

Out in the middle of nowhere across the street from the bus terminal is the misnamed *Alojamiento Central*. There is a bus stop at the front door, however, and it's only ten minutes from town on Micro A. It's very basic, but costs only US$2.50 per person. Just 100 metres further on is the similar *Alojamiento Austria* where the long-distance bus drivers stay when they're in town. It's the same price as the Central but a bit cleaner.

Midway between the bus terminal and town, near the railroad track, is the very clean *Alojamiento Chuquisaca* which also charges US$2.50 per person for basic accommodation.

The equally basic *Alojamiento La Plata* at Ravelo 32 is rapidly gaining popularity among bare-bones budget travellers. It's got hot water and at US$2.50 per person is a comfortable and central place to stay.

Places to Stay - Middle

The *Residencial Bolivia* at San Alberto 42 is a convenient and central location but it isn't special. They justify the price of US$5 per person with the fact that they offer private baths. Hot showers are also available.

If you want a bit of luxury, for US$15 single or US$20 double, try the *Hostal Libertad* - also on San Alberto. You've got television, telephone, piped-in music, private baths, lots of space, and a refrigerator stocked with chocolates, wine, and soft drinks (they cost extra, of course) in each room. In addition, they offer room service for breakfast. This is the nicest mid-range accommodation in town since the others - the *Grand Hotel* and the *Hotel Londres* - are similar in price and quality to the Bolivia.

Places to Stay - top end

The *Hostal Colonial* on Plaza 25 de Mayo rates four stars by the Bolivian rating system but expect to pay twice the amount for accommodations similar to those at the Hostal Libertad, which is described above.

The beautiful old *Crúz de Popayán* which rates three stars, but is at least as nice as the Colonial, is at Loa 881.

Places to Eat

After braving the culinary deserts of Potosí, you'll find that Sucre should bring welcome relief with its relatively wide variety of eating establishments and quality of food available. If you're coming from anywhere else, you'll still find this a pleasant place, food-wise.

For breakfast, the *PIP* on Calle San Alberto is highly recommended for its excellent bread, baked fresh every morning. They also serve coffee and hot salteñas after 8.30 or 9 am. If you'd like to wash it down with a glass of milk, the *Pil Dairy* across the street in front of the market sells litre pouches as soon as the daily shipment arrives.

Another of the best places to buy salteñas is the nameless shop on España between Camargo and San Alberto where they cost only 25c. For an American-style breakfast, go to the restaurant at the Hostal Libertad or the Hostal Colonial.

If a fruit salad sounds appealing, some of the best around can be found in the food stalls at the market. You have to search around for them because they're in a section devoted only to fruit and fruit concoctions. One and a half salads will cost you only 50c - it's a Bolivian tradition to reward a satisfied customer with half as much again as a gesture of gratitude.

There seems to be a problem with chicken in Sucre, I tried several different restaurants and never found one that was completely satisfying. At *Pollos a la Canasta* in front of the main market, it was grossly underdone and effectively inedible but the owners couldn't see fit to pop it back in the pressure cooker for a few minutes. At *Pollos Campeón* on Ravelo it was dry, tough, and cold. At *Pollos Hawaii*, which was the best of the lot, it was so overpriced and the service was so poor that I decided to give up on the foul fowl for awhile and look at other options.

Both *Pecos Bill Pizzeria* on Avenida Argentina and *Pizza Napolitana* on the Plaza seem to do a good job. The latter plays good British and American music and serves as a local hangout for the under-21 and university crowd. Drinks and coffee are a bit expensive but a pizza large enough to fill you up costs only US$1.50.

Nicer restaurants with a variety of Bolivian and International dishes are found at *Leblón* on the corner of San Alberto and Arce and at *Las Vegas* on the main plaza. Many travellers have been disappointed with the latter, but it remains a reasonably priced alternative to fast food.

For a snack, go to the friendly *Snack Paulista* (on Calle Ortíz) near the main plaza which serves good humintas and superior chicken empanadas. For those who prefer their snacks frozen, *Helados Cri Cri* on Calle Estudiantes serves the best ice cream in town and is highly recommended by many travellers.

If you're looking for typical Bolivian snacks and lunches, *El Sol* at Colón 423 has been repeatedly recommended.

If you'd like to go dancing and meet some of the younger folks in Sucre, try *El Sótano* a disco in the Parque Bolívar or *El Cuerno* on Calle España. Both close on Mondays.

Getting There & Away

Air The office of *Lineas Aereas Imperiales* (tel 25931), which is the only line serving Potosí (via Cochabamba), is on the main plaza. The LAB office (tel 21140) is at Bustillos 121-127. Their information number at the airport is 24445. The airport, five km north of town, can be accessed by micro or taxi.

Bus The long distance bus terminal is quite a way from the centre and not within comfortable walking distance. Micro A does the run from Calle Junín, just north-east of Camargo, for 10c but it is often full beyond tolerable capacity and with luggage it would be a nightmare. The best bet is to splurge on a taxi which will cost about US$1.50 to or from the terminal.

Trans-Pullman La Paz and *10 de Noviembre* both do the run to Potosí at 8 and 10.30 am daily. The six-hour trip costs US$4. Trans-Pullman La Paz goes on to Oruro on their 10.30 am trip and leaves again at 6 pm. From Oruro, they continue to La Paz. Both 10 de Noviembre and Trans-Pullman La Paz serve Tupiza and Villazón at 10.30 am daily and on Tuesdays the latter goes to Tarija.

To Vallegrande, *Unificado* departs at 6 pm Thursdays. *Flota Chaqueña* goes to Camiri on Tuesday and Friday at 7 am for US$17.50.

There is service to Santa Crúz on Monday, Tuesday, Thursday, Friday, and Saturday at 5 pm on *Andes Bus*. The fare is US$12.50.

Micros to many of these destinations, particularly Potosí, leave when full from the Indian market near the railroad tracks at Avenida Ostria.

If you're leaving from the main bus terminal you pay 75c for the privilege, which goes for the upkeep of the building. If your bus leaves early in the morning, some flotas will want you to leave your luggage by the previous night for loading.

To points southward such as Tarabucó, Padilla, Tomina, or Camiri, there are trucks and micros that leave when full from the top of Calle Grau. They charge about the same as Flota Chaqueña does, but if the bus is full you've got an option.

There are rumours that a small bus serves Uyuni from Sucre on Wednesdays at 7 am, but I can't imagine how rough this trip might be if it exists at all.

Soltrans, whose office/terminal is near Pizza Napolitana, just off the main plaza, offers comfortable service to Potosí twice daily for US$6.50.

Rail

Express trains go to La Paz on Monday

and Thursday at 2.50 pm for US$9 and US$6.50 for first and second class. To Villazón and Tupiza they leave on Saturdays at 3 am. All trains out of Sucre must pass through Potosí.

The railroad station is across the little plaza/traffic circle north-west of Parque Bolívar on Cabrera.

Getting Around

If you're in a hurry and want to see the best of Sucre quickly, *Teresita S Tours* (tel 23206) – downstairs from the Hostal Libertad) offers city tours and also excursions to Tarabuco and Potosí.

There are a number of micros which ply the streets of the city and all of them seem to congregate at or near the market between runs. They're usually very crowded but since the town is so small, you won't have to spend much time aboard. The fare is 10c. The two most useful routes are the one which climbs the steep hill to the top of Avenida Grau to the Recoleta and the Tarabuco-bound-truck stop, and Micro A which goes to the main bus terminal.

Unfortunately, taxi drivers in Sucre have a reputation for being a bit unscrupulous, but this is probably thanks to the appeal the town has to so many foreigners. I think a lot of drivers are taking advantage of the pesos/bolivianos confusion so count your change carefully. A taxi ride to the cemetery or the transportation terminals will cost US$1.50. To the airport and La Glorieta, expect to pay double that.

TARABUCO

Although it's been 'discovered' for a long time now, Tarabuco should not be missed. It lies a dusty two hours, 65 km, to the south-east of Sucre at an elevation of 3200 metres. It therefore has a mild climate just a little cooler than that of Sucre itself.

On 12 March 1816, Tarabuco was the site of the Battle of Jumbati in which the village folk defended themselves under the leadership of Doña Juana Azurduy de Padilla and liberated the town from the Spanish forces.

The majority of Tarabuco's inhabitants are involved in agriculture or textiles. The colourful handmade clothing and weavings produced in Tarabuco and environs are the most renowned and well-executed in all Bolivia and they attract visitors and art lovers from all over.

The best and most popular time to visit Tarabuco is during the colourful Indian market which takes place each Sunday morning. There you can buy beautiful native artesanía – armadillo shell charangos, pullovers, coca pouches, ponchos, and most of all weavings featuring geometric and zoomorphic designs. Be forewarned that it's all very touristy and even well-bargained prices are high.

Even if you're not interested in major investments here, it's worth going anyway to see the colourful and unique costumes of the strolling and charango-playing campesinos. The wares laid out in stalls around the main plaza and on the side streets are so colourful that they lend a festive and lighthearted atmosphere to the entire place.

In commemoration of the Battle of Jumbati, each March the village stages *Phujllay* (which means 'amusement' or 'play' in Quechua). Over the years it's become one of the three most important annual fiestas in Bolivia. Over 60 communities show up in local costume.

The celebration begins with a Quechua mass and procession followed by the *Pukhara* ceremony, a Bolivian version of Thanksgiving. Folkloric dancers and musicians perform throughout the two-day weekend fiesta. If you're going to be in the area in March, ask at the Sucre tourist office for specific dates or write to them (preferably in Spanish) at *Instituto Boliviano de Turismo*, Potosí 102, Sucre, Bolivia.

A smaller local celebration called *Fiesta del Virgen de Rosario* takes place

in October to the tune of bullfights, masses, and parades.

Places to Stay & Eat

During Phujllay your chances of finding accommodation in Tarabuco are slim to none so be sure to take camping equipment if you plan to stay the night. During the rest of the year, lodging is available at the *Hotel Prefectural* for US$2 per person and at *Alojamiento Florida* for half that. The former is on the main plaza and the latter only half a block off it. The restaurant under the Hotel Prefectural serves good lunches and beer or soda for US$1.25. Snack foods are available in the streets during the market.

Getting There & Away

Trucks and micros leave from the top of Calle Calvo in Sucre between 6.30 and 9.30 Sunday mornings. They charge US$1 for the trip which requires at least two hours along very dusty roads. It's a good idea to wear sunglasses to keep the dust out of your eyes or you won't be able to enjoy any of the beautiful scenery en route. Trucks return to Sucre from the top of the main plaza in Tarabuco between 2 and 3.30 pm Sundays.

There are quite a few agencies in Sucre which do day tours to Tarabuco for less than US$20. A very helpful agency is the Teresita S Tours on San Alberto under the Hostal Libertad.

Southern Highlands

Drier, more desolate, and more isolated than the valleys of Cochabamba, Potosí, and Sucre, the Southern Highlands of Western Tarija and South-eastern Potosí Departments have come to call themselves the 'Andalusia of Bolivia' and it doesn't require much imagination to understand why. Anyone familiar with the Iberian peninsula will immediately notice the resemblance. The dry, eroded badlands, the neatly-groomed vineyards and orchards, the white stucco and red tile buildings, and the lilting sing-song nature of the local dialect all serve to fuel the proud self-image the southerners, particularly Tarijeños, have of their highland portion of the country. Even the Tarija River has recently been renamed Guadalquivir!

Further to the west near the edge of the Southern Altiplano in the south-east corner of Potosí Department lies the spectacular red rock country that surrounds the friendly growing city of Tupiza. To the south, in the southernmost 'toe' of Bolivia one finds the oil-bearing veins and the lush sugar cane-producing valleys that are situated away from the border town of Bermejo.

Although they may successfully be cultivated, the valleys and basins in this southern area are narrower than they are further north. Therefore, the farms of the region tend to be long and ribbon-like and more difficult to access than those of Sucre and Cochabamba and historically this area never rose to the agricultural prominence that its soils and climate would otherwise permit. Despite its grand

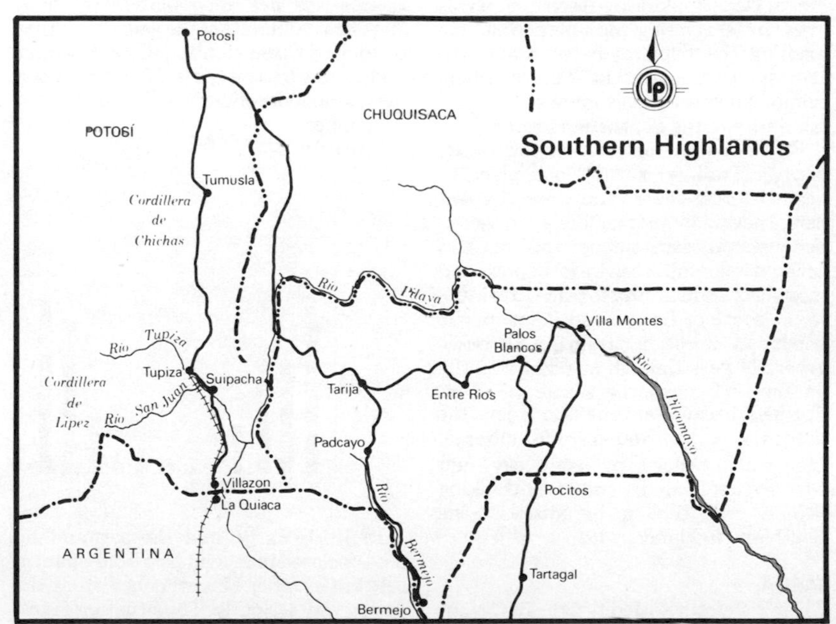

delusions about spiritual kinship with Andalusia, quite a few Bolivians in the more urbanised parts of the country simply regard the South as the 'Backwater' of Bolivia and tasteless jokes popular elsewhere are retold in La Paz with 'Tarijeño' replacing 'Irish', 'Polack', 'Newfie', or what have you.

Highly regional, southerners are eager to point out to Bolivians elsewhere that in 1810, the year following Chuquisaca's 'first cry of independence in the Americas', part of this region actually did declare its independence from Spain and operated briefly under a sovereign government with its capital at Tarija.

Having been relatively isolated, the people of this section have historically identified and traded more with Argentina, their neighbour to the south, than with the rest of Bolivia. That is now changing with a recent influx of *mineros despedidos*, unemployed miners. Victims of layoffs and labour strife in the mines of Oruro and Potosí Departments are resettling in this area in staggering numbers and are swelling the populations of the urban centres, particularly in Tupiza where mining plays an important role due to its proximity to the Southern Altiplano.

For those who want to leave the beaten 'Gringo Trail', this is a good place to begin. During the several weeks I spent here, I never saw another foreign traveller. Few visitors passing through this area stop because it doesn't receive a lot of press and most folks are in a hurry to reach Argentina to the south or La Paz and Potosí to the north. In addition, trains and buses generally pass through at night and the darkness obscures the scenic wonders. Too bad, because anyone who enjoys the outdoors, a year-round mild climate, good wine, geology, palaeontology, and friendly, educated, and free-thinking people, will find a paradise in the Southern Highlands.

TARIJA

There's a distinct Mediterranean flavour about Tarija which is evident in the climate, architecture, and vegetation. Around the main plaza grow stately date palms and the landscape immediately surrounding the city has been wildly eroded by wind and water into convoluted badlands reminiscent of parts of the Spanish Meseta.

The influence of Bolivia's Indian element is minimal in this city and the Tarijeños, who today call themselves 'Chapacos' are proud to be accused of considering themselves more Spanish or Argentine than Bolivian. The Chapacos, some of whom are descended from Argentine gauchos, are generally lighter-skinned and more European in appearance than most Bolivians elsewhere.

Tarija was founded on 4 July 1574, under the name of *La Villa de San Bernardo de Tarixa* by Don Luis de Fuentes y Vargas under the orders of Viceroy Don Francisco de Toledo.

The city lies at an elevation of 1924 metres and has a population of about 60,000. The climate of the valley is similar to that of Cochabamba although winter nights may be a bit cooler. The dry season here, as in most of Bolivia, is from April to November.

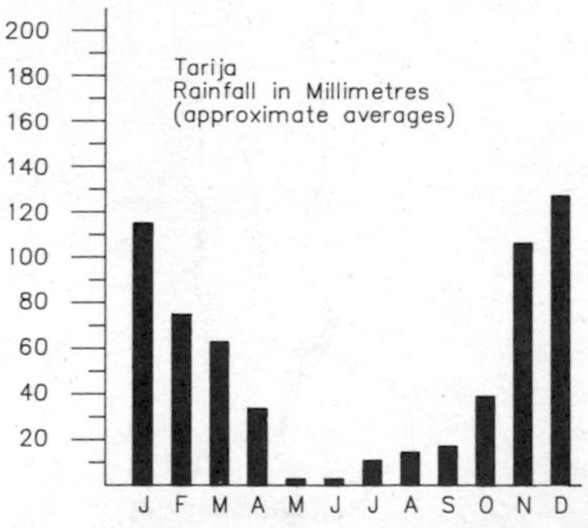

In 1810, Tarija and the surrounding area declared independence from Spanish rule but as far as I know, nobody took the action very seriously. The situation didn't erupt into armed warfare until 15 April 1817, at the *Batalla de la Tablada* in which the Chapacos won a significant victory over the Spanish forces. The departmental holiday is still celebrated on 15 April each year.

When Bolivia's independence was established in 1825, Tarija joined as part of the Bolivian Republic, having contributed its manpower over the years to that struggle, also.

Although there's no single overwhelming attraction to draw visitors to the area, Tarija is most definitely worth a visit. The surrounding badlands are chock full of the fossilised remains of prehistoric animals and ancient hunting tools can be found in the hills. In addition, Tarija is known for its numerous annual fiestas and the unique musical instruments used to celebrate them. And of course one finds here the usual Bolivian gamut of churches, parks, and museums that round out the picture.

Overall, Tarija is a peaceful, clean, friendly, and well-educated city that is free of the usual flurry that surrounds more touristy locales; consequently it's a lovely place to spend a few days relaxing and enjoying the sun.

Information

The tourist office on Calle Saracho near Bolívar is marginally helpful but the spiel they'll give you is memorised and specific questions throw them off balance. They do give out city maps which show street plans only – no points of interest are marked and street names are not legible.

Consulate If you need a visa for Argentina, the consulate is on the corner of Bolívar and Ballivián. The maximum wait is 48 hours but visas are often issued on the spot.

Changing Money The only place in town that will habitually exchange travellers' cheques is *Comercial Marconi*, a vendor of large appliances on the corner of Campos and Bolívar. The best time to go is after mid-day and before 5 pm during which time they have enough cash on hand to make exchanges. A couple of the travel agencies in town will change travellers' cheques if there is sufficient demand for dollars.

The two casas de cambio on Calle Bolívar between Sucre and Campos will give a competitive rate for dollars cash.

Churches

The *Convento San Francisco* between the streets of Ingavi, Colón, Campos, and Madríd was founded in 1606 and today it is a national monument and houses the major library in Tarija.

The *Cathedral*, one block off the Plaza Luís de Fuentes (main plaza) at the end of Calle Madríd is rather ordinary inside. It contains the remains of Luís de Fuentes, the founder of Tarija, and other Tarijeños prominent in the city's history. The church was constructed in 1611 and enhanced in 1925.

The most interesting church in town is the *Iglesia de San Roque* which sits on the hill at the end of Calle General Bernardo Trigo. It's fairly recent in construction, having been completed in 1887, but it's an imposing structure and serves as a landmark which is visible all over Tarija.

A nice overall view of the city is to be had from the garden of the *Iglesia de San Juan* at the top of Calle Bolívar. The church was constructed in 1632. It was here that the Spanish signed their surrender to the Liberation Army after the Batalla (Battle) de la Tablada on 15 April 1817.

Archaeology & Palaeontology Museum

The *Archaeology and Palaeontology Museum* is operated by the university. The entrance is on the corner of Bernardo Trigo and Virginio Lema one block from the main plaza. It was undergoing careless renovation in early 1987 and many of the display pieces were damaged in the

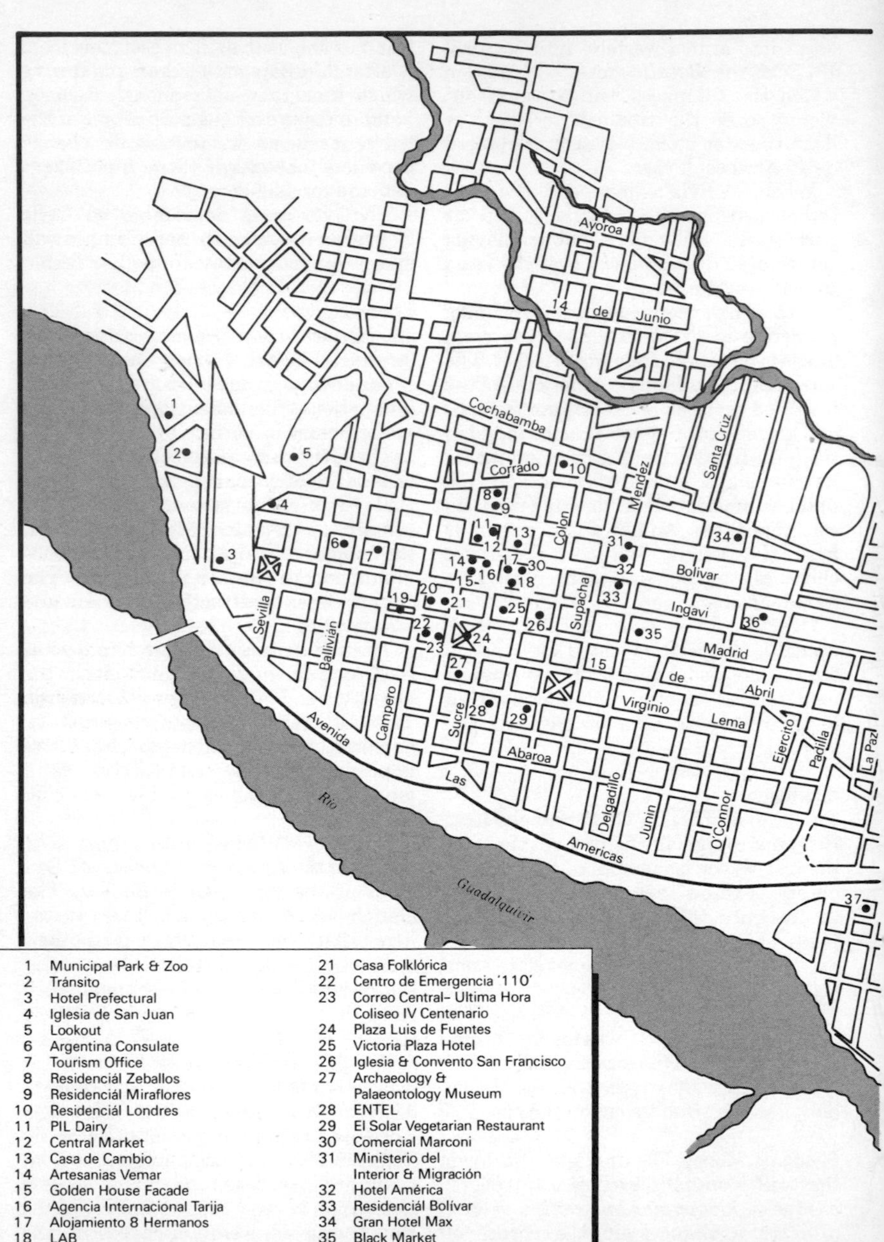
Ayoroa
14 de Junio
Cochabamba
Corrado
Santa Cruz
Mendez
Colon
Bolivar
Ingavi
Supacha
Sevilla
Ballivián
Madrid
15 de Abril
Virginio Lema
Campero
Sucre
Avenida Las Americas
Abaroa
Delgadillo
Junin
O'Connor
Ejercito
Padilla
La Paz
Río Guadalquivir
1 Municipal Park & Zoo
2 Tránsito
3 Hotel Prefectural
4 Iglesia de San Juan
5 Lookout
6 Argentina Consulate
7 Tourism Office
8 Residenciál Zeballos
9 Residenciál Miraflores
10 Residenciál Londres
11 PIL Dairy
12 Central Market
13 Casa de Cambio
14 Artesanias Vemar
15 Golden House Facade
16 Agencia Internacional Tarija
17 Alojamiento 8 Hermanos
18 LAB
19 Cathedral Metropolitana
20 TAM Office
21 Casa Folklórica
22 Centro de Emergencia '110'
23 Correo Central– Ultima Hora Coliseo IV Centenario
24 Plaza Luis de Fuentes
25 Victoria Plaza Hotel
26 Iglesia & Convento San Francisco
27 Archaeology & Palaeontology Museum
28 ENTEL
29 El Solar Vegetarian Restaurant
30 Comercial Marconi
31 Ministerio del Interior & Migración
32 Hotel América
33 Residenciál Bolívar
34 Gran Hotel Max
35 Black Market
36 Castle
37 Bus Terminal

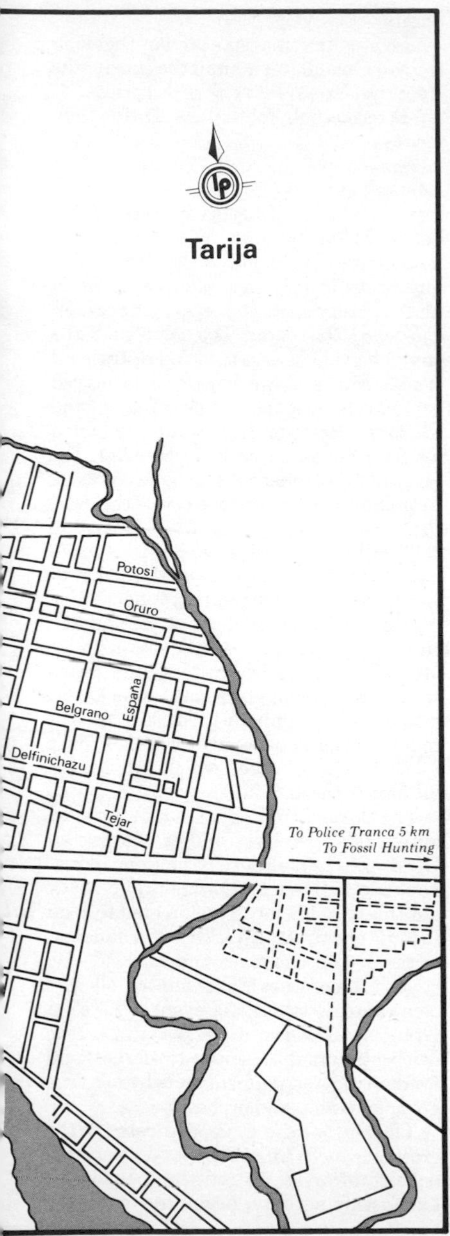

process but once it's all put back together, it will be a good place to get an overview of the prehistoric creatures and the early peoples that inhabited the Tarija area.

They have well-preserved remains of all the animals – *megatherium*, *mastodon*, early horses, and *glyptodon* – including a nearly complete glyptodon carapace and tail. Accompanying these are interesting artistic representations of how these animals must have looked in the flesh. On the archaeological side of the museum ancient tools, weapons, and pottery from throughout southern Bolivia are displayed.

Palaeontologist and local fossil expert, Ronald Randall, is a New Zealander who's spent 25 years in the Tarija area and has hunted and collected specimens all over Bolivia. He maintains a small museum in his home and is willing to show his finds and explain them to anyone who might be interested. He uses the Creationist theory to explain the rise and disappearance of prehistoric animals and even for a hard-core evolutionist like myself, it's an interesting discussion. Most impressive, however, is his natural talent for identifying and locating underlying fossils in very plain-looking rock. To arrange a visit to his museum, phone him at tel 5108 in Tarija.

Fossil Hunting

The Tarija area is a paradise for amateur palaeontologists who'd like to try their hand at fossil collecting. The area to the north of town in the *quebradas* (dry washes), near the airport and across the highway along the pipeline, is littered with remains of prehistoric creatures, primarily early horses, mastodons, megatheriums (giant ground sloths), and three-metre-long armadillo-like creatures called glyptodons. If you go looking, take good hiking footwear with lots of tread because the terrain is difficult and the unconsolidated silt can be very slippery. If possible, take some sort of geologist's pick or a similar instrument so you can carefully extract any fragile specimens you may find.

Many of the fossils are just lying loose or sitting on pedestals of sediment. Since the area is so severely eroded and each rainfall changes the face of the land it's uncommon to find a complete skeleton here. The parts have been sloshed around for thousands of years and deposited rather haphazardly in these sedimentary layers. On occasion, though, a fairly complete animal does turn up.

If you know what you're looking for, you're guaranteed to find more than you could ever cart off. The small blue 'stones' that are found lying all over the place are actually well-fossilised fragments of mastodon bones, tusks, and teeth. The crumbly rosettes you'll see in piles or embedded in sediment are pieces of glyptodon carapace, and the small rounded chalk-like 'pebbles' are from the hide of megatherium. Crania, pelvic, bones, and long bones of all these creatures can be found throughout the area but they are normally quite fragile because most of them haven't been well petrified. It's probably best not to try to unearth them because most of them will crumble into dust without the support of surrounding soil. If you encounter any significant or well-petrified finds, Mr Randall requests that you note the location and report them to him at tel 5108, Tarija, for further investigation.

Zoo

The zoo is in a park at the western end of town, but like most in South America, it is unkempt and the animals appear to be in pretty poor condition. They've got pumas, monkeys, a bear, a rhea which runs around loose, and a cage full of condors. The condor cage is too small for even one bird, let alone seven, and overall the place is pretty depressing. The surrounding park, however, is pleasant and there's a nice children's playground near the zoo. It's a 10 to 15 minute walk from the centre and admission is free.

Sports

There's a municipal sports complex along the Río Guadalquivir amid the eucalyptus trees which line Avenida Americas. It offers basketball, football, and other field sports.

Fiestas

Any discussion of fiestas in Tarija must be preceded by one of local musical instruments which play an integral role in any fiesta in this city. Unique to Tarija and vicinity are the *erke*, the *violín chapaco*, the *caña*, the *caja* and the *camacheña*. The erke is a wind instrument made from a cow's horn and is played exclusively between New Year's and Carnival. Between Easter and the *Fiesta de San Roque* in early September, the favoured instrument is the violín chapaco. From San Roque until the end of the year, the camicheña, a type of flute, is used in celebration. The caja, which is a drum played with one hand is used during all fiestas as is the caña, a three-metre-long cane pole with a cow's horn on the end. It's similar in appearance and sound to an alphorn. Charangos, guitars, and flutes which are popular elsewhere in the Andes also figure prominently in the music-making. The traditional dance of Tarija is *La Rueda* (The Wheel) which is danced at all fiestas throughout the year.

The Carnival of Tarija is one of the most animated in Bolivia and if the one in Oruro proves too touristy for your liking, you'd do well to trip down here and check out this one. It's mostly dedicated to good fun and the streets fill with joyful dancing, original and unusual music, and the colourful costumes of the country folk who come into town for the event. There's a Grand Ball in the main plaza after the celebration and the entire town shows up for dancing and performances by folkloric groups, bands, and orchestras.

The *Fiesta de la Crúz*, dedicated to the cross on which Christ died, is oddly enough a celebration of 15 days and nights of exhausting activity, beginning on 3 May each year. Music is provided by ensembles of cajas, cañas, and violínes which accompany dances and processions.

Undoubtedly, the best-known festival of Tarija is the *Fiesta de San Roque*, who is the patron saint of the city and also the patron saint of dogs. Although the *Día de San Roque* falls on 16 August, the celebration actually begins on the first Sunday of September.

The impressive costumes typical of this fiesta include silk scarves of brilliant colours, colourful half-length shirts, and head-dresses of polychrome feathers and ribbons. The entire effect is topped off with glittering sequins and other small bright objects. The fiesta begins with a procession of costumed dancers, musical groups, and even well-dressed canine participants, and continues for three days thereafter.

One other significant annual event is the *Fiesta de las Flores* a religious celebration dedicated to the *Virgen de Rosario*. It begins the second Sunday in October at the Iglesia de San Juan. A procession of the faithful led by an image of the Virgin of Rosario leaves the church and is showered all along its route with flower petals thrown by the spectators. Throughout the day the locals attend a colourful fair and bazaar in which they spend lavishly for the benefit of the Church.

What to Buy

The best handcrafted souvenirs typical of Tarija would naturally be the unique musical instruments played in the area. Unfortunately, it's difficult to carry a caña or a caja around in your pack, but the smaller ones can be mailed home with little difficulty. The problem lies in finding a place that sells them. *Artesanías Vemar* which is highly touted by the tourist office has little more than tacky elementary school crafts and there's nothing of real interest. Try the *Casa Folklórica* on the corner of Madríd and Trigo or ask around at the market for the name of someone who designs and makes the particular instrument you're looking for.

Places to Stay - bottom end

Of all the lower-range accommodation available in Tarija, the *Residencial Bolívar* on Bolívar is probably the best value for the money. It's clean, friendly, and tidy and has hot showers, a snack restaurant, a TV room, and a pleasant and sunny courtyard. They charge US$4 per person without private bath or US$6 per person with. Avoid the restaurant for breakfast, however, as it is grossly overpriced.

Similar accommodation can be had across the street at *Hotel América*. You can't miss it – the large obtrusive sign out front is a classic example of overkill advertising. It's not quite as clean as the Bolívar but they have hot water and both a good restaurant and noisy bar downstairs. A room without bath costs US$3 per person. A private bath costs US$5.

Alojamiento 8 Hermanos at No 782 Mariscal Sucre is very ordinary but pleasant. They charge US$3 per person for a room without bath. Hot water is available. *Alojamiento El Hogar* offers similar accommodations at similar prices but it's out across the street from the bus terminal, a bit of a walk from the centre.

The *Residencial Miraflores* charges US$2.75 and US$3 for Bolivians and foreigners respectively for dorm-style rooms without baths. Individual rooms cost US$3.25 for Bolivians and US$3.50 for foreigners.

The *Residencial Zeballos* has an even more confusing pricing scheme. A single room with private bath costs US$6.50 for Bolivians and US$8 for foreigners. A single without private bath is US$4 for Bolivians and US$5 for foreigners. Doubles with private bath cost US$10 for foreigners and US$9 for Bolivians. Doubles without bath are US$6 for Bolivians and US$7 for foreigners. I stopped short of asking about triples. At any rate, they told me that if business is slow, they'll let foreigners stay at the Bolivian price.

Places to Stay – middle

The *Residencial Familiar* at 649 Sucre is clean and has a pleasant atmosphere. All rooms have private bath and cost US$6.50 per person.

Slightly upmarket is the *Victoria Plaza Hotel* on the main plaza. As you might expect, two-tier pricing is in effect here. For a room with private bath and phone, Bolivians pay US$15 per person and foreigners US$20. There is an attached restaurant downstairs and the overall atmosphere, for Tarija anyway, is a little ritzy.

Camping

The best place to camp if it's not raining is in the quebradas of the fossil-hunting area near the airport. Alternatively, the far bank of the Río Guadalquivir offers some nice spots to pitch a tent.

Places to Eat

The best food in town is undoubtedly served at *El Solar Vegetarian Restaurant* on Colón near Virginio Lema. I can't recommend it enough – even meat-eaters will like it. It's not only friendly and inexpensive, but the portions are larger than a normal person can eat in one sitting. A typical lunch consisting of salad, soup, a main course, herb tea, and dessert costs only US$1.25. Dinners are equally reasonable.

The *Snack Daniela* on Mendez near Bolívar is also recommended. From the outside, it may look like nothing but a hole in the wall but the inside is very nice. They serve excellent roasted chicken which comes with chips and fried rice for only US$1.50. They open at 7 pm.

There are a couple of restaurants downtown which are popular with locals. The *Restaurant Chapaca* on the plaza is a bit dirty but is nice for lunch or a snack. *Arlequín* is expensive but is very clean and serves good dinners. *Snack Pio-Pio* serves as a local youth hangout. They have fairly good chicken and chips for the same price as Snack Daniela but the portions are smaller and not as tasty.

The restaurant in *Hotel América* does typical Bolivian dinners for a reasonable price but you may have to put up with a few drunks who frequent the bar there.

For ice cream, try the *Heladería Victoria* on the main plaza.

Around the north-east corner of the market can be found some very good pastries and snacks not available in other parts of Bolivia, including some delicious and fattening crepe-like concoctions called *panqueques*.

Fresh milk is available from the *Pil Dairy* on the corner of Bolívar and Trigo.

Don't forget to sample some of the local wines while visiting Tarija.

Getting There & Away

Air The *Oriel Lea Plaza Airport* is just east of town along the main highway. While it would be quite a long walk, it can be reached by taxi from the centre in 10 minutes. Tarija is served by *Lloyd Aereo Boliviano* from La Paz, Sucre, Cochabamba, Santa Crúz and Yacuiba. Their office (tel 2282) is at Ingavi 0-0236. TAM (tel 2734) flies to Yacuiba, Villa Montes, and Santa Crúz. They are located at the corner of Sucre and Ingavi.

Bus The main bus terminal is on the east end of town on Avenida Américas. Though it's within walking distance of the centre, it would seem a long way carrying a heavy pack.

If you're headed south toward Bermejo and Aguas Blancas, Argentina, both *Padcaya* and *Expreso Guadalquivír* leave at 8.30 am and 7.30 pm daily. *Flota Chapaco* leaves at 8.30 am and 7 pm daily but all these flotas play musical passengers so you may not have a reservation on the one whose ticket you bought. It pays to arrive early and ask. The fare each way is

US$7 and the trip takes six to eight hours.

To Yacuiba which is the border town across from Pocitos, Argentina, *Flota Trans-Gran Chaco* leaves on Monday, Friday, and Sunday at 5 pm. The trip takes about 12 hours over a fantastically beautiful route that is unfortunately done at night.

Flota 10 de Noviembre leaves for Sucre, Potosí, Oruro, and La Paz on Monday, Thursday, and Saturday at 5.30 pm. *Velóz del Sud* leaves for La Paz on Monday, Tuesday, Thursday, and Saturday at 5 pm and for Potosí on Sunday, Monday, Wednesday, and Friday at 6 am. *San Lorenzo* serves La Paz on Monday, Wednesday, Thursday, and Friday at 5 pm.

To Villazón, the border town across from La Quiaca, Argentina, *Velóz del Sud* leaves on Monday, Wednesday, Saturday, and Sunday at 9 am and *Expreso Villazón* goes on Monday, Thursday, and Saturday at 8.30 am.

If you're going to Villa Montes, a route served almost exclusively by petrol trucks, wait at the tranca east of town for a ride. This will prove a fairly terrifying road but the scenery is indescribable. Between Entre Ríos and Palos Blancos you'll keep experiencing the strange sensation that you've been mysteriously transported back to the American West of the late 1800s. Near the end of the trip, the road passes through the amazing Pilcomayo Gorge. Plan on 20 to 24 hours for this 279-km trip during the dry season. During the wet, either fly or go the long way around through Argentina.

An alternate way to reach Villa Montes is to take the Yacuiba bus to Palos Blancos and hitch a ride from there. All the petrol truck drivers stop at the bar in Palos Blancos to get drunk on Argentine wine before braving the Pilcomayo Gorge. If that's not a comforting thought, I don't know what is.

For trucks to Potosí, Villazón, Yacuiba, or Bermejo, take a taxi to the appropriate tranca and wait for a vehicle going your way. Use the north tranca for Villazón and Potosí and the south-east for Yacuiba and Bermejo. Expect maximum discomfort and to pay only slightly less than you would on the flota.

Getting Around

Tarija is so small that it's possible to walk just about anywhere you'd like to go, but there are numerous taxis which cost only 30c to anywhere within the centre, including the long-distance bus terminal. To the airport, expect to pay at least 50c and several dollars to the fossil-hunting areas or the trancas.

BERMEJO

Bermejo is a hot, sticky, and dusty (or muddy) town 270 km south of Tarija with little to offer the visitor but an entry/exit stamp to/from Bolivia in his or her passport. The southernmost town in Bolivia, it lies on the banks of the Río Bermejo at the south-west end of Bolivia's oil-bearing geologic formation. There's a YPFB (that's *Yacimientos Petrolíferos Fiscales Bolivianos*, if you're interested) compound here which keeps many of the town's 15,000 or so residents busy.

Bermejo also lies in the heart of a major sugar-cane-producing region and there's a refinery just out of town. Up the river five km from YPFB, an international bridge spans a canyon of the Río Bermejo creating a highway link with Argentina on the other side.

The 'ant trade' mentioned in the chapter on the Villazón area is alive and well here, too. In fact, the whole scene is so ludicrous that the shenanigans that go on there can turn into quite an entertaining comedy of errors (and it's something to watch while standing in the stagnant queue at Argentine Immigration). The Argentine officer very formally eyeballs the folks passing through the gate into his country as if he didn't know what they were doing there. Often, he'll confiscate any suspicious-looking empty sacks they

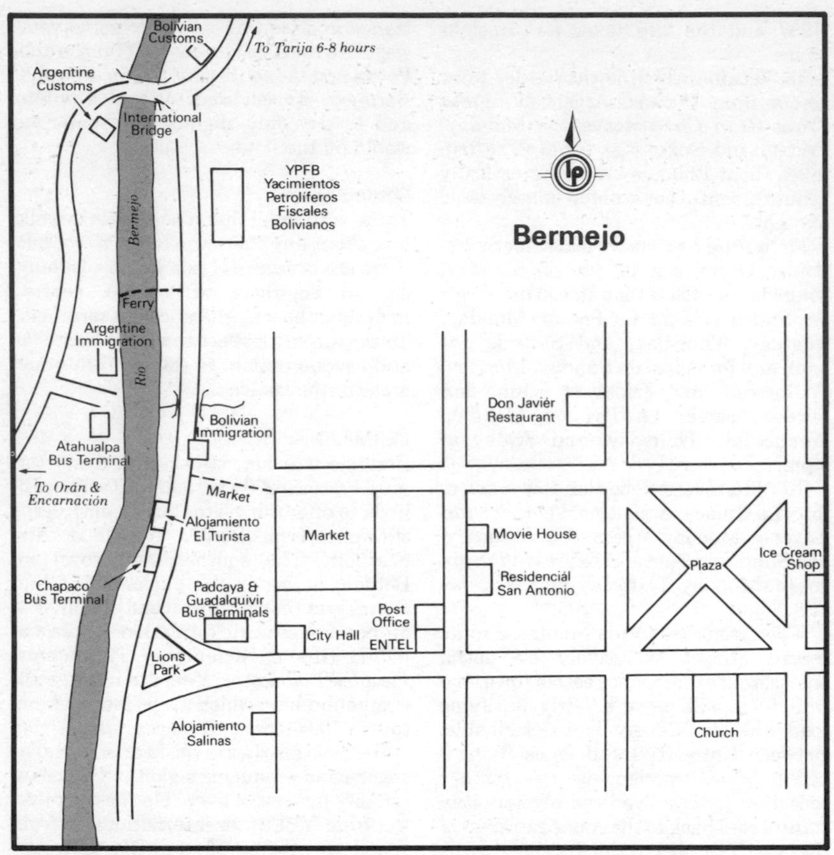

may be carrying lest they be used for some illicit purpose, such as a means to transport 'contraband' back across the river. Most of the 'ants' just smile, defiantly take back the sacks, and march on through the gate without another word.

As soon as all those containers are filled with wine, noodles, rice, and what have you, they play the game to get back through the control, passing through the gate while the officials are conversing or literally looking the other way. Once in awhile, something is confiscated or a sack of noodles is 'accidentally' broken on the ground but everyone just laughs about it. They'll all be back the next day to try again. While this can all be very amusing to watch, it's also a little depressing when you realise that the unrealistic import tax on these things has put them out of reach of average Bolivians and without the 'ant trade', no one could afford to buy staple items which Bolivia does not produce.

Information

Changing Money The main street in Bermejo is lined with casas de cambio but none of them change travellers' cheques so be sure to have Argentine australes, cash dollars, or bolivianos on hand when you arrive here. All the casas de cambio offer different rates for cash – ask at several before handing over the money.

Crossing the Border The border post on the Bolivian side is open from 7 am to 4 pm 'más o menos' as the locals will tell you. Argentina is one hour later than Bolivia time-wise, but the post there is open during the same hours, 8 am to 5 pm local time.

After getting an exit stamp, you can hitch a ride to the bridge and walk across (this is the hard way) or take the ferry across the river between Bermejo and Aguas Blancas, the settlement on the Argentine shore. The trip costs 25c and the boats leave when full, which is about every 30 seconds. Get your entrance stamp at the immigration post on the opposite side (see map for locations).

Places to Stay

In Bermejo you don't have much choice of accommodation. The *Residencial San Antonio* is very basic but clean, with no private baths. It costs US$4.50 per person. The owners are friendly and there's a decent restaurant attached.

The *Alojamiento El Turista* near the immigration office is clean and offers private baths and hot water. If both of these are full, as they often are, you may have to resort to the third choice – a filthy alojamiento just off the main street in a brick building. There's no sign so just ask for *Alojamiento Salinas*. They charge US$3 per person but avoid it if at all possible. At two bits it would be overpriced.

In Bermejo the power is turned off all night and into the morning. The tap water is murky and quite unsafe and I'm sure it's drawn straight from the river.

Places to Eat

Both the *Don Javiér* on the plaza and *Residencial Don Antonio* serve standard Bolivian fare for equally standard prices. Nothing is outstanding – just lomo, chicken, soup, and rice. There is, however, a good ice cream shop on the plaza.

Getting There & Away

From Bermejo to Tarija, all flotas leave from their respective terminals at 7.30 pm and cost US$7. The trip will take from six to eight hours.

From Aguas Blancas, buses to Orán leave hourly from the terminal across from the immigration office. The fare is US$1 and it takes about an hour. From Orán, you can connect to Salta, Jujuy, Tucumán, Tartagal (for Pocitos and Yacuiba), and even Asunción. The Asunción bus leaves once a week on Saturday afternoons.

Since there are no hotels in Aguas Blancas, you must stay in either Bermejo or Orán.

Those travelling to Argentina from Bolivia should expect several thorough searches by customs and police, especially at this border crossing. They are drug-paranoid over there and no youngish-looking foreigner will escape suspicion. If you're carrying a camera, radio, walkman, or other electronic device, register it with immigration upon entering Argentina to avoid its confiscation by unscrupulous officials later on.

TUPIZA

In the background runs the Tupizan range, very red, or better, a ruddy sepia, very distinct, and resembling a landscape painted by an artist with the animated brilliance of Delacroix or by an impressionist like Renoir . . . In the tranquil air, translucent, flows the breath of smiling grace . . .

Carlos Medinaceli, Bolivian Writer

If anyone were to ask me what I considered the nicest place in all Bolivia, without hesitation or qualification I would answer 'Tupiza'. Anyone who loves the desert

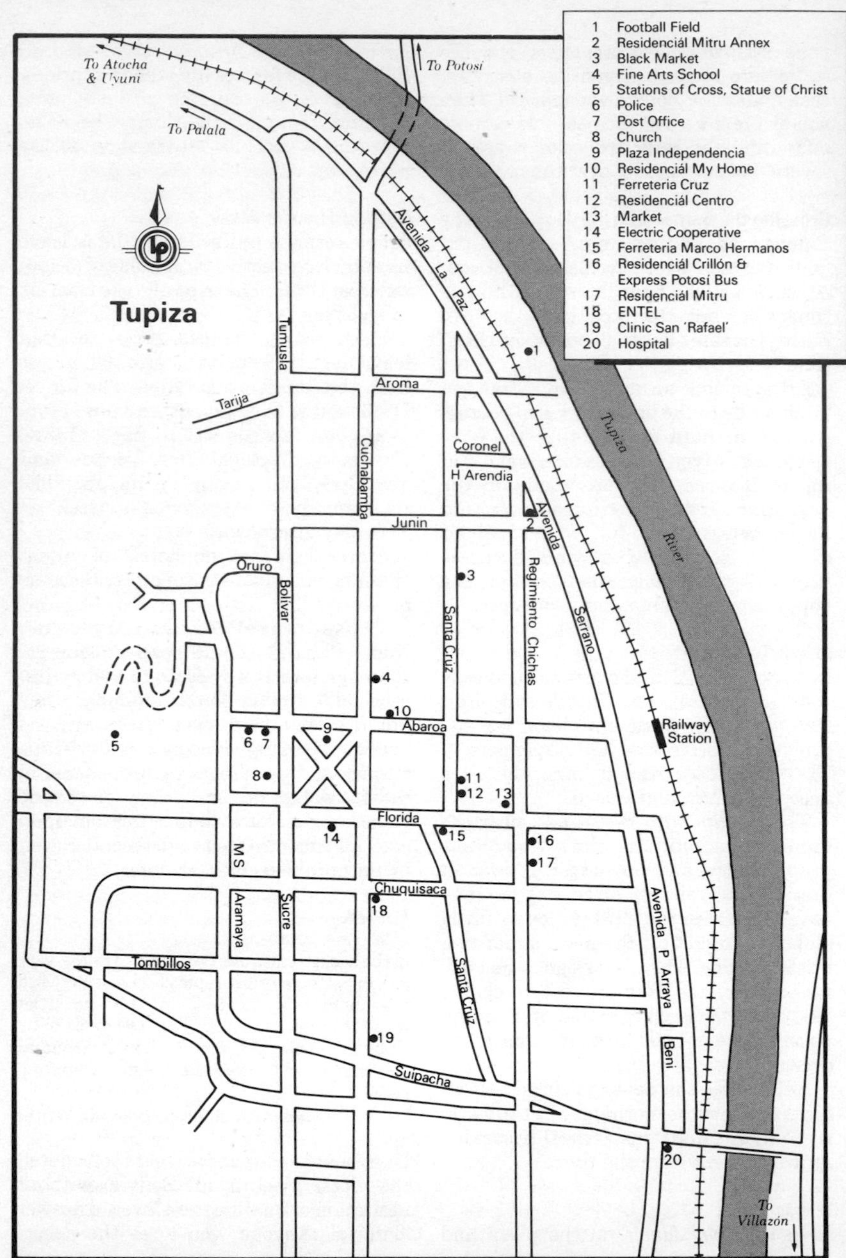
Tupiza
1 Football Field
2 Residenciál Mitru Annex
3 Black Market
4 Fine Arts School
5 Stations of Cross, Statue of Christ
6 Police
7 Post Office
8 Church
9 Plaza Independencia
10 Residenciál My Home
11 Ferreteria Cruz
12 Residenciál Centro
13 Market
14 Electric Cooperative
15 Ferreteria Marco Hermanos
16 Residenciál Crillón & Express Potosí Bus
17 Residenciál Mitru
18 ENTEL
19 Clinic San 'Rafael'
20 Hospital
To Atocha & Uyuni
To Potosí
To Palala
Avenida La Paz
Tumusla
Aroma
Tarija
Cuchabamba
Coronel
H Arendia
Junin
Avenida Serrano
Tupiza River
Oruro
Bolívar
Santa Cruz
Regimiento Chichas
Abaroa
Railway Station
Florida
M S
Aramaya
Sucre
Chuquisaca
Tombillos
Avenida P Arraya
Beni
Suipacha
To Villazón

landscapes of the American South-west, the wilderness of the Kimberley Ranges, or the Stone Forests of Kunming, China, will also love Tupiza.

The capital of Sud Chichas, a province of Potosí Department, Tupiza is the most literate and educated city of all Bolivia with 90% of the population able to read and write. It's also a comparatively young city - half of its 20,000 inhabitants are under the age of 20 and its growth rate is one of the highest in the country.

Tupiza lies at an altitude of 2950 metres in the narrow valley of the Tupiza River, surrounded by the rugged Cordillera de Chichas. The climate is mild year-round with most of the rain falling between November and March. During July and August, the days are hot, dry, and clear, but night-time temperatures can drop to below freezing.

The original tribe inhabiting this valley and the surrounding mountains called themselves Chichas. They left archaeological evidence of their existence here but there is actually very little known about their culture or their language. It is assumed that they were a unique group, separate from the tribes living in neighbouring areas of southern Bolivia and northern Argentina, but anything unique about them was destroyed between 1471 and 1488 when the Incas, under the leadership of Tupa' Inca Yupanqui, annexed the region into the Empire. In turn, the Chichas' homeland was used by the Incas as a military nucleus from which to gather forces and organise armies to conquer the Humahuaca, Diaguitas, and Calchaquíes tribes of northern Argentina.

After the Spanish conquered the Inca Empire, the entire southern half of that domain was given to Diego de Almagro by decree of Carlos V, the king of Spain. By the time Almagro and company arrived in the Tupiza Valley on a familiarisation expedition in October of 1535, the Chichas culture had been forgotten, completely absorbed into that of the Quechuas. Almagro stayed briefly in the Valley then moved southward toward Chile, bent on exploring the rest of his newly-acquired spoils.

Though the official date of the founding of Tupiza is 4 June 1574, and an official decree states that its founder was captain Luis de Fuentes (who also founded Tarija), it's all pure conjecture. The origin of the name is similarly hazy. The current spelling was derived from *Tope'sa* or *Tucpicsa* but no one has a clue what the word meant. It has been suggested that it probably meant 'red rock' in Chichas since that seems to be the salient feature of the area, but that too is just a guess.

The Chichas area took part in the tumultuous Campesino Rebellion of 1781. In Tupiza, Luis de la Vega, who approved of the uprising, mobilised the local militia and proclaimed himself governor of Chichas, Lipez, Cinti, and Porco, encouraging rebellion against the Spanish authorities. This mob was successful in executing the Spanish Corregidor of Tupiza and levelling his house, but the rebellion was effectively quelled before it really got underway. There were at the time 4000 Indian troops en route to Tupiza under the leadership of Pedro de la Crúz Condori. Their mission was to help organise and carry out massive violence against the government but the army was intercepted by the Spanish commander Rosequín before it reached Tupiza.

On 7 November 1810, the first victory in Upper Peru's struggle for independence from Spain was realised at the Battle of Suipacha which was fought just to the east of the Tupiza Valley. Likewise, the last decisive battle of that 15-year-long war took place at Tumusla, in the northern end of the Chichas province on 9 December, 1824.

From the time of founding through the War of Independence the Spanish population of Tupiza grew steadily, lured to the area by the favourable climate and suitable agricultural and grazing lands. Later on, the discovery of minerals in the Cordilleras de Chichas and Lipez attracted even more and with them came the Indians who would be doing most of the work. Unlike the rest of Bolivia where the Indian strains dominate, the current residents here are of predominantly Spanish descent although the Quechua and Chichas influence is evident.

In 1840, Argentine revolutionaries fleeing the tyranny of the brutal dictator Juan Manuel Rosas escaped into Tupiza and were incorporated into the community. More recently, campesinos are moving into town from the countryside and 800 out-of-work miners and their families have already settled there with 1500 more expected in the near future. The favourable conditions in the area also attract immigrants from other parts of the country.

Economically, the town is dependent primarily on agriculture and mining. The main crop is maize and mines in the vicinity produce antimony, lead, silver, bismuth, and a little tin. A YPFB plant five km out of town also provides employment and the only antimony smelter in Bolivia operates along a dry tributary of the Tupiza River.

Despite its often tumultuous past and its favourable economic situation of late, the main attraction here is still natural – the rainbow-coloured rocks and mountains, clear wild rivers, cactus forests, multi-hued chasms of rugged spires and pinnacles, beautiful sunsets and brilliant blue skies, varied and abundant wildlife. This is beginning to sound like a tourism promo! Indeed, those who are properly equipped and know how to appreciate the wilderness outdoors will undoubtedly recognise the appeal of this place and since so few visitors have passed through here, you can expect a sincere welcome from the friendly Tupiceños.

Information

Changing Money Neither bank in Tupiza will change money. The two hardware stores, *Ferretería Crúz* on Avenida Santa Crúz and *Ferretería Marco Hermanos* on the corner of Santa Crúz and Florida, are both reputable and will change dollars cash. Various small shops in town will exchange cash dollars, bolivianos, and Argentine australes.

The *Electric Coöperative* on Plaza Independencia will exchange both dollar notes and travellers' cheques for the same rate. Go to the second storey cashier's window.

Market The *mercado de ferias* takes place on Monday, Thursday, and Saturday mornings along Avenida Chichas. The *Mercado Negro* (Black Market) where you can buy just about anything imaginable occupies the block between Chichas, Santa Crúz, Junín, and Abaroa. It is open daily.

Finca Chajrahuasi

Just out of town across the river is this old abandoned farmstead which was owned by Carlos Victor Aramayo, one of the three 'tin barons' of Bolivia. Today it is overgrown with weeds and in quite the state of disrepair. Aramayo, who had maintained his business in Bolivia using Bolivian labour, was heaped into the same category as the absentee Simon Patiño. When his mines were nationalised in 1952, Aramayo had to flee to Europe to escape the wrath of his countrymen. His property today is used as a football field but it is apparent that this was once a very comfy estate.

Bellas Artes

La Escuela de Bellas Artes (School of Fine Arts) occupies the 16th century mansion of the Eguía family. The building itself is in pretty poor condition, but efforts are underway to renovate it. Inside there is a small art museum and a limited but beautiful library of old literature and reference books in Spanish, English, and French.

Cerro Chorolque

The short trail to the top of Cerro

Top: Cerro Rico-Potosí (TM)
Left: On the summit of Huayna Potosí (TM)
Right: Condoriri in the Cordillera Real (TM)

Top: Copacabana (DS)
Bottom: Ruins on Isla de La Luna – Lake Titicaca (DS)

Chorolque, flanked by Stations of the Cross, is a pleasant morning or evening walk when the low sun brings out the fiery reds of the surrounding countryside. The hill, which is crowned by a statue of Christ, affords a good overall view of the town.

Places to Stay

The *Residencial Crillón* on Chichas near Florida is clean and basic and costs US$1.50 per person. In the same range, but not so clean, is the *Sede Social Ferroviaria*, an authentic place on Abaroa near the train station.

The *Residencial Centro* on Santa Crúz costs US$2.50 per person and it's clean with a nice restaurant and hot water.

A place that's recommended by locals is the *Residencial My Home* at 288 Aboroa. It costs US$1.50 per person and has a reputedly good restaurant attached. The name sounds cosy, anyway.

The nicest place in town is probably the *Hotel Residencial Mitru* and *Mitru Annex*. It's extremely clean and friendly, but their 'hot' showers are actually tepid. Still, it's a bargain at US$3 per person.

Places to Eat

The only really good sit-down restaurants are in the hotels. The one in the *Residencial Mitru* is good but overpriced. The restaurants in the *Residenciales Centro* and *My Home* are both recommended by locals.

Across the street from the train station are street vendors who sell very nice meals of salad, potatoes, rice, and a main dish for less that US$1. Similar meals can be found in the little cubbyholes in the same area.

The several food stalls in the market are cheap and are especially good for breakfast. The local humintas are some of the best I've had in Bolivia.

Getting There & Away

The *Expreso Potosí* office is in the same building as the Residencial Crillón on Chichas. You can buy a ticket here to Potosí, but the bus leaves from in front of the train station at 7.30 pm daily. To Villazón, it leaves in the morning and costs US$1.50. There is no bus service direct to Tarija from Tupiza – you must go through Villazón.

Although I love this place, it is after all Bolivia and the railroad situation here is as bad as everywhere else. Plan on hassles and long waits when trying to buy tickets out of here. If you want to go the boxcar route, the trains do carry them as far as Uyuni but it would be a bitterly cold ride and I think I'd prefer a ticket queue to a night of shivering in a cold boxcar. Even with lots of clothes and a sleeping bag it can get uncomfortable.

On Thursday, Friday and Saturday, express trains leave for La Paz at around 7 pm. The first class fare is US$9.20 and second is US$6.15. On Monday and Thursday, they only go as far as Oruro. First class costs US$6.32 and second costs US$4.20, departing also at 7 pm.

Only second class seats are available to Potosí and Sucre for US$3.28 and US$4.62, respectively. Trains leave on Friday at about 2.15 pm.

There are daily trains to Villazón which leave at 7 pm and cost US$1.50 first class and US$1 second class.

AROUND TUPIZA

Tupiza's real appeal lies in the country that surrounds it and compared to other wilderness wonders in Bolivia, it's relatively easily accessible to those without private transport. Thanks to mining activities on the Altiplano, 100 km or so west of Tupiza, there's a surprisingly good network of roads criss-crossing that mountainous territory. Although no public transport ventures into the vicinity, you can flag down one of the many trucks that service the mines, foundries, geologic camps, and health posts out there. It's also possible to walk from the town into the wilderness. Just three or four km up the Quebrada de

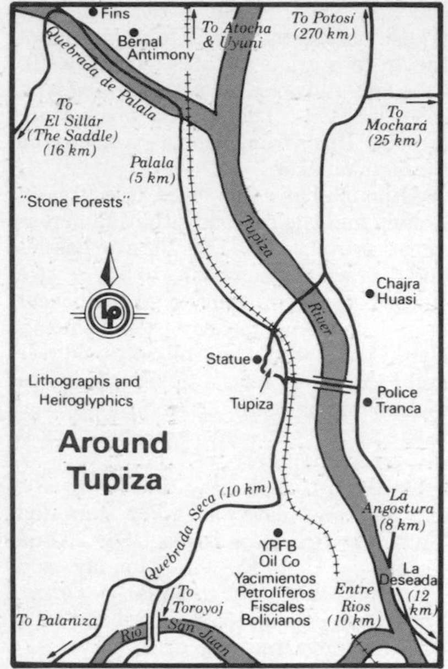

Palala you can get a good idea of what the country has to offer.

There are no trails, per se, but hiking opportunities are endless for those experienced in cross-country travel. In addition to the roads, there are ridges, dry washes, and canyons which provide routes into the never-never. If you'll be doing any hiking away from the roads, be sure to carry a compass and wear shoes that can withstand assault by all sorts of prickly desert vegetation. Topographic maps of the area may be acquired in La Paz at the mapping office or the *Military Geographical Institute*. Alternatively, you may be able to scare one up by asking around town. City Hall, the Electric Coöperative, and the mining companies immediately come to mind as possible sources of information.

Unless you're planning to follow a reliable source of water like the Río Tupiza or the Río San Juan, you'll need to carry all the water you'll need while hiking, which in this desert climate will be at least three litres per person per day. And speaking of water, if it looks like rain anywhere in the vicinity, stay out of the dry washes. As in desert areas everywhere, flash flooding is a real danger.

It will be possible to pitch a tent just about anywhere but common sense will dictate that you avoid canyons or dry washes.

Archaeology

Throughout the country around Tupiza you'll find not only amazing geologic formations but also fossilised remains of prehistoric animals, ancient stone tools and spearheads, and hieroglyphs and lithographs drawn by the ancient people of the region, possibly the Chichas or their predecessors. It seems that no one has ever done sufficient investigation to determine which group is responsible for these things. In the interest of future research, please leave things as you find them.

Quebrada de Palala

During the rainy season, the *Quebrada de Palala* is a tributary of the Río Tupiza but during the rest of the year it's used as a highway into the back country. Beginning just north of town, this route passes tall and thin red rock formations called fins. Beyond the red rocks are several colourful hills, coloured greenish blue and violet by lead and other mineral deposits. At this point, the route turns left and climbs another wash through cactus and scrub brush. If you keep following the road up the steep mountain, you'll reach a place called *El Sillár*, The Saddle, in which the road straddles a narrow ridge between two mountains. Throughout this area are rugged amphitheatres of pillars and eroded spires which closely resemble China's Stone Forest. The distance from Tupiza to El Sillar is 16 km.

Quebrada Seca

To the south of town near the YPFB plant

the road turns off into *Quebrada Seca* meaning simply 'dry wash'. It follows the wash through some spectacular red rock country until it reaches an intersection. The right fork climbs the hill toward the village of Palaniza and the left fork crosses the Río San Juan and eventually gets lost in the side canyons opening into the main channel. This is a particularly beautiful route and I've seen condors soaring above Quebrada Seca.

La Angostura

Although this is along the main route to Villazón, it's an impressive spot. Where the Río Tupiza narrows to squeeze through this tight opening in the rock, the road passes through a tunnel in the formation called *La Angostura*, which means 'The narrows'. Along the route to La Angostura notice the diggings in yellowish soil along the road. Gold is found here in profitable quantities and the locals often mine it. Also, look up at the ridge on the right side of the road (headed south) for the formation called *Bolívar* which resembles a profile of the Liberator.

A nice view can be had at the pulloff at *Entre Rios*, which is the confluence of the Río San Juan and the Río Tupiza just beyond La Angostura, about 10 km from town.

La Deseada

The name *La Deseada* means 'The Desired'. This shady little spot beside the Río Tupiza serves as a favourite picnic area for the residents of Tupiza and it has a nice broad flat area for tent camping near the riverbank. To get there, walk across the bridge on Calle Beni in town and hitch a ride in one of the many trucks which pass the tranca on the road going to Villazón. La Deseada is 12 km from Tupiza but all the drivers will know where to drop you off.

Other

There are countless other interesting trips, mountains, canyons, rivers, and rock formations in the area. Most of them are unnamed and await discovery by someone prepared to appreciate them.

Santa Crúz

Since 1950, Santa Crúz has mushroomed from a backwater cattle-producing town of 30,000 to its' present position as Bolivia's second city with over 600,000 people – and still growing phenomenally. Despite its size, this cosmopolitan city still retains traces of its dusty past, evident in its wide streets, its frontier architecture, and its small-town atmosphere.

In Santa Crúz you'll find people from all corners of the earth and many walks of life – Japanese businessmen, German-speaking Canadian Mennonites, Indian restaurateurs, escaped Nazis, Arabs, foreign oil workers, cocaine traffickers, campesinos from highland Bolivia, and disenchanted refugees from the nuclear powers. In addition, the amount of money that obviously floats around this place will amaze you. Nowhere else in Bolivia will you see so many 12-bedroom homes, Toyota 4WDs, BMWs, and other play-things not normally associated with the Bolivian scene. This explains why Santa Crúz is now one of the most expensive cities on the continent for low-budget travellers, more expensive even than such reputed money-munchers as Montevideo and Beunos Aires.

Santa Crúz de la Sierra was founded in 1561 by Ñuflo de Chaves, a Spaniard who'd come from the area that is now Paraguay. The original site of the settlement was some 270 km east of the foothills of the Cordillera Oriental. Around the end of the 16th century, when that proved too vulnerable to attack by local Indian tribes, the city was moved 220 km west to its current site, 50 km east of the hills.

The original purpose for Santa Crúz' existence was to supply the rest of the colony with tropical and sub-tropical agricultural products such as rice, cotton, sugar, and fruit. The prosperity lasted until the late 1800s when transportation routes were opened up between La Paz and the Peruvian coast. Imported goods then became cheaper than those produced in Sant Crúz and hauled over the mule trail that connected it with Cochabamba.

It wasn't until 1954 when the highway was completed that Santa Crúz began to spring back from the economic depression imposed by its remoteness. The completion of the railway line to the Brazilian frontier in the mid-1950s also served to open trade routes eastward. Santa Crúz was suddenly in a position to thrive. Tropical agriculture immediately returned and the city began a flurry of growth that would continue unabated to the present day.

Not surprisingly, the rich agricultural potential of the Santa Crúz area has attracted not only optimistic settlers from the Bolivian highlands, but also a rice-growing Okinawan colony, a settlement of Italians, and thousands of Platt-Deutsch-speaking Canadian Mennonites who came to the area fleeing governmental problems in their former colony in Belize. Others are arriving daily.

The climate of Santa Crúz can be described as tropical, but since the city sits in the transition zone between the Amazon rainforests to the north and the dry Chaco plains to the south, it enjoys more sun and less-stifling temperatures than the humid and rainy Beni region. Even so, expect some rain to fall every day. In the winter, rainfall will come mostly in the form of the 10-minute downpour but in the summer a single deluge can go on for days. The Santa Crúz climate is also characterised by constant heavy winds that rarely subside for any length of time. At times during the winter, cold winds called *surazos*, out of the Pampa or Patagonia, blow in and bring surprisingly chilly temperatures.

Santa Crúz today is a big city at the edge of a wilderness. Its lush vegetation

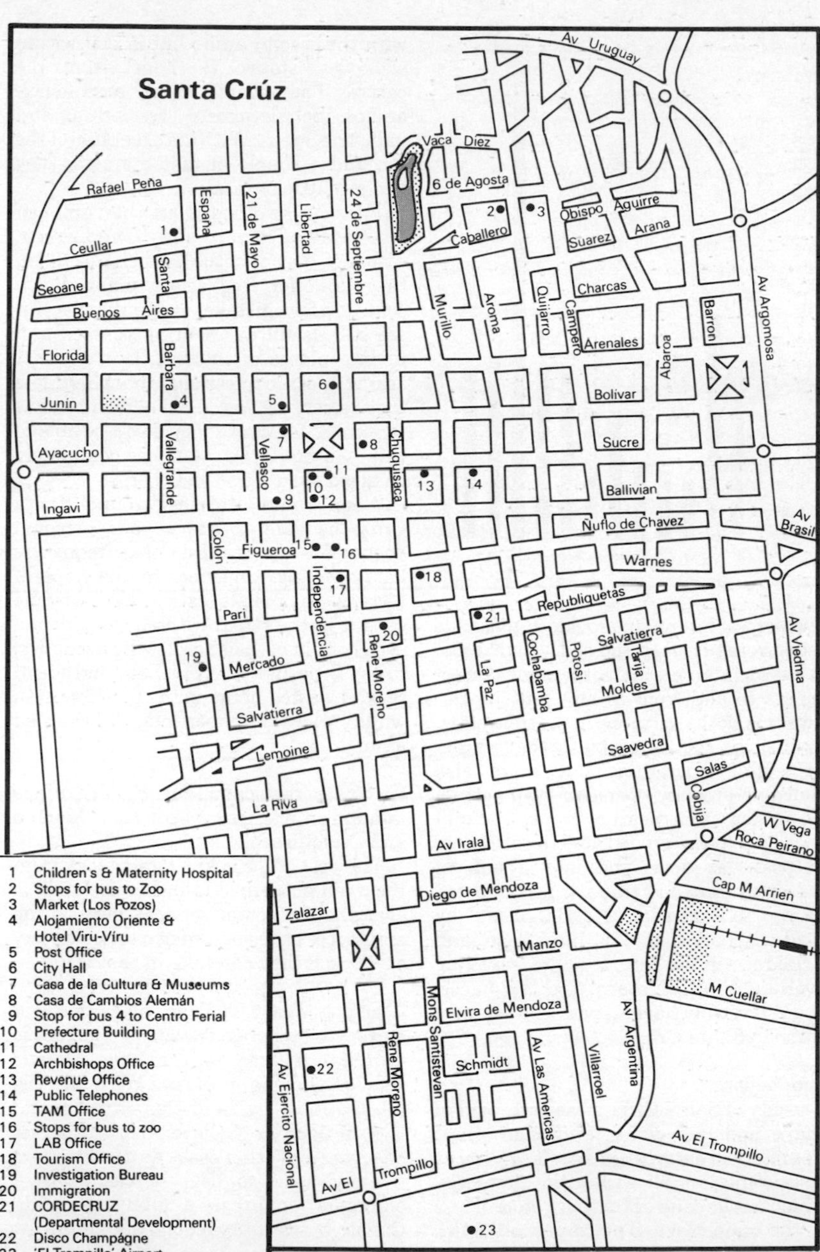

Santa Crúz
Av Uruguay
Vaca Diez
6 de Agosta
Rafael Peña
Ceullar
España
21 de Mayo
Libertad
24 de Septiembre
Caballero
Obispo Aguirre
Arana
Suarez
Seoane
Santa
Buenos Aires
Charcas
Murillo
Aroma
Quijarro
Campero
Barron
Av Argomosa
Florida
Barbara
Arenales
Abaroa
Junín
Bolivar
Ayacucho
Vallegrande
Vellasco
Chuquisaca
Sucre
Ingavi
Ballivian
Ñuflo de Chavez
Av Brasil
Colón
Figueroa
Warnes
Independencia
Pari
Republiquetas
Av Viedma
Rene Moreno
Salvatierra
Cochabamba
Potosi
Tarija
Mercado
La Paz
Moldes
Salvatierra
Saavedra
Lemoine
Salas
La Riva
Cobija
W Vega
Roca Peirano
Av Irala
Cap M Arrien
Diego de Mendoza
Zalazar
Manzo
M Cuellar
Mons Santistevan
Elvira de Mendoza
Av Argentina
Rene Moreno
Schmidt
Av Las Americas
Villarroel
Av Ejercito Nacional
Av El Trompillo
Av El Trompillo
1 Children's & Maternity Hospital
2 Stops for bus to Zoo
3 Market (Los Pozos)
4 Alojamiento Oriente & Hotel Viru-Víru
5 Post Office
6 City Hall
7 Casa de la Cultura & Museums
8 Casa de Cambios Alemán
9 Stop for bus 4 to Centro Ferial
10 Prefecture Building
11 Cathedral
12 Archbishops Office
13 Revenue Office
14 Public Telephones
15 TAM Office
16 Stops for bus to zoo
17 LAB Office
18 Tourism Office
19 Investigation Bureau
20 Immigration
21 CORDECRUZ (Departmental Development)
22 Disco Champágne
23 'El Trompillo' Airport

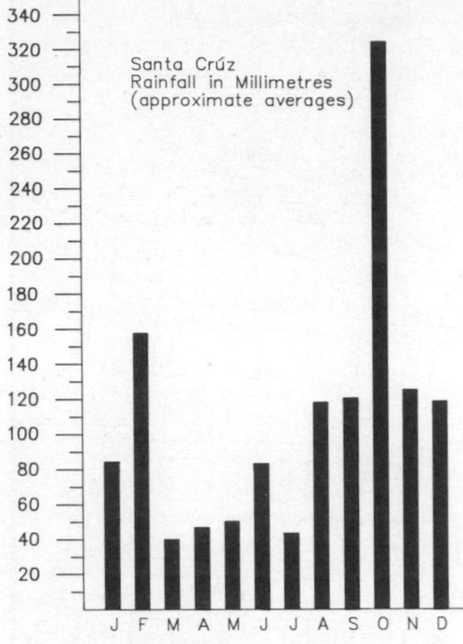

and agreeable climate provide appreciable relief from the stark and chilly highlands. It has an international airport with direct flights to and from Miami, but jungle-dwelling sloths still hang in the trees of the main plaza. It is the centre for the cocaine-smuggling operations but it is also Bolivia's primary source of rice, cotton, and other warm-weather crops. The city that was once an isolated agricultural outpost has developed into a hub of transportation and trade. It is connected by rail to Argentina and Brazil and by road with Cochabamba, the Chaco, and Trinidad – in the Beni. If you're travelling overland to or from any of these places, you'll probably have to pass at least once through Santa Crúz.

Information

The city of Santa Crúz is basically oval in shape and laid out in *anillos* or rings. Commercial enterprises, hotels, and most restaurants are all within the first ring, which has its centre of activity more or less at the main plaza. The train station lies with the second anillo but is still within walking distance (½ hour) from the centre. The second, third, and fourth anillos include mostly residential and industrial areas. With the exception of the zoo and a couple of nice markets, they contain little of interest.

The tourist office is on the corner of Ñuflo de Chavez and Chuquisaca. Although it's one of the less helpful offices, they do offer free street plans which contain a few mistakes and omissions, but are still useful in orienting yourself and finding places of interest. Don't bother asking specific questions, though, unless they're very basic (i.e. 'Where is the bus terminal?') because they won't be able to help you unless the staff has completely changed since I was last there.

When you're walking around Santa Crúz, be sure to carry your personal documents at all times. Police frequently harass young foreigners in the hope of picking up a little extra cash. Anyone caught in the street without documents, even in front of their hotel, will be required to pay the usual 'fine' of US$50 and spend several wasted hours in the police station while relevant paperwork is shuffled around.

Post & Communication The ENTEL office is found on Warnes between René Moreno and Chuquisaca.

The post office is just half a block from the main plaza on Junín. Beware of over-charging for postal services here as the employees have been known to pocket any extra cash they can take in that way.

Changing Money The only place that will currently exchange travellers' cheques is *Cambios Alemán* on the René Moreno side of the main plaza. With all the international trade in this city, I found this difficult to believe, but the street changers and other casas de cambio seem to only want to deal in cash. Street changers congregate along Avenida Cañoto between Ayacucho and Junín, at the intersection of Cañoto and Irala near the bus terminal, and around the main plaza. Casas de Cambio, however, offer the same rates for cash as the street changers and they're quite a bit safer. Strangely enough, the numerous travel agencies in town don't seem to be interested in changing dollars.

Consulates A few of the most useful consular addresses in Santa Crúz include:

Argentina
  Banco de la Nación Building Junín 22
Brazil
  Suarez de Fiqueroa 127 (tel 44400)
Paraguay
  Sucre 677
Perú
  Calle La Paz 726
West Germany
  Corner of El Trompillo & Chaco (tel 44569)
USA
  Bolívar 342 Edificio Oriente, 3rd Floor, No 306 (tel 30725)

Books English language books can be found at *Los Amigos del Libro* on René Morenos across from the cathedral and at *Libreria El Ateneo* on Junín. The former has a wide selection of popular paperbacks and souvenir publications while the latter offers only second-hand paperbacks. Both, however, are very expensive. Desperate for something to read, I paid US$15 for a paperback clearly marked US$4.95 on the cover (and that was after bargaining!). It's that import tax again . . .

At both the above-mentioned places, it's also possible to find classic literature in Spanish but it isn't cheap either.

Cathedral

The cathedral on Plaza 24 de Septiembre is worth a look. It's very nice architecturally and not at all gaudy. Notice particularly the woodwork on the ceiling and the silverwork around the altar.

The *Cathedral Museum* inside the church is open Tuesday and Thursday from 10 am to noon and 4 to 6 pm and on Sunday from 10 am to noon and 6 to 8 pm. Admission is US$1. It contains quite a collection of religious icons and artefacts but very little art. The most interesting items herein are the many gold and silver relics from the Jesuit Guarayos missions north-east of Santa Crúz. They've also got one of the world's smallest books, a thumbnail-sized volume which contains the Lord's prayer in several languages, and a collection of religious vestments and medallions.

Casa de la Cultura

The full name of this departmental museum/arts complex is *Casa de la Cultura Raúl Otero Reiche*. Located on the main plaza, it contains fossils, minerals, pottery and other indigenous artefacts, a childrens' library with nice educational dioramas, and a small art museum. Some of the art, especially that representative of modern Bolivia, is quite good.

Zoo

This is one of the few zoos in South America that is worth the time and money. They've got a nice collection of South American animals which all appear to be humanely treated and well-fed. The woolly llamas do seem to be a bit over-dressed and irritable in this climate, however.

The zoo also has some endangered and exotic species like tapirs, pumas, jaguars, and the South American spectacled bear. Sloths, which are too slow and lazy to try to escape, wander around loose or hang upside down in the trees all day.

To get there, take the bus from the stop indicated on the map or from *Parque El Arenal*. Admission is US$1.

Parque El Arenal

This park with its pleasant lagoon is a good spot for a picnic or just relaxing. On an island in the centre of the lake is a large raised-relief mural with a collage of historical and modern-day aspects of

Santa Crúz. The park is clean and nicely landscaped.

Botanical Garden

Although the tourist office promotes it and will carefully explain how to get there, you should probably know that the Botanical Garden no longer exists because it was destroyed in a flood several years ago. Although plans to renovate it are currently in the works, the project seems to be moving along very slowly. Ask locally about the progress out there (but not at the tourist office) before making a special trip to see it.

Dunas de Palmar

These large sand dunes, about an hour south of Santa Crúz near the village of Palmar, can only be reached by private vehicle. There's also a nice freshwater lake where the locals go to swim, so you may be able to catch a ride out on the weekend.

What to Buy

The *Mercado los Pozos* near Parque El Arenal is good for inexpensive basketry and a variety of unusual tropical fruits. Try some of the more exotic ones like *guaypurú* and *ambaiba*.

There are artesanía shops scattered all over town and in keeping with local custom, they are expensive. They sell some beautiful Western-style clothing made of llama and alpaca wool, but if you're looking for genuine indigenous articles, the Altiplano is a better place to look.

Carvings of *morado* and *guayacán* wood are unique to the Santa Crúz area and look very good, but again, they are not cheap. Morado is much less expensive than guayacán, but you should still expect to pay at least US$20 for a nice piece of work. Relief carvings on *tari* nuts are also interesting and make easily-transported souvenirs.

The local Indians make beautiful macrame *llicas* or bags of root fibres which are nearly identical in both use and design to the famous *bilums* of New Guinea.

The leatherwork available in Santa Crúz is expert, but unfortunately most pieces are adorned with silly touristy designs and slogans. There are also some lovely ceramic pieces for sale but carrying them can be a problem.

Places to Stay - bottom end

The infamous two-tier pricing scheme is in effect in Santa Crúz but the differences in rates for Bolivians and foreigners aren't as great as they are elsewhere. Since prices in general are higher here than in the rest of Bolivia, the bottom end on the accommodation scale will include anything under seven dollars per person.

There isn't really one place that stands out overwhelmingly as the travellers' hotel in Santa Crúz but several are marginally popular. In my opinion, the best value is the *Hotel Copacabana* at 217 Junín. It's ultra clean and costs only US$6 per person with shared bath or US$12.50 per person with private bath. The *Alojamientos Santa Barbara* and *24 de Septiembre*, both on Calle Santa Barbara, are a bit dirty but they seem to be very popular with young Bolivians. Single rooms cost US$6 and doubles US$8, neither with private bath.

Alojamiento Oriente at 364 Junín is both a clean and friendly place and they'll watch your luggage while you travel about. The rooms surround a nice green courtyard and it's very quiet. They charge US$6 single and US$4 per person double without private bath. Rooms with a bath cost double that but hot water is available.

On Calle 21 de Mayo, the *Florida Hotel* is a bit grotty but considering that a room with private bath costs only US$6.50 single or US$11 double, it's good value.

In the same range as the Florida is the *Residencial Paulista* near the 7 Calles Commercial Centre. It's a bit dark and gloomy but it's halfway between the bus terminal and the centre, making it relatively convenient to both.

The cheapest place in town is without a doubt the *Alojamiento 15 de Octubre*, near the bus terminal on Calle Guaraní, which costs only US$3 per person. It's very basic with cold showers and communal baths only but it has laundry facilities and the proprietors are very friendly and helpful. Rooms don't lock but there's always someone on hand to keep an eye on things. Just down the street, but slightly upmarket, is the *Alojamiento Panamericano* which charges US$5 per person.

If you're looking for the cheapest places closer to the centre, try one of the *posadas* like *Posada El Turista* on the 400 block of Calle Junín. This is a good place to crash and nothing more, and is not particularly clean. If you don't have an aversion to scum, try *Posada Sucre* on Vallegrande. It's cheap and ought to be cheaper.

Places to Stay - middle

It seems that the nicest middle-range accommodation available is the *Hotel Italia* on René Moreno. Both clean and central, it offers fans, private phones and baths, and hot showers for US$12.50 single and US$21 double.

The *Hotel Viru-Viru* at 338 Junín costs only US$10 single and US$16.50 double, with breakfast included. It's very clean, with private baths and telephones.

The *Hotel Bibosi* across the street from the Copacabana on Junín is almost as nice as the Italia. All rooms have fans, telephones and private baths and cost US$10 for a single or US$16.50 double. Free coffee is also available. It's a clean and cheery place and I'd recommend it as good value for the price.

Alojamiento Ferrocarril across from the train station falls into the middle range, only because hundreds of people sleep outside at the station waiting for tickets and a soft warm bed begins to look pretty good at any price around midnight. Be warned, however, that if you leave the queue for any reason, including a short nap, you may not be able to get back in without bloodshed because all the people who've cut into the queue while you were gone won't know you're not trying to do the same.

Places to Stay - top end

The *Hotel Los Tajibos* is probably the nicest hotel in all Santa Crúz. With beautiful bars, fountains, pools and tropical gardens it's very appealing and the only drawback is that it's not central. Located out on the third anillo on Avenida San Martín, it's a good distance from town. To make reservations, phone 30022 in Santa Crúz or 351070 in La Paz or write to Hotel Los Tajibos, Casilla 335, La Paz, Bolivia.

Not quite in the five-star range but still very nice is the *Hotel Las Américas* on Calle 21 de Mayo, 400 block. It's got television, air conditioning, private baths and refrigerators, telephones, and a central location. There is an attached bar and restaurant downstairs. Surprisingly, it only costs US$30 for a single, US$35 for a double, and US$40 for a triple. Budget travellers who'd like to spring on a little luxury will find good value here.

Places to Eat

Such a cosmopolitan city as Santa Crúz will not disappoint when it comes to culinary matters. There are quite a few places to choose from and the food is of high quality, but be prepared to pay dearly at the nicer places.

For breakfast *Lucerna/Niky* on Calle Junín has good coffee, chocolate, salteñas, and typical American and European-style breakfasts, but it is far too expensive and they add 10% service on top of it.

If you don't want to spend a lot of money for breakfast in the markets you can try *jugo de papaya/guineo/naranja con leche* – that's papaya/banana/orange juice with milk – whipped up in a blender and served cold. For about 40c you can drink 1½ glasses, but be warned that it's addictive. It's hard to leave after only that much.

The markets generally serve pretty good meals during the day, also, but you may be put off by the extreme heat inside.

Another good place for a morning snack and coffee is *Bonanza* on Calle Junín across from the post office.

Snack Jet Set on the corner of Beni and Charcas is a small informal place to grab a snack. There are a number of other such places around Los Pozos market. For anyone into roasted chicken, chips and fried bananas, just take a stroll down Avenida Cañoto where there are dozens of similar fast food chicken restaurants.

Pizzeria La Bella Napoli on Independencia, six blocks south of the main plaza, offers excellent pseudo-Italian food in a rustic atmosphere and the prices are reasonable. Another delightfully 'ethnic' place is the *London Grill* on Calle Beni. It's a typical English pub, smack in the middle of Bolivia, complete with meat-oriented British cuisine, a dart board (and other essential decor), and lots of grog. There's a warm friendly atmosphere and (naturally) it's a good place to meet other travellers.

Another place where foreigners from all over tend to congregate is at *Gandhi's* on Calle Junín next door to the Bonanza. No, it's not a vegetarian restaurant, but the owner is an Indian who's spent many years in Bolivia and somehow acquired the nickname 'Gandhi'. It's good for juice, hot drinks, and snacks, and for dinner they serve up a variety of Indian curry dishes and *surabí*, a type of catfish unique to this area of eastern Bolivia and Paraguay. If you'd like your curry hot, you'll have to request it that way or they'll serve the mild variety that Bolivians seem to like better. A variety of other Indian fare is available, also. All meals cost US$3.

For a simple but tasty meal, try *Restaurant Oki* on 21 de Mayo or *El Dorado* on the main plaza. They serve good, filling lunches for US$1.75.

For surubí fans, *Churros Amadeo* on 21 de Mayo (just west of the main plaza) is unsurpassed in Santa Crúz. Their prices are reasonable and their food is excellent. The *surubí al ajo* (surubí in garlic) is highly recommended! The *New Hong Kong Restaurant* on Ballivián and the *China Town* on Velasco are two of the most reasonable *chifas* in town.

There are quite a few places around town to find good ice cream and related concoctions but the locals recommend *Helados Pomn* on Figueroa near Independencia and *Helados Cucimba* on Figueroa and René Moreno.

Discos

Santa Crúz discos are known throughout Bolivia as being some of the most liberal in the country. There are many to choose from, but the locals consistently recommended *Champágne* on Ejército near de Garay, *Swing* five km away on the highway to Cochabamba, *Fizz* near the zoo in the third anillo, and *Crazy Horse* more centrally located on Calle Junín beside Hotel Viru-Viru. They generally open around 9 pm and stay open 'till the wee hours of the morning. Without a private car, the only way to access the ones away from the centre is by taxi because the city micros don't run this late at night.

Getting There & Away

Air The new Santa Crúz International Airport is at Viru-Viru 15 km from town. It's half an hour by micro from the main bus terminal or slightly less by taxi. Micros leave when full – every few minutes – and cost only US$1. This airport is notorious for drug plants so if you're subjected to any police searches there, keep a close watch over what's going on.

Santa Crúz is linked by LAB to just about every corner of Bolivia. LAB also offers direct flights to or from Miami, Buenos Aires, São Paulo, and Asunción. In addition, some Santa Crúz travel agencies sell 3-day round-trip excursion tickets to such hot spots as Bogotá, Amsterdam, and Miami. It doesn't take long to figure out how this is justified! The Santa Crúz/Miami flight has gained such a reputation for trafficking that it should be avoided unless you're prepared for a long and thorough shakedown and strip search at Miami Airport.

TAM has service to Camiri and most major towns of the Oriente – San José de Chiquitos, Roboré, Puerto Suarez, and San Ignacio, to name a few.

If you're going to Brazil and don't want to fuss with the train, keep in mind that LAB flights to Puerto Suarez on the border are normally booked up two to three weeks in advance. Even though it doesn't guarantee anything, be sure to make reservations and purchase your ticket well before your intended departure date. An alternate method of getting to Brazil is to catch LAB's once-weekly flight to San Matías where you can cross the border to Cáceres. From there, buses are available to Cuiabá and thence to São Paulo and the rest of the country.

The LAB office in Santa Crúz is on the corner of Figueroa and René Moreno, two blocks from the Plaza. The TAM office is only a block away on the corner of Figueroa and Independencia.

The International Departure Tax in Santa Crúz is US$15 if paid in US currency and US$7.50 in bolivianos.

Bus There are quite a few flotas – *El Dorado*, *Copacabana*, *Panamericana*, *San Francisco*, etc – which leave for Cochabamba from the main terminal between 4.30 and 5 pm daily. From Cochabamba, almost all of them have connections to La Paz, Oruro, Sucre, and Potosí. Flota Copacabana accepts travellers' cheques in payment for passage.

To Trinidad, *Flota Puñata* leaves on Wednesday and Saturday at 6 pm but the trip is often cancelled during the rainy season. The trip costs US$13.50. There is a *Trans-Beni* bus which leaves on Wednesday and Saturday at 4.30 pm for only US$12.50. Its terminal is on Calle Ingavi one block west of Cañoto.

The *Unificado* bus goes to Camiri on Tuesday, Thursday, Friday, and Sunday at 7 pm. The fare is US$10.50. To Samaipata, Unificado leaves from the main terminal at 4 pm daily and costs US$3.50

There are micros which leave for Montero every 10 minutes or so for US$1.05. If you're going to one of the smaller towns north of Santa Crúz, you'll first have to go to Montero and catch a colectivo or micro from there.

Rail The rail line between Santa Crúz and Quijarro, a settlement on the Brazilian border across from the bustling city of Corumbá, is popular with travellers as a means of getting to Brazil from Bolivia. The journey is a beautiful one, passing through lush jungle, Chaco scrub, and oddly-shaped mountains to the steamy, sticky Pantanal area near the frontier. The many cattle ranches, agricultural projects, logging operations, and Mennonite colonies along the railway are all indicators of the current thrust into development of the long-neglected Oriente. Despite all the economic changes and growth in the area, there is still a diverse and abundant supply of wildlife and vegetation. Colourful flowers, birds, and butterflies thrive in the warm, moist conditions and larger species, though rarely seen, aren't far away.

There's a daily train that is scheduled to depart at noon but if it's not cancelled altogether, it's normally hopelessly delayed. Three classes of service are available – Pullman, First, and Second – but it's difficult to distinguish between them. There's a distinctly bovine feeling that comes over anyone who boards this train. The roof and the boxcars have their drawbacks but they're much more comfortable than the coaches.

There is a ferrobus service that leaves on Monday, Thursday, and Saturday but a seat is very hard to come by. Numerous railroad people told me that ferrobus tickets must be reserved one week in advance but the procedures for doing that are very hazy at best. There are four ticket windows at the station and one is marked 'ferrobus'. There's always a queue waiting beside it and I suppose if you camped out in the queue long enough, someone may show up with some tickets. I'm not putting you on – this is the way things are.

The train tickets are a little easier to come by because you must buy the ticket on the day of departure. In theory the window opens at 9 am to sell tickets for the noon train, but plan on spending at least one night in the queue if you want to get a seat. Also, be prepared to fight for your place in the queue because latecomers show up at 4 am, shove their way into the front of the queue, and if the police and military haven't yet arrived to keep order, the situation turns into a powder keg. If you'd rather avoid this situation, you can ride in the bodegas (boxcars) and purchase a second class ticket from the conductor when he comes by. The regular second class fare to Quijarro is US$6 at the window, but the conductor will charge 20% more.

If you're going south toward Argentina, there's a ferrobus to Yacuiba on Monday, Wednesday, and Friday. A *tren rápido*, or fast train, leaves on the same days. First class to Yacuiba on the ferrobus is US$10.50. Second class is only US$7.50. On the train first class costs US$5.50 and second is US$4. From Santa Crúz the boxcars are just about empty but on the return journey they are full of Argentine contraband and not as comfortable. When buying a ticket to Yacuiba, be sure to get in the proper queue at the train station. This line, which is not as popular as the one to Brazil, has its own ticket window and there aren't as many hassles in getting a seat.

Getting Around

Taxis in Santa Crúz are quite a bit higher priced than in the highland regions of Bolivia but are still cheaper than in the Beni. You can expect to pay US$1.50 for a ride to anywhere within the first anillo or to the train station. A taxi to the airport at Viru-Viru will cost around US$10 but try to bargain them down.

There is a good system of city micros in Santa Crúz. They connect the transportation terminals and all the anillos with the centre. The fare is 25c per ride. Other micros to small settlements around Santa Crúz leave from the north end of the bus terminal when they are full.

MONTERO

The rapidly growing community of Montero is in the flat agricultural lands north of Santa Crúz. With a population of 60,000, it's one of the largest cities in the lowland areas of Bolivia. The immediate vicinity of Montero is planted in such cash crops as bananas, sugar cane, and rice. In addition, soybeans, sesame, and peanuts are cultivated and used in the production of vegetable oils.

Montero is 50 minutes by micro from Santa Crúz bus terminal but the only reason to come here at all would be en route to somewhere else. It serves as a jumping-off point for several interesting day trips and since hotel prices here are about half what they are in Santa Crúz, it's financially appealing, also.

Information

Post & Communications Montero has both an ENTEL office and a post office. The post is not reliable at all and posting a letter here is equivalent to flushing it down the loo.

Market The market in this town is incredible. Incredible because I haven't the slightest doubt that it is the filthiest in all Bolivia. If the trash, insects, and discarded animal parts don't make you retch, the sewage, dogs, and festering stagnant water will. This place should be avoided unless you just want the experience of seeing something so repulsive.

Excursions A trip to Okinawa, the

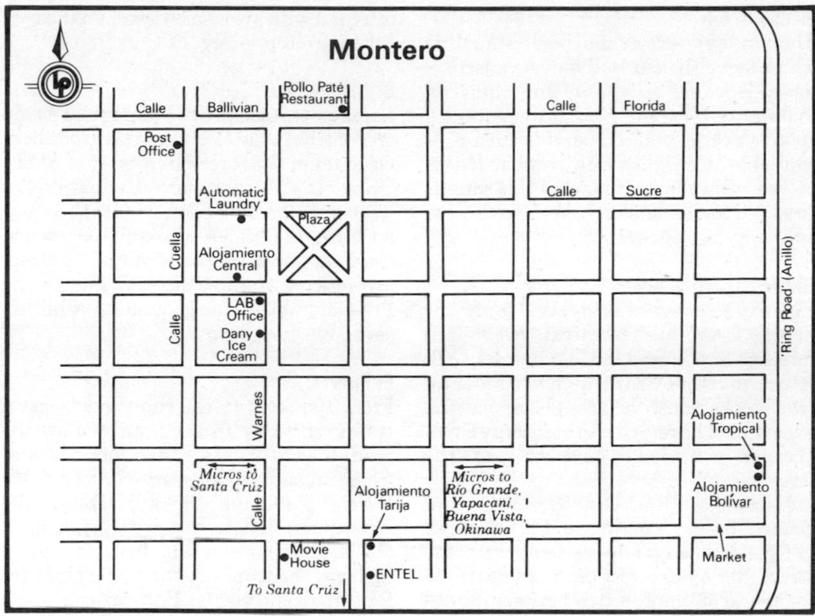

Japanese rice-growing colony to the east of Montero makes an interesting excursion, but the colony itself is on the wane these days as disillusioned settlers migrate to greener pastures. Not far beyond Okinawa is Puerto Banegas, locally known as Río Grande, where you can catch a boat to Trinidad. Micros from Montero to the river cost US$2. Apart from going in person to Río Grande, there's really no way to ascertain when boats will be leaving for Trinidad.

A nice trip that is very popular with locals is to the Río Surutú where there is a nice sandy beach ideal for picnics and camping during the dry season. From Montero, take the micro to Buena Vista and from there walk the three km to the river.

Another recommended day trip is to the bridge at the Río Yapacaní 85 km from Montero. Along the river is a row of 'temporary' eating establishments which serve surubí and other fresh fish from the river. During the rainy season, these buildings normally are washed away by flooding so they must be rebuilt each year. Needless to say, don't bother going between November and March and don't expect too much luxury.

Places to Stay

The only accommodation available in Montero can be found in several very basic alojamientos. The good news is that they are only half the price of equivalent accommodation in Santa Crúz. *Alojamientos Central*, *Tarija*, *Bolívar*, and *Tropical* are all marked on the map, but the Central appeared to be the cleanest and most pleasant of these.

Near the Alojamiento Central is a self-service laundromat which may prove useful, especially since clothing hung out in this humid climate will often sour before it's dry.

Places to Eat

There are quite a few cubbyhole restaurants which serve the old Bolivian standards – lomo, chicken, *milanesa*, and the like. *Pollo Paté* on Calle Florida does pretty good chicken and chips. Ice cream is available at *Helados Dany* and at *Kivón* on the main plaza. If none of this sounds good, go to the market where you'll lose your appetite altogether.

Getting There & Away

There's a micro that leaves from the Santa Crúz bus terminal every ten minutes and costs US$1.05 one way. To return to Santa Crúz, the micros line up two blocks south of the plaza, leaving when full. The return trip costs only US$1 because you don't have to pay the terminal tax.

Micros to Río Grande, Yapacaní, Beuna Vista, Okinawa, and other small villages in the area leave from the same street four blocks west of the market.

On the 50-minute trip between Santa Crúz and Montero, notice the interesting sculpture in the middle of the traffic circle in Warnes. It's a very colourful portrayal of a man with an oxen-drawn banana cart called appropriately '*El Carretero*'.

SAMAIPATA

Samaipata itself is little more than a tiny settlement in the foothills of the Cordillera Oriental about three hours west of Santa Crúz. It's a popular destination of weekend school trips from Santa Crúz and for lowland families who'd like to escape the heat for a couple of days. The real attraction of the area lies in *El Fuerte*, the Pre-Columbian ruins found on a hilltop seven km from town.

El Fuerte

From the town to the ruins is at least a two-hour walk. To get there, follow the road toward Santa Crúz for two km. There, a sign which reads *Ruinas de El Fuerte* points up the hill. Follow the subsequent signs saying *Ruta* to the top of the hill, about five km from the main highway. Entrance to the site is US$1 for foreigners and 50c for Bolivians.

There are no actual buildings at El Fuerte. What you'll find is a stone 100 metres long with seats, tables, *hornillos*

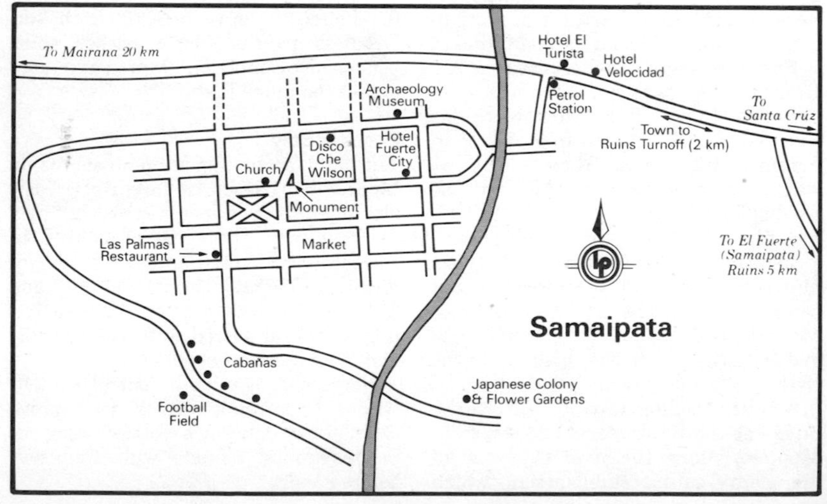

(niches), troughs, tanks, and conduits all carved into it. There is also a *cueva* which is actually more a tank than a cave only a short walk downhill from the main site. These ruins are attibuted to the Incas but actually very little is known about their purpose or their history.

The view from the ruins over the surrounding countryside is also worthwhile as it takes in much of the transitional zone between the highlands to the west and low lying areas to the east.

Archaeology Museum

The small museum in town is an interesting place to visit but it offers very little in the way of explanation of the Samaipata site. They do have a few Tiahuanaco artefacts and some local pottery. Admission is 50c for foreigners and 25c for Bolivians.

Japanese Colony

The Japanese colony on the hillside above Samaipata is a very pleasant and friendly place to visit. They grow many varieties of vegetables and flowers and they have some beautiful Japanese gardens. The colonists are both proud and happy to show visitors around some of their projects.

Places to Stay

The *Hotel Fuerte City* is as clean and friendly a place as you're likely to find and I'd recommend it to anyone. The accommodation is very basic with no private baths or hot water but meals are available if you arrange them in advance. They charge US$3.25 per person.

The *Hotel El Turista* and *Hotel Velocidad* both have restaurants which are really the only places to eat in town. Since they're on the main highway they're always noisy due to constant truck and bus traffic. A room in either costs US$3.50 per person.

Quite a bit upmarket are the *Cabañas Alemanes* which are popular with the wealthier sector of Santa Crúz society. They're very nice with cooking facilities, refrigerators, private baths, great views, indoor heating, and lots of quiet. They must be reserved in advance through *Vimpex Travel* in Santa Crúz. Ask for Mrs Aida McKenney. A cabin costs US$35 per day for up to six people. Each additional person up to eight will cost US$5 extra. If you've got a group, this is definitely the way to go.

If you're looking for a bit of nightlife, the *Disco Ché Wilson* is very popular with visitors from Santa Crúz.

Getting There & Getting Around

From Santa Crúz, the *Flota Unificado* leaves daily at 4 pm and costs US$3.50 for the three-hour, 118 km trip to Samaipata. Getting to Cochabamba is a little tougher because buses stop in Mairana about 20 km down the road. To get to Mairana, flag down a truck in front of the Hotel El Turista. The Santa Crúz/Cochabamba buses stop in Mairana for a dinner break between 7 and 7.30 pm daily. If you miss the bus, there's a basic hotel, the *Urkupiño*, along the main highway there.

If you don't feel like walking to the ruins from Samaipata, there are small trucks that go up when the road is dry enough to be negotiable. Ask at the Archaeology Museum about availability of transport or simply flag one down as it passes.

Southern Lowlands

The vast, sparsely-populated Southern Lowlands take in all of crescent-shaped South-eastern Bolivia. Today, the region is bounded roughly by the foothills of the Cordillera Oriental, The Guarayos Hills, and the international boundaries of Brazil, Paraguay, and Argentina.

The land is generally flat, broken only by long low ridges and odd monolithic mountains. A lot of this territory lies soaking under vast marshes like the Bañados de Izozog deep in the wilderness, and the Grán Pantanal along the Brazilian frontier. Mostly, though, it is characterised in the south by the hostile, thorny scrubland of the Grán Chaco melting gently into the low jungle-like savannas and forests along the rail line. Although other populations exist in the transitional zones, the only city of the true Chaco is Villa Montes, a small settlement on the Santa Crúz to Yacuiba railway that claims the distinction of being the hottest spot (literally) in Bolivia.

With the release of the recent film, *The Mission*, about Jesuit missionary activities in South America, there has been an awakening of interest in their work in the interior regions of the continent.

When all this was still unsurveyed and largely unorganised territory, the Jesuits established an autonomous religious state in Paraguay and spread outward, founding missions in the wilderness to the north, previously unexplored by Europeans. The north was inhabited by numerous tribes of hunting and gathering Indians – the Chiquitanos, the Moxos, the Guaranies, and others.

Each mission became an experiment with community life for a group of people who had lived by wits from time immemorial, and the Jesuits set up what they considered to be the best possible community hierarchy. Each unit, called a *reducción* was headed by two or three Jesuit priests. They set up military units also, and for a time, the Jesuit armies were the strongest and best-trained in South America. The reducciones themselves provided a formidable barrier/buffer zone between the Spanish in the west and the Portuguese in Brazil.

Over the years, a trade network was established with the Quechua and Aymará to the west and soon cotton, honey, beeswax, and artwork were being exchanged for raw silver mined in the highlands. The Indians, traditionally hunters and gatherers, were taught agriculture by the priests and forced to produce food in this manner. With Jesuit training, they also became accomplished artisans and produced outstanding work in both silver and wood.

In addition to economic ventures, the Jesuits promoted education and culture among the tribes. Extremely able artists, the Indians handcrafted musical instruments – the renowned violins and harps featured in Chaco music today – and learned to play Italian baroque music. In the remotest of settings, they gave concerts, dances, and theatre performances which could have competed on a European scale.

It goes without saying that the Indians were also thrust into Christianity heart and soul. Local cultures were suppressed and the people were coerced into European lifestyles and modes of thought. Therefore, very little is known about the pre-Jesuit cultures of the South American interior.

Perhaps the most impressive work done by the missions is represented in the beautiful mission churches which survive in this South-eastern part of Bolivia. More than in any other region under Jesuit influence, those in this area have been preserved and restored. The nicest and most accessible of these can be seen in San Ignacio, San Javier, San José de

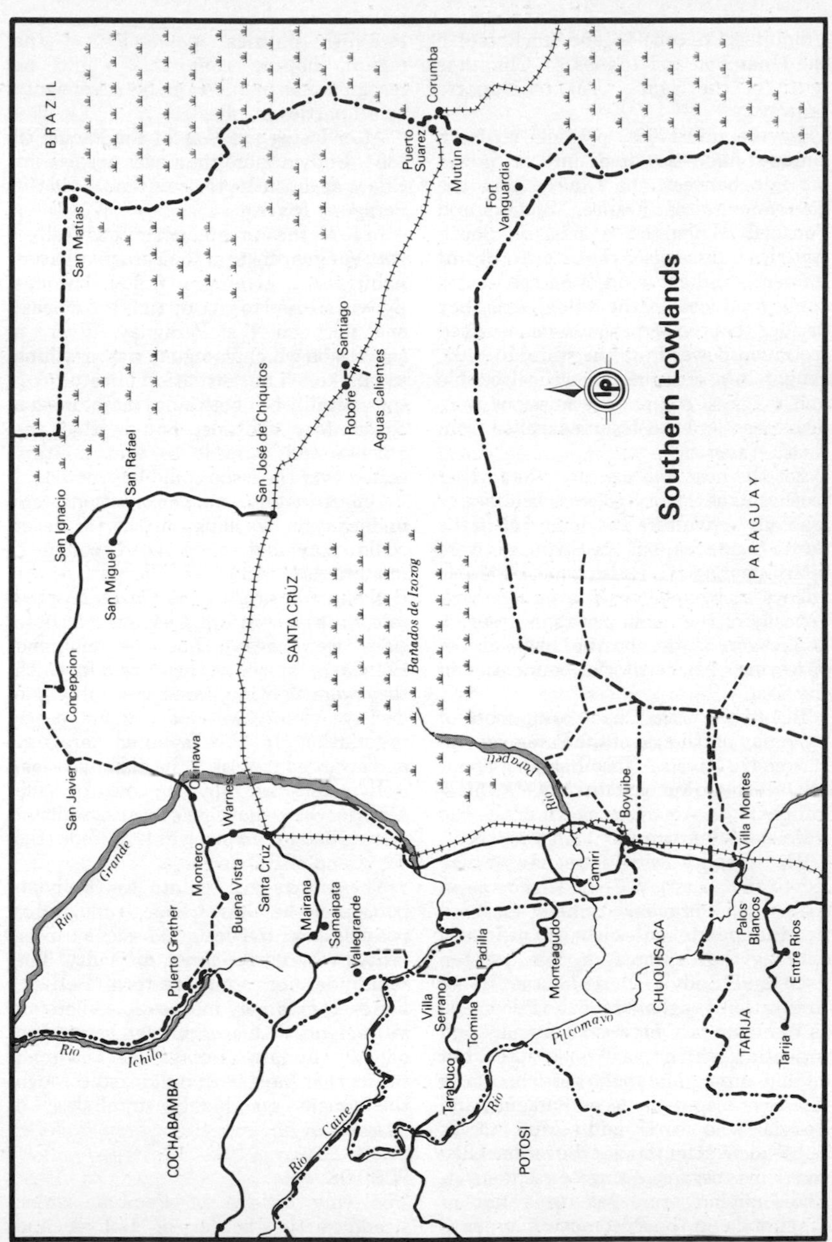
Southern Lowlands
BRAZIL
PARAGUAY
San Matias
Puerto Suarez
Corumba
Mutún
Fort Vanguardia
Santiago
Roboré
Aguas Calientes
San José de Chiquitos
San Rafael
San Ignacio
San Miguel
Concepcion
San Javier
Okinawa
Warnes
Montero
Buena Vista
Santa Crúz
SANTA CRÚZ
Bañados de Izozog
Río Parapeti
Boyuibe
Camiri
Villa Montes
Mairana
Samaipata
Vallegrande
Puerto Grether
Río Grande
Río Ichilo
COCHABAMBA
Villa Serrano
Padilla
Monteagudo
Tomina
Tarabuco
Río Caine
Río
Pilcomayo
POTOSÍ
CHUQUISACA
TARIJA
Palos Blancos
Entre Rios
Tarija

Chiquitos, Concepción, and San Rafael in the Guarayos and Llanos de Chiquitos north of the Santa Crúz to Quijarro railway.

By the mid-1700s, political strife in Europe had escalated into a power struggle between the Church and the governments of France, Spain, and Portugal. When the Spanish in South America fully realised the extent of Jesuit influence and got wind of all the wealth being produced in the wilderness, they decided that the perpetrators had usurped too much power from the state. In 1767, caught in a crossfire of political babble and religious dogma, the missions were disbanded and the Jesuits expelled from South America.

For the next half century, the further reaches of the Spanish colonies were largely ignored. Agriculture was doing well in the Santa Crúz area, but the Spaniards were more intent upon colonising the hospitable valleys and exploiting the mineral-rich deposits of the highlands than ensuring possession of the hostile lowlands or surveying hazy territorial boundaries in the East.

Before the 1938 Chaco War, most of Paraguay north-east of the Paraguay and Pilcomayo Rivers – encompassing about 240,680 square km – and the 168,765 square km chunk of Argentina north of the Río Bermejo, lay within Bolivian territory.

The dispute with Paraguay, which led to the Chaco War, had its roots in 1842 when Paraguay formally declared its independence without officially defining the demarcation line between itself and Bolivia. In 1878, the Hayes Arbitration designated the Río Pilcomayo as the boundary between Paraguay and Argentina, which was duly accepted, but all that empty land to the north became a matter of dispute between Paraguay and Bolivia who both laid claim to it. Subsequent attempts at arbitration failed and Bolivia began pressing for a settlement. The Bolivian army set up a fort at Piquirenda on the Pilcomayo in order to establish physical possession of the region, hoping that this would be recognised as unquestionable sovereignty by all parties involved.

After losing the War of the Pacific in 1884, Bolivia more than ever needed the Chaco as an outlet to the Atlantic via the Paraguay River.

In 1928, the Paraguayan military seized Fort Vanguardia near the Paraguay River. Arbitration attempts failed because Bolivia refused to give up rights to at least one port on the Paraguay River, a concession which Paraguay was unwilling to make. The situation heated up considerably but both sides maintained a conciliatory attitude, hoping that the other would concede so that military action over the issue could be averted.

Unfortunately, while negotiations were underway in Washington (the US never could stay out of a good conflict), unauthorised action on the part of the Bolivian military in the Chaco erupted into full-scale warfare. Casualties on both sides were heavy but the highland Bolivians, unused to the terrain in which they were fighting, fared miserably. No decisive victory was reached but peace negotiations in 1938 favoured Paraguay and awarded it most of the disputed area. Bolivia retained only the town of Villa Montes where that side's most significant victory had taken place in 1934 under the command of Bilbao Rioja.

These days access into the Bolivian portion of the Grán Chaco is rough but possible, and the Jesuit Missions can be visited without too much difficulty. The remainder of south-eastern Bolivia, however, is largely inaccessible. The few settlements with airstrips can be reached only by private aircraft and the mud tracks that have been bulldozed through the jungle are highly unreliable, if passable at all.

POCITOS

The tiny village of Pocitos, which straddles the border of Bolivia and

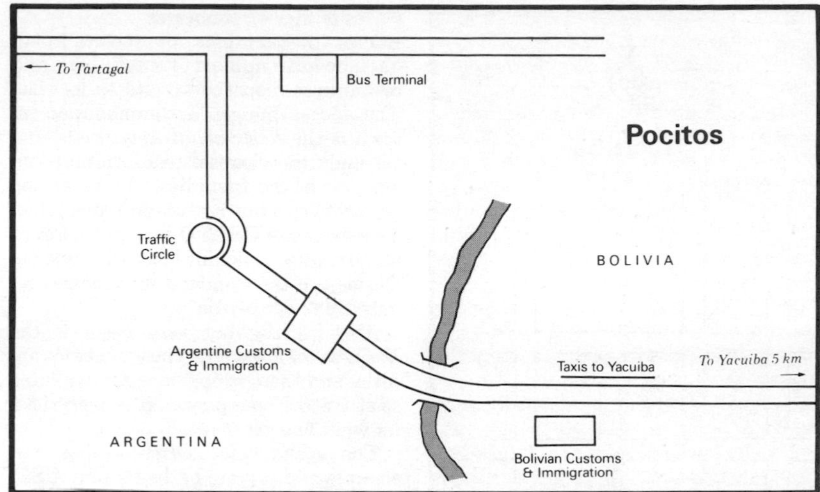

Argentina, is little more than a point of exit/entry between those two countries. From the Argentine side there are buses every two hours or so to Tartagal and Encarnación. In the latter, connections may be made to Salta/Jujuy, Orán, and even Buenos Aires. There are also railroad connections between Pocitos, Argentina, and Buenos Aires.

From the Bolivian side, taxis queue up along the main street awaiting passengers to Yacuiba. The fare between Pocitos, Bolivia and Yacuiba is 35c per person regardless of the number of people.

If you're entering Bolivia here, it is not possible to get more than a 30-day stamp from the Bolivian Immigration because they simply don't have one. Neither is there a consulate for either country.

From the Argentine bus terminal to the immigration offices is only a five-minute walk.

YACUIBA

In the transition zone between the Chaco and the highly agricultural Argentine Pampa, Yacuiba serves as the effective easternmost point of entry/exit along the Bolivian/ Argentine frontier.

Yacuiba is the terminus for the railway to Santa Crúz which was constructed with Argentine capital according to the terms of a treaty between the two countries made on 10 February, 1941. Bolivia agreed to export all its surplus petroleum to Argentina in exchange for this 580-km railroad which would approach the terminal of the Buenos Aires-Pocitos line already in place. The project was begun immediately but it wasn't completed until the 1960s. Now the entire line is in use.

Yacuiba is also the terminus of a 10,000-barrel-per-day YPFB oil pipeline from Camiri to the Argentine frontier.

The town and the surrounding area are really of very little interest but you may find yourself sitting here for a couple of days awaiting a train or a bus out.

Information

Changing Money There are five or six casas de cambio along the main north-south street in Yacuiba. None of them will exchange travellers' cheques, so going northward you'll have to wait until you get to Camiri or Santa Crúz and going southward until Embarcación, Argentina. Although all of these exchange houses

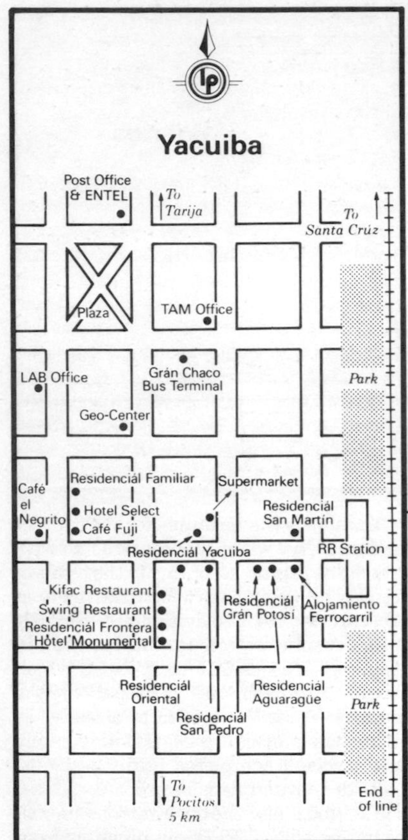

offer similar rates for dollars, bolivianos, and australes, be particularly careful calculating and counting the amount you should get. I was exchanging australes for bolivianos and one casa de cambio here tried to give me considerably less than their posted rate. When I questioned the amount they told me that I was evil for trying to rip them off until I called the manager and straightened things out. Don't be intimidated by such practices or you'll probably get taken.

Places to Stay – bottom end

Being the terminus of the railroad, Yacuiba has a number of hotels, bars, and restaurants disproportionate to its size. The nicest budget accommodation in town is the *Residencial Aguaragüe*. It's certainly the cleanest place around and also one of the friendliest. There are no private baths but hot water is available. Twin beds cost US$2.50 per person. *Cama matrimonial* or double beds are US$4.50. Dorm-style three and four-bed rooms cost only US$2 per person.

Also friendly but very basic is the *Residencial Frontera*. The bathrooms are filthy and there is no hot water available so at US$3.50 per person, it is overpriced for what you get.

The *Residencial Oriental* has hot showers and private baths for only US$5 single and US$8 double and it's marginally clean.

The cheapest accommodation available is at the *Residencial Grán Potosí*, *Alojamiento Ferrocarríl*, *Residencial San Martín*, and *Residencial Familiar*. They're all very basic with shared baths and cold showers, all charging US$2.50 per person.

The *Residencial Yacuiba* costs US$3 per person but they have hot water. Double beds with private bath are available for US$10.

The *Residencial San Pedro* costs US$5 for a double without bath and US$10 with bath. They don't have any single rooms and if you're alone they want you to pay for a double anyway.

Places to Stay – middle

The only nicer accommodation in Yacuiba is the very clean *Hotel Monumental* on the main North-South street next door to Residencial Frontera. All rooms have private bath and hot water for US$10 per person.

Places to Eat

All the locals recommend *El Negrito* for the best food in town. It is very good and also reasonably priced but the service is dreadfully slow. They serve the old Bolivian standbys - fish, chicken, and beef dishes with the usual trimmings.

Both *Geo-Center* and *Swing* are popular local hangouts with the under-21 crowd but they serve passable food, too. I'd also recommend *Kifac*, across from the military compound, which is one of the few places in town to buy breakfast. Its homey atmosphere is pleasant.

Getting There & Away

By air, Yacuiba is served by TAM from Tarija and by LAB from Camiri and Santa Crúz. If you don't want to spend a gruelling 12 to 24 hours on the bus from Yacuiba to Tarija, the fare is only US$14 each way, about the same as the bus. The airline offices are both marked on the map.

The *Flota Trans-Grán Chaco* goes to Tarija twice a week. If you're going to Villa Montes and want to see some spectacular scenery, take the flota to Palos Blancos and hitch a ride with a petrol truck from there into Villa Montes. Alternatively, there are trucks which take the more direct route to Villa Montes following the foothills of the Cordillera Oriental.

There's a fast train to Santa Crúz that leaves on Tuesday, Thursday, and Saturday at 12.35 pm. First class fare to Santa Crúz is US$5.50, second is US$4. To Villa Montes only, the fares are US$2 and US$1.25.

The ferrobus, much of which is often reserved for the military, leaves on Tuesday, Thursday, and Saturday at 9.30 pm. The fare to Santa Crúz in first and second class is US$10.50 and US$7.50. To Villa Montes costs US$2.50 and US$2. A mixed freight and passenger train leaves on Monday and Friday at 7.20 pm. Only second class is available.

If you have a second class ticket on one of the trains, you might consider riding in the boxcars to Santa Crúz. It's bound to be quite uncomfortable riding with all the freight normally stuffed into them but there are some interesting conversations to be had with the contrabandists who transport their goods this way. There's nothing risky about it - smuggling is considered an honourable profession around these parts.

PALOS BLANCOS

Consisting of a few bars and scattered houses overlooking a beautiful river, Palos Blancos is one of those places simply oozing with character and not much else. It's a real town that could pass for a Hollywood western movie set and standing on the main street, you can almost see Butch and Sundance storming into town in a cloud of billowing dust.

The church here is one of the most rustic and charming in all Bolivia - a tumbledown, old, whitewashed mud building in a colourful red and green landscape. An arch of cowbells outside is used to call the faithful to worship and the donation box in front is surrounded by wildflowers and prayer requests.

There's no formal accommodation in town, but camping opportunities are limitless. There are lots of sites along the river. Alternatively, you can ask around for a place to stay with one of the locals. If you do, be sure to read the warning under 'Chagas' in the Health Section of the Facts for the Visitor chapter.

Minimal food services are available at the stores and bars across from the church.

All transport between Villa Montes, Yacuiba, and Tarija must pass through Palos Blancos so finding a ride in or out should be no problem during the dry season (from March to October).

VILLA MONTES

Villa Montes, Bolivia's only significant outpost in the true Chaco, is known for several reasons. First of all, it prides itself on being the hottest place in the country - which isn't difficult to believe when the mercury rises above the 40° mark and a hot dry wind coats everything with a thick layer of red dust. Secondly, this town (and

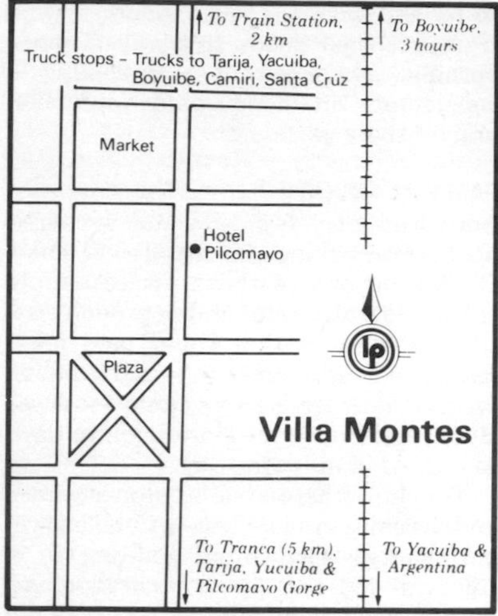

the entire Chaco) is famous for its wildlife, particularly the small buzzing varieties. Ravenous flies and mosquitos thrive and anyone who is at home 'beyond the black stump' should feel very comfortable here.

Most importantly, however, Villa Montes is known for its excellent fishing and is popular with anglers from all over Bolivia and neighbouring countries. At El Choro Grande Falls on the Rió Pilcomayo, the fish are prevented from swimming further upstream and *surubí*, *sábalo*, and *dorado* are abundant and easily caught. The dorado is particularly interesting because it is the only fish which has a hinge at the front of its jawbone, allowing the mouth to open wider horizontally. If you like fish but aren't into fishing, there are restaurants seven to 10 km from town along the Pilcomayo Gorge that serve some of the best you'll ever eat for about US$2.50.

During the Inca times, tribes of Guaranies immigrated to this area from what is now Paraguay and today their descendants make up most of the indigenous population of the town. This small and lonely outpost continued pretty much unnoticed until it emerged as a major strategic stronghold of the Bolivian army during the Chaco War. The Paraguayans knew that it was necessary to take Villa Montes in order to capture an undisputed victory in the conflict and in 1935, the Battle of Villa Montes took place. Under the command of General Bernardino Bilbao Rioja and Major Germán Busch, the Bolivians enjoyed their most significant victory of the war. The momentum gained in that battle allowed them to recapture portions of the eastern Chaco and some of the Santa Crúz oil fields previously lost to Paraguay.

Places to Stay

The *Hotel Pilcomayo* on the main street doesn't have a sign out front so you'll have to ask in order to get the right doorway. It's very basic but it's probably the best budget accommodation in town at US$2.50 per person. The *Hotel El Rancho* across the street from the railroad station two km out of town is more expensive but nicer.

Getting There & Around

By air, TAM flies to and from Tarija. Flights take 45 minutes and cost only US$14.

By rail, Villa Montes is two hours north of Yacuiba and ten hours south of Santa Crúz. The railroad station is two km north of town.

If you're looking for transport to Tarija, Yacuiba, Boyuibe, Palos Blancos, Camiri, or Santa Crúz, trucks park along the strip marked *Parada de Camiones* at the north end of the market. If you're headed south or would just like to spend a day seeing the Pilcomayo Gorge, you can also take a taxi to the tranca five km south of town and wait for a truck headed in the right direction.

The taxi fare from the centre to the railroad station is 50c per person.

BOYUIBE

Barely large enough to be considered a

town, Boyuibe sits along the Yacuiba-Santa Crúz rail line three hours north of Villa Montes and seven hours south of Santa Crúz on the fringes of the Grán Chaco. It serves primarily as a point of transit. To the south a road goes to Villa Montes and the route from Camiri to Paraguay passes through here, also.

If you're hoping to find a truck over the very difficult route into northern Paraguay, you'll probably have to spend at least a day or two in Boyuibe and probably longer. Transport to Camiri, Villa Montes, and Yacuiba stops in front of the *Tránsito* office along the main street.

The train to the south passes at about 1 am on Tuesday, Thursday, and Saturday. Going northward, it passes on Monday, Wednesday, and Friday at night.

Places to Stay

There are two hotels in Boyuibe, the *Hotel Chaqueño* and the *Hotel Guadalquivír*. Both are little more than a bed to crash in, but due to scarcity of accommodation and long waits for transportation they cost US$4 per person.

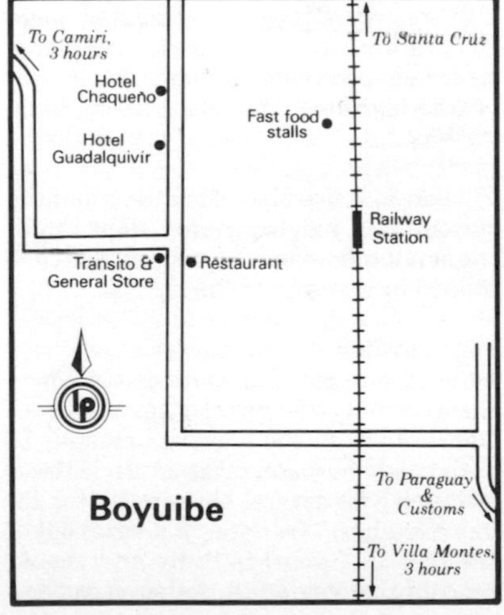

To Paraguay

If you want to attempt the overland trip to Paraguay, Boyuibe is the logical place to start from. There is no public transport and the road is rough and sandy. In the wet season, it is impassable altogether because the roadbed turns to slimy mud or quicksand. There are trucks which travel this road about once a week during the dry season but there is no actual schedule and you could be waiting for a very long time. Nevertheless, you could also get lucky. I found one after waiting only five hours. Petrol trucks no longer do this run because the cost of fuel is now equal in Bolivia and Paraguay, making it an unprofitable venture. If that situation changes, this route will begin to see a little more activity. Passengers from Boyuibe to Mariscal Estegarribia in Paraguay can expect to pay about US$20 each for the 24 to 30 hour (under optimum conditions) trip.

If you have access to a very hardy private vehicle, this trip may be attempted individually. There are no spares or fuel available until well into Paraguay, road conditions change with each rainfall, and traffic is intermittent at best so don't jump into such a venture without some serious preparation. A supply of fuel, water, food, spare parts, tyres, and so on is essential. Before setting out, be sure to get a free exit stamp from the customs office just outside Boyuibe.

While the scenery along this level route may get a bit monotonous, the Chaco region is worth seeing for its colourful variety of flora and fauna. Butterflies and birds are abundant, but this is also one of the final strongholds of some large South American mammals – like the tapir and the jaguar. The little peccary (locally called *javelí*) can sometimes be seen, too.

The vegetable life of the region is quite unusual and won't disappoint either. The thorny scrub of the Chaco landscape is enlivened by brilliant flowering trees and bushes such as the yellow *carnival* bush, the yellow and white *huevo*, and the pink or white thorny bottle tree, locally known as the *tomoroche* or *palo borracho*. In addition to these, you'll find many species of cactus and the red-flowering *quebracho* or 'break-axe' tree. Its beautiful wood is so heavy that it won't float. Quebracho wood has historically been one of the primary exports of the Chaco region.

As nice as it is to look at, the Chaco is unfortunately not optimum for exploration on foot. Its dense and thorny character makes it virtually impenetrable to those of us who walk upright.

CAMIRI

On the edge of the Chaco with a favourable climate, Camiri has grown phenomenally in recent years due to lucrative employment opportunities with YPFB, affectionately known locally as just '*Yacimientos*'. Though it has come to be called 'The Oil Capital of Bolivia', it is historically just as important for natural gas as for petroleum production.

In 1955, two pipelines were constructed to carry natural gas and petroleum to Yacuiba on the Argentine frontier. The following year, a 1½ million dollar natural gas reinjection plant was built by YPFB atop Cerro Sararenda. Its purpose was to recover liquid petroleum gas by reinjecting natural gas into oil-bearing formations. Another plant (this one to process liquid petroleum gas) was built and began functioning in 1968. A refrigeration and dehydration plant was put into operation at nearby Taquiparenda in 1983 for the recovery of liquid petroleum, but decreased production led to its being closed after only three years in operation. Since then, Camiri has seen ups and downs in the industry but it remains Bolivia's centre of fossil fuel production.

Camiri is also a military garrison town, a fact which visitors will tune into immediately. If they plan to stay in a hotel, all visitors to Camiri must register with immigration upon arrival (see map) and then report to the military police for a permit to stay in town. For your trouble, you get a stamp in your passport and sweaty palms while a lineup of military and police officers suspiciously eyeball you and question your motives for being in town. This procedure is free, by the way, so don't let them talk you into paying for it. If you're driving in a private vehicle, you've got to go through the same procedure for permission to leave.

In Camiri as in all Oriente towns, watch closely during all searches of your luggage. There have been reports of drug plants here.

Information

Changing Money *Hotel Ortuño* will exchange travellers' cheques at an excellent rate, one of the best in Bolivia. The small store next door to the Hotel Ortuño changes dollars cash for the same rate.

Things to See & Do

Camiri residents are very proud of the YPFB plant at the edge of town. There's no formal tour available but it you'd like to have a look around inside, turn up at about 8 am and ask for someone who can show you the facility and explain what goes on there.

Just north of town on the road to Sucre there are racquetball courts in a large wedge-shaped building about 200 metres off the highway. This place seems to be very popular with locals and military personnel.

There is a nice view of the town and the surrounding jungle covered slopes from the small hill above the market, which is topped by a statue of Christ.

Places to Stay

Despite its reputation as an energy town, there is not enough electric power in Camiri to fulfil the growing demands so each neighbourhood takes a turn without electricity for several hours a day for 15-day stretches. The water that oozes out of the taps in Camiri is filthy and should probably be avoided altogether. It can be a

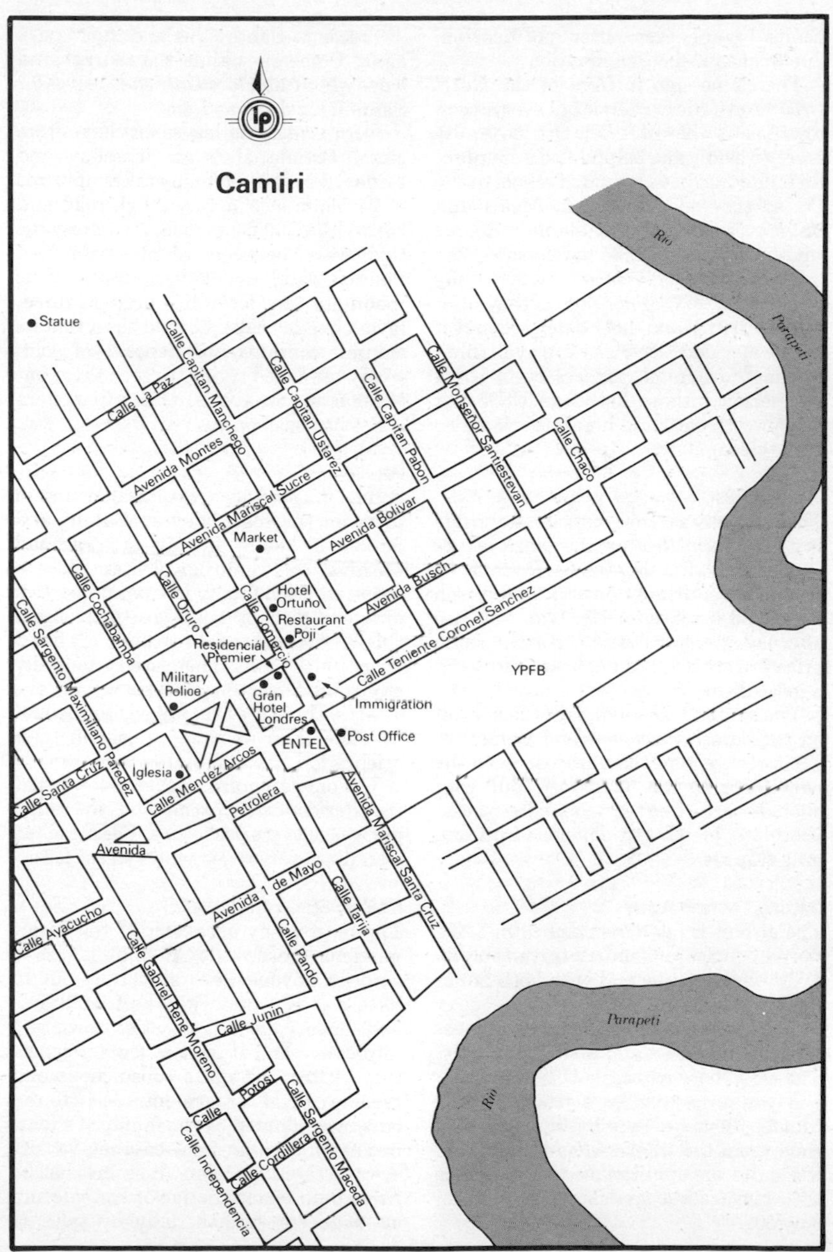
Camiri
Statue
Calle La Paz
Calle Capitan Manchego
Calle Capitan Ustarez
Calle Capitan Pabon
Calle Monseñor Santiestevan
Calle Chaco
Rio Parapeti
Avenida Montes
Avenida Mariscal Sucre
Avenida Bolivar
Market
Avenida Busch
Calle Cochabamba
Calle Oruro
Calle Comercio
Hotel Ortuño
Restaurant Poji
Calle Teniente Coronel Sanchez
Calle Sargento Maximiliano Paredez
Residenciál Premier
Military Police
Grán Hotel Londres
Immigration
YPFB
ENTEL
Post Office
Iglesia
Calle Santa Cruz
Calle Mendez Arcos
Petrolera
Avenida Mariscal Santa Cruz
Avenida
Avenida 1 de Mayo
Calle Tarija
Calle Ayacucho
Calle Gabriel Rene Moreno
Calle Pando
Calle Junin
Parapeti
Calle Potosi
Calle
Calle Sargento Maceda
Calle Cordillera
Calle Independencia
Rio

health-hazard even after purification, due to chemical contamination.

There's no sign in front of the *Hotel Ortuño* on Calle Comercio but everyone in town knows where it is. The Ortuño family is very friendly and helpful and a couple of their children have attended school in the US so they speak English. Meals and private baths are available. Rooms without bath cost US$5 per person.

The *Residencial Premier* is exceptionally clean. For US$7.50 per person they offer private baths and hot water whenever both water and electricity are available.

The *Grán Hotel Londres* costs US$4 per person without bath and US$5 per person with bath and hot water. It's also fairly clean.

Places to Eat

There are only a couple of good restaurants in town. *Pollo Rico* on the plaza serves roasted chicken in the evening. *Restaurant Poji* on the corner of Comercio and Busch does good lunches for US$1.25. You can also eat at *Hotel Ortuño*. For the same price you get soup, salad, bread, rice, and a meat dish.

The best buy, as usual, is at the market on the corner of Bolívar and Comercio. The street vendors there are just about the only place to buy breakfast, but your choices are limited to coffee, tea, chocolate, bread, and delicious fruit and milk frappés.

Getting There & Away

The airport is just outside of town along the road to Sucre. Camiri is served only by TAM which connects it with both Santa Crúz and Sucre.

To Boyuibe, there is a micro that leaves from Barrio San Antonio at 3 pm daily. The three-hour trip costs US$1.50.

If you're looking for a truck to Villa Montes, Boyuibe, Yacuiba, or Tarija, they leave from the tranca when they're full. It's quite an uphill walk to the tranca with luggage but you can go by taxi for only 50c.

Trucks to Santa Crúz and Sucre park along Comercio beside the market and leave when full. *Flota Unificado* leaves for Santa Crúz daily at 7 am.

Flota Chagueña leaves for Sucre from Hotel Ortuño at 7 am Tuesday and Friday. The trip normally takes upwards of 24 hours over a very rough road and costs US$17.50 per person. If you're going this way, between Monteagudo and Padilla watch for a very conspicuous mountain that looks like a fallen three-layer birthday cake. Legend has it that its summit contains rich deposits of gold. Many have died trying to reach them but as far as anyone knows, nobody in modern times has been on top.

Padilla

Padilla is a friendly agricultural mountain town on the road between Camiri and Sucre. If you're in the area around Carnival, this would be a pleasant place to spend it. Each family in town prepares a different dish or beverage (most often chicha) to bring to the feast and it's like a big pot luck affair. There aren't normally any tourists, as far as I know, but the locals assured me that any visitors would be more than welcome to join in their celebration.

The only accommodation in town is at the *Residencial Cascada* on the main plaza beside the post office. The attached restaurant serves good but typical fare.

SAN JOSE DE CHIQUITOS

The most easily accessible of the Jesuit missions, San José de Chiquitos is sure to surprise anyone who takes time out to have a look around it. The friendliness and beauty of this frontier town are impressive and it sees so few foreigners that visitors are quite conspicuous and receive royal treatment. We found ourselves adopted by the family of a local businessman who insisted that we eat every meal in his home. It seems that he wrote pulp science fiction on the side and we were entertained daily by tales of

Captain Death Rays and the Giant Vampire. Thrilling stuff!

Flanked on the south by a low escarpment and on the north by flat soggy jungle, San José is rapidly developing into the cattle ranching centre of the deep Oriente and most of its population is either involved in ranching or the buying and selling of contraband foodstuffs from Brazil. As a matter of fact, San José, like most of the Oriente, economically and culturally looks toward Brazil rather than La Paz and you'll hear nearly as much Portuguese as you will Spanish here.

San José de Chiquitos was named after the Chiquitanos Indians who were the original inhabitants of this area. The Jesuits arrived sometime in the mid-1740s and the magnificent mission church that today dominates the town was begun around 1748.

Information

Changing Money Although there's no place to exchange travellers' cheques, the small corner store two blocks from the main plaza (see map) will exchange dollars cash if they have sufficient bolivianos on hand.

You'll probably be limited by cash availability to about US$50 at a time.

Jesuit Mission church

The mission church in San José de Chiquitos is not just another ho-hum South American monument to colonialism. Even confirmed church-haters cannot fail to be impressed by the architectural design of this one which is unique in all South America. Similarities have been noted between it and religious structures in both Poland and Belgium but there is no conclusive evidence as to the origin of its exterior design. The main altar, however, is nearly identical to those of other Jesuit missions in the vicinity.

The church compound occupies an entire block with several buildings and courtyards arranged inside. The bell tower was finished in 1748, the Death Chapel is dated 1752, and the *parroquio* or living area was completed 1754. All construction work was done by the Chiquitanos themselves using Jesuit plans. The doors, some of the altar work, and one magnificent bench seat were all hand-carved in wood by expert Chiquitano artisans.

A massive restoration project is currently underway under the direction of Swiss architects Hans Roth and Ekhard Kühne.

The bottle trees on the huge plaza in front of the church are full of sloths and noisy parrots, while the ground beneath is hopping with frogs and large toads. Be sure to note the rather odd and erotic fountain off to one side of the plaza. It's a safe bet to say that you won't find anything like this in highland Bolivia.

Chiquitano Monument

The people of the area seem to be proud of the indigenous heritage of San José and to prove it they've put up a monument at the entrance to town. It portrays an archetypal Chiquitano maiden with her obligatory water jar but it's a tasteful work of art, nonetheless.

Pool & Waterfall

Just a 4½ km walk from town there is a resort, of sorts, with a murky green swimming pool where the locals go to cool off. Admission costs US$1 per adult and 50c for minors. The walk itself, however, is probably more appealing than the pool. Along the way you'll have the opportunity to see cattle ranches, jungle vegetation, and even an old abandoned schoolhouse. At one point, the road passes through an archway, obviously designed by the same person who did the fountain. Be sure to carry insect repellent on this walk and wear something substantial on your feet and legs. The ants are ferocious!

A very pleasant waterfall, which is the source of San José's drinking water, is above the pool, a short walk through the jungle. It's a cool, shady spot out of the often blistering tropical heat, but due to swarms of biting insects you probably won't want to spend a lot of time there.

Places to Stay

The *Alojamiento San Silvestre* across from the railroad station costs US$3.50 per person for a single or double room. The showers are cold, but in this climate you'll welcome them.

Nearer the centre, across the street from the church is the *Hotel Victoria* which also costs US$3.50 per person. The doors to the rooms don't lock and the owner is quite a bitchy old lady but the staff is friendly enough and they'll keep an eye on your things while you're out and about.

If you'd prefer to camp out, ask the priest at the church if you can pitch a tent in the courtyard there.

Places to Eat

There's a reasonable restaurant next door to the Alojamiento San Silvestre and some very nice kiosks near the train station which serve inexpensive lunch and dinner specials.

The chicken restaurant across the plaza from the church serves pretty awful food but if you arrive late, it may be the only thing open.

My favourite place is a restaurant/bar two blocks from the main plaza which serves good meals and drinks in a pleasant open courtyard.

Getting There & Away

Although there's a rather complicated overland route to San José, the best and easiest way to get there is on the Santa Crúz to Quijarro train. The trip from Santa Crúz takes eight hours which means that if the train leaves Santa Crúz more or less on time, you can theoretically get here before dark the same day. The fare to San José de Chiquitos from Santa Crúz is US$2.50 first class or US$1.50 second class. Going the other direction the train leaves Quijarro at 6 am daily and should arrive in San José at least 12 hours later. The ferrobus going east passes on Monday, Thursday, and Saturday and going west on Sunday, Wednesday, and Friday but getting a reserved ticket from an intermediate point like this is almost impossible.

All air service to San José is on LAB from either Santa Crúz or Puerto Suarez.

AROUND SAN JOSÉ DE CHIQUITOS

Mennonite Colony

Although its probably best not turned into a tourist attraction like similar places have been in the eastern US, a visit to the Mennonite Colony 42 km north of San José is as interesting a cultural experience as you're ever likely to have.

The Mennonites of this colony originally came from Saskatchewan, Canada, but only the older people remember the place and the younger ones have no idea where Canada is. They set out from their homeland in search of a place where they could practise their religion, farm their land, and live out peaceful and self-sufficient lives apart from the influences of modern society. They originally found such a place in Belize, Central America, but hassles with the government there in the mid-70s sent them looking for a new home.

Seeing the great agricultural potential of the Bolivian Oriente, thousands of them came to the wilderness east of Santa Crúz. They cleared vast tracts of jungle and created a rustic slice of the North American midwest in the heart of Bolivia. So far the Bolivian government has appreciated the role they've played in opening up previously uninhabited territory but as more and more highland Bolivians begin to eye the potential of the Oriente, it remains to be seen how long this situation will last.

These highly traditional people speak a dialect of German called *Platt-Deutch* which is actually more of a mixture of German and Dutch. Despite their Canadian roots, very few speak English and most of them don't even speak Spanish. Wherever you go in this part of South America (quite a few Mennonites have also established colonies in Paraguay, Brazil, and Argentina) you'll be able to recognise the *Menonos*, as the locals call them, by their dress. The men all wear hats and identical blue or green overalls. The women, who are required more or less to blend into the background, all wear knee-length dresses and head coverings.

Mennonite homes are simple farmhouses. Most of the farming is done by hand or by draft animals and they travel from place to place in horse-drawn carts, as motorised vehicles are prohibited.

The merchants in San José de Chiquitos carry on trade with the colony, buying milk, cheese, butter, and poultry from the Mennonites on a regular basis. Normally at least one truck does the run each day.

Getting There & Away

If you'd like to ride along and have a look at what's going on in the colony, wait at the tranca across the railroad tracks (see map) before 9 am. The round trip will cost between US$2.50 and US$5 per person.

If you do go, try to respect the privacy of the colonists. Most of them prefer not to have their photos taken and many, especially the women, don't really want anything to do with the outside world at all, which is precisely the reason they came to this remote place to begin with.

This is, of course, not the only Mennonite colony in Bolivia. There are others scattered all over this region and northward into the Beni, and a particularly high concentration around the city of Santa Crúz.

Other Jesuit Missions

To the north of San José de Chiquitos in the Llanos de Chiquitos and the Guarayos Hills there are several other accessible Jesuit missions which can be visited with a little effort and expense.

The first village founded in the region was San Javiér, 230 km over dirt roads from San José. Although the mission was begun in 1692, the church wasn't constructed there until the mid-1700s. The first church that was completed in all the missions was at San Rafael, which was built between 1740 and 1748. Today, the mission church at San Rafael has been completely restored and the interior is particularly beautiful with original paintings and woodwork intact.

The church at Concepción, which is 160 km north-west of San José has also been restored, but it looks like a sort of religious Disneyland with gaudy plastic decor and lots of kitsch inside.

All three of these, San Javiér, San Rafael, and Concepción were originally designed by Martin Schmidt, a Swiss missionary, musician, and architect who worked in the area in the 1700s.

The church that is generally considered the most beautiful of the Jesuit missions in Bolivia was not designed by Schmidt but its style reflects his influence. San Miguél, 140 km from San José, is probably the most accurately restored of them all and its artwork and wood carvings are superb.

At the other major mission site in the area the original Jesuit church (San Ignacio) has been replaced by a modern one but the village, still inhabited primarily by Indians, is interesting to visit.

Getting There & Away

Both LAB and TAM offer twice-weekly air service between Santa Crúz, Concepción, and San Ignacio. Alternately, you can travel overland by truck from San José de Chiquitos but it will cost between US$30 and US$50 per person each way to any of the other mission villages. To arrange transport, wait at the tranca early in the morning. There is a truck going to San Ignacio or one of the other missions nearly every day during the dry season (March to October).

ROBORÉ

The village of Roboré – four hours east of San José de Chiquitos, along the railway – began in 1916 as a military outpost and even today, the military presence is a bit over-whelming. You can imagine what happens when a lot of bored soldiers posted in the middle of nowhere learn that a couple of gringos have wandered into a town that rarely sees outsiders at all. We were constantly harassed by machine-gun-toting teenagers who had nothing better to do than peruse our documents and try to cause as many problems as they could.

Anyone planning to stay overnight in the town will have to register with the military police before they'll be allowed to stay at the hotel and were it not for a couple of interesting things to see in the area, I'd advise anyone to give this place a wide berth and let these kids keep their mindless games to themselves.

Things to See & Do

Just a short distance from Roboré, 20 km or so, is another Jesuit mission. Santiago is the most accessible one still inhabited by the Indians and in the cultural sense, it is even more interesting than San José de Chiquitos. A taxi from town to the village

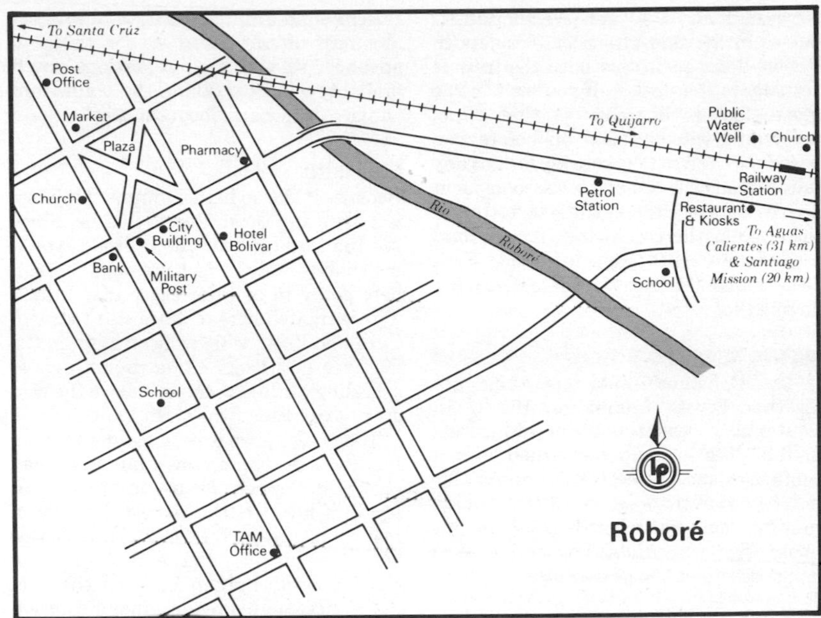

will cost at least US$25 but if you have a group, this would probably be the best way to go. Military vehicles do the run sporadically from the east end of town and cost only US$1.50 per person.

At Aguas Calientes, 31 km east of Roboré, there are 40° to 41° medicinal baths which are very popular with the Bolivians. The Santa Crúz-Quijarro train stops in Aguas Calientes, so if you'd like to see it, it's possible to forego Roboré altogether. It's also possible to get there by truck which leaves from the east end of town and costs US$1.50 per person. If you want to spend the night here, you'll have to camp out.

The Roboré River which passes through town is cool and clean and offers some very pleasant and refreshing swimming.

Places to Stay

The only hotel in Roboré is the *Bolívar*, just half a block from the plaza. They charge US$4 per person for a room with shared bath or US$5 each for private bath. As I mentioned previously, foreigners must obtain permission from the military to stay here.

If you'd rather not fuss with the military at all, ask to see Padre José at the church near the railroad station. He'll let you camp out in the garden there and also provide you with some very interesting company. He's an Austrian priest who's spent over thirty years in this remote part of Bolivia (and before that, many years in South China) and if you speak German, Spanish, or Mandarin, he can tell you all sorts of amazing stories about the area.

Getting There & Away

Both TAM and LAB fly into Roboré from Puerto Suarez, San Matías, the Jesuit missions, and Santa Crúz. If you'd rather travel by rail, the eastbound train passes in the wee hours of the morning, usually between 1 and 1.30 am. Westbound, it passes in the mid-afternoon. Tickets in Roboré don't go on sale until the train is actually in the station. If you wait in the queue to buy a ticket at that time, everything will be filled up before you board the train so it's probably best to hop into a coach or a boxcar as soon as it arrives and pay the extra 20% to buy a ticket from the conductor. The normal second class fare to Quijarro is US$3. First class is about US$4. To Santa Crúz it's double that.

PUERTO SUAREZ

If the Bolivians could get their act together Puerto Suarez on the Grán Pantanal – a treasure house of wild animal and birdlife – could be turned into a profitable and attractive town. At this point, however, it is a filthy, sticky, muddy, malaria-infested hole. In his book, *The Incredible Voyage*, Tristan Jones describes the place aptly:

> . . .it is fit for neither man nor beast. I will go further and say that it is the asshole of the Americas, North and South. It consists of a few unpainted, rotting wooden shacks slouched around railroad sidings, the lines of which are overgrown with jungle and alive with mosquitoes. On each side of the siding is a noisy fog-ridden swamp of fetid, stagnant water that stinks to high heaven. During the twilight hours millions of mosquitoes rise off it, crowding the night air so thickly that there is hardly room between them to see the giant moths which smash headlong into every light they can find. Over all this hovers a smothering, dank heat, making for an experience rather like putting your head into an oven full of rotting rats.

This descriptive passage was written ten years ago and since, then, nothing has changed. I can think of absolutely no reason for anyone wanting to spend any time here. There are a few artesanías in town but they are mostly for the benefit of Brazilians who take day trips over from Corumbá and want to prove they've set foot on Bolivian soil.

LAB and TAM do frequent runs between Puerto Suarez and Santa Crúz but flights are most often booked up for weeks in advance, so without reservations you'll probably wind up taking the train from Quijarro a few km down the tracks.

QUIJARRO

Because it sits on higher ground, Quijarro is a little nicer than Puerto Suarez. Since it's the terminus for the railroad, you'll invariably find yourself passing through here going to or from Corumbá, Brazil. You're treated here to a beautiful view of Corumbá itself, which sits on a hill in the distance and looks like a dream city of sparkling white skyscrapers above the vast green expanses of the Grán Pantanal.

Today, Quijarro is nothing more than a muddy,little border town but that may change in the near future. In Mutún just south of here are the richest deposits of iron manganese on the continent. Although it's now just in the early stages of development, Bolivia believes the iron manganese may provide a major solution to the current economic crisis in the country. It also realises that it has to be quick about developing it.

Historical precedent has taught Bolivia to be paranoid of its neighbours in matters such as this. Concern that the country's giant neighbour to the east may take more than an admiring interest in them is justifiable, especially because these deposits are so near the frontier.

Crossing the Border

When the train pulls into Quijarro, there is always a lineup of taxis waiting to take you to the border which is about two km from the station. It's necessary to bargain with these taxi drivers because the initial price they'll quote you will be some exorbitant figure. They're banking that foreigners won't know the distance to be travelled and may agree to pay what they ask. The going rate will be between US$1 and US$1.50 per person which may still seem a bit steep but then it costs 25c just to take a shit at the public toilets in Quijarro.

It's probably best to exchange money on the Bolivian side since the black market in Corumbá is a little hard to find. The Brazilian authorities are cracking down on illicit trade in foreign currency and exchange locations keep moving around. The money changers at the frontier will only accept US$ cash and they are not at all interested in bolivianos. Since it looks like the Brazilian *cruzado* is destined to follow in the footsteps of its predecessor, the *cruzeiro*, it would be impossible to quote any sort of reliable exchange rate. Currently, the cruzado is inflating at a rate of about 200% annually. In June, 1987, the official cruzado was going for 38.6 per dollar. On the black market, you could get about 57. Your best bet is to ask travellers going the opposite direction what a fair rate will be.

Some travellers report being required to pay 50c for a Bolivian exit stamp. Others have had to pay US$2.50 to leave the country here. Still others paid nothing. It probably just depends on which officer is on duty at the time. I have heard rumours that some nationalities are required to pay an exit fee but the Bolivian embassy in the US couldn't confirm this.

Just across the bridge you'll be subjected to a luggage search, but Brazilian immigration is at the federal police post in the Corumbá railroad station. For 10c a city bus will take you into Corumbá, about five km from the border. Everyone entering Brazil from Bolivia is required to have a yellow fever vaccination certificate or they won't be admitted to the country. There is a vaccination clinic in Corumbá but it is only open one hour per day, Monday to Saturday, and not at all on Sunday. A couple of Argentine citizens employed both the beg and bribe methods when I was there and neither succeeded in convincing the authorities to waive this requirement.

There are two trains daily to Campo Grande and thence to São Paulo, but if you've got the time, Corumbá is worth a couple of days. For US$10 to $20 you can spend several hours cruising around the Pantanal, an immense marshland full of diverse wildlife. It's also possible to travel by boat from here to Cuiabá in the northern part of the Mato Grosso. During the dry season, a bus does the same trip.

There are luxurious buses which connect Corumbá with Campo Grande and from there to São Paulo and Rió de Janeiro, but they fill up quickly so it's a good idea to make a reservation as soon as you arrive in town if you plan to go this route.

If you need a place to stay in Corumbá, try the *Hotel Central* which charges US$3 per person.

There's a Bolivian consulate at 812 Rua Antonio Mario Coelho, but it's closed on weekends. There's no Brazilian consulate on the Bolivian side, however. The nearest one is in Santa Crúz.

Getting There & Away

From Santa Crúz to Quijarro there is a tentative Express train, leaving at noon daily, and it reaches the frontier in about 20 hours. First class fare for the entire trip is US$10. Second class costs US$6. Going the opposite direction, the train leaves Quijarro at 6 am daily. You'll have the same problems getting tickets here as you do in Santa Crúz so be prepared for a bit of a wait.

There is a ferrobus which goes from Quijarro to Santa Crúz on Wednesday, Friday, and Sunday. It costs US$14.50 for a first class ticket and US$13.50 for second. From Santa Crúz to Quijarro, it leaves on Monday, Thursday, and Saturday and does the run in considerably less time than the train. Securing a ticket can be extremely difficult.

If you're travelling by train to or from Quijarro, be sure to have plenty of mosquito repellent on hand. There are often long and unexplained stops in low-lying, swampy areas and the zillions of skeeters get voraciously hungry.

Amazon Basin

Although it's a thousand km upstream from the Great River itself, Bolivia's portion of the Amazon Basin better represents the dreamy image most travellers associate with that river than the real thing does. While the accessible portion of Brazil's rainforest is largely an eroded wasteland of stumps and its remotest riverbanks are heavily populated, just across the border in Bolivia the stereotypical Amazon is alive and well. There, one will find the deep, mysterious and scarcely inhabited Eden (though it's also been called the Green Hell) that one sees on the glossy pages of 'National Geographic'.

The Amazon Basin, however, plays a far greater role in the overall scheme of things than just a source of amusement and wonder for those fortunate enough to behold it. Most of us are so accustomed to hearing the grim predictions meted out by the scientific world regarding this region that we have ceased to be shocked or concerned by them, but even so, they bear repetition.

At the present rate of destruction, the entire Amazon Basin biosphere will be history within 20 years. A goodly chunk of South America will be summarily carted off and dumped into the Atlantic Ocean and the resulting moonscape will have witnessed a mass extinction of animal and vegetable species on a scale unknown since the demise of the dinosaurs. And that is just the beginning - we're all familiar with the depressing predictions regarding the world's climate, oxygen supply, ozone layer and pharmaceutical potential should such a thing occur.

On a slightly more optimistic note, in August 1987 it was announced that a US-based environmental organisation called *Conservation International* made Bolivia an offer it could scarcely refuse. It agreed to pay US$650,000 of Bolivia's US$4 billion foreign debt in exchange for conservation of a 1½ million hectare preserve near the Beni River in the northern part of the country. Bolivia will retain management of the land but wildlife will be protected and haphazard development curtailed - at least in theory. A country with such an uncertain present has little incentive to consider the future.

Bolivia already has quite a few theoretical parks and preserves on the books but boundaries are loosely-defined and conservation enforcement is non-existent. Little-explored and relatively ignored, Bolivia's jungled lowlands have only recently begun to figure in the consciousness of the Bolivian government. With all the eyeballing of potential fortunes to be had in the wilderness, it will be interesting to see whether or not Bolivia will keep up its end of the conservation bargain when it's not so convenient to do so.

Historically, the Beni, Pando and surrounding areas have passed through stages of activity. The original inhabitants of the region were a number of jungle-dwelling tribes, many of whom still live there today. Some of the westernmost tribes were conquered by the Incas and annexed into the Imperialist Inca Empire. The first significant European penetration of these lowlands was staged by the hardy Jesuits who also opened up the eastern lowlands to Christianity and European domination. After the Jesuits were expelled from South America in 1767, the vast steamy plains of northern Bolivia saw little activity for 50 years.

According to Alcides D'Orbigny, the young French naturalist who extensively explored the South American interior during the early 1830s, those missionaries that came to fill the 'void' left by the expulsion of the Jesuits did little more than turn the Beni Indians into Christian

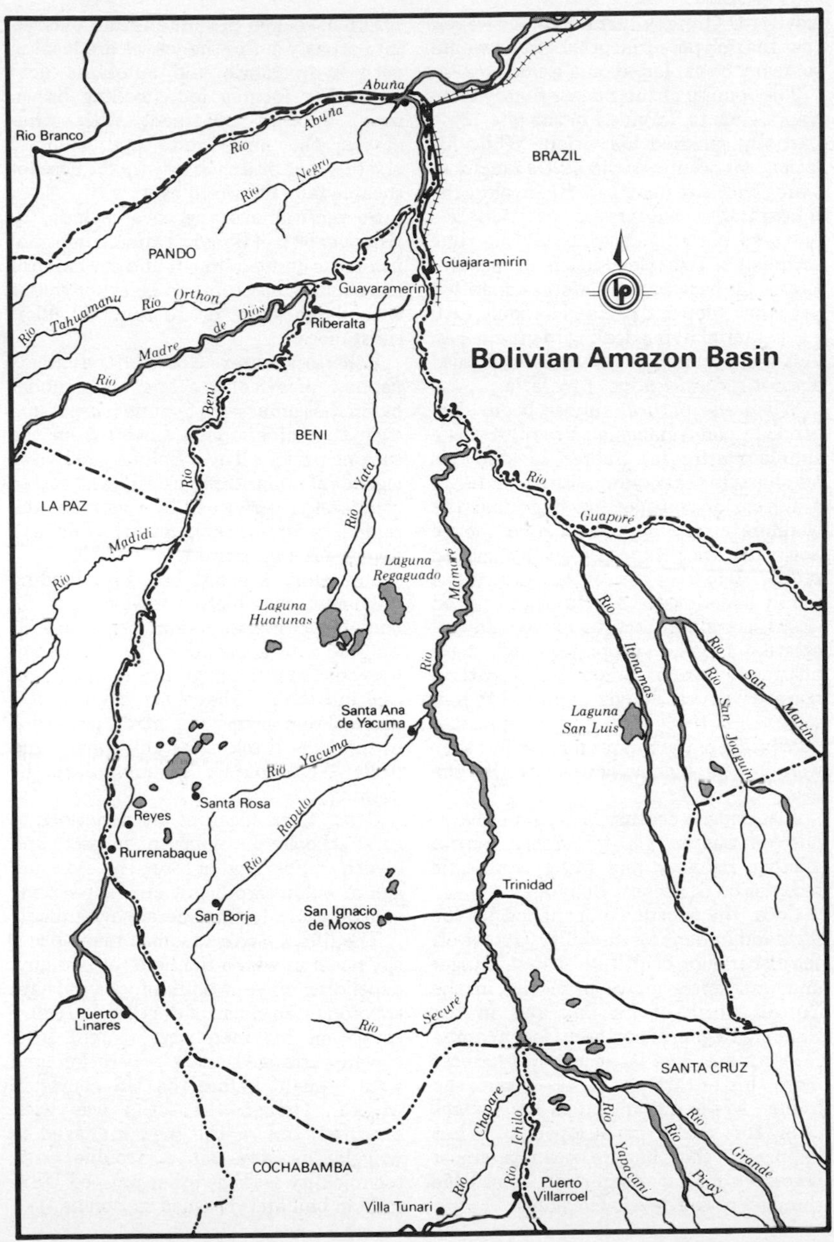
Bolivian Amazon Basin
BRAZIL
PANDO
BENI
LA PAZ
SANTA CRUZ
COCHABAMBA
Abuña
Rio Branco
Guajara-mirin
Guayaramerin
Riberalta
Santa Ana de Yacuma
Santa Rosa
Reyes
Rurrenabaque
San Borja
San Ignacio de Moxos
Trinidad
Puerto Linares
Puerto Villarroel
Villa Tunari
Río Abuña
Río Negro
Río Tahuamanu
Río Orthon
Río Madre de Diós
Río Beni
Río Yata
Río Madidi
Río Mamoré
Río Guaporé
Río Itonamas
Río San Martín
Río San Joaquín
Río Yacuma
Río Rapulo
Río Securé
Río Chapare
Río Ichilo
Río Yapacani
Río Piray
Río Grande
Laguna Regaguado
Laguna Huatunas
Laguna San Luis

slaves. D'Orbigny predicted, however, that the rich potential of the region would someday be exploited on a grand scale.

The coming of the Suarez family from Santa Crúz to Trinidad in the late 1800s partially satisfied his vision. While his father was occupied with cattle ranching, young Nícolas Suarez set off to explore the inhospitable wilderness of Bolivia's northern hinterlands which at the time included a sizeable portion of western Brazil. He became intimately acquainted with the region and decided he could earn a substantial living dealing in quinine, an anti-malarial remedy that is still used against certain strains of malaria.

When the natural rubber boom descended upon Amazonian Brazil, it was a simple matter for Suarez to shift his emphasis to that commodity and arrange a system of transporting it around the Mamoré rapids into Brazil and thence down the Río Madeira to the Amazon proper. Before the turn of the century, the family had amassed a fortune and owned about six million hectares of lowland real estate. A good proportion of these holdings was in the remote Acre Territory, however, which Bolivia managed to lose to Brazil in 1903. With Acre went a large percentage of the Suarez fortune but they were by no means devastated by the loss.

Just under a century later, a relative of Nícolas Suarez was to largely control another industry and bring worldwide recognition to darkest Bolivia.

Coca, the substance cherished by the highland Indians for its ability to stave off the discomforts of altitude, thirst, hunger and uneasiness grows primarily in the Yungas north of La Paz and in the Chapare Region of northern Cochabamba Department. The latter region produces more bitter-tasting leaves than the former, so the Indians prefer the Yungas coca for daily consumption. What happens to the Chapare coca has almost become a matter of common knowledge throughout the developed world.

Dried, soaked in kerosene and mashed into a pasty pulp, the leaves are treated with hydrochloric and sulphuric acid until they form a foul-smelling brown base. Further treatment with ether creates the pure white hydrochloride crystals that find their way up the noses of cocaine fans the world over.

So profitable is the cocaine industry that over 60% of Bolivia's annual informal income is derived from it and the name of the country has come to be synonymous with large-scale production of illicit substances.

Roberto Suarez Gomez, the great-nephew of Nícolas Suarez the rubber baron, has amassed a fortune (surpassing even that of his great uncle) from the cocaine trade. All over Bolivia you'll hear legends of philanthropic deeds and acts of compassion performed by this man who rapidly became an enigma and a folk hero among his compatriots.

One story I heard had him landing unannounced (which is the way he usually lands) in a Piper aircraft at Reyes airport, walking into a particularly poor neighbourhood and flinging large quantities of cash into the air to be collected by the local people. From there, he reportedly proceeded to the local drinking establishment and declared open bar for the remainder of the evening.

Other tales speak of his donations to rural schools, development projects and health clinics. And of course he, now and again, made significant and self-serving contributions to the federal government.

The life of Suarez Gomez reads like a spy novel in which the hero (or bad guy, depending on your point of view) always stays one step ahead of the CIA. In 1980, a couple of his men were caught in a cleverly-arranged 'sting' operation and were brought before the US courts in Miami. Though the setup was well-executed, one of the men managed to wriggle his way out of trouble on a technicality and the other jumped US$1 million bail and returned to Bolivia.

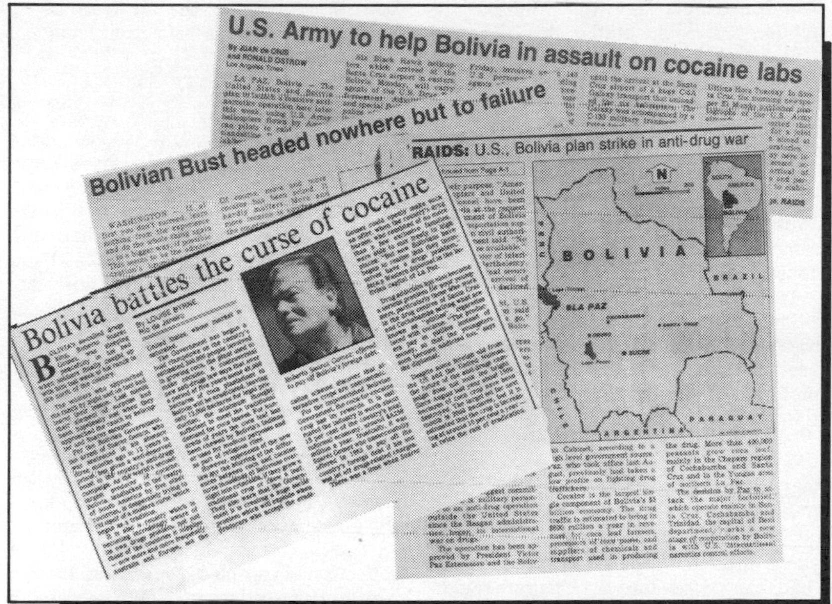

By the mid-1980s, US yuppiedom was consuming so much Bolivian cocaine that the North American government decided something had to be done about it. Realising that it would be unpopular to bomb the cocaine producers among their own population, the US pointed an accusing finger at Bolivia and threatened drastic action if that government would not cooperate with US military action aimed at curtailing the production of Bolivia's most lucrative export. Victor Paz agreed (grudgingly, I'm sure) when Rambo – er – Ronald Reagan and his buddies across the Potomac proposed some joint cleaning up of the remote reaches of the Beni and Chapare regions.

Fortunately or unfortunately, again depending upon your perspective, the operation was prematurely leaked to the press and the jungle processing labs were given sufficient warning to pack up and clear out before the bombs arrived. Only minor damage was done and the US government found itself in a rather embarrassing situation.

In 1987 the Bolivian army failed in their attempt to arrest the elusive Suarez Gomez when they ruined their 'element of surprise' by raiding his ranch by helicopter. In mid 1988, however, they were much more successful. In his absence, the Bolivian Government had sentenced Suarez Gomez to 12 years in prison and the Bolivian soldiers sent to get him, this time quietly and under cover of night, managed to arrest the cocaine king while he was still in his bed.

Despite all this discussion, northern Bolivia is not all cocaine and jungle. Cattle ranching is still carried out on a large scale, especially around Trinidad. The ancestry of some of the Beni herds traces back to Jesuit times, though most of the cattle raised today are Asian Indian zebu cattle imported through Brazil.

The main highways of the region are the

Amazon tributaries – the Mamoré, the Ichilo, the Beni, Madre de Diós and Guaporé, to name but a few – that elsewhere would be considered great rivers in their own right. Along these jungle waterways, riverboats, barges, buckets and bathtubs serve as the primary means of transportation for passengers, freight, vehicles and livestock. Villages are thin on the ground and some remote tribes have had only minimal contact with modern civilisation.

In short, this is very much a different Bolivia than the one seen in La Paz and the rest of the highlands, but what goes on here over the next few years will have profound effects upon the remainder of the country.

VILLA TUNARI

If you'd like to enjoy the type of scenery everyone goes to the Yungas to see, but you'd rather not experience the terrifying road, then travel into the Chapare region from Cochabamba. From high mountain lakes to deep, steaming valleys and the seemingly endless tropical forests of the Amazon Basin, the trip to Villa Tunari is spectacular.

The flooding of late 1985 and early 1986 that sent Lake Titicaca overflowing its banks also had a profound effect in this region. Most of the bridges along this route were either damaged or washed out altogether. While repairs are going on, traffic just has to wing it without bridges and there are several very hairy river crossings. When you see the heaps of concrete rubble (and at one point a 30 metre chunk of highway!) that litter the river bottom, you can begin to imagine the amounts of water we're talking about here. Until repairs are made, an overland trip into the Chapare during the rainy season is out of the question.

Villa Tunari itself is actually just a tropical resort for cold-weary highlanders. It's a quiet and relaxing spot to rent a cabaña, swim in jungle rivers and soak in hot springs. When the air feels like a sauna, however, this last activity may not be so appealing.

Getting There & Away

From Cochabamba you'll need to take a bus marked 'Chapare' which leaves from 9 de Abril and Oquendo near Lake Alalay. The first bus of the day leaves at 6.30 am and subsequent buses leave when full. The fare to Villa Tunari is US$2.50 and the trip takes about six hours. There are lots of police checks along this route.

Puerto Villarroel

The muddy jungle settlement of Puerto Villarroel lies three to four hours northeast of Villa Tunari and serves as one of the major river ports of Northern Bolivia. Although it consists of nothing but a collection of tumbledown wooden hovels, a military installation, a YPFB plant and an area that could be loosely described as a port, this town serves as both a vital transportation terminal and as a popular gateway to the Amazon lowlands. For anyone who just wants a quick look at the jungle, the trip to Puerto Villarroel is an easy two-day round trip from Cochabamba.

The most important advice that can be offered to anyone visiting this place is to bring lots of good insect repellent. The second most important advice is to wear strong old shoes with lots of tread. Even in the dry season, the muddy streets of Puerto Villarroel will crawl up past your ankles and threaten to devour your footwear, so anything not well-secured to your feet will fall prey and probably be lost forever.

Places to Stay

There are only two hotels in Puerto Villarroel and both can be described as very marginal accommodation.

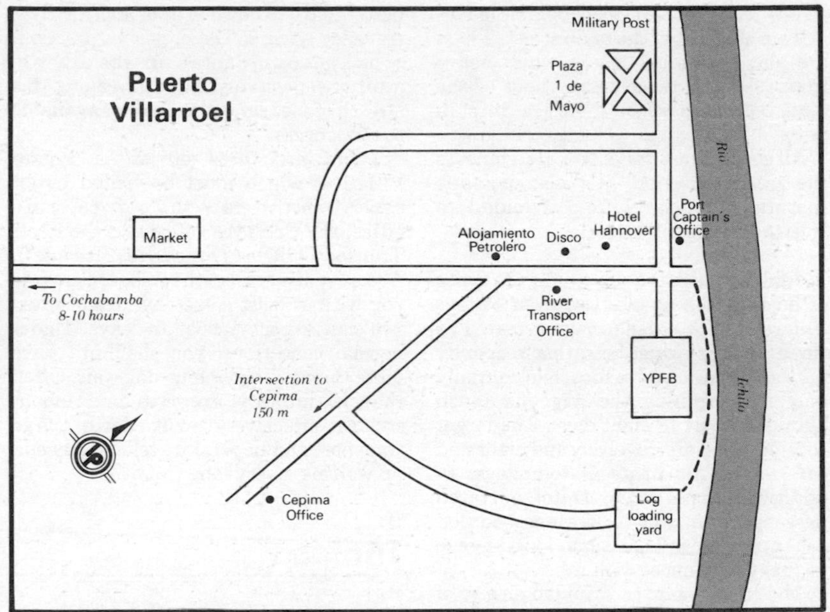

At the *Alojamiento Petrolero* the rooms are constructed of raw boards and scraps of wood pieced together into a leaky structure that seems to be more or less public domain. The doors don't lock and people walk in and out of your room at will. When I was there, one such visitor was a local drunk who staggered in and decided to spend the rest of the night there singing, yelling and slobbering on the floor. There aren't any showers but there is a toilet in the middle of a banana grove. For these conditions you'll pay US$2 per person.

The *Hotel Hannover* is quite a bit nicer. It's got a pleasant shady courtyard, lawn furniture, a restaurant and a disco/bar. The latter, however, causes problems. Unless you want to stay up dancing, you'll stay awake fuming all hours of the night with your head stuffed under your pillow in an attempt to muffle some of the mega-decibel noise.

Places to Eat

There are half a dozen fairly nice restaurants housed in the shacks along the main street. They're all expensive when compared to Cochabamba and they offer little variety but if you don't mind fish or chicken, you'll be able to find nourishment. For good empanadas, snacks, hot drinks and juice, try the market on the main street.

If you like to dance, as I mentioned before, there is an obnoxious disco next to the Hotel Hannover which plays both Latin and European/American music. Those staying at the Hannover may ultimately decide that it's a case of if you can't beat them, join them.

Getting There & Away

The bus that passes through Villa Tunari from Cochabamba continues on to Puerto Villarroel. The fare for the entire trip is US$10.

The return bus to Cochabamba leaves at 7 am sharp from the main street. There are also occasional trucks which leave from the same place at any hour of the day, especially when there's a ship in port.

Although most travellers are going in the other direction, it's also possible (naturally) to travel from Trinidad to Puerto Villarroel by river.

To Trinidad There are three different types of boats which do the run from Puerto Villarroel to Trinidad (or vice versa). The small family-run cargo boats that frequently putter up and down the Río Ichilo normally only travel during the day and reach Trinidad in six to eight days. The larger commercial craft travel day and night and can do the run in about four days. In addition, there is a Dutch-operated passenger ship which does unscheduled runs up and down the river but you have to be lucky to connect with it.

The average fare to Trinidad on any of these boats is about US$30 with food included. The quality of food will vary from boat to boat, of course, but overall the diet will consist largely of fish, dried meat, fruit and turtle eggs. Even if you do buy a passage with food, it's an extremely good idea to carry along some emergency rations just in case the shipboard cuisine proves too unpalatable or unexciting for your tastes. It's also possible to buy passage without food; this should cost about US$15 per person.

A mosquito net is an absolute must, especially if you're on one of those boats that ties up for the night. It would also behove you to carry either drinking water or water purification tablets, preferably iodine-based, to treat the murky river water that you'll certainly be subjected to.

On some boats, a hammock will be required for sleeping due to limited floor space. On others, you can stretch out in a sleeping bag on the deck, the roof or even the cargo. Although hammocks are available in Cochabamba, it may be better to try to buy one from another river traveller going in the opposite direction, or pick one up in Santa Crúz where they're a bit cheaper. Very few boats along this stretch of the Ichilo make cabins available to passengers.

There are three offices in Puerto Villarroel which must be visited by all cargo transporters – the port captain's office, the CEPIMA office and the River Transport Office (*Transportes Fluviales*). A stop by any or all of these should provide you with at least a sketchy idea of when you can expect a boat to leave. Under normal conditions, you shouldn't have more than a three or four-day wait. Often though, military exercises and labour strikes effectively shut down cargo transport and hopeful travellers may end up waiting a very long time.

Trinidad

Like greyhounds chasing the elusive rabbit, the Spanish wandered all over the Americas following whispered legends and rumours of the mystical city of unimaginable wealth which they called *El Dorado*, 'the Gilded'.

One such tale was of Paititi, an incredibly opulent land east of the Andean Cordillera near the source of the Río Paraguay. It was said to be governed by a particularly affluent king called *El Grán Moxo*. Though the would-be looters combed and scoured the region for a trace of the coveted booty, they found but a few primitive and hostile tribes and their muddy jungle villages. There was not a single street paved with gold, nor a single royal treasury brimming with precious gems and metals. In the mid-1600s, they gave up and went searching elsewhere for El Dorado.

The Spanish may have found nothing that interested them in the Moxos, as the region was and is called after the mythical king, but the Jesuits did. The area was

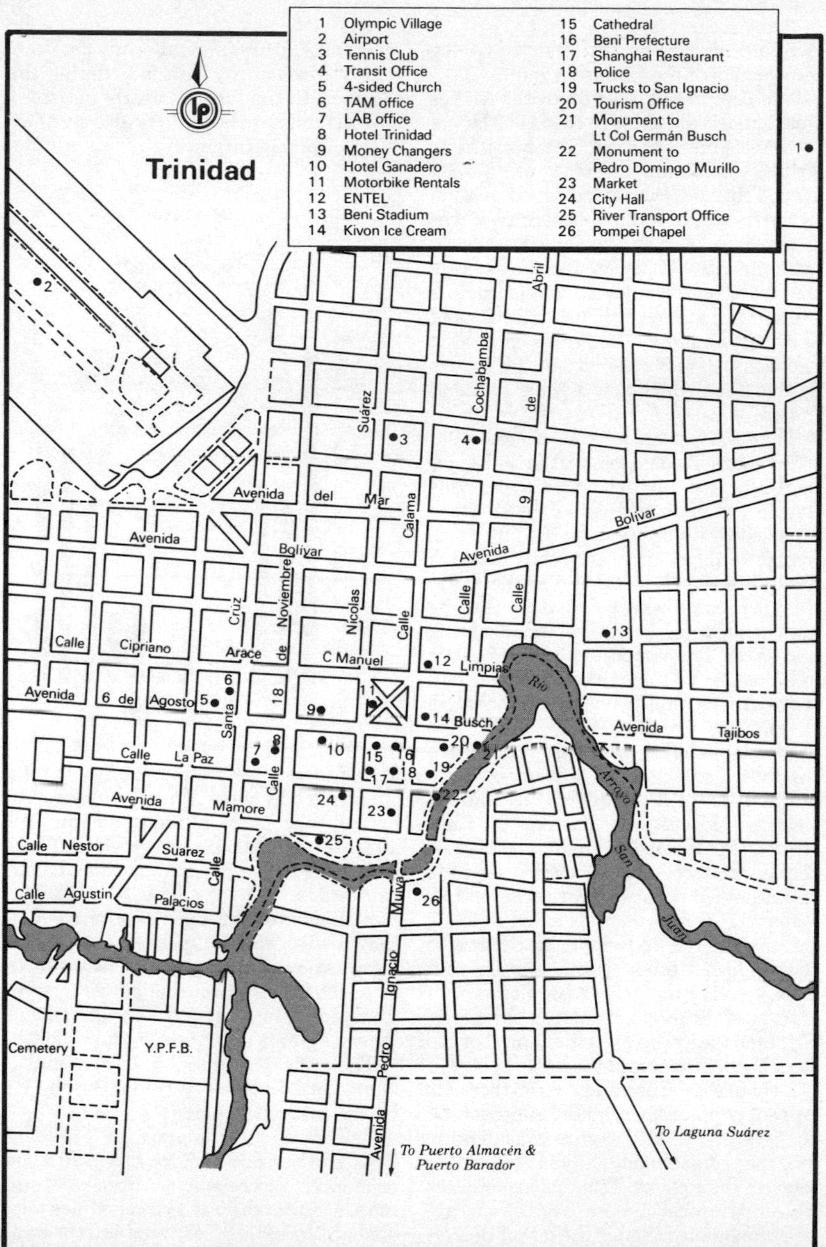
Trinidad
1 Olympic Village
2 Airport
3 Tennis Club
4 Transit Office
5 4-sided Church
6 TAM office
7 LAB office
8 Hotel Trinidad
9 Money Changers
10 Hotel Ganadero
11 Motorbike Rentals
12 ENTEL
13 Beni Stadium
14 Kivon Ice Cream
15 Cathedral
16 Beni Prefecture
17 Shanghai Restaurant
18 Police
19 Trucks to San Ignacio
20 Tourism Office
21 Monument to Lt Col Germán Busch
22 Monument to Pedro Domingo Murillo
23 Market
24 City Hall
25 River Transport Office
26 Pompei Chapel
Avenida del Mar
Avenida Bolívar
Calle Cipriano Arace
C Manuel Limpias
Avenida 6 de Agosto
Calle La Paz
Avenida Mamore
Calle Nestor Suarez
Calle Agustin Palacios
Avenida Busch
Avenida Tajibos
Santa Cruz
18 de Noviembre
Nicolas Suárez
Calle Calama
Calle Cochabamba
Calle 9 de Abril
Calle Muiva
Avenida Pedro Ignacio
Río Arrayo San Juan
Cemetery
Y.P.F.B.
To Puerto Almacén & Puerto Barador
To Laguna Suárez

rich in souls ripe for the plucking by the messengers of the Christian god.

The first Jesuit mission in the Moxos was founded at Loreto in 1675. The city of La Santísima Trinidad, 'the Most Holy Trinity', came into existence on 13 June 1686. Trinidad, the second Jesuit mission in the flatlands of the Southern Beni was founded by Father Cipriano Barace. It was originally constructed on the banks of the Mamoré River at a site 14 km from its present location. In 1769, floods and pestilence along the river made it necessary to move the city to the Arroyo de San Juan which now divides Trinidad in two.

The Jesuits set up a society there similar to the one they would establish in the Llanos de Chiquitos and the Guarayos Hills during the century that followed. They imposed Christianity upon the unwitting 'pagan' inhabitants and taught them European ways – metal and leatherwork, weaving and basketry, writing, reading and printing of literature, woodcarving and so on. They imported herds of cattle and horses to the remote outpost and thanks to the prolific vegetation that grew there, the animals fared well. The descendants of these herds still thrive throughout the vicinity of Trinidad.

The Jesuits also taught the Indians tropical agriculture. Thanks to their efforts, the Beni today produces bananas, coffee, tobacco, cotton, cacao, peanuts and a host of other warm weather crops. When the Jesuits were expelled in 1767, the missionaries and opportunistic settlers that followed brought only slavery and disease to the indigenous peoples.

At an altitude of 237 metres, the city of Trinidad today serves as the capital of the Beni Department and the nerve centre of just about everything that goes on there. Its current population is rapidly approaching 40,000 and it's likely to grow considerably over the years to come. Only 14° of latitude south of the equator, Trinidad experiences a humid tropical climate. The seasons are less pronounced than in the rest of Bolivia and temperatures are uniformly hot year-round. Most of the rain falls during the summer, in the form of nearly incessant downpours, but the winters also see their share of precipitation.

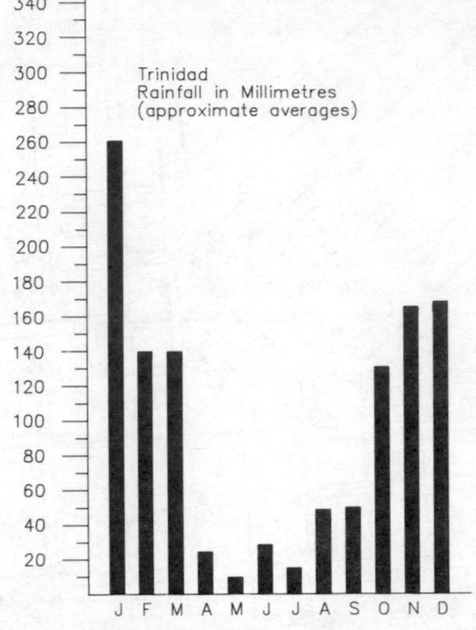

Information

Trinidad does have a tourist office but it's open very odd hours. There's supposed to be someone there all morning and all afternoon but this is rarely the case. Your best bet is to drop by between 2 and 3 pm as it seems to be the hour when they're most likely to turn up. For your trouble, they'll give you some basic but useful information and a city plan. They seem to be much better at touting hotels though, than providing directions to vague out-of-the-way points of interest in the vicinity.

The office is upstairs in the multi-storey building on Avenida Busch, 1½ blocks east of the plaza.

Beware of street names in Trinidad. That is to say, don't get too flustered if you encounter discrepancies from map to map. Many of the city's street names were changed in 1987. Most maps and the local population still use the old names while new maps use the revised names. Fortunately, the city isn't too big and the confusion caused by this will be only short-lived. Of note, Avenida Mariscal Santa Crúz was changed to Avenida Pedro Ignacio Muiva and Calle Junín is now Calle Pedro de la Rocha.

Changing Money Street changers may be found on Avenida 6 de Agosto between Nícolas Suarez and 18 de Noviembre, but they will only exchange cash dollars.

The only place in Trinidad that will even consider changing travellers' cheques is the *Hotel Ganadero*. It helps if you're staying there, of course, but you may be able to persuade them with a hard luck story.

Jungle Trips

Although it's very difficult to arrange a jungle trip on your own, there are several tourism agencies in Trinidad which offer hunting, fishing and safari excursions of varying lengths into the surrounding area. *Turismo Moxos* (tel 21141) at Avenida 6 de Agosto 745 is probably the best known. They arrange trips to San Ignacio de Moxos and Loreto as well as canoe and horseback safaris into lesser-known parts.

Garza Tours (tel 20603) is at Avenida 6 de Agosto 787. *Trinitours* (tel 22766) is on the east side of the main plaza. If you'd like to arrange a tour in advance, *Inditour* (tel 350265 La Paz) is on the bottom floor of the Seguros Bolívar Building, Mariscal Santa Crúz 1289 in La Paz.

River Trips

Of all possible river trips in Bolivia, the ones here provide the greatest diversity of plant species and animal life. They are also the ones that best portray the Amazon mystique and the purity of its solitude.

Although the scenery changes little, it's difficult to get bored with it. The longer you travel through it, the deeper you'll be gazing into the darkness of the forest, the more closely you'll be scanning the riverbanks for signs of movement, the more naturally you'll be conversing with your fellow travellers (including the pink dolphins following the boat), and the more intensely you'll be staring at and calculating the patterns in the water. Free of the pressures and demands of active travelling, you'll have the opportunity to relax and savour some of the things that send people tramping off to places like Bolivia.

Even those not planning to travel by river may find it worthwhile to make the trip to Puerto Almacén to eat fresh fish at one of the riverside restaurants or to Puerto Barador to watch the pink dolphins playing in the water.

If you're looking for transport along the Río Mamoré or Ibaré to Guayaramerín or southward to Puerto Villarroel (Cochabamba) or Río Grande (Santa Crúz), the first place to look is the river transport office, *Transportes Fluviales*, on Mamoré between Pedro de la Rocha and 18 de Noviembre. If they don't have anything, don't despair, there are alternatives.

It would be worthwhile to check out the situation at Puerto Almacén, on the Río Ibaré eight km from town; or Puerto Barador, on the Río Mamoré 12 km from town. There are no buses, and taxis will cost in the vicinity of US$15 each way, but trucks leave frequently from Pedro Ignacio Muiva, 1½ blocks south of the bridge. The fare to either port will cost about US$1 per person.

In Puerto Almacén, check the *Capitanía del Puerto* for departure schedules. In Puerto Barador, you will have to ask about the boat. If you're travelling up the Mamoré to Guayaramerín, you can expect to pay about US$50 per person including food. If you can arrange passage on a boat that travels through the night, mosquito nets are only recommended but if you tie up for the night, they are essential. Be sure to talk with the captain about sleeping arrangements before you set out. Hammocks are available in

Trinidad but if you have a sleeping bag, it will suffice on most runs and will probably be more comfortable since the jungle nights get surprisingly chilly. Food along this route will consist mainly of *massaca*, *charque*, rice, noodles and bananas in every conceivable form. Since the trip will take at least four to five days, some supplemental nourishment will be greatly appreciated.

Laguna Suarez

This hard-bottom lake only five km from town is excellent for swimming, especially on a hot, sticky day. There is no public transport so you'll have to walk, hire a motorbike or hitch.

Places to Stay

The nicest hotel in town, and the one used by those travelling to the Beni on 'business', is the *Hotel Ganadero* on Avenida 6 de Agosto. It rates four stars on the Bolivian system and although it's nice, the service is poor, the staff is sour-faced and it's too expensive. A single room costs US$30, a double is US$35, a triple is US$40, and a suite (suitable for honeymoons, they say) goes for US$50. Officially, foreigners are supposed to pay an additional US$5 but with a little coaxing you'll have no trouble securing the Bolivian rate.

For your money, the Ganadero offers a few luxuries such as a rooftop pool, a bar/night club, air conditioning(!), television and piped-in music. Avoid the laundry service, however, or you'll need medical attention upon receiving the bill.

One of the nicest budget hotels is the *Hotel Yacuma* on the corner of Calle La Paz and Santa Crúz - er - Avenida Muiva. It's nice and clean and a room without bath costs about US$4 per person.

The *Hotel Trinidad*, on Calle 18 de Noviembre, costs US$4.50 per person but it's very nice accommodation for the price (in Trinidad, anyway). There are no private baths available but it offers hot showers and a friendly garden atmosphere.

Places to Eat

Strangely enough, two of the best places to eat at in Trinidad are Chinese restaurants. The *El Dragón*, on Joaquín de la Sierra, and the *Shang Hai*, on Calle Pedro de la Rocha just half a block from the plaza, offer pseudo-Chinese cuisine. A filling meal at one of these places will cost about US$5 per person and after you've sloshed down a cool *Tsingtao* or two, your bill will double. Trinidad is not one of the easier places to be frugal.

Since this is the heart of cattle country, there are a couple of places which specialise in beef. If you'd like to splurge on a nicely-done meat and potatoes ensemble, try the expensive *Hotel Ganadero* dining room. After dinner you can have a drink at the bar beside the rooftop pool and enjoy the commanding view of Trinidad and all the boundless jungle that surrounds it.

For those who must stick to a budget no matter what, there are good snacks and sandwiches available at the eatery on the corner of Nícolas Suarez and 6 de Agosto.

For ice cream try *Kivon* on the corner of Calama and Busch.

If your budget is such that you are shocked by the prices at even the small nondescript greasy spoon establishments scattered throughout the town, there's always the market. The fruit there, especially the grapefruit, oranges and bananas, is very good.

Getting There & Away

From La Paz, LAB has three non-stop flights per week to Trinidad and three flights back to La Paz. There are also air connections on both LAB and TAM to all major and some minor towns and settlements of the Beni and Pando. LAB flies nonstop to Santa Crúz and Cochabamba too.

There is a twice weekly bus that travels to and from Santa Crúz from March to October, but during the rainy season your chances of getting through are very slim indeed.

For another alternative, see 'River Transport' in this section.

Getting Around

If you've got any spunk at all, don't be lured into taking a taxi from the airport to town; it's one of the biggest ripoffs in Bolivia. For the very walkable distance of 1½ km, taxis charge US$10. If you can't bear to walk, however, the taxi is your only option because Trinidad doesn't have a city bus system and it's very difficult to balance a large pack while perched on the back of a motorcycle taxi.

Once you're settled in somewhere, consider hiring a motorbike to get out and see the area around town. The motorbike taxi drivers will all be happy to take the day off and hire out their bikes if the price is right.

This normally hashes out to about US$25 to US$30 per 24-hour day. All you'll need to operate a motorbike is a driving licence from home.

SAN IGNACIO DE MOXOS

This Moxos Indian village 89 km west of Trinidad was founded on 1 November 1689 by the Jesuits and was originally named Loyola, after the founder of the Jesuit order.

The tranquil little village is an agricultural settlement where the people speak a unique indigenous language known locally as *Ignaciano*. Near the town there's a nice lake for swimming or fishing. Each 31 July, San Ignacio stages a fiesta.

Access to San Ignacio is by trucks which leave in the morning from the east end of Calle La Paz near the river. All along the route there is good jungle scenery.

The trip takes four to five hours from March to October, but during the summer the road is impassable and the only way in is by air.

Guayaramerín

Guayaramerín, on the alligator infested Río Mamoré opposite the Brazilian town of Guajará-mirim, is a rail town where the railroad never arrived. The line that would have connected the Río Beni town of Riberalta and the Brazilian city of Pôrto Velho was completed only as far as Guajará-mirim on the other side of the border.

The original intention of this railroad was to compensate Bolivia for the loss of the Acre Territory which Brazil annexed in 1903 and to provide Bolivia with an outlet to the Atlantic via the Río Madeira. Today the line is used only occasionally as a tourist novelty. A museum in Guajará-mirim tells the story of the Madeira-Mamoré railway and houses some artefacts that railroad buffs will especially appreciate.

Guayaramerín is actually the terminus for river transport along the Mamoré because a few km north of the town the river is fraught with rapids and small waterfalls which render it unnavigable.

Historically, the area was a centre of rubber production and Nícolas Suarez, who made a fortune from the boom before the turn of the century, had his rubber exporting headquarters at the head of the rapids. From Cachuela Esperanza he transported the cargo overland past the rapids to the Río Madeira, from where he shipped it downstream to the Amazon, the Atlantic and finally on to markets in Europe and North America.

Guayaramerín today, with a population of about 14,000, is a small river port and an entry point to or from Brazil. It is also the eastern terminus of the best highway in northern Bolivia. This 90-km road connects Guayaramerín with Riberalta and provides a transportation shortcut between the Beni and Mamoré river systems. Despite its good condition it is, like most Bolivian roads, still impassable when it's been raining a lot.

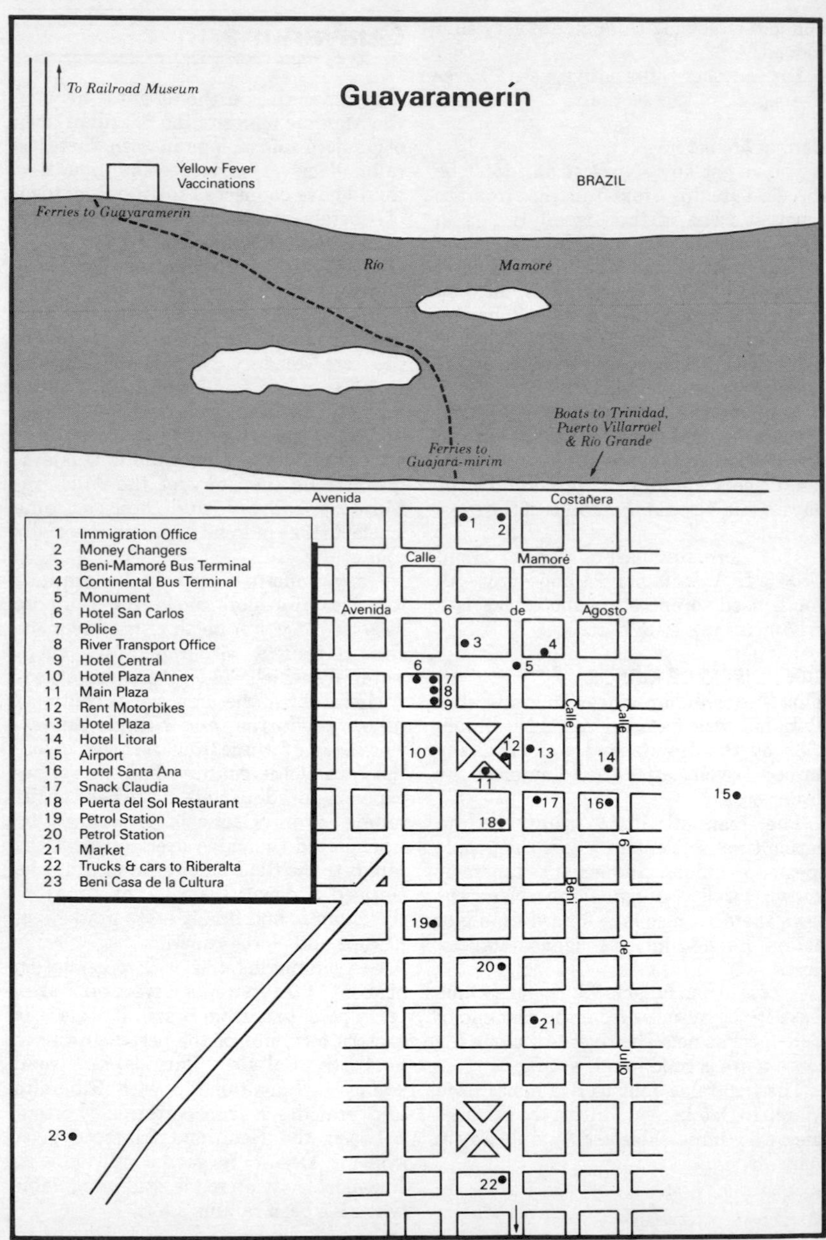
To Railroad Museum
Guayaramerín
Yellow Fever Vaccinations
BRAZIL
Ferries to Guayaramerín
Río
Mamoré
Boats to Trinidad, Puerto Villarroel & Río Grande
Ferries to Guajara-mirim
Avenida
Costañera
Calle
Mamoré
Avenida
6
de
Agosto
Calle
Calle
16
Beni
de
Julio
1 Immigration Office
2 Money Changers
3 Beni-Mamoré Bus Terminal
4 Continental Bus Terminal
5 Monument
6 Hotel San Carlos
7 Police
8 River Transport Office
9 Hotel Central
10 Hotel Plaza Annex
11 Main Plaza
12 Rent Motorbikes
13 Hotel Plaza
14 Hotel Litoral
15 Airport
16 Hotel Santa Ana
17 Snack Claudia
18 Puerta del Sol Restaurant
19 Petrol Station
20 Petrol Station
21 Market
22 Trucks & cars to Riberalta
23 Beni Casa de la Cultura

Unlike Riberalta, Guayaramerín retains a strong frontier atmosphere and is a typically friendly jungle town.

Information

Consulates There is a Brazilian consulate in Guayaramerín, one block south of the main plaza. It's open from 9 am to noon on weekdays. US citizens need visas to travel in Brazil beyond Guajará-mirim.

If you're coming from Brazil into Bolivia and need a visa, there is a Bolivian consulate in Guajará-mirim. It's a small, unassuming cubbyhole upstairs in the *Alfa Hotel* building on Rua Leopoldo de Matos.

It's a bit difficult to find because there's no sign, but the Portuguese words *onde fica* (pronounced AWN-gee FEE-ca), meaning 'where is', will go a long way in Guajará-mirim. In addition, on this side of the river the ubiquitous Spanish *gracias* becomes *obrigado* (bree-GAH-doo) if you're a man, or *obrigada* (bree-GAH-dah) if you're a woman.

The consulate, by the way, is open only on weekday mornings.

Changing Money Travellers' cheques in US$ may be exchanged at the *Hotel San Carlos*. Cash dollars, Brazilian cruzados or bolivianos are changed by a number of aggressive *cambistas* that hang around the port area.

Crossing the Border

Even if you're not planning to travel there, one of the things you can do from Guayaramerín is pop across the Río Mamoré into Brazil and spend a little time in Guajará-mirim.

Motorboats leave from the port on either side of the river every few minutes. The odd thing is that from Bolivia to Brazil they cost 75c per person but going in the opposite direction, the fare is US$1.25. You may travel back and forth across the river at will but if you're going beyond the frontier area, you'll have to deal with border formalities.

If you're leaving Bolivia from here, you have to have your passport stamped at *Migración* near the port in Guayaramerín and again at the *Policia Federal* at 842 Avenida Dr Antonio C da Costa, five blocks from the port in Guajará-mirim.

As usual, everyone needs a yellow fever vaccination certificate to enter Brazil here. If you don't have one, there is a very convenient and relatively sanitary clinic at the port on the Brazilian side. The medical staff use an air gun rather than a hypodermic needle so it's safe. Brazil has one of the worst AIDS problems in the world and they really are trying to do something about it.

The contrast between the twin towns will be striking. While the Bolivian town is a dusty frontier settlement, the Brazilian city is a bustling metropolitan area complete with a variety of restaurants, shops, parks and traffic.

For a little culinary variety, try some Brazilian favourites like *arroz e feijão* (ar-OZ ee fay-ZHOWNG), which is literally rice and beans; *feijoada* (fay-ZHWA-da), a popular meat dish; or *churrasco* (shoo-RAS-coo), which is steak that is infinitely better than what is available across the river. You can wash it all down with *cachaça* (ca-SHA-sa), which is a powerful liquor; or delicious *Brahma* or *Antartica guaraná* soda.

Brazilian junk food is usually fairly greasy, but it's a change. Try *ovo recheado* (AW-voo heh-SHYA-doo), *pasteis* (pas-TAYS), or *kibe* (KEE-bee) doused in *molho de pimento* (MAWL-yoo jhee pee-MAYN-too). The latter is *HOT* sauce made of cayenne pepper and other fiery ingredients and it's very good.

Places to Stay

The nicest and mellowest place to stay in Guayaramerín is undoubtedly the *Hotel Litoral* near the airport. It's got private baths, refreshing tepid showers, is very clean and it's a bargain at only US$5 per person. In the courtyard they've got a snack bar and a television which seems to be always playing Brazilian *novelas* (soap operas) to a full house.

Across the street, the *Hotel Santa Ana* offers pretty much the same amenities but they charge US$6 per person.

The *Hotel Central* and *Hotel Plaza* both cost US$5 per person but rooms are without private bath. They're a bit run down and only offer cold showers. Overall, I'd deem them not good value for the money.

The *Hotel San Carlos* is the upmarket place to stay. It's got a very nice restaurant, a swimming pool and hot water at all times. A single room costs US$15; a one-bed double is US$20; a two-bed double goes for US$25; and a gimmicky room called the Suite will cost US$30. All rooms have private baths, of course.

Places to Eat

A good place for breakfast or dinner is the *Hotel San Carlos* dining room which is run by Brazilians and offers good if overpriced food.

The best quick and typical meals in town can be had at the *Snack Claudia* just off the main plaza. They've got good variety and reasonable prices (for the Beni, anyway).

The *Puerto del Sol* is usually recommended by locals but I reckon it's grossly overrated. The food is only average and serious 'gringo pricing' is the norm.

Getting There & Away

LAB has three flights a week from La Paz which make a stop in Trinidad en route. From Guayaramerín, they continue on to Riberalta and then return to La Paz.

From the port, ships leave almost daily for Trinidad, four to seven days up the Mamoré. For information regarding departures, the port captain's office has a notice board which lists any activity in or out of town. Further details about this route can be found in the section on Trinidad.

There are two bus companies in Guayaramerín, *Transportes Beni-Mamoré* and *Transportes Continental*. In theory, they each leave twice daily at 9 am and again at 3.30 pm, but this is most often not the case. Normally, only one or the other will leave once a day and if the tickets are not sold out the run is cancelled completely and irate would-be passengers are given a lame excuse.

The excuse I received was that a bridge was damaged and the road was closed until the following day. In the next breath, they suggested I try to find a truck to Riberalta, which I did. The damaged bridge which had closed the road was not only not damaged it was non-existent.

When the bus is running, it costs US$5 per person for the two-hour journey to Riberalta. There are trucks which leave from the main street 2½ blocks beyond the market (see map) which cost the same but make the trip in less time. If you'd like to travel a bit more comfortably, cars charge US$7.50 and you're spared exposure to the choking red dust that seems to get into everything.

From Guajará-mirim across the river, there are buses several times daily to Pôrto Velho from where it's possible to find transport to anywhere in Brazil. The border city is also served by *Varig/Cruzeiro* airlines which connect it to other Brazilian urban centres, mostly via Pôrto Velho.

Getting Around

You'll quickly discover that there are no automobile taxis in Guayaramerín, but then the town is so small you can walk just about anywhere you'd like to go.

Those who want to do some exploring of the surrounding area can hire a motorbike from the main plaza for about US$20 per 24-hour day. A particularly nice place to visit is the natural swimming hole near the tranca four km west of town along the Riberalta road. The water is clear and refreshing and it's a favourite local picnic spot.

Riberalta

It seems that Riberalta boasts more private vehicles per capita than any other town in Bolivia and all these vehicles come in the form of tiny, buzzing Japanese motorbikes. The Riberaltans' idea of a night out on the town is to pile as many people onto the bike as possible, cruise down to the centre and spend a few hours doing laps around the main plaza.

If you sit at the sidewalk café beside the plaza, drink a few beers and stare at all this activity long enough, you'll begin to get the sensation that the needle playing your life's recording has somehow gotten stuck in one groove. The same faces, the same bikes, the same events are played out over and over!

The city of Riberalta has a rapidly-increasing population that is currently about 50,000. This is one of the few hot, sticky, dusty and bug-infested South American towns that can, nevertheless, be accurately described as pleasant (that's if pouring rain isn't turning the place into a muddy quagmire).

It's an educated and relatively modern town with a new church on the square, social clubs, three cinemas and a generally mellower attitude than most other Bolivian places. It sits at an elevation of 175 metres on the banks of the Río Beni near its confluence with the Madre de Diós, making it a transportation hub of sorts.

Originally, Riberalta was one of the centres of rubber production in northern Bolivia and during the rubber boom it thrived. When that industry declined due to increasing competition from Asian countries and the development of synthetics, Riberalta resorted to growing, producing and exporting oil from Brazil nuts, an enterprise which still goes on today.

Information

Changing Money Although there is no place in town to exchange travellers' cheques, Brother Casimiri at the vichary (see map) will change cash and personal cheques. Several small stores around town will also change cash but at a lower rate.

Things To Do

If you're travelling by boat to or from Puerto Linares or Rurrenabaque, you'll probably be spending a day or two in Riberalta. There's not really a lot for the tourist to do there but you can hire a motorbike and explore the surrounding jungle tracks and trails or go for a swim in the river. Before attempting the latter, however, it's probably best to seek out a piranha-free area. The locals will know where it's safe to swim.

At Puerto Beni-Mamoré, within walking distance of the centre, you can watch the hand-carving and construction of small boats and dugouts by skilled craftsmen who've been at it for many years. In addition, two km east of the plaza along Ejército Nacional you can visit an old rubber plantation, see coffee and Brazil nuts being roasted and visit a carpentry.

Above all else, Riberalta is one of those places that simply invites you to kick back and relax. During the heat of the day, all strenuous activity is suspended and the locals tend to search out the nearest hammock. Tourists would probably be advised to follow their example if they don't want to suffer heat-related maladies.

On every clear night though, the place comes to life with the previously-mentioned cruising motorbikes. Amid the buzz of activity, however, don't fail to notice the spectacular Amazonian sunsets which can normally be counted upon to provide an impressive show.

Places to Stay

Undoubtedly the nicest place to call home in Riberalta is the *Residenciál Los Reyes* near the airport. The attitude of this place is so friendly and helpful and the establishment itself is so atypically clean that I'd recommend it to anyone passing

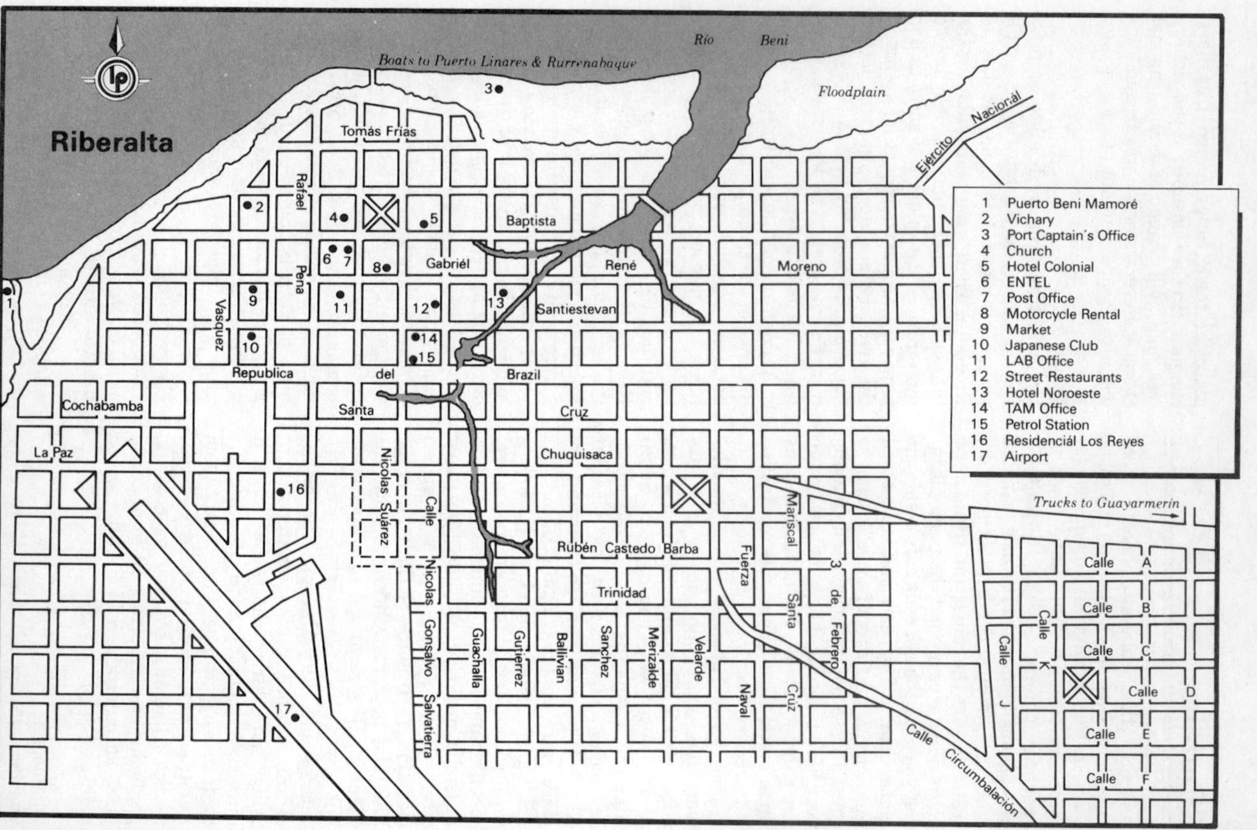
Riberalta
1 Puerto Beni Mamoré
2 Vichary
3 Port Captain's Office
4 Church
5 Hotel Colonial
6 ENTEL
7 Post Office
8 Motorcycle Rental
9 Market
10 Japanese Club
11 LAB Office
12 Street Restaurants
13 Hotel Noroeste
14 TAM Office
15 Petrol Station
16 Residenciál Los Reyes
17 Airport
Río Beni
Floodplain
Boats to Puerto Linares & Rurrenabaque
Ejército Nacionál
Trucks to Guayarmerín
Calle A
Calle B
Calle C
Calle D
Calle E
Calle F
Calle K
Calle J
Calle Circumbalación
3 de Febrero
Mariscal Santa Cruz
Fuerza Naval
Velarde
Merizalde
Sanchez
Ballivian
Gutierrez
Guachalla
Calle Nicolas Gonsalvo
Salvatierra
Nicolas Suárez
Baptista
René Gabriél
Moreno
Santiestevan
Cruz
Chuquisaca
Rubén Castedo Barba
Trinidad
Republica del Brazil
Santa
Tomás Frías
Rafael Pena
Vasquez
Cochabamba
La Paz

through town. It costs US$7.50 per person for a room with private bath or US$5 per person without. For the money, you also get hot or cold showers, fans, a meticulously clean snack bar, free coffee and a cool and shady area to while away the heat of the afternoon.

If that's full, you can stay at the *Hotel Noroeste* for the same price but it's not nearly as nice, lacking most of the items listed as assets at the Los Reyes.

The *Hotel Colonial*, though friendly, has quite a few problems, not the least of which is that it's positively screaming with tiny 747s. The helpful owner will be happy to fumigate your room if you request it but the chemical leaves a foul smell and a floor littered with corpses of the dead and dying. It can't be too healthy for humans, either. In addition to mosquito problems, the showers are definitely sub-standard, the rooms are sub-clean and there's not even a fan to circulate the stifling, stagnant air.

The only redeeming feature about this place that tries to pass itself off as a nice hotel is the breakfast. For US$1.25 per person, you can eat steak, eggs, biscuits with jam and butter, fruit, coffee and just about anything else you'd care to order. In case you're not familiar with prices in the Beni, this would be considered the best bargain in town. The rooms, however, are another story. At US$7.50 per person (with bath), they're anything but a good deal.

Places to Eat

The *Restaurant Oriental* just off the plaza serves good inexpensive lunches but there's little variety. The name is a little misleading as 'oriental' in Spanish means 'eastern', as in 'eastern' Bolivia, so don't go expecting fried rice and sweet & sour pork! Their repertoire includes egg sandwiches, lomo and chicken with the usual trimmings.

The *Cola* on the main plaza is very popular with the locals but it's more of a sandwich/snack shop than a restaurant. The *Club Social*, also on the plaza, offers a variety of nicer cuisine, including well-prepared steak, chicken and fish, but their attitude is a bit high-strung.

The ice cream shop next door to the Club Social is very good for juices, milkshakes, flan and sandwiches as well as ice cream. The sidewalk seating area also provides an advantageous place to watch the nightly Kawasaki derby on the plaza.

Two blocks away from the plaza there are numerous outdoor street restaurants, or should I say in-the-middle-of-the-street restaurants, which serve a variety of inexpensive dishes in a barbecue-style atmosphere.

As I mentioned in the 'Places to Stay' section, the *Hotel Colonial* is unsurpassed for breakfast.

While you're visiting the northern Beni, you may want to try *carne de jochi* which is a local delicacy. Jochi, which in English is called agouti, is a large rodent which inhabits these jungles.

For an unusual meal, try the *Japanese Club* near the market. They are only open intermittently but they do a variety of Chinese, Japanese and local dishes.

Getting There & Away

By air, both LAB and TAM serve Riberalta and there are several weekly flights to La Paz, Santa Crúz, Trinidad, Guayaramerín and Cobija but during the rainy season you may well be stuck here for some time. The Riberaltans tell me that during the summer, flights on both lines are often cancelled for weeks on end.

When the road to Guayaramerín is closed, the only way out of Riberalta is up the Río Beni and even then, heavy rains may wreak havoc with the port area and eliminate that option too. In short, Riberalta is probably best avoided between the soggy months of November and March.

Buses run to Guayaramerín daily at 6.30 am and cost US$5. Although both flotas *Continental* and *Beni-Mamoré* schedule the trip, normally only one or the other actually goes. Alternately, wait for a truck just outside of town along the road toward Guayaramerín. This dusty ride also costs US$5 per person.

A road to Cobija is scheduled to open sometime soon! Reportedly, half-track military vehicles have already been able to do the trip. Another penetration-standard road is in the works to connect Riberalta to La Paz.

Boats leave frequently from the port on the Río Beni for the five-day minimum trip to Puerto Linares in La Paz Department. From Puerto Linares, it's only a matter of finding a truck to get to La Paz, which is very easy. The Beni, arguably the most important river in Bolivia, passes through countless twisting km of virgin jungle. This is the longest single river trip available in Bolivia. The port captain's office, where departure information is posted, is found at the northern end of Calle Guachalla. Expect to wait no longer than a day or two for a boat going your way.

Getting Around

Although everything in Riberalta is within reasonable walking distance of the centre, there are motorbike taxis which will take you anywhere in town for 25c. It's also possible to hire a motorbike to check out the surrounding river and rainforest country. There are plenty of tracks and trails cut across the landscape and it's nice to explore a little and see what you may find.

Motorbikes may be hired from the *taxistas* which hang out on the corner of Nícolas Suarez and René Moreno. The going rate is about US$25 per 24-hour day.

Cobija

Cobija, the capital of the remote Pando Department, was once the booming rubber-producing centre of north-western Bolivia. When the rubber industry declined, however, Cobija's fortunes came crashing down heavily with it. The town was reduced to a forgotten hamlet of 5000 people, tucked away in the furthermost corner of the republic. The only map I could find of Cobija was about 10 years old and many of the streets marked thereon were hopelessly overgrown with jungle. If this trend continues, the town may be swallowed up in just a few years.

Although there are a few interesting things to see in the area, including rubber and Brazil nut plantations, and a number of lakes and places to view jungle wildlife, transportation is difficult and Cobija's hinterland is not easily accessed.

The very adventurous can hire a motorised dugout and head off upriver from nearby Porvenir to visit some of the very primitive Indian villages around the Peruvian border but this is not recommended without a guide and some experience at navigating overgrown and convoluted tropical waterways.

Cobija serves as a port of entry with Brasileia and Acre in Brazil across the International Bridge. Cobija at present has no surface link with the rest of Bolivia but a highway to Riberalta should be open by the time this book is published. Another to La Paz has been bulldozed but remains impassable.

With 1770 mm of precipitation falling annually, Cobija is the rainiest spot in Bolivia.

Information

Consulate For US citizens and others who need a visa to enter Brazil, there is a consulate in Cobija on the corner of Calle Beni and Fernandez Molina.

Immigration Bolivian Immigration is located in the Prefectural building on the main plaza. The office opens at 9 am on weekdays.

Changing Money Street changers will change cash dollars, bolivianos and Brazilian cruzados. To exchange travellers'

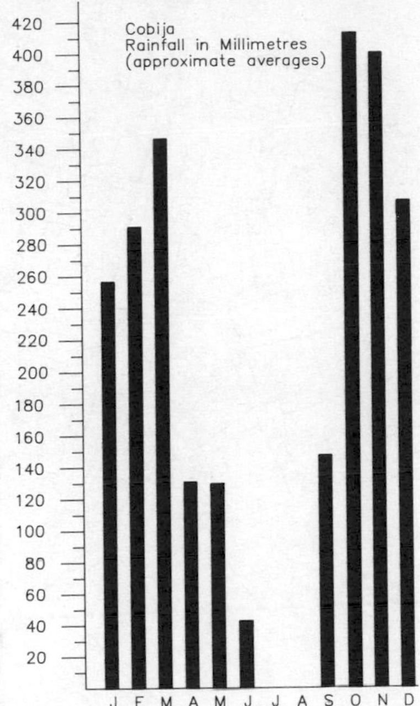

cheques, you'll have to try the jewellery shop on Calle Cornejo opposite the small plaza or *Casa Mendez* on Calle Beni.

If you're exchanging money in Brasileia, over the border, be sure to check the bank for the official rate before handing over any money to a shopkeeper. On the black market you should be able to get 20 to 40% higher than the official rate but you won't be able to exchange travellers' cheques.

Crossing the Border

If you're going to or coming from Brazil, you'll have to get entry/exit stamps from the *Migración* in Cobija and the *Policia Federal* in a suburb of Brasileia.

A yellow fever vaccination certificate is required of everyone entering Brazil from Cobija but at the time of writing, there was no vaccination clinic in Brasileia so you'll have to track down a private physician if your records are not in order.

Since it's a rather long up and down walk from Cobija across the bridge to Brasileia, you may want to take the big orange bus that runs back and forth across the border every 45 minutes or so. It costs US$1 and drops you about one km down the road from the Policia Federal. From there, you'll probably have to take a taxi to the *Rodoviario* (haw-doo-VYAHR-yu), the bus terminal, where you can find buses to Río Branco and from there to points all over Brazil.

Places to Stay

The *Hotel Prefectural* which costs US$7.50 per person is a bit run down but it's still the nicest accommodation in town and you'll be particularly grateful for the empathy of the person who installed the electric fans in each room. Only cold showers are available but all rooms have private baths.

The *Residencial Frontera* is clean and relatively inexpensive at US$3.50 per person. No private baths are available. *Residencial Cobija* is similar in quality but it only costs US$3 per person and it's the cheapest nice place to stay in Cobija. Although *Alojamiento 25 de Noviembre* costs less, it's a nasty, claustrophobic little place and should be avoided if possible.

The *Hostería Sucre* is very pleasant but it's a little expensive considering they only offer shared baths. It does have a peaceful common area with refrigerator, refreshments and cold drinking water (boiled) available at all times. With an American-style breakfast included, it costs US$10 per person. Without the breakfast, it's US$7.50.

Places To Eat

Finding food in Cobija can be very tricky. For breakfast, nothing can compare to the *Hostería Sucre* where they serve up papayas, bananas, scrambled eggs, coffee, chocolate, bread, jam, butter and so on.

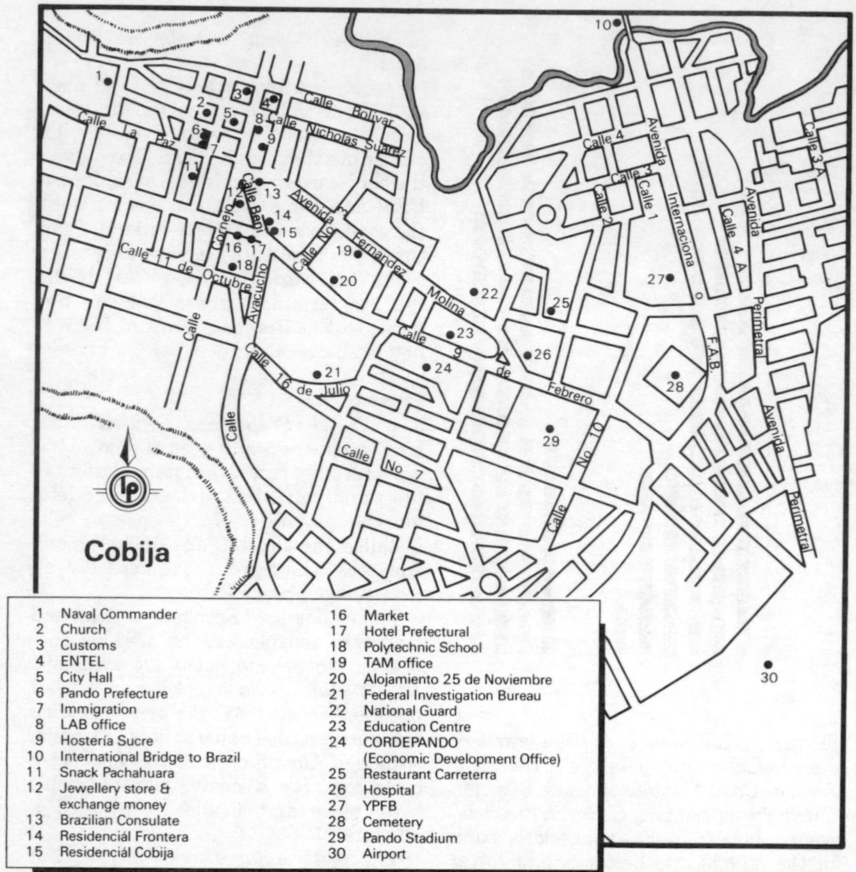

For US$2.50 per person, you'll get more than you can eat.

Probably the best general restaurant, but also the most expensive, is the *Paceño*. It was last seen on the corner of Cornejo and 6 de Agosto but it's going to move to Calle Racua sometime in the near future. Unfortunately, the management of this place is rather disagreeable.

Snack Pachahuara is a good place for a quick sandwich, empanada or cold drink.

The mysterious *Restaurant Carreterra* is advertised all over town but it's located in the maze of trails between the YPFB plant and Avenida Fernandez Molina. It is reputed to be good but I never found it open. Maybe you'll have better luck.

In the early morning, the market sells some pretty good chicken empanadas but that's about all in the way of prepared food. Lots of tinned Brazilian products are available though, so if you have a stove, you may be able to whip up something different. Most people would not want to touch the 'fresh' meat that's available in the market – but there is a variety of fresh fruit and vegetables.

Getting There & Away

LAB and TAM both serve Cobija and have twice-weekly connections to Riberalta and Trinidad. TAM has a thrice-weekly flight to La Paz, but from November to March the run is usually cancelled and often several weeks pass without a flight. LAB also goes to La Paz but with four intermediate stops – Riberalta, Guayaramerín, Trinidad and Cochabamba.

If you fly into Trinidad, don't stand around too long waiting for your luggage to be unloaded. It's all piled into the back of a pickup and taken to the appropriate airline office in town (see map) for collection there.

As was mentioned before, there is no surface transportation from Cobija to the rest of Bolivia without travelling literally thousands of km through Brazil. If you're headed toward Brazil, there are buses that leave four times daily from the terminal in Brasileia. All buses go to Río Branco, the capital of Acre, but from there it's easy to find buses to Pôrto Velho which has connections to Manaus and all of Brazil.

Mountaineering in Bolivia

Climbing in Bolivia, like the country itself, is a lesson in extremes. The weather can be impossibly wet or as dry as any in the world. Even in the dry season temperatures can fluctuate over 40°C in a single day of climbing. Roads lead close to many of the fine peaks, but in a land of strikes, crowded public transport and constant flux, just finding the truck or bus to get you there can lead to headaches rivalling those caused by soroche.

Whatever the frustrations though, the beauty and variety of the aptly named Cordillera Real (Royal Range) more than makes up for them. Most people who wish to explore Bolivia's mountains will find the 150 km long range just east of La Paz offers the easiest access and most spectacular climbing of any in the country.

Providing delightful contrast, the range separates the stark Altiplano on its west from the fertile green Yungas falling away to the Amazon on its east. To the north lies the inaccessible Cordillera Apolobamba and to the south the more distant Quimsa Crúz, which boasts Bolivia's best climbing rock. Six peaks of the Cordillera Real rise above 6000 metres and there are many more gems in the 5000-metre range. While few are 'walk-ups', due to the altitude, glaciers, ice or steep snow, most are well within reach of the average climber.

During the dry season, May to September, the Cordillera is blessed with some of the most stable weather a hiker or climber could ask for. Precipitation is minimal and winds are mild. Due to the elevation and lack of cloud cover, however, temperatures are extreme with daytime highs of up to 30°C at the lower elevations and night time lows of -15°C above 5000 metres. These conditions lead to incredibly stable snow conditions so the Real is a good place to learn snow climbing on the peaks or to perfect technique on one of the steeper faces or gullies.

The few dangers of climbing in Bolivia mainly relate to the altitude and the lack of any kind of rescue possibilities. Because the Cordillera is relatively easy to access, and acclimatisation doesn't occur over the long period of time it takes to reach the high altitude, soroche is a constant threat. (Refer to the section on soroche under Health in the Facts for the Visitor chapter.)

Mountain Sickness, by Peter Hackett, is one of the most practical books available, as it's field oriented and easily transportable. I carry it with me whenever I go high.

Luckily, those spending much time in Bolivia before climbing will have a good head start on acclimatisation. Those just arriving would do well to spend at least a few days to a week in La Paz or hiking in the nearby area, staying as high as possible.

Once you're acclimatised to the Altiplano's relatively thin air, remember there are still 2500 more metres of even thinner air lurking above, so climb smart. Drink plenty of fluids (three to four litres daily), sleep as low as possible and descend at any sign of serious altitude sickness *before* a headache, troubled breathing or lethargy turn into life threatening pulmonary or cerebral oedema.

Don't forget to always treat your water. I don't know how many times I've been miles from any habitation or road, just below the peaks, thinking the water would be safe from any animal wastes, only to see llamas or alpacas way up above me, even as high as the snowfields and glaciers. Far from any roads or towns is no place to get the trots.

If you should get sick or injured, rescue cannot be expected. While many of the routes are frequently climbed, solitude is still one of the joys of Bolivian alpinism, so be prepared to get yourself out of trouble. Rescue groups or helicopters simply do not exist.

MAPS & GUIDES

Planning can be one of the most frustrating parts of climbing in Bolivia. Maps are of poor quality, miserably small scale and often difficult to obtain. Even the elevations of the peaks is murky with reported altitudes varying as much as 600 metres.

Bradt Enterprises (409 Beacon St, Boston, MA 02115 USA) or Overmead (Monument Lane, Chalfont St Peter, Bucks SL9 OHY, England) sometimes carry topographical maps useful to the aspiring Bolivian alpinist.

Michael Kelsey's *Guide to the World's Mountains* (310 East 950 South, Springville, UT 84663 USA) has maps and trip descriptions that are helpful.

The *American Alpine Club Journal* is a good source for particular route information. For alpine history of the area look for the long out of print *Climbing and Exploration in the Bolivian Andes* by Conway or *Summit* magazine between the July-August 1982 and the July-August 1983 issues.

Once you're in Bolivia maps are far easier to obtain than they used to be when you had to visit the intimidating Bolivian military headquarters. The civilian map office in La Paz is at the corner of Colombia and 16 de Julio in the Edificio Camara Nacional de Comercio. Also check Los Amigos del Libro, 1430 Calle Mercado in La Paz, for the *Southern Cordillera Real* a dated but excellent climbing guide or, if you're competent in Spanish, *La Cordillera Real de los Andes, Bolivia*.

EQUIPMENT

Scrambling in Bolivia's Andes can be done with little more than what the average adventure traveller normally carries – a sturdy pair of shoes, a good layering of clothes, hat and gloves, water bottle, day pack, etc.

If the higher peaks beckon, however, more serious equipment will make climbing safer and easier. Bring any climbing gear with you as what little is to be found in Bolivia is expensive and/or poor quality. Remember, you'll have to carry this stuff on the plane, bus, truck, mule or back, so 'light is right'. While you're not climbing, your gear can be left with a reliable hotel. Following is a list of general recommendations for clothing and gear.

Clothing

Loose fitting layers are best for the constantly changing temperatures. A sturdy, dark, wind coat that can take the abuse of buses, trucks, mules and the resulting constant dust is important. Bolivia is one of the few places in South America where down is practical.

Camping

Ensolite pad – important for insulating from cold or rocky ground.

Sleeping bag – down or synthetic, good to –5°C (you can always put on more clothes if it gets colder!).

Tent – useful for occasional snotty weather, adds warmth.

Pack – a large capacity, internal frame (external frames exposed to Bolivian buses don't last long).

Water bottles – at least two one-litre containers.

Head lamp – important for those pre-dawn starts; bring plenty of batteries and bulbs as locally available ones are of poor quality.

Food

While the convenience food you may be used to is not easily available, perfectly adequate dried foods such as *Knorr* soups, rice, instant coffee, etc. can be bought locally. Those going to Bolivia for just a few weeks climbing may want to bring freeze-dried; otherwise, buy it at the markets.

Cooking

Kerosene or multi-fuel stoves such as MSR are best as white gas and butane gas cartridges are difficult to obtain.

Large pot for melting snow and another for cooking (mixing the two can produce some pretty funny-looking water which means you don't drink as much which can lead to dehydration which can lead to mountain sickness which – you get the picture).

A teflon fry pan is a nice luxury for frying up the ubiquitous potato.

Water purification – the system of your choice; remember giardia, dysentery, hepatitis and all their ilk lurk in the mountains, too.

Climbing

Amount and kind of gear obviously depends on just how serious you want to get, but the following would suffice for the normal routes on almost any peak in the Real. Remember, most routes are over snow and/or ice, often in glacier form. This gear won't do you any good if you don't know how to use it. Climbing, like most camping gear, can often be sold to locals or other travellers for more than you could get back home.

Harness or webbing.

Three to five 'biners, one locking.

Ice axe and protector.

Crampons and protectors.

Nine or 11 mm rope.

Two or three ice screws and snow pickets or flukes.

Ice hammer – particularly for the more difficult climbs (Condoriri, Illampu, Illimani, Ancohuma).

Prusiks – for crevasse rescue.

Sun protection

Top quality sun cream and glasses are essential, don't scrimp here! A baseball hat with bandana makes an effective 'Lawrence of Arabia' sun shield.

ROUTES

Following are some trip descriptions for five of Bolivia's more famous mountains. Access and route information may change overnight so always ask for recent information. The *Club Andino Boliviano* (refer to the La Paz chapter for more info) is a good source for current information.

Illimani This 6460 metre giant overlooking La Paz is probably the most famous of Bolivia's peaks. It was first climbed by a party led by Conway, the pioneer alpinist of the 19th century.

From La Paz, take a bus or truck going to Palca, Ventilla or towards the Bolsa Negra Mine. Buses leave for Ventilla from the Plaza Belzu. Alternately, try to catch a truck from the Transito just past Calacota (or Cota-Cota).

From Ventilla head east toward the Bolsa Negra Mine for about 15 km. There will be a right turn leading to the Urania Mine; take this very deteriorated road for about 27 km to an old bridge with a hut ruin above.

The climb is fairly straightforward. Follow the faint path up through rock and scree to the major ridge between the glaciers staying on its right side at first, later running the ridge crest. After about eight hours a plateau called *Nido de Condores*, 'Nest of the Condors', will be gained. This is the normal camping spot at about 5600 metres. The major difficulty is the ice fall at about 6000 metres. The normal route seems to be around to its left but when we were there, we found it more direct to bypass it on the right. From the ridge top, turn south for an easy if breathless stroll to the summit.

Huayna Potosí The 6088-metre high Huayna Potosí is probably the most popular major peak in Bolivia due to its ease of access and imposing beauty. Buses and trucks make the regular run to the mine of Milluni, via Alto La Paz.

From the Transito at Milluni it is about six km up to Zongo Pass and another two to Laguna Zongo along a fairly well frequented road. From the lake, cross the dam and follow the pipe to a small reservoir, continuing up to a moraine. Stay left of the ice fall and gain the glacier, trending right, towards the snow ridge. Ascend this to between 5500 and 5700 metres where there are several places to camp (the higher ones receive more sun).

It is about six hours from there to the summit, staying right if crevasses warrant. This is the easiest of the climbs described in this section and is suitable for beginner climbers.

Condoriri Condoriri is a beautifully

sculpted mountain with twin wing-like ridges flowing from either side of the summit pyramid. At 'only' 5648 metres this is the smallest of the peaks discussed here, but arguably the most difficult. Without a vehicle, access is not easy.

Take a bus or truck to Milluni, via Alto La Paz. From the Transito charter a vehicle or walk west about 24 km to Tuni Lake. From there follow the rough road which circles south around the lake and continues up a drainage trending north. Follow this to a second lake where there are several good campsites. A saddle to the left (west) of the slopes above the lake will allow you to skip the icefall and give easy access to the glacier. Head to the summit pyramid, back again to the right, to access a gully in the front edge of the east face. This will take you through a rock band to a notch, and from there to the summit ridge and on to the top. The summit ridge is very exposed with huge, airy sheets of rime.

Ancohuma This is the highest peak in the Sorata Massif, towering to 6427 metres in the remote northern edge of the Cordillera Real. It was not climbed until 1919 and still remains very challenging.

The peak is accessed via the tropical paradise of Sorata. From this lovely little town you will want to hire a truck for the long traverse to the Candeleria Mine. A few kilometres further is the quiet village of Cooco where a llama train can be hired to take you to the lake basin east of the peaks at about 4500 metres. It will take at least two days for these various transportation arrangements to get you to the lakes.

From there head west up to the glacier following the drainage up through loose moraine. Camp should be made below the north ridge, the normal route. After a circuitous path through a crevasse field, a steep pitch or two of ice will gain the north ridge. An exposed but fairly easy ridge walk will take you to the summit.

A fascinating way back to La Paz is via the 'Gold Diggers Way', exposing an incredible cross-section of Bolivia from the glaciated heights to the jungle lowlands. From Ancoma (halfway between Sorata and Cooco) follow the old Inca trail for about four days down the Tipuani Valley to the mining town of Unutuluni where a truck can be caught to Guanay. From there buses go on back to La Paz. It is best to have the climbing gear sent back to Sorata rather than heave it all the way out the up-and-down route to Unutuluni.

Sajama Those wishing to climb at some time other than the dry season may wish to try their luck on Sajama, the hulking volcano south-west of La Paz on the northern edge of the Atacama Desert. At 6520 metres it is Bolivia's highest peak, challenging mainly because of its difficult access and high altitude.

Access is usually via Oruro and Turco to Lagunas or the town of Sajama. It can also be reached along the Arica road from Patacamaya between Oruro and La Paz. The mountain is climbed from the north, south (from Lagunas), or west (from Sajama) with two to three days necessary to reach the summit. Dust and sandstorms can be a problem when the wind kicks up. Carry lots of water, though once on the snow cap there will be plenty available in the form of ice.

There are many other peaks to entice the experienced climber and whether you choose one of those described here or one of the lesser known and less-travelled ones, climbing in the Bolivian mountains is always an adventure.

Author's Note

Todd Miner, who prepared this section is coordinator of Alaska Wilderness Studies at the University of Alaska Anchorage. He leads frequent trekking and climbing expeditions to the Andes and offers mountaineering courses there for those who wish to travel economically. For more information, contact him at Alaska Wilderness Studies, 2533 Providence Drive, Anchorage, Alaska 97508 USA.

Index

Abbreviations

Argentina (A)
Chile (C)
Peru (Peru)
Paraguay) (P)

Map references in **bold** type

MAPS

Temperature

To convert °C to °F multipy by 1.8 and add 32

To convert °F to °C subtract 32 and multipy by ·55

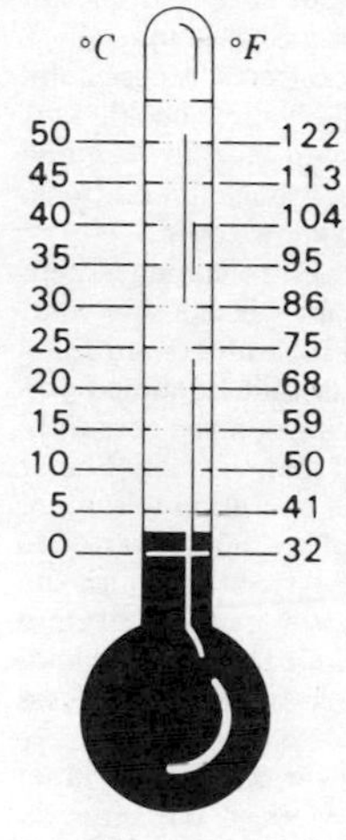

Length, Distance & Area

	multipy by
inches to centimetres	2.54
centimetres to inches	0.39
feet to metres	0.30
metres to feet	3.28
yards to metres	0.91
metres to yards	1.09
miles to kilometres	1.61
kilometres to miles	0.62
acres to hectares	0.40
hectares to acres	2.47

Weight

	multipy by
ounces to grams	28.35
grams to ounces	0.035
pounds to kilograms	0.45
kilograms to pounds	2.21
British tons to kilograms	1016
US tons to kilograms	907

A British ton is 2240 lbs, a US ton is 2000 lbs

Volume

	multipy by
Imperial gallons to litres	4.55
litres to imperial gallons	0.22
US gallons to litres	3.79
litres to US gallons	0.26

5 imperial gallons equals 6 US gallons
a litre is slightly more than a US quart, slightly less than a British one

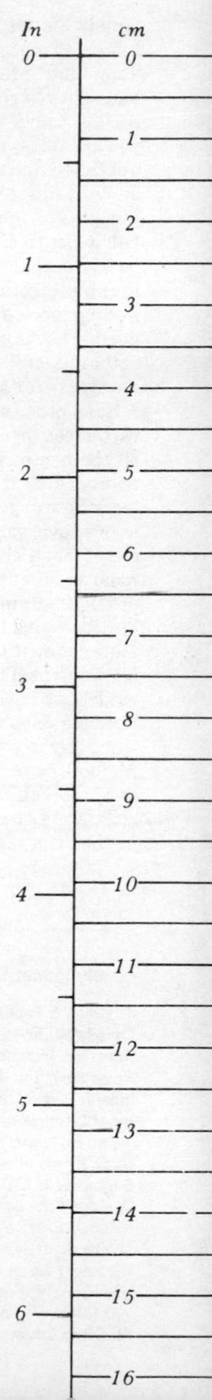

Lonely Planet

Lonely Planet published its first book in 1973. Tony and Maureen Wheeler had made a lengthy overland trip from England to Australia and, in response to numerous 'how do you do it?' questions, Tony wrote and they published *Across Asia on the Cheap*. It became an instant local best-seller and inspired thoughts of a second travel guide. A year and a half in South-East Asia resulted in their second book, *South-East Asia on a Shoestring*, which they put together in a backstreet Chinese hotel in Singapore in 1975. The 'yellow book', as it quickly became known, soon became *the* guide to the region and has gone through five editions, always with its familiar yellow cover.

Soon other writers started to come to them with ideas for similar books – books that went off the beaten track and took an adventurous approach to travel, books that 'assumed you knew how to get your luggage off the carousel,' as one reviewer described them. Lonely Planet grew from a kitchen table operation to a spare room and then to its own office. It also started to develop an international reputation as the Lonely Planet logo began to appear in more and more countries. In 1982 *India – a travel survival kit* won the Thomas Cook award for the best guidebook of the year.

These days there are over 60 Lonely Planet titles. Nearly 30 people work at our office in Melbourne, Australia and another half dozen at our US office in Oakland, California.

At first Lonely Planet specialised exclusively in the Asia region but these days we are also developing major ranges of guidebooks to the Pacific region, to South America and to Africa. The list of walking guides is growing and Lonely Planet is producing a unique series of phrasebooks to 'unusual' languages. The emphasis continues to be on travel for travellers and Tony and Maureen still manage to fit in a number of trips each year and play a very active part in the writing and updating of Lonely Planet's guides.

Keeping guidebooks up to date is a constant battle which requires an ear to the ground and lots of walking, but technology also plays its part. All Lonely Planet guidebooks are now stored and updated on computer, and some authors even take lap-top computers into the field. Lonely Planet is also using computers to draw maps and eventually many of the maps will be stored on disk.

The people at Lonely Planet strongly feel that travellers can make a positive contribution to the countries they visit both by better appreciation of cultures and by the money they spend. In addition the company tries to make a direct contribution to the countries and regions it covers. Since 1986 a percentage of the income from each book has gone to aid groups and associations. This has included donations to famine relief in Africa, to aid projects in India, to agricultural projects in Nicaragua and other Central American countries and to Greenpeace's efforts to halt French nuclear testing in the Pacific. In 1988 over $40,000 was donated by Lonely Planet to these projects.

Lonely Planet Distributors

Australia & Papua New Guinea Lonely Planet Publications, PO Box 88, South Yarra, Victoria 3141.
Canada Raincoast Books, 112 East 3rd Avenue, Vancouver, British Columbia V5T 1C8.
Denmark, Finland & Norway Scanvik Books aps, Store Kongensgade 59 A, DK-1264 Copenhagen K.
Hong Kong The Book Society, GPO Box 7804.
India & Nepal UBS Distributors, 5 Ansari Rd, New Delhi – 110002
Israel Geographical Tours Ltd, 8 Tverya St, Tel Aviv 63144.
Japan Intercontinental Marketing Corp, IPO Box 5056, Tokyo 100-31.
Netherlands Nilsson & Lamm bv, Postbus 195, Pampuslaan 212, 1380 AD Weesp.
Singapore & Malaysia MPH Distributors, 601 Sims Drive, #03-21, Singapore 1438.
Spain Altair, Balmes 69, 08007 Barcelona.
Sweden Esselte Kartcentrum AB, Vasagatan 16, S-111 20 Stockholm.
Thailand Chalermnit, 108 Sukhumvit 53, Bangkok 10110.
UK Roger Lascelles, 47 York Rd, Brentford, Middlesex, TW8 0QP
USA Lonely Planet Publications, PO Box 2001A, Berkeley, CA 94702.
West Germany Buchvertrieb Gerda Schettler, Postfach 64, D3415 Hattorf a H.
All Other Countries refer to Australia address.

Lonely Planet Guides to the Americas

Alaska – a travel survival kit
A definitive guide to one of the world's most spectacular regions – including detailed information on hiking and canoeing.

Canada – a travel survival kit
Canada offers a unique combination of English, French and American culture, with forests mountains and lakes that cover a vast area.

Chile & Easter Island – a travel survival kit
Chile has one of the most varied geographies in the world, including deserts, tranquil lakes, snow-covered volcanoes and windswept fjords. Easter Island is covered, in detail.

Ecuador & the Galapagos Islands – a travel survival kit
Ecuador is the smallest of the Andean countries, and in many ways it is the easiest and most pleasant to travel in. The Galapagos Islands and their amazing inhabitants continue to cast a spell over every visitor.

Mexico – a travel survival kit
Mexico has a unique blend of Indian and Spanish culture and a fascinating historical legacy. The hospitality of the people makes Mexico a paradise for travellers.

Peru – a travel survival kit

The famed city of Machu Picchu, the Andean altiplano and the Amazon rainforests are just some of Peru's attractions. All the facts you need can be found in this comprehensive guide.

South America on a shoestring

An up-dated edition of a budget travellers bible that covers Central and South America from the USA-Mexico border to Tierra del Fuego. Written by the author The New York Times called "the patron saint of travellers in the third world".

Baja California – a travel survival kit

Mexico's Baja peninsula offers a great escape, right at California's back door. This comprehensive guide follows the long road south from raucous border towns like Tijuana, to resorts, untouched villages and deserted villages.

Colombia – a travel survival kit

Colombia is the land of emeralds, orchids and El Dorado. You may not find the mythical city of gold, but you will find an exotic, wild and beautiful country.

Lonely Planet Guidebooks

Lonely Planet guidebooks cover virtually every accessible part of Asia as well as Australia, the Pacific, Central and South America, Africa, the Middle East and parts of North America. There are four main series: 'travel survival kits', covering a single country for a range of budgets; 'shoestring' guides with compact information for low-budget travel in a major region; trekking guides; and 'phrasebooks'.

Australia & the Pacific

Australia
Bushwalking in Australia
Papua New Guinea
Bushwalking in Papua New Guinea
Papua New Guinea phrasebook
New Zealand
Tramping in New Zealand
Rarotonga & the Cook Islands
Solomon Islands
Tahiti & French Polynesia
Fiji
Micronesia

South-East Asia

South-East Asia on a shoestring
Malaysia, Singapore & Brunei
Indonesia
Bali & Lombok
Indonesia phrasebook
Burma
Burmese phrasebook
Thailand
Thai phrasebook
Philippines
Pilipino phrasebook

North-East Asia

North-East Asia on a shoestring
China
China phrasebook
Tibet
Tibet phrasebook
Japan
Korea
Korean phrasebook
Hong Kong, Macau & Canton
Taiwan

West Asia

West Asia on a shoestring
Turkey

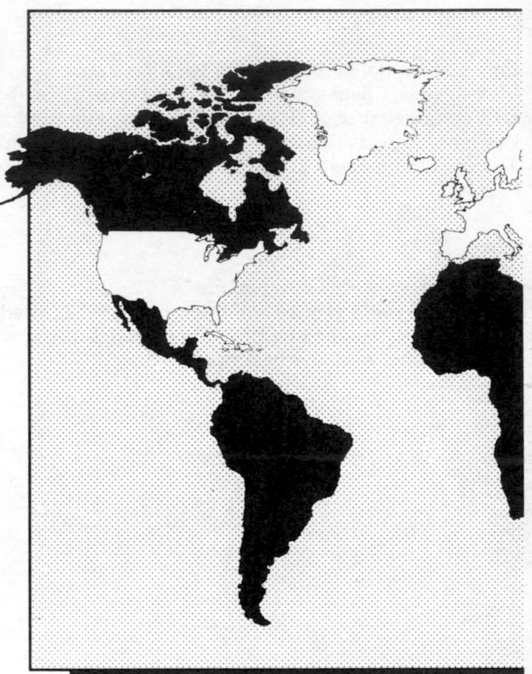

Mail Order

Lonely Planet guidebooks are distributed worldwide and are sold by good bookshops everywhere. They are also available by mail order from Lonely Planet, so if you have difficulty finding a title please write to us. US and Canadian residents should write to Embarcadero West, 112 Linden St, Oakland CA 94607, USA and residents of other countries to PO Box 88, South Yarra, Victoria 3141, Australia.

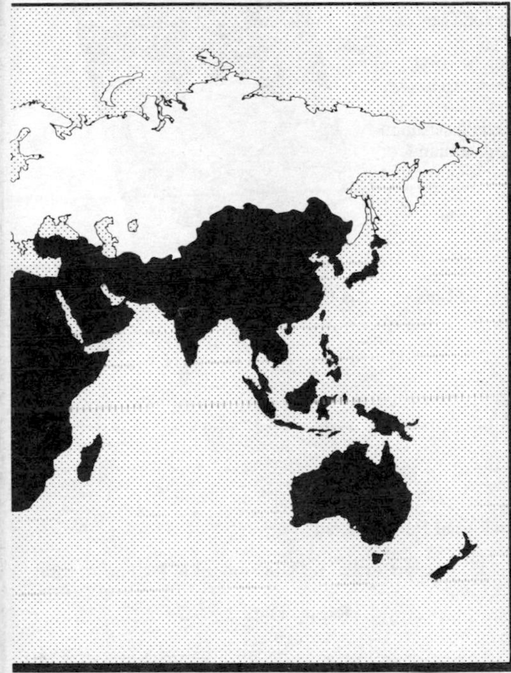

Indian Subcontinent

India
Hindi/Urdu phrasebook
Kashmir, Ladakh & Zanskar
Trekking in the Indian Himalaya
Pakistan
Kathmandu & the Kingdom of Nepal
Trekking in the Nepal Himalaya
Nepal phrasebook
Sri Lanka
Sri Lanka phrasebook
Bangladesh

Africa

Africa on a shoestring
East Africa
Swahili phrasebook
West Africa

Middle East

Egypt & the Sudan
Jordan & Syria
Yemen

North America

Canada
Alaska

Mexico

Mexico
Baja California

South America

South America on a shoestring
Ecuador & the Galapagos Islands
Colombia
Chile & Easter Island
Bolivia
Peru

Lonely Planet Update

We collect an enormous amount of information here at Lonely Planet. Apart from our research there's a steady stream of travellers' letters full of the latest news. For over 5 years much of this information went into a quarterly newsletter (and helped to update the guidebooks). The new paperback *Update* includes this up-to-date news and aims to supplement the information available in our guidebooks. There will be four editions a year (Feb, May, Aug and Nov) available either by subscription or through bookshops. Subscribe now and you'll save nearly 25% off the retail price.

Each edition has extracts from the most interesting letters we have received, covering such diverse topics as:

- how to take a boat trip on the Yalu River
- living in a typical Thai village
- getting a Nepalese trekking permit

Subscription Details

All subscriptions cover four editions and include postage. Prices quoted are subject to change.

USA & Canada – One year's subscription is US$12; a single copy is US$3.95. Please send your order to Lonely Planet's California office.

Other Countries – One year's subscription is Australian $15; a single copy is A$4.95. Please pay in Australian $, or the US$ or £ Sterling equivalent. Please send your order form to Lonely Planet's Australian office.

Order Form

Please send me

☐ One year's subscription – starting next edition. ☐ One copy of the next edition.

Name (please print) ....

Address (please print) ....

....

....

Tick One

☐ Payment enclosed (payable to Lonely Planet Publications)

Charge my ☐ Visa ☐ Bankcard ☐ MasterCard for the amount of $ ....

Card No .... Expiry Date ....

Cardholder's Name (print) ....

Signature .... Date...

US & Canadian residents

Lonely Planet, Embarcadero West, 112 Linden St, Oakland, CA 94607, USA

Other countries

Lonely Planet, PO Box 88, South Yarra, Victoria 3141, Australia